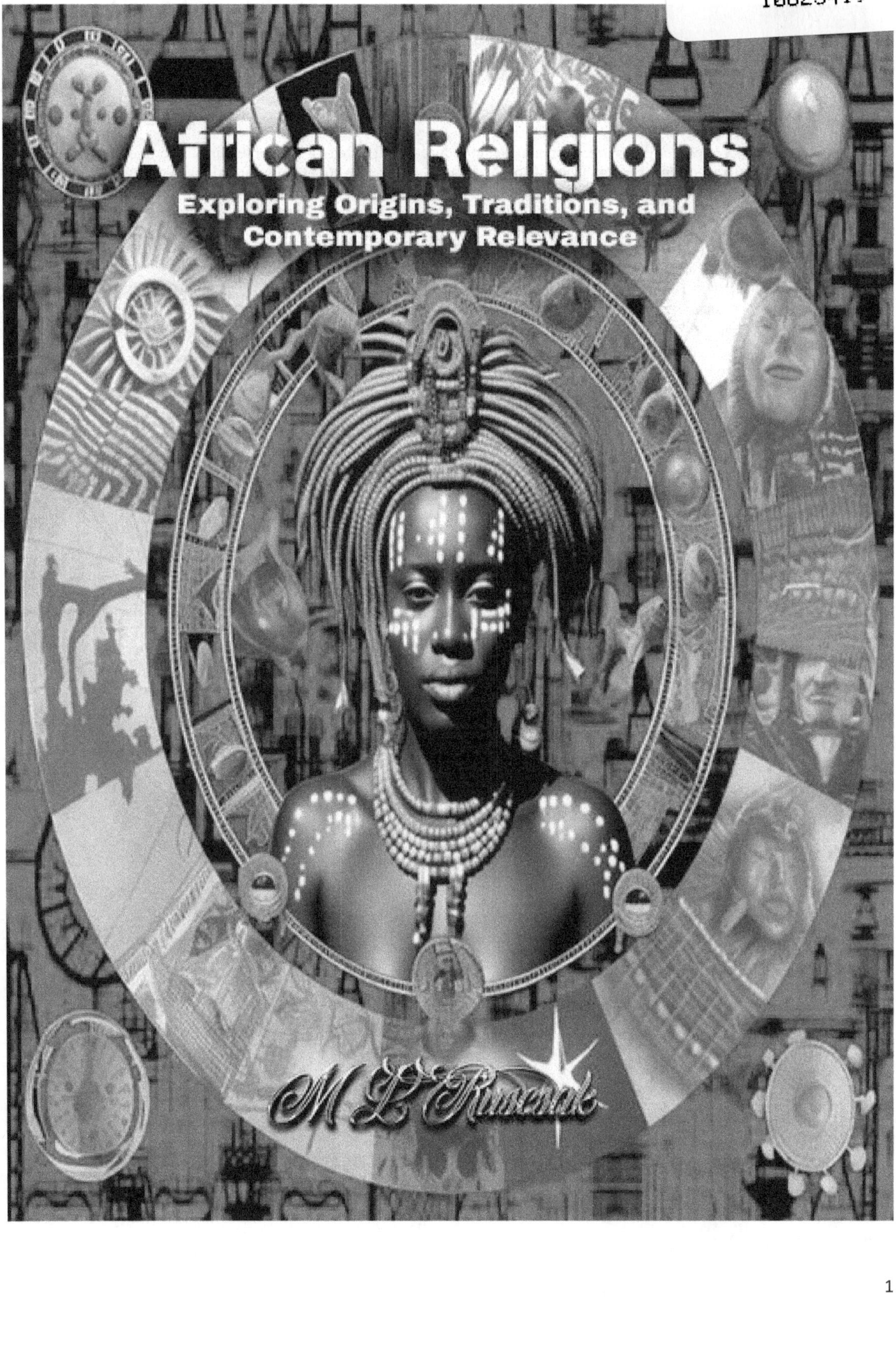

African Religions
Exploring Origins, Traditions, and Contemporary Relevance

M L Rusenko

African Religions

Copyright © 2023 by Trient Press

Trient Press
3375 S Rainbow Blvd
#81710, SMB 13135
Las Vegas,NV 89180
Ordering Information:
Quantity sales. Special discounts are available on quantity purchases by corporations, associations, and others. For details, contact the publisher at the address above.
Orders by U.S. trade bookstores and wholesalers. Please contact Trient Press: Tel: (775) 996-3844; or visit www.trientpress.com.
Printed in the United States of America
Publisher's Cataloging-in-Publication data
Ruscsak, M.L
A title of a book : African Religions: Exploring Origins, Traditions, and Contemporary Relevance

ISBN
Hard Cover   979-8-88990-017-7
Paper Back   979-8-88990-019-1
Ebook   979-8-88990-018-4

Exploring Origins, Traditions, and Contemporary Relevance

Introduction

Part 1: Theories on the Origins of Religion

Chapter 1: Overview of the different theories on the origins of religion
Chapter 2: Animism and ancestral worship as precursors to religion
Chapter 3: The evolution of religion from shamanism to organized religion
Chapter 4: Critiques of the different theories
Chapter 5: Contemporary theories on the origins of religion

Part 2: African Religions: An Introduction

Chapter 6: Overview of African religions and their diversity
Chapter 7: The influence of colonialism and globalization on African religions
Chapter 8: African traditional religions and their role in society
Chapter 9: The relationship between African religions and other religions
Chapter 10: The role of African religions in African societies

Part 3: African Traditional Religions

Chapter 11: The concept of African Traditional Religions (ATRs)
Chapter 12: Characteristics of ATRs and their practices
Chapter 13: The diversity of ATRs across different African societies
Chapter 14: The role of divination and spiritual practices in ATRs
Chapter 15: The impact of Christianity and Islam on ATRs

Part 4: The Role of Ancestors in African Religions

Chapter 16: The concept of ancestors in African religions
Chapter 17: The role of ancestors in African societies and their practices
Chapter 18: The relationship between living individuals and their ancestors
Chapter 19: Ancestral veneration and its significance in African religions
Chapter 20: Ancestral healing and its role in spiritual wellbeing

Part 5: African Diasporic Religions

Chapter 21: Overview of African diasporic religions, such as Vodou, Santeria, and Candomble
Chapter 22: The history and development of African diasporic religions

Chapter 23: The relationship between African diasporic religions and African religions
Chapter 24: Key practices and beliefs in African diasporic religions
Chapter 25: The role of African diasporic religions in contemporary societies

Part 6: African Feminist Theologies

Chapter 26: Overview of African feminist theologies
Chapter 27: Key themes in African feminist theologies
Chapter 28:The intersection of gender and religion in African societies
Chapter 29: African women's spiritual practices and their significance
Chapter 30: The role of African women in religious leadership

Part 7: Conclusion and Future Directions

Chapter 28:Key insights and takeaways
Chapter 29:Future directions for the study of African religions and the origins of religion
Chapter 30: The role of African religions in contemporary society
Chapter 31: The potential for interfaith dialogue and collaboration
Chapter 32: The importance of preserving and promoting African religious traditions

Exploring Origins, Traditions, and Contemporary Relevance

INTRODUCTION

Religion has played a significant role in human societies for thousands of years. It has shaped culture, beliefs, and values, providing a framework for understanding the world and the purpose of life. The academic study of religion explores the nature and diversity of religious phenomena across cultures, time, and space. In this book, we will examine the origins, traditions, and contemporary relevance of African religions.

The Academic Study of Religion

The academic study of religion is an interdisciplinary field that draws on theories and methods from various disciplines, such as anthropology, sociology, history, philosophy, psychology, and religious studies. Scholars in this field seek to understand the beliefs, practices, and institutions of religions and their social, cultural, and political contexts. They investigate the relationship between religion and other aspects of human life, such as identity, morality, power, and globalization.

The interdisciplinary nature of the field allows for a multifaceted approach to the study of religion. For example, anthropologists may focus on the rituals and practices of a particular religious group, while historians may analyze the historical development of religious institutions, and sociologists may examine the social and political factors that shape religious beliefs and practices. By using multiple approaches, scholars can gain a more comprehensive understanding of religion and its role in human societies.

Origins of Religion

The study of the origins of religion is a complex and contested field. Scholars have proposed various theories to explain how religion emerged in human societies. Some theories suggest that religion emerged as a response to natural phenomena, such as the fear of death, the need for order, or the desire for control over the environment. Others argue that religion emerged as a result of social factors, such as the need for social cohesion, the desire for power, or the influence of charismatic leaders.

One approach to understanding the origins of religion is to study the practices and beliefs of traditional societies, such as hunter-gatherer or pastoralist societies. These societies often have complex religious practices that are closely tied to their daily lives and worldview. For example, many traditional African religions view the natural world as sacred and believe that humans have a responsibility to maintain a harmonious relationship with nature.

Another approach to understanding the origins of religion is to analyze the historical development of religious traditions. Many of the world's major religions have evolved over time through a process of syncretism, in which different religious beliefs and practices merge and adapt to new social and cultural contexts. For example, African diasporic religions such as Vodou, Santeria, and Candomble emerged through the syncretism of African and European religious traditions during the slave trade era.

The relevance of studying the origins of religion

Studying the origins of religion is important for several reasons. First, it provides insight into the cultural and historical context in which religions emerged, helping us understand how they have shaped and been shaped by human societies. Second, it enables us to identify common themes and patterns across different religious traditions, highlighting the universality of human experience and the diversity of human expression. Third, it allows us to critically examine our own assumptions and biases about religion and to appreciate the complexity and richness of religious diversity.

In this book, we will explore the origins, traditions, and contemporary relevance of African religions. We will examine the role of African religions in shaping culture, identity, and social relations, and we will analyze the diversity of religious practices and beliefs across the African continent. By engaging with this topic, we hope to deepen our understanding of religion and its role in human societies and to appreciate the rich and complex tapestry of religious diversity across the world.

PART 1: THEORIES ON THE ORIGINS OF RELIGION

Welcome to Part 1 of our exploration of African religions: Theories on the Origins of Religion. In this section, we will delve into the various theories proposed to explain how religion emerged and evolved throughout human history. We will start by providing an overview of the different theories, including animism and ancestral worship as precursors to religion, and the evolution of religion from shamanism to organized religion.

As we examine these theories, we will also explore the critiques that have been made of them, highlighting the strengths and weaknesses of each. Finally, we will delve into contemporary theories on the origins of religion, taking into account the latest research and developments in the field.

By the end of this section, you will have a deeper understanding of the complex and multifaceted nature of religion and its origins, as well as the ongoing debates and discussions in the academic study of religion. So let's dive in and explore the fascinating world of the origins of religion.

Exploring Origins, Traditions, and Contemporary Relevance

CHAPTER 1: OVERVIEW OF THE DIFFERENT THEORIES ON THE ORIGINS OF RELIGION

Religion is a fundamental aspect of human existence, present in virtually every society throughout history. Despite its ubiquity, the origins of religion remain a topic of debate and speculation among scholars. Understanding the origins of religion is essential for understanding the human experience, as it sheds light on the ways in which people have interpreted and made sense of the world around them throughout history.

The study of the origins of religion is a complex and interdisciplinary field, drawing on insights from anthropology, archaeology, psychology, sociology, and other disciplines. Scholars in this field seek to answer questions such as: How did religion arise? What factors influenced its development? How has religion evolved over time? These questions have proven challenging to answer, as the origins of religion are shrouded in the mists of prehistory and are difficult to discern through the limited archaeological and textual evidence that has survived.

Overview of different theories on the origins of religion

Over the centuries, scholars have proposed numerous theories to explain the origins of religion. These theories can be broadly categorized into two groups: those that focus on psychological and cognitive factors, and those that focus on social and cultural factors.

Psychological and cognitive theories propose that religion arose as a result of inherent human cognitive and psychological tendencies. For example, some scholars argue that religion developed as a way for humans to make sense of the natural world and to cope with the uncertainty and unpredictability of life. Others suggest that religion developed as a way to satisfy human needs for connection, meaning, and purpose.

Social and cultural theories propose that religion developed as a result of social and cultural factors, such as social organization, political power, or economic structures. For example, some scholars argue that religion developed as a way to establish and maintain social cohesion and order, while others suggest that religion developed as a way for rulers and elites to maintain their power and authority over the masses.

Some of the major theories of the origins of religion include:

Animism: This theory proposes that religion arose as a result of early humans' belief in spirits inhabiting natural objects and phenomena, such as trees, rocks, and rivers.

Ancestral worship: This theory proposes that religion developed as a way to honor and communicate with the spirits of deceased ancestors, who were believed to have the power to influence the living world.

Shamanism: This theory proposes that religion developed as a result of the practices of shamans, who were believed to have the ability to communicate with spirits and to mediate between the human and spirit worlds.

Evolutionary theories: These theories propose that religion developed as a result of human evolution, with religion evolving from primitive forms such as animism and ancestral worship to more complex and organized forms such as polytheism and monotheism.

Critiques of the different theories

Each of these theories has its strengths and weaknesses, and scholars continue to debate their relative merits. Some critics argue that the psychological and cognitive theories fail to take into account the cultural and social factors that shape religion, while others argue that the social and cultural theories fail to account for the innate human tendencies that give rise to religion. Some critics also argue that the evolutionary theories are overly simplistic and fail to account for the diversity and complexity of religious beliefs and practices around the world.

Contemporary theories on the origins of religion

In recent years, scholars have proposed a number of new theories and perspectives on the origins of religion. Some of these perspectives draw on advances in cognitive science and evolutionary biology, while others draw on insights from postcolonial and feminist theory.

One example of a contemporary theory of the origins of religion is the idea of "biocultural evolution." This theory proposes that religion developed as a result of the interplay between biological and cultural factors, with religion evolving in response to both the innate cognitive

African Religions

Introduction to the study of the origins of religion

The origins of religion have been a subject of debate and inquiry for centuries. In this section, we will explore the various theories and ideas surrounding the emergence of religion and the significance of understanding its origins.

Introduction to the study of the origins of religion:
Religion has played an integral role in human societies throughout history. It has influenced the way people think, behave, and interact with one another. The study of religion has been an essential part of the academic world for many years, as scholars seek to understand the nature of religious beliefs and practices. One area of study that has received significant attention is the origins of religion. This field of inquiry seeks to explore the origins of religious beliefs and practices and how they have evolved over time.

✧ **Overview of different theories on the origins of religion:**

There are several different theories on the origins of religion. These theories range from the idea that religion emerged as a result of the need to explain natural phenomena to the idea that religion developed as a means of social control. One of the earliest and most influential theories is animism, which posits that everything in the natural world possesses a spirit or soul. Animism is often considered a precursor to religion and is seen as the basis for many early religious beliefs.

Another important theory is ancestor worship, which suggests that early humans believed in the existence of a spiritual world and that the spirits of deceased ancestors could influence the living. Shamanism, which is the belief in a spiritual world that can be accessed through the use of altered states of consciousness, is also considered an important precursor to religion.

Other theories include the idea that religion emerged as a way of understanding the natural world, as a means of dealing with death and the afterlife, and as a way of providing social cohesion and order. Each of these theories offers a different perspective on the origins of religion and highlights the complex nature of this field of study.

✧ **Explanation of the importance of understanding the origins of religion:**

Understanding the origins of religion is crucial for several reasons. First, it allows us to gain insight into the beliefs and practices of different cultures and societies throughout history. By studying the origins of religion, we can better understand how religion has evolved over time and how it has influenced the development of human societies.

Second, understanding the origins of religion can help us to better understand the psychological and social factors that influence religious belief and practice. By studying the origins of religion, we can gain insight into the role that religion plays in people's lives and the ways in which it impacts their thinking, behavior, and social interactions.

Finally, understanding the origins of religion is essential for promoting religious tolerance and understanding. By gaining a deeper understanding of the beliefs and practices of different religions, we can learn to appreciate the diversity of human experience and promote greater respect and understanding between people of different faiths.

In conclusion, the study of the origins of religion is an important area of inquiry that offers insights into the nature of religious beliefs and practices. By exploring the different theories on the origins of religion and understanding the significance of this field of study, we can gain a deeper appreciation for the role that religion has played in human societies throughout history.

Overview of different theories on the origins of religion

The question of the origins of religion has been a subject of fascination and debate for centuries. Scholars and researchers from various disciplines have attempted to provide answers to this complex and multi-faceted question. In this chapter, we will explore the different theories on the origins of religion, including animism and ancestral worship, shamanism, and organized religion. We will also examine the critiques of these theories and the contemporary perspectives that have emerged.

Animism and ancestral worship as precursors to religion

Animism is the belief that all living and non-living things possess a spirit or soul. This worldview is often associated with hunter-gatherer societies and early agricultural communities. According to this theory, animism was the first stage of religious development, where early humans attributed spiritual qualities to natural phenomena such as animals, trees, and rocks. This belief system laid the foundation for more complex religious practices, including ancestor worship.

Ancestor worship is the veneration and honoring of one's ancestors as a way of connecting with the spirit world. In many traditional societies, ancestors are believed to have a powerful influence on the living and are seen as intermediaries between the living and the divine. The practice of ancestor worship was widespread in ancient societies and continues to be a part of many modern religions.

Ancestor worship is a common feature of many African religions and is often accompanied by elaborate rituals and ceremonies. Ancestors are believed to play an important role in providing guidance, protection, and blessings to their descendants. In many African societies, ancestors are also seen as the guardians of cultural traditions and are believed to have a special responsibility for ensuring the well-being of the community.

In some African religions, ancestors are seen as spiritual beings who can communicate with the living through divination and other forms of spiritual communication. Divination is the practice of seeking knowledge of the future or the unknown through supernatural means. It is a common practice in many African religions and is often performed by priests, diviners, or other religious specialists.

In addition to animism and ancestor worship, many African religions also place a strong emphasis on the role of spirits and deities. Spirits are believed to be powerful supernatural beings that can have a profound impact on human life. They are often associated with natural phenomena such as mountains, rivers, and trees, and are believed to possess specific qualities or powers.

Deities, on the other hand, are often seen as more abstract concepts or forces that govern the natural world and human affairs. In some African religions, deities are associated with specific elements such as water, fire, or earth, while in others they are seen as the embodiments of important moral principles such as justice, compassion, or wisdom.

Overall, the unique features of African religions reflect the diversity and complexity of African culture and history. These religions have played a crucial role in shaping African identity, promoting social justice and ecological sustainability, and inspiring a rich tradition of art, music, and literature.

The evolution of religion from shamanism to organized religion

Shamanism is a religious practice that involves a practitioner, known as a shaman, who communicates with the spirit world on behalf of the community. Shamans are believed to have the ability to enter altered states of consciousness and connect with spirits, often through the use of hallucinogenic plants. Shamanism is a widespread practice among traditional societies and is considered by many scholars to be one of the earliest forms of organized religion.

Exploring Origins, Traditions, and Contemporary Relevance

As societies became more complex and organized, religion evolved into more formalized institutions, such as temples and priesthoods. This development led to the emergence of organized religions such as Hinduism, Buddhism, Judaism, Christianity, and Islam. These religions have more structured beliefs, practices, and hierarchies, and are characterized by a more systematic approach to religious practice.

As organized religions developed, they often incorporated elements of earlier religious practices and beliefs. For example, many traditional beliefs and practices were incorporated into Hinduism, which developed in the Indian subcontinent around 2,500 years ago. Buddhism, which emerged as a distinct religion in the same region, also drew on earlier religious traditions.

Judaism, Christianity, and Islam, which are often referred to as the Abrahamic religions, are monotheistic religions that emerged in the Middle East. They share a belief in one God and draw on the Old Testament of the Bible, which includes stories and teachings from earlier Jewish traditions. Christianity and Islam, in particular, have spread around the world and have been adapted to a wide variety of cultural contexts.

Despite their differences, all of these religions share certain common features, such as a belief in the existence of a divine being or beings, a set of moral and ethical principles, and a system of religious practices and rituals. They also play an important role in shaping cultural identity and promoting social cohesion within their communities.

Critiques of the different theories

Despite the popularity of these theories, they have also faced criticisms from scholars and researchers. Some have argued that these theories reflect Western biases and assumptions about the nature of religion, and fail to take into account the diversity of religious practices and beliefs found in non-Western societies. Others have argued that these theories neglect the role of politics, economics, and social factors in the development of religious institutions.

Contemporary theories on the origins of religion

In recent years, scholars have developed new theories on the origins of religion that incorporate a more interdisciplinary approach. One such theory is the cognitive theory of religion, which suggests that religious beliefs and practices are a product of human cognitive processes. Another theory is the evolutionary theory of religion, which proposes that religion evolved as a mechanism to promote cooperation and social cohesion in early human societies.

The study of the origins of religion is a complex and multifaceted field that requires a multidisciplinary approach. By examining the different theories and critiques of the origins of religion, as well as the contemporary perspectives that have emerged, we can gain a deeper understanding of the role that religion plays in human society.

Explanation of the importance of understanding the origins of religion

The study of the origins of religion is a crucial aspect of understanding the human experience. Religion has played a significant role in shaping human societies, cultures, and behaviors throughout history. From the earliest known civilizations to the present day, religion has been a central aspect of human life, providing meaning, purpose, and guidance to individuals and communities.

By understanding the origins of religion, we gain insight into the human experience and the ways in which our beliefs and behaviors have been shaped by the cultural and environmental contexts in which we live. This understanding can help us to better appreciate the diversity of human experience and to develop a greater sense of empathy and understanding towards others who may hold different beliefs.

Furthermore, the study of the origins of religion can provide valuable insights into the ways in which human societies have developed over time. It can help us to understand how social, economic, and political factors have influenced the evolution of religion, and how religion has in turn influenced these same factors. This understanding can be particularly useful for those working in fields such as anthropology, sociology, and political science.

In addition, understanding the origins of religion can have practical applications in contemporary society. By understanding the historical and cultural contexts in which religious beliefs and practices developed, we can better appreciate the significance of these beliefs and practices to those who hold them. This can be particularly useful for those working in fields such as education, healthcare, and social work, where knowledge of different religious traditions can help professionals better serve the needs of diverse populations.

Overall, the study of the origins of religion is an important and valuable area of inquiry that can provide insight into the human experience, the development of human societies, and contemporary issues facing our diverse and complex world.

CHAPTER 2: ANIMISM AND ANCESTRAL WORSHIP AS PRECURSORS TO RELIGION

In this chapter, we will explore the concept of animism and ancestral worship as precursors to religion. Animism is a belief system that attributes souls or spirits to non-human entities, such as animals, plants, and natural phenomena. Ancestral worship, on the other hand, is the veneration of ancestors as spiritual beings who can intercede on behalf of the living.

The idea that animism and ancestral worship were precursors to religion has been a topic of debate among scholars for many years. Some argue that these beliefs provided the foundation for later religious systems, while others view them as distinct practices that do not fit neatly into the category of religion.

We will begin by examining the concept of animism and how it has been practiced in various cultures throughout history. We will also explore the ways in which ancestral worship has been a part of many different belief systems and how it has evolved over time.

Throughout this chapter, we will consider the ways in which animism and ancestral worship have been viewed as precursors to religion. We will explore the arguments for and against this idea and discuss the controversies surrounding this perspective.

By understanding the origins and evolution of these practices, we can gain insight into the development of religion and how it has influenced cultures throughout history. We will also consider how the study of animism and ancestral worship can help us better understand contemporary religious practices and the ways in which they are shaped by cultural and historical contexts.

Through a critical analysis of the theories surrounding animism and ancestral worship, we can engage in deeper discussions about the nature of religion and its role in human society. By the end of this chapter, students will have a comprehensive understanding of these beliefs and their significance in the development of religious systems.

African Religions

Explanation of animism and ancestral worship

Animism and ancestral worship are often considered as precursors to religion. In this section, we will explore the concepts of animism and ancestral worship, their historical and cultural significance, and how they relate to the development of religion.

Animism is a term used to describe the belief that all things, both animate and inanimate, have a spirit or soul. This belief system is often associated with traditional and indigenous cultures, where the natural world is seen as a living, breathing entity that is intertwined with the human experience. In animistic cultures, everything from animals and plants to mountains and rivers are believed to possess their own unique spiritual essence. This is often expressed through the use of rituals and ceremonies, which are designed to honor and connect with the spirits of the natural world.

Ancestral worship, on the other hand, is the belief that one's ancestors continue to exist in a spiritual realm after death and can exert influence over the living. This belief system is often associated with traditional and indigenous cultures, where the family and community are seen as a vital part of the human experience. In ancestral worship cultures, ancestors are revered and honored through the use of ancestor altars, ancestral rituals, and offerings of food and drink.

Both animism and ancestral worship are deeply rooted in the human experience, and have played an important role in shaping the development of religion throughout history. One of the key ways in which these belief systems have influenced the development of religion is through the concept of animatism.

Animatism is the belief in a universal life force or energy that animates all things. This life force is often referred to as mana, prana, or qi, depending on the culture in question. In animistic cultures, mana is believed to be present in all living things, and is seen as the source of spiritual power and vitality. This concept is closely related to the idea of animism, as both concepts emphasize the spiritual essence of the natural world.

The idea of animatism has had a profound influence on the development of religion, particularly in the early stages of human history. For example, many of the world's oldest religions, such as Hinduism and Taoism, are based on the concept of animatism. In these religions, the concept of mana or qi is central to spiritual practice, and is believed to be the source of spiritual power and healing.

Another way in which animism and ancestral worship have influenced the development of religion is through the use of sacred objects and rituals. In many traditional cultures, objects such as stones, feathers, and bones are believed to possess spiritual power and are used in rituals and ceremonies. These objects are often seen as a conduit for spiritual energy, and are used to connect with the natural world and the spirits of ancestors.

Similarly, many traditional cultures use rituals and ceremonies to honor and connect with their ancestors. These rituals often involve offerings of food and drink, and are designed to establish a connection with the spiritual realm. This idea of connecting with the spiritual realm through ritual and ceremony is a key aspect of many religions, and can be seen in practices such as prayer and meditation.

Despite the significance of animism and ancestral worship in the development of religion, these belief systems have also been the subject of criticism and controversy. One of the key criticisms of animism is that it is often seen as primitive and superstitious. This criticism is based on the assumption that animistic beliefs are based on a lack of scientific understanding, and that they are therefore inferior to more modern religious beliefs.

Another criticism of animism and ancestral worship is that they can be seen as culturally insensitive. This criticism is based on the idea that animistic beliefs and practices can be misappropriated or misunderstood by outsiders, leading to misunderstandings and disrespect for indigenous cultures.

Despite these criticisms, animism and ancestral worship remain an important part of many cultures around the world, and continue to influence the development of religion today. Many scholars argue that animism is not primitive or inferior, but rather a sophisticated and complex system of beliefs that reflects the deep relationship between humans and the natural world.

Furthermore, the idea that animistic beliefs are based on a lack of scientific understanding is a flawed assumption, as many animistic cultures have sophisticated and nuanced understandings of the natural world. For example, indigenous cultures in the Americas have a deep understanding of the medicinal properties of plants, and have developed complex systems of healing based on this knowledge. Similarly, many African cultures have developed complex agricultural practices based on a deep understanding of the natural world and its cycles.

In addition, the idea that animistic beliefs are culturally insensitive is also problematic, as it assumes a Western perspective that views indigenous cultures as inferior or primitive. In reality, many indigenous cultures have a deep respect for the natural world and have developed complex systems of belief and practice that are deeply rooted in their cultural heritage. By dismissing these beliefs as primitive or superstitious, we risk perpetuating colonial attitudes and disrespecting the rich cultural traditions of indigenous peoples.

Overall, while animism and ancestral worship have been subject to criticism and controversy, they remain important and relevant belief systems that continue to shape the development of religion today. By understanding the complexities and nuances of these belief systems, we can gain a deeper appreciation for the diversity of human experience and the profound ways in which humans relate to the natural world.

How animism and ancestral worship are considered precursors to religion

Animism and ancestral worship are often considered precursors to religion because they both involve the veneration of spiritual beings, and they both seek to explain the mysteries of the natural world. In this section, we will explore the ways in which animism and ancestral worship laid the foundation for the development of religion.

Animism is a belief system that holds that all living and non-living things have a spirit or soul. According to animism, everything in the world, from rocks and trees to animals and humans, is animated by a spiritual essence. This spiritual essence is not the same as the physical body, but rather an intangible force that gives life to the physical form.

The animistic worldview is based on the idea that everything in the world is interconnected, and that all beings are part of a larger, universal energy. This energy is often referred to as "mana" or "chi," and it is believed to flow through all things in the world. According to animistic belief, by living in harmony with this energy, humans can achieve balance and wellbeing.

The concept of ancestral worship is closely tied to animism. Ancestral worship involves the veneration of ancestors and the belief that they continue to influence the world beyond death. In many cultures, ancestors are believed to be able to communicate with the living, and they are often seen as powerful spiritual entities who can offer guidance and protection.

The practice of ancestral worship is based on the idea that the dead continue to exist in some form after death. This belief is often rooted in the animistic worldview, which holds that all beings have a spiritual essence that transcends the physical body. According to this belief, when a person dies, their spirit or soul continues to exist, and it may continue to play a role in the world beyond death.

Exploring Origins, Traditions, and Contemporary Relevance

Both animism and ancestral worship played a significant role in the development of religion. Many of the earliest religious practices were based on animistic and ancestral beliefs, and these beliefs continue to influence religious practices around the world.

For example, many indigenous religions are based on animistic and ancestral beliefs. In many Native American cultures, for example, animism is central to religious practice. The belief in a universal life force that animates all things is seen as the basis for spiritual and physical health. Similarly, ancestral worship is an important part of many African religions, where ancestors are believed to play a central role in the spiritual world.

In addition to influencing indigenous religions, animism and ancestral worship also influenced the development of more organized religions. For example, many of the early religions of the ancient world, such as the religions of Egypt and Mesopotamia, were based on animistic and ancestral beliefs. In these religions, gods were often seen as powerful spiritual entities that were responsible for the natural world, and they were often associated with specific natural phenomena, such as the sun, moon, and stars.

As organized religions developed, they often incorporated elements of animism and ancestral worship into their belief systems. For example, many religions have a belief in a spiritual realm beyond the physical world, which is often similar to the animistic concept of mana or chi. Similarly, many religions incorporate the veneration of saints, which can be seen as a form of ancestral worship.

Despite the significant influence of animism and ancestral worship on the development of religion, these belief systems have also been the subject of criticism and controversy. Some critics argue that animistic and ancestral beliefs are primitive and superstitious, and that they have no place in modern society. Others argue that these beliefs can be misappropriated or misunderstood, leading to cultural insensitivity and disrespect for indigenous cultures.

In conclusion, animism and ancestral worship are considered precursors to religion because they both involve the veneration of spirits and ancestors, which played a significant role in shaping early human beliefs and practices. These belief systems provided a framework for understanding and interacting with the natural world, and for establishing social and cultural norms.

The animistic worldview, which sees all things as having a spiritual essence or energy, has been influential in many religious and spiritual traditions. It has also been an important source of inspiration for ecological and environmental movements, as it emphasizes the interconnectedness of all things and the importance of living in harmony with nature.

Ancestral worship, on the other hand, played a key role in the development of family and clan structures, as well as social and political systems. By venerating their ancestors, early humans were able to establish a sense of continuity and belonging, as well as a system of values and ethics.

While these belief systems have been criticized as primitive and superstitious, they continue to be practiced and valued by many people around the world. As with all belief systems, it is important to approach animism and ancestral worship with respect and cultural sensitivity, and to appreciate their ongoing relevance and significance in the modern world.

As students of religion, it is important to understand the historical and cultural context in which these belief systems arose, as well as their continued influence on contemporary religious and spiritual practices. By studying animism and ancestral worship, we can gain a deeper appreciation for the diversity and complexity of human religious experience, and develop a more nuanced understanding of the role that spirituality and culture play in shaping our beliefs and values.

Examples of animism and ancestral worship in different cultures

Animism and ancestral worship have been present in many different cultures throughout history, and continue to be practiced in various forms today. In this section, we will explore some examples of animism and ancestral worship in different cultures around the world.

✧ **African Traditional Religion**

African Traditional Religion is a term used to describe the various religious traditions practiced by different ethnic groups in Africa. Many of these traditions involve animistic beliefs and practices, such as the veneration of ancestors and the belief in a spiritual essence or life force. For example, the Akan people of Ghana believe in a Supreme Being known as Nyame, as well as a pantheon of lesser deities and ancestral spirits. Offerings and sacrifices are made to these deities and ancestors in order to gain their favor and protection.

✧ **Native American Religion**

Many Native American tribes practice forms of animism and ancestral worship. For example, the Navajo people believe in a complex system of deities and spirits, including the Holy People, who are venerated through ceremonies and offerings. The Hopi people also believe in a pantheon of deities, including the kachinas, who are said to represent natural elements such as rain and corn.

✧ Chinese Religion

Chinese religion is a term used to describe the various religious traditions practiced in China, including Confucianism, Taoism, and Buddhism. Many of these traditions involve animistic beliefs and practices, such as the belief in chi or life force, which is said to flow through all living things. Ancestral worship is also an important aspect of Chinese religion, as it is believed that the spirits of the dead can provide guidance and protection to their living descendants.

✧ Shintoism

Shintoism is the indigenous religion of Japan, and is based on animistic beliefs and practices. Shintoists believe in a pantheon of kami, or spirits, that inhabit the natural world. These kami can be found in various forms, such as rocks, trees, and animals. Ancestral worship is also an important aspect of Shintoism, as it is believed that the spirits of one's ancestors can offer protection and guidance.

✧ Hinduism

Hinduism is a major religion practiced in India and other parts of South Asia. It involves a complex system of deities and beliefs, many of which are animistic in nature. For example, Hindus believe in a life force known as prana, which flows through all living things. Ancestral worship is also an important aspect of Hinduism, as it is believed that the souls of the dead can influence the lives of their living descendants.

These are just a few examples of animism and ancestral worship in different cultures around the world. While the specific beliefs and practices may vary from culture to culture, the underlying principles of honoring and venerating the spirits of the natural world and one's ancestors are often shared.

Criticisms and controversies surrounding the idea of animism and ancestral worship as precursors to religion

Criticisms and controversies surrounding the idea of animism and ancestral worship as precursors to religion are not new, and they continue to be discussed and debated by scholars and practitioners alike. These criticisms are often based on the assumption that animistic and ancestral beliefs are primitive and superstitious, and that they have no place in modern society. However, there are also concerns about cultural sensitivity and the potential for misunderstandings and misappropriations of indigenous beliefs and practices.

One of the primary criticisms of animism and ancestral worship is that they are often seen as primitive and superstitious. This criticism is based on the assumption that animistic beliefs are based on a lack of scientific understanding, and that they are therefore inferior to more modern religious beliefs. Critics argue that animistic beliefs are based on a magical or mystical worldview, which is incompatible with modern scientific understanding of the world.

Another criticism of animism and ancestral worship is that they can be seen as culturally insensitive. This criticism is based on the idea that animistic beliefs and practices can be misappropriated or misunderstood by outsiders, leading to misunderstandings and disrespect for indigenous cultures. For example, some people may view the practice of ancestor worship as primitive or barbaric, without understanding the cultural significance and complexity of these beliefs.

There are also concerns about the potential for misappropriation of indigenous beliefs and practices. For example, some New Age practitioners may appropriate indigenous beliefs and practices without understanding their cultural context or historical significance, leading to cultural disrespect and misunderstanding. Additionally, some critics argue that the commercialization of indigenous spiritual practices, such as the sale of smudge kits or other ceremonial objects, is exploitative and disrespectful to the cultures from which these practices originate.

However, it is important to note that not all scholars and practitioners agree with these criticisms. Some argue that animism and ancestral worship are valid and important aspects of human spirituality, and that they have value as cultural and historical artifacts. For example, some proponents of eco-spirituality argue that animistic beliefs and practices are essential to understanding our relationship with the natural world, and that they can help to foster a greater sense of environmental awareness and stewardship.

Additionally, it is important to recognize the diversity and complexity of indigenous beliefs and practices. While there are certainly some shared characteristics among animistic and ancestral beliefs, there are also significant variations and differences across cultures and regions. For example, the concept of mana in Polynesian cultures is different from the concept of chi in Chinese culture, and both are different from the concept of wakanda in Native American cultures.

Exploring Origins, Traditions, and Contemporary Relevance

In conclusion, while animism and ancestral worship are considered precursors to religion and have played an important role in the development of human spirituality, they are not without controversy and criticism. Scholars and practitioners must be mindful of the potential for cultural insensitivity and misappropriation, and must approach these beliefs and practices with respect and understanding. Ultimately, the study of animism and ancestral worship can help to shed light on the diversity and complexity of human spirituality, and can offer insights into our relationship with the natural world and with each other.

CHAPTER 3: THE EVOLUTION OF RELIGION FROM SHAMANISM TO ORGANIZED RELIGION

Religion has been a defining feature of human society for thousands of years, shaping our cultures, beliefs, and values. But how did religion evolve from its earliest forms to the complex, organized systems we see today? The answer lies in the history of shamanism and its transformation into organized religion.

Shamanism is one of the earliest known forms of religious practice, dating back to the Paleolithic era. The word "shaman" comes from the Tungus tribe of Siberia and refers to a person who has access to the spirit world and can communicate with supernatural beings. In shamanic belief systems, the shaman serves as a mediator between the physical and spiritual worlds, using various techniques such as drumming, dancing, and chanting to enter a trance state and connect with the spirits.

Shamanism is characterized by its animistic beliefs, which hold that everything in the world, from animals and plants to rocks and rivers, has a spirit or soul. These spirits can be communicated with and manipulated for various purposes, such as healing, divination, and protection. Shamanism also often involves the use of psychoactive plants and substances, such as ayahuasca and peyote, to induce altered states of consciousness and facilitate communication with the spirits.

Over time, shamanism began to evolve and adapt to changing cultural and social conditions. As human societies became more complex and hierarchical, shamanic practices began to take on more organized and formal structures. This process gave rise to what is known as "proto-religion," which emerged in the Neolithic era and involved the development of rituals, myths, and beliefs centered around specific deities or spiritual entities.

Proto-religion eventually gave way to organized religion, which emerged in various parts of the world and is characterized by highly structured and codified belief systems, hierarchies of authority, and centralized institutions such as churches, mosques, and temples. Organized religions also often involve the creation of texts, such as the Bible, the Quran, or the Vedas, that serve as authoritative sources of doctrine and practice.

Exploring Origins, Traditions, and Contemporary Relevance

The evolution of religion from shamanism to organized religion is a complex and multifaceted process that has been shaped by a variety of cultural, social, and historical factors. However, there are several key themes and trends that can be identified across different regions and periods.

One important factor in the evolution of religion is the process of urbanization and state formation. As human societies became more complex and hierarchical, with the emergence of cities and centralized political institutions, religion began to take on a more formal and institutionalized character. This process is exemplified by the rise of the great religious traditions of the Axial Age, such as Hinduism, Buddhism, Confucianism, and Judaism, which emerged in response to the challenges and opportunities of urban life.

Another important factor in the evolution of religion is the influence of philosophical and intellectual movements. As human societies developed more sophisticated systems of thought and inquiry, religion began to be influenced by philosophical and intellectual movements such as the Greek rationalist tradition, the Chinese Daoist and Mohist schools, and the Indian Upanishadic and Buddhist traditions. These movements challenged traditional religious beliefs and practices, leading to the development of new forms of spirituality and religious thought.

A third important factor in the evolution of religion is the process of globalization and cultural exchange. As human societies became more interconnected through trade, migration, and conquest, religion began to be influenced by outside cultural and religious traditions. This process is exemplified by the spread of Christianity and Islam, which emerged in specific cultural and historical contexts but were able to adapt and spread to other regions through the process of cultural exchange and syncretism.

Despite the many changes and transformations that have occurred in the evolution of religion, some elements have remained consistent across different religious traditions. For example, many religions have a belief in a supernatural or spiritual realm, as well as a set of practices or rituals designed to connect with this realm. Additionally, many religions have a set of moral or ethical principles that guide human behavior and interaction.

The evolution of religion from shamanism to organized religion has been a complex and multifaceted process that has taken place over thousands of years. By examining the different factors that have influenced this evolution, we can gain a deeper understanding of the ways in which religion has shaped human history and culture. In the following chapters, we will explore these different factors in more detail, focusing on their role in shaping the development of different religious traditions and practices.

Chapter 3 will explore the evolution of religion from shamanism to organized religion, tracing the development of key religious practices and beliefs over time. We will begin by examining the role of shamanism in early human societies, and how this practice laid the groundwork for the development of more complex religious traditions. We will then look at the emergence of organized religion in different regions of the world, including the Middle East, India, and China. Finally, we will explore the ways in which globalization and cultural exchange have influenced the development of religion in the modern world, and how this ongoing process continues to shape religious practices and beliefs today.

As we delve into the evolution of religion, it is important to approach this topic with an open and critical mind, recognizing that different religious traditions have their own unique histories and cultural contexts. By studying these traditions in depth, we can gain a deeper appreciation for the rich diversity of human spirituality and the many ways in which religion continues to shape our world today.

Explanation of shamanism as an early form of religious practice

Shamanism is an early form of religious practice that has been observed in many cultures throughout history. Shamanism can be defined as a practice in which individuals, known as shamans, enter altered states of consciousness in order to communicate with spirits and the divine. Shamans act as intermediaries between the physical world and the spirit world, using their abilities to heal, divine, and perform other spiritual tasks.

The practice of shamanism can be traced back to the Paleolithic era, and has been found in cultures all over the world, including the Americas, Asia, Africa, and Europe. Despite the many variations in shamanic practice across cultures, there are several common elements that define the practice.

One of the most common features of shamanism is the belief in spirits. These spirits are believed to inhabit the natural world and can be found in animals, plants, rocks, and other natural objects. The shaman believes that by entering an altered state of consciousness, they can communicate with these spirits and gain knowledge and power from them.

Another key feature of shamanism is the use of ritual and ceremony. Shamans use various tools and objects in their rituals, including drums, rattles, feathers, and crystals. These objects are used to help the shaman enter an altered state of consciousness and communicate with the spirits. Shamanic ceremonies often involve dancing, chanting, and other forms of physical movement.

In addition to communicating with spirits, shamans also have the ability to heal. In many cultures, the shaman is the primary healer, using their spiritual abilities to treat physical, emotional, and psychological ailments. Shamans may use a variety of techniques in their healing work, including herbal remedies, massage, and energy healing.

Shamanism also emphasizes the importance of community and social connection. In many cultures, the shaman serves as a spiritual leader and advisor, providing guidance and support to members of the community. The shaman may also be responsible for maintaining social harmony and resolving conflicts within the community.

Despite its many similarities across cultures, shamanism can take on many different forms depending on the specific cultural context. For example, in some cultures, the shaman is a hereditary position passed down through families, while in others, anyone with the ability to enter an altered state of consciousness can become a shaman.

In addition, the specific rituals and practices of shamanism can vary widely. For example, some shamans may use psychoactive plants to enter an altered state of consciousness, while others may use drumming or other forms of sensory stimulation.

Despite its many variations, shamanism remains an important and influential form of religious practice. Many modern spiritual movements, including the New Age movement and neo-shamanism, have been influenced by shamanic practices and beliefs. As humanity continues to evolve and change, it is likely that shamanism will continue to play an important role in spiritual and religious practice.

Examples:

Research the use of shamanism in the indigenous cultures of South America and discuss the common elements that define shamanic practice in these cultures.

Explore the role of the shaman in traditional Siberian cultures and compare and contrast it with the role of the shaman in Native American cultures.

Compare and contrast the use of psychoactive plants in shamanic practice with the use of meditation and other spiritual practices in modern spiritual movements.

Exercises:

Compare and contrast the role of the shaman in traditional cultures with the role of religious leaders in modern organized religions. How have these roles evolved over time?

Research the ways in which shamanic practices have been appropriated and misappropriated by non-indigenous people and cultures. What are the ethical implications of this?

Explore the scientific basis for the use of psychoactive plants in shamanic practice. How do these plants affect the brain and consciousness, and what are the potential risks and benefits of their use?

Research the ways in which shamanism has been incorporated into modern Western spirituality and self-help movements. How has this affected the perception and practice of shamanism?

Compare and contrast the ways in which shamanism and organized religion address the problem of evil and suffering in the world. How do these approaches differ, and what are the implications for understanding the nature of the divine and human experience?

Reflect on your own spiritual or religious practices and beliefs. Are there any elements of shamanism or other early forms of religious practice that resonate with you?

How might these elements inform your understanding of spirituality and the divine?

How shamanism evolved into organized religion

Shamanism is often considered an early form of religious practice, and its influence can be seen in many of the world's major religions. However, as human societies became more complex and organized, shamanic practices began to evolve into more formalized religious systems.

One of the earliest examples of this transformation can be seen in the development of the ancient Egyptian religion. Although the early Egyptians practiced a form of animism that shared many similarities with shamanism, the religion gradually evolved into a more formalized system centered around the worship of a pantheon of gods and goddesses. This transformation was likely driven in part by the growing complexity of Egyptian society, which required a more centralized and organized form of religion to maintain social order.

Similarly, the early Vedic religion of India also evolved from a more shamanic form of spirituality into a complex system of ritual and sacrifice centered around the worship of numerous deities. This transformation was likely influenced by the development of the caste system and the growing importance of social hierarchy in Indian society.

In many cases, the transformation of shamanic practices into organized religion was also influenced by outside cultural and religious traditions. For example, the ancient Greek philosopher Pythagoras is often credited with introducing the concept of a soul that exists beyond death into Western thought. This concept, which had parallels in shamanic beliefs about the afterlife, had a profound influence on the development of Western religions such as Christianity and Judaism.

Similarly, the spread of Buddhism from India to China and other parts of Asia led to the development of a rich and complex system of religious beliefs and practices that blended elements of shamanism, animism, and other spiritual traditions. In many cases, these new religious systems incorporated local shamanic practices and beliefs, further blurring the line between shamanism and organized religion.

Despite these changes, however, many of the core elements of shamanic practice continued to play an important role in organized religion. For example, many religious rituals and ceremonies involve altered states of consciousness, such as meditation or prayer, that are similar to the trance states induced by shamanic drumming or psychoactive plants. In addition, many organized religions place a strong emphasis on the importance of community and social connection, which are also central themes in shamanic practice.

Despite the many ways in which shamanism has influenced the development of organized religion, however, it is important to recognize that these two forms of spirituality are not necessarily mutually exclusive. Many people continue to practice both shamanism and organized religion, either separately or in combination, as a way of connecting with the divine and exploring the mysteries of the universe.

Examples:

Research the influence of shamanic beliefs and practices on the development of Christianity and Judaism. How have these religions incorporated elements of shamanism into their own beliefs and practices?

Explore the role of shamanism in the development of ancient Chinese religion, particularly the influence of the Daoist and Confucian traditions on shamanic beliefs and practices.

Compare and contrast the use of psychoactive plants in shamanic practice with the use of entheogens in organized religions such as Christianity, Hinduism, and Buddhism. How do these different spiritual traditions view the use of these substances, and what role do they play in spiritual practice?

Examples of shamanism and organized religion in different cultures

Shamanism and organized religion have taken on many different forms throughout history and across cultures. In this section, we will explore some examples of shamanic and organized religious practices in various cultures and examine how they have evolved over time.

Native American Religions

Native American religions are some of the most well-known examples of shamanic practices in the world. Many Native American cultures have a long history of shamanic practices, which include the use of psychoactive plants, drumming, and chanting to induce an altered state of consciousness. These practices are often used by shamans to communicate with spirits and ancestors, as well as to heal and provide guidance to members of the community.

In many Native American cultures, shamanism has evolved into organized religious practices that incorporate elements of Christianity and other religions. For example, the Native American Church, which is widespread among Native American tribes in the United States, combines traditional shamanic practices with Christian beliefs and practices.

African Religions

African religions also have a long history of shamanic practices, which vary widely depending on the specific culture. In many African cultures, the shaman serves as a healer, diviner, and mediator between the living and the dead. The shaman may also use psychoactive plants or other methods to enter an altered state of consciousness and communicate with spirits and ancestors.

Exploring Origins, Traditions, and Contemporary Relevance

Many African religions have also developed into organized religions with hierarchies of priests and other religious leaders. For example, in the Yoruba religion of Nigeria, the shamanic practices of divination and spirit communication have evolved into a complex system of religious beliefs and practices with a priesthood and organized worship.

Hinduism

Hinduism is another example of a religion with shamanic roots that has evolved into an organized religion over time. The earliest forms of Hinduism were based on shamanic practices and the worship of nature spirits and ancestors. Over time, Hinduism evolved into a complex system of religious beliefs and practices with a caste system, a pantheon of gods and goddesses, and a rich tradition of religious texts and scriptures.

Today, Hinduism is one of the world's major religions, with over a billion followers worldwide. It incorporates a wide range of beliefs and practices, from the worship of deities to the practice of meditation and yoga.

Buddhism

Buddhism is another example of a religion that has evolved from shamanic roots into an organized religion. The historical Buddha, Siddhartha Gautama, was a shamanic practitioner who sought enlightenment through meditation and other spiritual practices.

Over time, Buddhism evolved into a complex system of beliefs and practices with a hierarchy of monks and nuns and a rich tradition of religious texts and scriptures. Today, Buddhism is one of the world's major religions, with millions of followers worldwide.

Neo-Shamanism

In recent years, there has been a growing interest in shamanic practices among people in the West. This has led to the development of a movement known as neo-shamanism, which incorporates elements of traditional shamanic practices into a modern spiritual context.

Neo-shamanism often involves the use of drumming, chanting, and other methods to induce an altered state of consciousness, as well as the use of psychoactive plants and other traditional shamanic tools. It is often practiced in a group setting, with a shamanic practitioner leading the group in spiritual practices and ceremonies.

Critics of neo-shamanism argue that it is a form of cultural appropriation that appropriates traditional shamanic practices without proper understanding or respect for the cultures from which they originate.

Conclusion

Shamanism and organized religion have taken on many different forms throughout history and across cultures. While they share some similarities, such as the use of ritual and belief in a spiritual realm, they also have distinct differences in terms of structure, hierarchy, and the role of intermediaries.

Shamanism, as an early form of religious practice, emphasizes direct personal experience of the spiritual realm and the importance of community and social connection. It has been practiced in many different cultures across the world and continues to influence modern spiritual movements.

Organized religion, on the other hand, often emphasizes the importance of adherence to a set of beliefs and practices, with a structured hierarchy of leaders and intermediaries. It has played a significant role in shaping the development of many cultures and societies throughout history.

Examples of shamanism and organized religion in different cultures show the diversity of religious practices and beliefs around the world. The indigenous cultures of South America, for example, have a rich tradition of shamanic practices, while ancient civilizations such as Egypt and Greece developed complex organized religions with gods and goddesses, priesthoods, and elaborate rituals.

In some cultures, shamanism has evolved into organized religion, as seen in the case of the Bön religion of Tibet, which incorporates shamanic practices into a structured religious system. In other cases, organized religions have incorporated shamanic elements, as seen in the use of entheogens in certain Christian sects.

Critics of neo-shamanism argue that it is a form of cultural appropriation that appropriates traditional shamanic practices without proper understanding or respect for the cultures from which they originate. This highlights the importance of respecting and understanding the cultural context of religious practices and beliefs.

In conclusion, shamanism and organized religion offer distinct perspectives on spirituality and religious practice. While they may have different structures and beliefs, they both provide individuals and communities with a sense of connection to the spiritual realm and a framework for understanding the world around them.

Exploring Origins, Traditions, and Contemporary Relevance

Understanding the history and diversity of religious practices can help us appreciate the complexity and richness of human experience and provide a basis for respectful engagement with other cultures and belief systems.

Examples:

Research the use of shamanism in the indigenous cultures of North America and discuss how it differs from shamanism in South America.

Compare and contrast the role of intermediaries in organized religion and shamanism.

Explore the impact of the spread of organized religion on indigenous shamanic practices in the Americas.

Discuss the incorporation of shamanic practices into organized religions, using examples such as the Bön religion of Tibet and the use of entheogens in certain Christian sects.

Criticisms and controversies surrounding the idea of the evolution of religion from shamanism to organized religion

Criticisms and controversies surrounding the idea of the evolution of religion from shamanism to organized religion have been present for decades. While some scholars argue that there is a direct line of development from shamanism to organized religion, others disagree, suggesting that the two are fundamentally different in nature and should not be compared or conflated.

One of the main criticisms of the evolutionary approach to religion is that it is based on a flawed assumption that there is a linear trajectory of development from simple to complex. This perspective is based on a Eurocentric view of history and assumes that Western societies are more advanced and sophisticated than non-Western cultures. However, this is a highly problematic view, as it ignores the rich and diverse religious traditions of non-Western cultures, many of which are just as complex and sophisticated as their Western counterparts.

Critics of the evolutionary approach also argue that it oversimplifies the development of religion, ignoring the many factors that contribute to the formation and evolution of religious traditions. For example, the evolutionary approach tends to focus on the role of individual visionaries and leaders in the development of religion, ignoring the importance of social, political, and economic factors in shaping religious beliefs and practices.

Moreover, critics argue that the evolutionary approach to religion tends to overlook the diversity of religious experiences and practices, assuming that all religious traditions are the same and follow a similar trajectory of development. This view fails to acknowledge the rich and complex diversity of religious traditions and practices, each with their own unique history, beliefs, and practices.

Another criticism of the evolutionary approach to religion is that it is often based on outdated and inaccurate information about shamanism and organized religion. For example, the idea that shamanism is a primitive form of religion that evolved into more advanced organized religions has been challenged by scholars who point out that many indigenous shamanic traditions are highly sophisticated and complex, with their own rich and diverse spiritual practices and beliefs.

Furthermore, some scholars argue that the idea of a direct evolutionary link between shamanism and organized religion is based on a narrow and Western-centric definition of religion that does not take into account the wide range of spiritual practices and beliefs found in non-Western cultures. This view suggests that the evolutionary approach to religion is based on a biased and limited view of the diversity of human religious experiences.

Despite these criticisms and controversies, the idea of the evolution of religion from shamanism to organized religion remains an important and influential theory in the study of religion. While there is much debate and disagreement among scholars about the validity of this approach, it continues to shape the way we understand and study the diversity of religious traditions and practices found throughout the world.

Examples of controversies surrounding the idea of the evolution of religion from shamanism to organized religion can be seen in various religious traditions and cultures. For example, some indigenous communities in South America and other parts of the world have rejected the idea that shamanism is a primitive form of religion that has evolved into more advanced organized religions. Instead, they argue that shamanic practices are an integral part of their cultural and spiritual heritage and should be respected and valued as such.

Similarly, some scholars and practitioners of Western esotericism have criticized the evolutionary approach to religion, arguing that it is based on a narrow and biased view of history and culture that fails to acknowledge the rich and diverse spiritual traditions of non-Western cultures.

In conclusion, while the idea of the evolution of religion from shamanism to organized religion is a useful framework for understanding the diversity of religious traditions and practices found throughout the world, it is important to approach this theory with a critical and nuanced perspective. By acknowledging the rich and diverse history of religious traditions and practices, we can gain a deeper understanding and appreciation of the complex and multifaceted nature of human spirituality.

CHAPTER 4: CRITIQUES OF THE DIFFERENT THEORIES

In the previous chapters, we have explored the various theories regarding the evolution of religion from shamanism to organized religion. While each theory presents a different perspective on the origins and development of religious practices, they are not without their criticisms and controversies. In this chapter, we will examine some of the critiques that have been raised against these theories, and explore their implications for our understanding of religion.

Critique of the Diffusionist Theory

One of the main criticisms of the diffusionist theory is that it relies too heavily on the assumption that cultural traits and practices are transmitted from one culture to another through diffusion. While it is true that cultures do interact and exchange ideas, it is important to acknowledge that this process is not one-way or deterministic. Cultures are dynamic and complex, and cultural exchange can occur through a variety of mechanisms, including migration, trade, conquest, and imitation.

Critics of the diffusionist theory argue that it oversimplifies the complex processes of cultural transmission and ignores the agency of individuals and groups in shaping and adapting cultural practices. Furthermore, diffusionism tends to reinforce a Eurocentric view of cultural development, where Western cultures are seen as the most advanced and influential, while non-Western cultures are portrayed as passive recipients of Western influence.

Critique of the Evolutionary Theory

The evolutionary theory has also faced criticism from various scholars who argue that it is based on a simplistic and reductionist understanding of cultural development. One of the main critiques of the evolutionary theory is that it assumes that cultural evolution is a linear and progressive process, where cultures move from primitive to advanced stages of development. This view is often criticized for being ethnocentric and for ignoring the diversity of cultural forms and practices.

Another criticism of the evolutionary theory is that it tends to focus on the external factors that shape cultural development, such as environmental factors, technological advancements, and economic changes, while neglecting the internal factors, such as human agency, creativity, and innovation. This approach can lead to a deterministic and reductionist view of cultural development, where human beings are seen as passive agents of cultural change, rather than active participants in shaping their own cultural practices.

Critique of the Psychologizing Theory

The psychologizing theory has been criticized for its emphasis on individual psychology and its neglect of social and cultural factors that shape religious practices. Critics argue that the psychologizing theory tends to reduce complex cultural practices to individual psychological motivations, such as the need for security, comfort, or meaning. This approach ignores the social and cultural dimensions of religious practices, such as the role of tradition, community, and cultural norms.

Furthermore, the psychologizing theory tends to rely on a narrow and reductionist understanding of human psychology, often drawing on Western psychological models that may not be applicable to non-Western cultures. This approach can lead to a universalizing and ethnocentric view of religious practices, where diverse cultural practices are reduced to universal psychological needs.

Critique of the Functional Theory

The functional theory has been criticized for its emphasis on the adaptive and functional aspects of religious practices, while neglecting their symbolic and expressive dimensions. Critics argue that the functional theory tends to reduce religion to its utilitarian functions, such as providing social cohesion, regulating behavior, and reducing anxiety. This approach ignores the symbolic and expressive aspects of religious practices, such as their aesthetic, artistic, and emotional dimensions.

Furthermore, the functional theory tends to assume a static and homogenous view of society, where social institutions serve stable and fixed functions. This view ignores the dynamic and contested nature of social institutions, where different groups and individuals may have different interests and interpretations of the same social institutions.

In conclusion, the different theories regarding the evolution of religion from shamanism to organized religion have provided us with a framework to understand the historical and cultural contexts in which religion has developed. While each theory has its own strengths and limitations, it is important to critically evaluate their assumptions and implications.

The diffusion theory highlights the role of cultural contact and exchange in shaping religious practices, but it may oversimplify the complex processes of cultural interaction and transformation. The adaptation theory emphasizes the functional benefits of religious practices for social cohesion and survival, but it may neglect the diversity and complexity of religious beliefs and practices.

The neo-shamanism movement draws inspiration from various shamanic traditions, but it also raises ethical and cultural issues of appropriation and authenticity. The critiques of the evolution theory remind us to consider the diverse and dynamic nature of religious practices, and the potential for multiple interpretations and interests within and across societies.

Therefore, a more nuanced and comprehensive approach is needed to understand the complexities and diversities of religious practices and their historical and cultural contexts. Such an approach should incorporate insights from various disciplines, such as anthropology, sociology, history, psychology, and ecology, and should be sensitive to the voices and perspectives of different cultural groups and individuals.

The next chapter will examine the role of ecology and spirituality in the contemporary environmental movement, and how different spiritual practices and beliefs can inform and inspire ecological awareness and activism.

Overview of criticisms and controversies surrounding the different theories on the origins of religion

Theories on the origins of religion have been a subject of debate for centuries, and there is still no consensus among scholars. The different theories offer varying perspectives on how religion emerged and evolved over time, with some tracing it back to shamanism, while others propose a more gradual development from animism to polytheism to monotheism. While each theory offers valuable insights into the development of religion, they are not without their criticisms and controversies.

One of the main criticisms of the shamanism-to-organized religion theory is that it is often based on a Western-centric view of religion. It assumes that shamanism is a primitive form of religion and that organized religion represents a higher form of development. This view has been challenged by scholars who argue that shamanism is a complex and sophisticated system of beliefs and practices that are just as valid and meaningful as organized religion.

Moreover, the shamanism-to-organized religion theory has been criticized for its oversimplification of the historical and cultural diversity of shamanic and organized religions. It tends to treat all shamanic practices and organized religions as homogenous and static, ignoring the rich and varied cultural contexts in which they exist.

Another criticism of the shamanism-to-organized religion theory is that it overlooks the agency and creativity of religious practitioners in shaping and adapting their beliefs and practices. Religious traditions are not simply passive recipients of cultural influences but actively engage with and reinterpret their cultural heritage.

The gradualist theory that posits a linear progression from animism to polytheism to monotheism has also been criticized for its simplistic and reductionist view of religion. It assumes that religion can be neatly categorized into discrete stages of development, ignoring the complexity and diversity of religious beliefs and practices across cultures and historical periods.

Furthermore, the gradualist theory has been accused of imposing a Western bias on the study of religion. It assumes that monotheism is the ultimate goal of religious development, which ignores the fact that many cultures have complex polytheistic or animistic traditions that are just as valid and meaningful as monotheistic religions.

Finally, the functional theory that views religion as serving a specific function in society has been criticized for its deterministic view of religion. It assumes that religion is solely driven by its function in society, ignoring the spiritual and personal motivations of religious practitioners.

In addition, the functional theory tends to assume a static and homogenous view of society, where social institutions serve stable and fixed functions. This view ignores the dynamic and contested nature of social institutions, where different groups and individuals may have different interests and interpretations of the same social institutions.

In conclusion, the different theories on the origins and evolution of religion have generated significant debates and controversies within the academic community. While each theory offers valuable insights into the development of religion, they are not without their criticisms and controversies. In the following chapters, we will explore in greater detail the criticisms and controversies surrounding each theory, providing a comprehensive and nuanced view of the subject.

Analysis of common critiques and objections to the different theories

Theories on the origins and evolution of religion have been a subject of academic inquiry for centuries. From the functionalist approach of Emile Durkheim to the cognitive approach of Pascal Boyer, different scholars have attempted to explain how religious beliefs and practices emerged and transformed over time. However, no theory is immune to criticisms and controversies. In this chapter, we will explore some of the most common critiques and objections to the different theories on the origins of religion, with a focus on the functionalist, cognitive, and evolutionary theories.

Critiques of the Functional Theory

The functional theory, which posits that religion emerged as a way to promote social solidarity and cooperation, has been criticized on several grounds. One of the most prominent criticisms is that it assumes a static and homogenous view of society, where social institutions serve stable and fixed functions. This view ignores the dynamic and contested nature of social institutions, where different groups and individuals may have different interests and interpretations of the same social institutions. For example, religion may not always serve to promote social solidarity, but may instead be used to justify social inequalities and conflicts.

Another criticism of the functional theory is that it overemphasizes the role of religion in promoting social integration and underemphasizes its role in promoting social differentiation. In other words, religion may not always serve to bring people together, but may instead serve to create divisions and hierarchies based on religious beliefs and practices. For example, the caste system in India is often justified by religious beliefs, but it also reinforces social inequalities and discrimination.

Critiques of the Cognitive Theory

The cognitive theory, which posits that religion emerged as a byproduct of cognitive mechanisms that evolved to solve other adaptive problems, has also been subject to criticism. One of the main critiques is that it reduces religion to a mere epiphenomenon of cognitive processes, without giving due consideration to the cultural and historical factors that shape religious beliefs and practices. In other words, the cognitive theory tends to overlook the social and historical contexts in which religious beliefs and practices emerge and evolve.

Another criticism of the cognitive theory is that it assumes a universal and static human nature, where all human beings share the same cognitive processes and mental structures. This view ignores the diversity and variability of human cultures and societies, where different groups and individuals may have different ways of perceiving and interpreting the world. For example, the concept of God in monotheistic religions may not be universal, but may instead reflect specific cultural and historical contexts.

Critiques of the Evolutionary Theory

The evolutionary theory, which posits that religion emerged as a result of natural selection and adaptation to the environment, has also faced criticism. One of the main critiques is that it relies on a simplistic and reductionist view of evolution, where complex and multifaceted phenomena are reduced to simple and linear processes. This view ignores the complexity and contingency of evolutionary processes, where multiple factors and interactions shape the emergence and evolution of traits and behaviors.

Another criticism of the evolutionary theory is that it tends to overemphasize the adaptive value of religious beliefs and practices, without considering their costs and trade-offs. In other words, religion may not always be a net benefit to individuals and societies, but may instead entail risks and liabilities. For example, religious conflicts and wars may have catastrophic consequences for human well-being and survival.

In conclusion, the different theories on the origins and evolution of religion have been subject to various critiques and controversies. These critiques and controversies reflect the diversity and complexity of human cultures and societies, where no theory can fully capture the richness and variability of religious beliefs and practices. Nevertheless, these critiques and controversies also provide opportunities for critical reflection and dialogue, where different perspectives and approaches can enrich our understanding of the human experience.

Examination of alternative theories and perspectives

The different theories on the origins and evolution of religion have been subject to numerous criticisms and objections. Some of these critiques are directed towards specific theories, while others are more general and target the assumptions and methods underlying the study of religion. These critiques and objections have led to the development of alternative theories and perspectives that challenge or complement the mainstream views.

This chapter will provide an overview and analysis of some of the most prominent alternative theories and perspectives on the origins and evolution of religion. We will examine their strengths and weaknesses, and compare them to the mainstream theories. We will also discuss how these alternative theories and perspectives contribute to our understanding of religion, and how they can inspire new research questions and approaches.

African Religions

Theories and Perspectives

Ecological perspectives on the origins and evolution of religion emphasize the role of the natural environment in shaping human beliefs and practices. These perspectives argue that the ecological conditions in which early human societies developed had a profound impact on their religious beliefs and practices. For example, the scarcity or abundance of resources, the presence or absence of natural disasters, and the proximity or isolation from other groups could all influence the development of religious beliefs and practices.

One of the most influential ecological perspectives is the bioregional approach, which argues that human cultures and religions are shaped by the unique features of their bioregion - the geographic area defined by its natural and cultural characteristics. According to this approach, different bioregions have different ecological challenges and opportunities, and therefore different ways of adapting to and making sense of the world. For example, a bioregion with abundant rainfall and fertile soil may develop a religion that emphasizes the importance of agriculture and the cyclical nature of growth and decay, while a bioregion with harsh winters and limited resources may develop a religion that emphasizes the importance of survival and endurance.

Ecological perspectives have been criticized for oversimplifying the relationship between the natural environment and human culture, and for neglecting the role of human agency and culture in shaping religious beliefs and practices. However, they have also inspired new research questions and approaches that integrate ecological and cultural factors in the study of religion.

Cognitive perspectives on the origins and evolution of religion emphasize the role of human cognition and psychology in shaping religious beliefs and practices. These perspectives argue that humans have evolved cognitive mechanisms that predispose them to perceive and interpret the world in religious terms, such as agency detection, theory of mind, and teleological thinking. According to these perspectives, religion is not a byproduct of cultural evolution, but a product of cognitive evolution.

One of the most influential cognitive perspectives is the theory of religion as an evolved adaptive illusion, which argues that religion is a byproduct of our evolved cognitive mechanisms for detecting and responding to social and environmental cues. According to this theory, religious beliefs and practices have no inherent truth value, but are rather adaptive illusions that enhance our survival and reproduction by providing us with a sense of control, meaning, and social cohesion.

Exploring Origins, Traditions, and Contemporary Relevance

Cognitive perspectives have been criticized for oversimplifying the complexity and diversity of religious beliefs and practices, and for neglecting the role of culture and social context in shaping religious experiences. However, they have also inspired new research questions and approaches that integrate cognitive and cultural factors in the study of religion.

Postcolonial and decolonial perspectives on the origins and evolution of religion emphasize the role of colonialism and imperialism in shaping the study and interpretation of religion. These perspectives argue that the Eurocentric and colonialist assumptions and methods underlying the study of religion have marginalized and distorted the perspectives and experiences of non-European and non-Western cultures and religions.

One of the most influential postcolonial perspectives is the critique of Orientalism, which argues that the Western study of non-Western cultures, including religion, is shaped by a colonialist and orientalist mindset that reinforces the superiority and domination of the West over the East. According to this critique, Western scholars have constructed a distorted and exoticized image of the East as backward, irrational, and mystical, which serves to justify Western imperialist projects and to marginalize and silence the voices and perspectives of the colonized peoples.

In the field of religious studies, this critique has led to a growing awareness of the need to decolonize the study of religion and to incorporate the perspectives and experiences of non-European and non-Western cultures and religions. Decolonial approaches to the study of religion emphasize the importance of centering the perspectives and voices of the colonized and marginalized peoples in the study of religion, and of challenging the Eurocentric and colonialist assumptions and methods that have dominated the field.

For example, some decolonial scholars argue that the concept of religion itself is a Eurocentric construct that has been used to impose Western categories and norms on non-Western cultures and religions. They argue that instead of studying religion as a discrete and universal category, we should adopt more nuanced and context-specific approaches that recognize the diversity and complexity of religious practices and beliefs across different cultures and historical contexts.

Other decolonial scholars have called for a more critical and reflexive approach to the study of religion, which recognizes the ways in which the study of religion has been shaped by power relations and political agendas. They argue that by exposing and challenging the political and ideological biases underlying the study of religion, we can create a more democratic and inclusive field that is open to a diversity of perspectives and voices.

In conclusion, the examination of alternative theories and perspectives on the origins and evolution of religion has highlighted the diverse and contested nature of this field of study. While the dominant theories have provided valuable insights into the historical and cultural development of religion, they have also been subject to a range of critiques and objections. By exploring alternative theories and perspectives, we can broaden our understanding of religion and challenge the assumptions and biases that have shaped the field. In the next chapter, we will explore some of the practical applications and implications of the study of religion, including its role in contemporary society and its potential for promoting social justice and environmental sustainability.

CHAPTER 5: CONTEMPORARY THEORIES ON THE ORIGINS OF RELIGION

In recent decades, there has been a surge of interest and research into the origins of religion. Advances in archaeology, genetics, neuroscience, and other disciplines have provided new insights into the development of human cognition, social behavior, and cultural practices, shedding light on the emergence and evolution of religious beliefs and practices. Moreover, the growing diversity and globalization of religious traditions have raised new questions and challenges for understanding the complex and dynamic nature of religion.

This chapter provides an overview of some of the most influential and innovative contemporary theories on the origins of religion. These theories range from evolutionary and cognitive models to sociological and cultural approaches, and they offer a variety of perspectives on the origins, functions, and meanings of religion. By examining these theories and their implications, we can gain a deeper understanding of the complex interplay between biology, culture, and history that has shaped human religiosity.

Analysis of Current Research and Findings on the Origins of Religion

One of the most important developments in the study of religion has been the integration of interdisciplinary research methods and approaches. For example, advances in genetics and archaeology have allowed researchers to trace the evolution and migration of human populations and their religious practices, providing new insights into the origins and spread of religion. Similarly, cognitive and neuroscience research has shed light on the cognitive processes underlying religious experiences and beliefs, illuminating the psychological and neurological foundations of religious behavior.

Some contemporary theories have emphasized the role of social and cultural factors in the development of religion. For example, the sociological approach to the origins of religion posits that religion emerged as a response to social needs and pressures, such as the need for social cohesion, identity formation, and conflict resolution. Similarly, the cultural approach argues that religion is a product of cultural evolution, shaped by historical and environmental factors, as well as cultural transmission and adaptation.

Other theories have focused on the cognitive and evolutionary roots of religion. The cognitive approach suggests that religion emerged as a byproduct of cognitive mechanisms that evolved for other purposes, such as social cognition, agency detection, or theory of mind. The evolutionary approach, on the other hand, proposes that religion evolved as an adaptive response to specific environmental or social challenges, such as ecological complexity, group competition, or moral dilemmas.

Relevance and Implications of Contemporary Theories on the Origins of Religion

The contemporary theories on the origins of religion have important implications for a wide range of fields, including anthropology, sociology, psychology, biology, and philosophy. For example, they can help us understand the complex interplay between biology and culture in shaping human behavior, and how this interplay has influenced the emergence and diversity of religious traditions. They can also inform debates about the relationship between religion and morality, the role of religion in social and political conflicts, and the potential for religious change and innovation.

Moreover, the contemporary theories on the origins of religion can provide valuable insights for practitioners and scholars in various religious traditions. By understanding the historical and cultural contexts of their own traditions, as well as the cognitive and social mechanisms underlying religious beliefs and practices, religious practitioners can gain a deeper appreciation for the diversity and complexity of human religiosity. They can also draw on these insights to develop new approaches to religious education, ritual, and social engagement.

Examples of Contemporary Theories and Their Application in Different Fields

There are many examples of contemporary theories on the origins of religion and their application in different fields. For example, the cognitive approach to the origins of religion has inspired new research on the relationship between religious experiences and brain activity, as well as the cross-cultural similarities and differences in religious cognition. Similarly, the evolutionary approach has led to new studies on the adaptive significance of religious beliefs and practices, as well as the relationship between religion and health.

In the field of archaeology, recent discoveries and analyses of material culture have provided new insights into the origins and development of religious beliefs and practices. For example, studies of ancient Egyptian burial sites have revealed the use of ritual and symbolic objects, such as amulets and funerary masks, which shed light on the religious beliefs and practices of this culture. Similarly, excavations of

Neolithic sites in Europe have uncovered evidence of ritual structures and artifacts, such as stone circles and figurines, which suggest the emergence of early religious practices.

The study of contemporary religions also provides a fertile ground for the application of contemporary theories on the origins of religion. For example, the study of new religious movements, such as Scientology or the Church of the Flying Spaghetti Monster, can shed light on the role of charisma, social networks, and cultural context in the formation and spread of religious ideas and practices. Similarly, the study of traditional religions, such as African diaspora religions or Native American religions, can contribute to the understanding of the role of colonialism, globalization, and cultural exchange in the shaping of religious beliefs and practices.

Contemporary theories on the origins of religion are also relevant to broader societal debates and issues. For example, the cognitive approach has been applied to understanding the psychology of religious violence, while the evolutionary approach has been used to examine the role of religion in promoting social cohesion and cooperation. Similarly, the study of the origins of religion can provide insights into the relationship between religion and environmentalism, or the ways in which religion shapes attitudes towards gender and sexuality.

In conclusion, contemporary theories on the origins of religion are a vibrant and growing field of study, with important implications for a wide range of disciplines and issues. By drawing on insights from neuroscience, anthropology, psychology, and other fields, contemporary theories offer new perspectives on the origins, development, and function of religion. Through the application of these theories in different fields and contexts, we can deepen our understanding of the diversity and complexity of religious beliefs and practices across time and space.

Overview of contemporary theories on the origins of religion

The study of the origins of religion has been a central topic in the field of religious studies for many years. However, the nature and origins of religion remain highly contested and have been subject to various interpretations and theoretical approaches. In recent years, a number of new and innovative theories have emerged that seek to shed light on the origins and evolution of religion. These theories draw on a range of disciplines, including cognitive psychology, evolutionary biology, anthropology, and archaeology, to name a few.

In this chapter, we will provide an overview of some of the most influential contemporary theories on the origins of religion. We will begin by exploring the cognitive approach, which argues that religion is a product of the human mind's inherent cognitive biases and limitations. We will then discuss the evolutionary approach, which posits that religion is a product of natural selection and has evolved to serve adaptive functions. Next, we will examine the social and cultural approach, which emphasizes the role of social and cultural factors in the origins and evolution of religion. Finally, we will discuss the symbolic approach, which views religion as a symbolic system that helps humans make sense of the world.

✧ The cognitive approach

The cognitive approach to the origins of religion emphasizes the role of the human mind in the development of religious beliefs and practices. Proponents of this approach argue that religion is a product of the cognitive biases and limitations that are inherent in the human mind. They suggest that the human mind is predisposed to believe in supernatural entities and forces and that this predisposition has been shaped by natural selection.

According to this approach, the human mind is limited in its ability to process and interpret information about the world. This limitation is due to the brain's limited capacity for processing information, as well as its tendency to rely on heuristics and shortcuts to simplify complex information. As a result, the human mind tends to categorize and simplify information about the world in ways that reflect its inherent biases and limitations.

Proponents of the cognitive approach argue that religion is a product of these cognitive biases and limitations. They suggest that the human mind is predisposed to believe in supernatural entities and forces and that this predisposition has been shaped by natural selection. They argue that the human mind has evolved to be sensitive to certain kinds of information, such as the presence of other minds and the existence of agency and intentionality in the world. These cognitive predispositions, they argue, have led humans to develop religious beliefs and practices that reflect these biases and limitations.

The cognitive approach has inspired a great deal of research into the relationship between religious experiences and brain activity, as well as the cross-cultural similarities and differences in religious cognition. It has also led to new insights into the role of ritual and symbolism in the development of religious beliefs and practices.

✧ The evolutionary approach

The evolutionary approach to the origins of religion posits that religion is a product of natural selection and has evolved to serve adaptive functions. Proponents of this approach argue that religion has evolved to serve a number of adaptive functions, such as providing a sense of social cohesion and promoting prosocial behavior.

According to this approach, religion has evolved because it confers some kind of fitness advantage on the individuals and groups that practice it. This advantage may take the form of increased cooperation, social cohesion, or a sense of purpose and meaning in life. The evolutionary approach suggests that religion has evolved to serve these functions because they increase the likelihood of survival and reproductive success.

The evolutionary approach has led to new studies on the adaptive significance of religious beliefs and practices, as well as the relationship between religion and health. For example, some studies have suggested that religious beliefs and practices can promote mental and physical health by reducing stress and anxiety and increasing social support.

✧ **The social and cultural approach**

The social and cultural approach to the origins of religion focuses on the role of social and cultural factors in the development and transmission of religious beliefs and practices. This approach emphasizes the importance of social and cultural context in shaping religious beliefs and practices, and suggests that religious phenomena can be understood as social and cultural constructions that reflect the values, norms, and practices of the societies in which they arise.

One of the key concepts in the social and cultural approach is the idea of religious pluralism, which refers to the coexistence and interaction of different religious traditions in a given society. According to this perspective, the emergence and evolution of religious traditions is influenced by the interactions between different groups and their cultural and social contexts. For example, the development of syncretic religions, which combine elements from different religious traditions, can be seen as a result of cultural contact and hybridization.

The social and cultural approach also emphasizes the importance of power relations in shaping religious beliefs and practices. According to this perspective, religious traditions can be seen as part of a broader system of power relations, in which certain groups have more influence and control over the definition and interpretation of religious meanings and practices. This can lead to the marginalization or suppression of certain religious traditions, or the privileging of others.

The social and cultural approach has been influential in a variety of fields, including anthropology, sociology, and cultural studies. It has led to new insights into the role of religion in shaping social and cultural practices, as well as the impact of social and cultural contexts on the development and transmission of religious beliefs and practices.

✧   **The cognitive approach**

The cognitive approach to the origins of religion focuses on the psychological and neurological processes that underlie religious beliefs and experiences. This approach suggests that religious phenomena can be understood as the result of cognitive processes, such as perception, memory, and reasoning, that are shaped by evolutionary and cultural factors.

One of the key concepts in the cognitive approach is the idea of the religious instinct, which suggests that humans have a natural propensity to seek out religious experiences and explanations. According to this perspective, religious beliefs and practices can be seen as the product of cognitive mechanisms that evolved to help humans make sense of their world and cope with uncertainty and ambiguity.

The cognitive approach has led to new research on the relationship between religious experiences and brain activity, as well as the cross-cultural similarities and differences in religious cognition. For example, studies have shown that religious experiences activate similar regions of the brain across different cultures and religious traditions, suggesting that there may be universal cognitive processes underlying religious experiences.

✧   **The ecological approach**

The ecological approach to the origins of religion focuses on the relationship between humans and their natural environment. This approach suggests that religious beliefs and practices can be understood as responses to ecological challenges and opportunities, such as environmental disasters, resource scarcity, and the need for cooperation and social organization.

One of the key concepts in the ecological approach is the idea of biophilia, which refers to the innate human tendency to seek connections with nature and other forms of life. According to this perspective, religious beliefs and practices can be seen as expressions of this biophilic tendency, as humans seek to establish meaningful relationships with the natural world.

Exploring Origins, Traditions, and Contemporary Relevance

The ecological approach has led to new research on the relationship between religion and environmentalism, as well as the role of religion in promoting sustainable and ecologically responsible behavior. For example, studies have shown that religious beliefs and practices can influence attitudes towards the environment, and that religious organizations can play an important role in promoting environmental activism and conservation.

Overall, contemporary theories on the origins of religion offer a wide range of perspectives and approaches to understanding the complex and multifaceted phenomenon of religion. These theories emphasize the importance of interdisciplinary and cross-cultural research, as well as the need to consider the multiple factors that contribute to the emergence and evolution of religious beliefs and practices.

Analysis of current research and findings on the origins of religion

The study of the origins of religion is a multidisciplinary field that involves scholars from diverse disciplines, such as anthropology, archaeology, psychology, cognitive science, biology, and history. Over the past few decades, there has been significant progress in understanding the origins of religion, thanks to advances in scientific methods, new theoretical frameworks, and the integration of multiple perspectives. In this section, we will analyze some of the current research and findings on the origins of religion.

Cognitive and neuroscientific studies

One of the most influential approaches to the origins of religion is the cognitive approach, which emphasizes the role of the human mind and brain in shaping religious beliefs and practices. According to this approach, religion is a natural and universal phenomenon that arises from the human brain's cognitive processes, such as perception, memory, reasoning, and social cognition. Researchers in this field use various methods, such as experimental studies, brain imaging, and cross-cultural comparisons, to investigate the cognitive and neural mechanisms underlying religious experiences and beliefs.

For example, studies using brain imaging techniques such as functional magnetic resonance imaging (fMRI) and electroencephalography (EEG) have shown that certain brain regions, such as the medial prefrontal cortex, the anterior cingulate cortex, and the temporal lobes, are activated during religious experiences and practices, such as prayer, meditation, and ritual. These studies suggest that religious experiences may be associated with changes in brain activity and connectivity, which may have adaptive functions, such as reducing stress, enhancing social bonding, and promoting prosocial behavior.

Other cognitive studies have focused on the cross-cultural similarities and differences in religious cognition, such as the concept of God, supernatural agents, and moral values. For example, researchers have found that many cultures have similar beliefs in supernatural agents, such as gods, spirits, and ancestors, which are often attributed with agency, intentionality, and moral values. These beliefs may have emerged from the human tendency to perceive patterns and agency in the environment and to anthropomorphize natural phenomena.

Evolutionary studies

Another influential approach to the origins of religion is the evolutionary approach, which emphasizes the adaptive functions of religious beliefs and practices in human evolution. According to this approach, religion may have evolved as a set of cognitive, emotional, and behavioral adaptations that helped humans cope with the challenges of social living, such as cooperation, conflict resolution, and group cohesion.

Researchers in this field use various methods, such as comparative analyses, experimental studies, and computational models, to investigate the evolutionary origins and functions of religion. For example, studies have shown that religious beliefs and practices are associated with various fitness benefits, such as increased social support, reduced stress, enhanced immune function, and improved reproductive success. These benefits may have contributed to the spread and persistence of religious beliefs and practices across different cultures and historical periods.

Other evolutionary studies have focused on the cultural transmission and variation of religious beliefs and practices, such as the role of cultural evolution, gene-culture coevolution, and cultural group selection. For example, researchers have found that religious beliefs and practices are often transmitted through social learning, such as imitation, teaching, and storytelling, and that cultural evolution may play a key role in shaping the diversity and complexity of religious traditions.

Archaeological and historical studies

Another important approach to the origins of religion is the archaeological and historical approach, which emphasizes the material and textual evidence of past religious practices and beliefs. According to this approach, religion is a cultural and historical phenomenon that can be traced back to the earliest human societies and can be studied through the analysis of artifacts, architecture, iconography, and texts.

Exploring Origins, Traditions, and Contemporary Relevance

Researchers in this field use various methods, such as excavations, surveys, and textual analysis, to investigate the archaeological and historical evidence related to religious practices and beliefs. Archaeological evidence includes objects, such as ritual artifacts, temples, and burial sites, while textual evidence includes religious texts, such as myths, hymns, and prayers. By analyzing these sources, researchers can gain insights into the beliefs, rituals, and social organization of past societies and their religious practices.

One of the key findings of the archaeological and historical approach is the diversity of religious practices and beliefs across time and space. For example, the ancient Egyptian religion, which lasted for over three thousand years, underwent numerous changes and adaptations, reflecting the political, social, and cultural transformations of Egyptian society. Similarly, the Hindu religion, which has a history of over four thousand years, has undergone significant changes and transformations, with the development of new rituals, doctrines, and beliefs over time.

Another important finding of the archaeological and historical approach is the role of religion in shaping social and political structures. For example, the emergence of complex societies and states in ancient Mesopotamia and Egypt was closely linked to the development of religious institutions and the centralization of religious authority. Similarly, the spread of Buddhism and Christianity in Asia and Europe, respectively, played a significant role in the formation of new cultural and political identities and the integration of diverse populations.

Recent research in this field has also focused on the interplay between religion and material culture, such as art, architecture, and landscape. For example, studies of the architecture of ancient temples and shrines have revealed the symbolic meanings and social functions of religious spaces, as well as the role of art and decoration in creating religious experiences. Similarly, research on the use of natural materials, such as plants and minerals, in religious rituals and healing practices has highlighted the importance of ecological and cultural factors in shaping religious practices and beliefs.

Despite the insights gained from the archaeological and historical approach, there are also limitations and challenges in interpreting the evidence. For example, the interpretation of artifacts and texts is often influenced by the biases and assumptions of the researchers, as well as the political and social contexts in which they work. In addition, the lack of written records and the destruction of archaeological sites and artifacts can limit our understanding of past religious practices and beliefs.

Overall, the archaeological and historical approach provides a valuable perspective on the origins of religion and its role in shaping human societies and cultures. By combining the analysis of material and textual evidence with theoretical frameworks and interdisciplinary methods, researchers can continue to uncover new insights into the diversity and complexity of religious practices and beliefs throughout history.

Discussion of the relevance and implications of contemporary theories on the origins of religion

The study of the origins of religion has important implications for a variety of fields, including anthropology, sociology, psychology, and philosophy. The various contemporary theories and approaches to the origins of religion have shed light on the nature of religion, its universality and diversity, and its role in human society and culture. In this section, we will discuss the relevance and implications of contemporary theories on the origins of religion for these fields.

Anthropology

Anthropology is the study of human societies and cultures. The study of the origins of religion is a central part of anthropology, as religion is an important aspect of human culture. The cognitive, evolutionary, social, and archaeological approaches to the origins of religion have all contributed to our understanding of religion as a cultural and historical phenomenon.

The cognitive approach has emphasized the universality of religious cognition and the ways in which the human mind is predisposed to religious beliefs and practices. This approach has helped anthropologists understand why religion is such a widespread and enduring feature of human culture.

The evolutionary approach has focused on the adaptive significance of religion and the ways in which religious beliefs and practices may have provided evolutionary advantages to early human societies. This approach has helped anthropologists understand the role of religion in human social organization and cooperation.

The social and cultural approach has emphasized the cultural and historical context of religion, and the ways in which religion is shaped by and shapes social structures and cultural values. This approach has helped anthropologists understand the diversity of religious beliefs and practices across different societies and cultures.

The archaeological and historical approach has emphasized the material and textual evidence of past religious practices and beliefs. This approach has helped anthropologists understand the development and evolution of religious beliefs and practices over time.

Exploring Origins, Traditions, and Contemporary Relevance

Sociology

Sociology is the study of human social behavior and institutions. The study of the origins of religion is relevant to sociology, as religion is a major social institution that shapes social norms, values, and behaviors. The various contemporary theories and approaches to the origins of religion have shed light on the ways in which religion shapes social organization and interaction.

The cognitive approach has emphasized the ways in which religious beliefs and practices provide social cohesion and identity. This approach has helped sociologists understand the role of religion in the formation and maintenance of social groups.

The evolutionary approach has emphasized the ways in which religion may have provided evolutionary advantages to early human societies, such as increased cooperation and conflict resolution. This approach has helped sociologists understand the role of religion in the development and maintenance of social order.

The social and cultural approach has emphasized the ways in which religion reflects and reinforces social norms and values. This approach has helped sociologists understand the ways in which religion shapes social attitudes and behaviors.

The archaeological and historical approach has emphasized the ways in which religion is shaped by and shapes historical and cultural contexts. This approach has helped sociologists understand the ways in which religion changes over time and across different societies and cultures.

Psychology

Psychology is the scientific study of human behavior and mental processes. The study of the origins of religion is relevant to psychology, as religion is an important aspect of human cognition and behavior. The various contemporary theories and approaches to the origins of religion have shed light on the ways in which religion is related to psychological processes and outcomes.

The cognitive approach has emphasized the ways in which religious beliefs and practices are shaped by cognitive processes, such as perception, memory, and attention. This approach has helped psychologists understand the ways in which religious beliefs and practices affect cognitive and emotional processes.

The evolutionary approach has emphasized the ways in which religion may have provided adaptive advantages to early human societies, such as reducing stress and anxiety. This approach has helped psychologists understand the ways in which religious beliefs and practices affect mental and physical health.

The social and cultural approach has emphasized the ways in which religion is shaped by social and cultural factors, such as social norms, values, and beliefs. This approach has helped psychologists understand the ways in which religion is related to social identity, intergroup relations, and attitudes towards out-groups.

For example, research has found that religious individuals tend to have more positive attitudes towards their own group and more negative attitudes towards out-groups, compared to non-religious individuals. This suggests that religion may play a role in shaping intergroup relations and attitudes.

Another important area of research in psychology is the study of religious experiences, such as mystical experiences and spiritual experiences. The cognitive approach has contributed to our understanding of the cognitive processes underlying these experiences, such as altered states of consciousness and the role of perception in religious experiences.

Moreover, the study of religious experiences is relevant to clinical psychology, as some individuals may experience religious or spiritual experiences as part of their mental health treatment. For example, some studies have found that religious or spiritual experiences can be beneficial for individuals with depression, anxiety, and addiction.

The study of the origins of religion is also relevant to the study of religious fundamentalism and extremism. Some scholars have argued that religious fundamentalism and extremism may be a response to cultural and social changes that threaten traditional religious beliefs and values. By understanding the ways in which religion is related to social and cultural factors, psychologists can better understand the psychological processes underlying religious fundamentalism and extremism, and potentially develop strategies for reducing its impact.

Overall, the study of the origins of religion has important implications for psychology, as it helps us understand the ways in which religion is related to cognitive, emotional, and social processes. This knowledge can inform psychological interventions and treatments for individuals with mental health issues, as well as inform strategies for promoting intergroup harmony and reducing the negative impact of religious fundamentalism and extremism.

Exploring Origins, Traditions, and Contemporary Relevance

Examples of contemporary theories and their application in different fields

Contemporary theories on the origins of religion have wide-ranging applications in various fields, such as anthropology, sociology, philosophy, and even neuroscience. In this section, we will examine some examples of how these theories have been applied in different fields.

Anthropology:

Anthropologists have long been interested in the study of religion and its role in human societies. Contemporary theories on the origins of religion have helped anthropologists understand the diversity of religious beliefs and practices across cultures and time periods. For example, the cognitive approach has been used to study the role of perception and memory in religious rituals and beliefs. The evolutionary approach has been used to study the adaptive advantages of religious beliefs and practices in early human societies. The social and cultural approach has been used to study the ways in which religion is shaped by social and cultural factors.

Sociology:

Sociologists have also been interested in the study of religion and its role in society. Contemporary theories on the origins of religion have helped sociologists understand the social and cultural factors that shape religious beliefs and practices. For example, the social and cultural approach has been used to study the ways in which religion is used to create and reinforce social norms and values. The cognitive approach has been used to study the ways in which religious beliefs and practices affect social behavior and attitudes.

Philosophy:

Philosophers have long been interested in the study of religion and its relationship to ethics and morality. Contemporary theories on the origins of religion have helped philosophers understand the ways in which religious beliefs and practices influence ethical and moral decision-making. For example, the cognitive approach has been used to study the ways in which religious beliefs and practices affect moral reasoning. The evolutionary approach has been used to study the ways in which religion may have provided adaptive advantages for the development of moral behavior in early human societies.

Neuroscience:

Recent advances in neuroscience have opened up new avenues for the study of religion and its relationship to the brain. Contemporary theories on the origins of religion have helped neuroscientists understand the ways in which religious beliefs and practices affect brain function and behavior. For example, the cognitive approach has been used to study the neural mechanisms involved in religious experiences and beliefs. The evolutionary approach has been used to study the ways in which religious beliefs and practices may have shaped the development of the human brain.

In conclusion, contemporary theories on the origins of religion have broad applications in various fields, from anthropology to neuroscience. These theories have helped researchers gain a better understanding of the diversity of religious beliefs and practices across cultures and time periods, as well as the ways in which religion is shaped by cognitive, evolutionary, and social and cultural factors.

Exploring Origins, Traditions, and Contemporary Relevance

PART 2: AFRICAN RELIGIONS: AN INTRODUCTION

The African continent is home to a diverse array of religious traditions that have played an important role in shaping the cultures and societies of the region. These religious traditions are often characterized by a close connection to the natural world, a strong emphasis on communal identity, and a rich mythology that reflects the history and experiences of the African people.

In this section, we will explore the key features and practices of African religions, including their historical development, cosmologies, and ritual practices. We will also examine the ways in which African religions have been impacted by colonization and globalization, and how they have adapted to changing social and political circumstances.

Through our analysis of African religions, we hope to provide students with a deeper understanding of the diversity and complexity of religious traditions around the world, as well as the ways in which religion intersects with social, cultural, and political dynamics. We also aim to challenge some of the stereotypes and misconceptions that surround African religions, and to highlight the ways in which they continue to shape and influence contemporary African societies.

CHAPTER 6: OVERVIEW OF AFRICAN RELIGIONS AND THEIR DIVERSITY

African religions refer to the spiritual practices, beliefs, and rituals of the various indigenous peoples of Africa. These religions have been practiced for thousands of years, and their origins are deeply rooted in the history, culture, and traditions of Africa. Today, African religions continue to thrive and evolve, and are an important part of the cultural heritage of the African continent.

In this chapter, we will explore the concept of African religions, their diversity, and some of the most prominent examples of African religions, including Yoruba, Santeria, Vodun, and Candomble. We will also discuss the similarities and differences between African religions and other spiritual paths.

The Concept of African Religions:

The concept of African religions is complex and multifaceted. It encompasses a wide range of spiritual practices and beliefs, including ancestor worship, divination, magic, healing, and ritual sacrifice. The beliefs and practices of African religions are deeply connected to the natural world, and reflect the deep reverence and respect that African peoples have for the earth and all living things.

One of the key characteristics of African religions is their diversity. There are over 3,000 ethnic groups in Africa, each with their own unique cultural traditions, languages, and spiritual practices. African religions are not monolithic, but rather reflect the incredible diversity and richness of the African continent.

The Diversity of African Religions:

The diversity of African religions is truly remarkable. There are many different types of African religions, each with their own unique practices and beliefs. Some examples of African religions include:

Yoruba Religion: The Yoruba religion is one of the most prominent African religions, and is practiced by millions of people in West Africa and around the world. The Yoruba religion is centered on the worship of a pantheon of deities known as orishas, who are believed to represent various aspects of the natural world.

Exploring Origins, Traditions, and Contemporary Relevance

Santeria: Santeria is a syncretic religion that developed in Cuba, and combines elements of Yoruba religion with Catholicism. Santeria is centered on the worship of orishas, and also incorporates the veneration of saints and the use of Catholic iconography.

Vodun: Vodun is an African religion that originated in the Dahomey region of present-day Benin. Vodun is centered on the worship of spirits known as vodun, who are believed to be able to intercede on behalf of humans in the spirit world.

Candomble: Candomble is an African religion that developed in Brazil, and is practiced by millions of people in South America. Candomble is centered on the worship of orixas, who are similar to the orishas of the Yoruba religion.

These are just a few examples of the incredible diversity of African religions. There are many other types of African religions, each with their own unique beliefs and practices.

Similarities and Differences with Other Spiritual Paths:

While African religions are incredibly diverse, they also share some similarities with other spiritual paths. For example, many African religions place a strong emphasis on community, and view spiritual practice as a collective endeavor. This is similar to the concept of sangha in Buddhism, which emphasizes the importance of community in spiritual practice.

Another similarity between African religions and other spiritual paths is the use of ritual and symbolism. African religions often incorporate complex ritual practices, such as drumming, dance, and chanting, as a way of connecting with the divine. Similarly, many other spiritual paths, such as Hinduism and Shintoism, also use ritual and symbolism as a means of spiritual expression.

Despite these similarities, African religions also have many differences with other spiritual paths. For example, African religions often have a strong connection to the natural world and incorporate nature-based spirituality into their practices. This is particularly evident in traditional African religions, where many deities and spiritual entities are associated with natural elements such as rivers, mountains, and animals.

Another difference is the way in which African religions view the concept of time. In many African cultures, time is seen as cyclical, rather than linear. This means that events are seen as recurring in a pattern, rather than progressing in a linear fashion.

African Religions

This cyclical view of time is often reflected in African religious practices, which emphasize the cyclical rhythms of nature and the importance of ancestral connections.

Additionally, African religions often place a strong emphasis on the importance of ancestors and ancestral traditions. Ancestors are viewed as important spiritual beings who can offer guidance and protection, and their spirits are often invoked in ritual practices. This emphasis on ancestral connections is less prevalent in many other spiritual paths.

It's also worth noting that African religions have been heavily influenced by colonization and missionary efforts, which have led to the blending of traditional African beliefs with elements of Christianity and Islam. As a result, many African religions today are syncretic, incorporating both African and Abrahamic religious practices.

Overall, the diversity of African religions is vast and complex, and cannot be easily generalized or stereotyped. Each tradition has its own unique practices, beliefs, and cultural contexts that contribute to its rich tapestry of spiritual expression.

The concept of African religions

African religions encompass a wide range of belief systems and practices that are deeply rooted in the diverse cultures of Africa. These religions have been shaped by the continent's complex history, including colonialism, slavery, and migration. Today, they are still practiced by millions of people throughout Africa and the African diaspora.

While African religions are diverse, they share some common characteristics. These include a belief in a Supreme Being or creator, ancestor veneration, and the use of ritual and symbolism. However, the specific beliefs, practices, and deities vary widely between different African religions and cultures.

In this section, we will explore the concept of African religions in more depth, including their history, diversity, and key beliefs and practices.

The History of African Religions

African religions have a long and complex history that spans thousands of years. In precolonial times, Africa was home to a rich tapestry of religious traditions, including animism, ancestor worship, and polytheism. These religions were deeply intertwined with African cultures and societies, shaping everything from social hierarchies to political systems.

Exploring Origins, Traditions, and Contemporary Relevance

With the arrival of colonial powers in the 19th and 20th centuries, African religions came under attack. Missionaries from Europe and America sought to convert Africans to Christianity, viewing African religions as primitive and superstitious. This led to the destruction of many traditional religious practices and artifacts, and the forced conversion of millions of Africans.

Despite these efforts, African religions have persisted to this day. Many Africans continue to practice traditional religions alongside Christianity and Islam, and the African diaspora has brought African religions to countries around the world.

The Diversity of African Religions

African religions are incredibly diverse, encompassing a wide range of belief systems, deities, and practices. While it is impossible to fully capture this diversity in one section, we will explore some of the most well-known African religions and their unique characteristics.

Yoruba Religion: The Yoruba religion is one of the most widespread African religions, with millions of practitioners in West Africa and the diaspora. It is centered around the worship of a pantheon of deities known as orishas, who are believed to control different aspects of the world. Yoruba religion also places a strong emphasis on ancestor veneration, and views death as a continuation of life.

Santeria: Santeria is a syncretic religion that developed in Cuba among enslaved Africans and their descendants. It combines elements of Yoruba religion with Catholicism, and is centered around the worship of orishas. Santeria practitioners also incorporate divination and healing practices into their spiritual work.

Vodun: Vodun, also known as Voodoo or Vodou, is a religion that originated in West Africa and is now practiced in Haiti and parts of West Africa. It is centered around the worship of a pantheon of deities known as lwa, who are believed to control different aspects of life. Vodun also incorporates ancestor veneration, divination, and healing practices.

Candomble: Candomble is a religion that developed in Brazil among enslaved Africans and their descendants. It combines elements of Yoruba religion, Bantu religion, and other African traditions, and is centered around the worship of orixas. Candomble also incorporates dance and music into its rituals, and places a strong emphasis on community and collective spiritual practice.

African Religions

Similarities and Differences with Other Spiritual Paths

While African religions are incredibly diverse, they also share some similarities with other spiritual paths. For example, many African religions place a strong emphasis on community, and view spiritual practice as a collective endeavor. This is similar to the concept of sangha in Buddhism, which emphasizes the importance of community in spiritual
practice.

Another similarity between African religions and other spiritual paths is the use of ritual and symbolism. African religions often incorporate complex ritual practices, such as drumming, dance, and chanting, as a way of connecting with the divine. Similarly, many other spiritual paths, such as Hinduism and Shintoism, also use ritual and symbolism as a means of spiritual expression.

Despite these similarities, African religions also have many differences with other spiritual paths. For example, African religions often place a greater emphasis on the ancestors and the spirit world, whereas other paths may focus more on personal enlightenment or union with the divine. African religions also tend to view the world as a holistic system, where all things are interconnected and interdependent. This is in contrast to some Western religious traditions, which may view the world as dualistic, with a clear separation between the spiritual and material realms.

Additionally, African religions often incorporate elements of syncretism, or the blending of different religious traditions. For example, the Yoruba religion in Nigeria has integrated elements of Catholicism into its practices, resulting in a syncretic form of worship known as Santeria. Similarly, Vodun in Haiti has blended elements of West African religions with Catholicism and indigenous spirituality. This syncretism has allowed African religions to adapt and survive in the face of colonization and forced conversion.

Another key characteristic of African religions is their oral tradition. Many African religions do not have a written scripture or dogma, but instead rely on the passing down of knowledge and wisdom through storytelling, proverbs, and other forms of oral communication. This has allowed for a great degree of diversity and flexibility within African religions, as they are able to adapt and evolve over time.

Despite the many differences between African religions and other spiritual paths, it is important to recognize their commonalities and seek to learn from one another. By studying the diverse spiritual practices and beliefs of different cultures, we can gain a greater understanding of the human experience and the many ways in which we seek to connect with the divine.

Exploring Origins, Traditions, and Contemporary Relevance

The diversity of African religions

The diversity of African religions is one of their defining characteristics. From the ancient Egyptian religion to the traditional beliefs of the San people of southern Africa, the continent's spiritual traditions are incredibly varied and complex.

One reason for this diversity is the vastness of the African continent, which spans over 11 million square miles and contains over 1.2 billion people. As a result, there are countless distinct cultures and languages throughout the continent, each with their own unique religious practices and beliefs.

Additionally, African religions have been shaped by centuries of interaction with other cultures, both within and outside of Africa. The spread of Islam and Christianity throughout the continent, for example, has had a significant impact on many African religions, leading to the creation of new syncretic traditions that blend elements of Christianity or Islam with traditional African beliefs.

Another factor contributing to the diversity of African religions is the different ways in which they are practiced. Some African religions are organized around a priesthood or hierarchy, with specific rules and rituals that must be followed. Others are more individualistic, with each person having their own unique relationship with the divine.

Despite this diversity, there are some common threads that run through many African religions. One of the most important is the idea of ancestor veneration. In many African cultures, ancestors are seen as powerful spiritual beings who can influence the course of human events. Ancestors are often believed to be able to provide guidance, protection, and blessings to their living descendants, and are therefore honored through offerings, prayers, and other forms of devotion.

Another common feature of African religions is the use of ritual and symbolism to connect with the divine. These rituals may involve music, dance, prayer, or the use of sacred objects, such as masks or talismans. They are often seen as a way of creating a bridge between the human and spiritual realms, and of communicating with the divine in a language that transcends words.

Perhaps most importantly, African religions are deeply rooted in the natural world. Many African cultures have a deep reverence for the land and its resources, and see themselves as stewards of the earth. This connection to the natural world is often expressed through rituals and ceremonies that celebrate the changing of the seasons, the cycles of the moon, and the rhythms of the earth.

African Religions

In short, the diversity of African religions is a testament to the richness and complexity of the continent's spiritual traditions. From the animistic beliefs of the San people to the sophisticated cosmologies of ancient Egypt, Africa's religious heritage is a source of inspiration and insight for people all over the world.

Examples of African religions, including Yoruba, Santeria, Vodun, and Candomble

African religions are diverse and complex, encompassing a wide variety of beliefs, practices, and traditions. While it is impossible to fully capture the richness and complexity of African religions in a single section, we can explore a few examples to provide a glimpse into the diversity of these spiritual paths. In this section, we will examine four African religions in more detail: Yoruba, Santeria, Vodun, and Candomble.

Yoruba Religion

The Yoruba people are one of the largest ethnic groups in West Africa, and their religion has a rich and complex history. The Yoruba religion is centered around the worship of Orishas, powerful spiritual beings who represent various aspects of the natural world and human experience. The Yoruba believe that these Orishas are capable of intervening in human affairs, and they offer prayers and offerings to them as a way of seeking their assistance and blessings.

One of the most distinctive features of the Yoruba religion is its complex system of divination. The Yoruba use divination to communicate with the Orishas and gain insight into the future. Divination involves casting a set of sacred objects, such as cowrie shells or kola nuts, and interpreting their patterns and positions to determine the Orisha's will.

In addition to divination, the Yoruba religion also places a strong emphasis on ancestor veneration. Ancestors are seen as important spiritual guides and protectors, and their wisdom and guidance are sought through offerings and rituals. Ancestral lineage is also an important aspect of Yoruba identity, and many Yoruba people trace their ancestry through the generations of their forebears.

The Yoruba religion has undergone significant changes over time, particularly through contact with other religions such as Christianity and Islam. This has resulted in the emergence of new forms of Yoruba religion, such as the syncretic religion of Santeria in Cuba and the United States.

Exploring Origins, Traditions, and Contemporary Relevance

The Orishas

The Yoruba religion recognizes a pantheon of over 400 Orishas, each with their own distinct personality and attributes. These Orishas are grouped into families or lineages, each with their own particular associations and characteristics. Some of the most important Orishas include:

✧ Eshu: The trickster god who is associated with crossroads and communication. Eshu is often depicted as a messenger and intermediary between humans and the other Orishas.

✧ Obatala: The creator god who is associated with purity and wisdom. Obatala is responsible for shaping the physical world and creating humans in his own image.

✧ Ogun: The god of iron and war who is associated with strength and perseverance. Ogun is often called upon for protection and assistance in times of conflict.

✧ Oshun: The goddess of love and beauty who is associated with the river. Oshun is often called upon for help with matters of the heart and fertility.

✧ Yemoja: The goddess of the ocean who is associated with motherhood and nurturing. Yemoja is often called upon for protection and guidance for children and families.

✧ These are just a few examples of the many Orishas recognized in the Yoruba religion. Each Orisha has their own stories, attributes, and associations, and they are honored through specific offerings, prayers, and rituals.

Divination

Divination is a central practice in the Yoruba religion, and it is used to communicate with the Orishas and gain insight into the future. There are several different forms of divination in the Yoruba religion, each with its own particular methods and tools.

One of the most common forms of divination is Ifa divination, which uses a system of 16 signs known as odu to provide guidance and insight. Ifa divination is typically performed by a trained diviner known as a babalawo, who interprets the odu based on the client's question or concern.

Another form of divination in the Yoruba religion is cowrie shell divination, which involves casting a set of cowrie shells and interpreting their patterns and positions. Cowrie shell divination is often used to provide more immediate answers to specific questions or concerns.

Ancestor Veneration

Ancestor veneration is another important aspect of the Yoruba religion, and it involves honoring and seeking guidance from one's ancestors. Ancestors are seen as important spiritual guides and protectors, and they are believed to have a continued presence in the lives of their descendants.

Ancestor veneration typically involves offerings and rituals to honor and appease the ancestors, such as pouring libations or setting up an ancestral shrine. Ancestral lineage is also an important aspect of Yoruba identity, and many Yoruba people trace their ancestry through the generations of their forebears.

Adaptations and Syncretism

The Yoruba religion has undergone significant changes over time, particularly through contact with other religions such as Christianity and Islam. This has resulted in the emergence of new forms of Yoruba religion, such as the syncretic religions of Candomble in Brazil and Santeria in Cuba.

Candomble emerged in Brazil during the 19th century as a result of the transatlantic slave trade. Yoruba slaves were brought to Brazil and forced to practice Christianity, but they also secretly maintained their traditional Yoruba religion. Over time, they began to fuse their Yoruba practices with elements of Catholicism, resulting in the creation of Candomble. In Candomble, the Orishas are worshipped alongside Catholic saints, and some Orishas are equated with specific Catholic saints. For example, the Orisha Ogun is associated with Saint George, while the Orisha Oxossi is associated with Saint Sebastian.

Santeria emerged in Cuba in the 20th century, also as a result of the transatlantic slave trade. Yoruba slaves were brought to Cuba and forced to practice Catholicism, but they also maintained their traditional Yoruba religion. Over time, they began to fuse their Yoruba practices with elements of Catholicism, resulting in the creation of Santeria. In Santeria, the Orishas are worshipped alongside Catholic saints, and some Orishas are equated with specific Catholic saints. For example, the Orisha Ogun is associated with Saint Peter, while the Orisha Elegua is associated with the crucifixion of Jesus.

These syncretic religions are examples of how the Yoruba religion has adapted and evolved over time in response to new cultural and historical contexts. While some may view the fusion of Yoruba religion with Christianity or Catholicism as a form of cultural assimilation or even oppression, others see it as a creative and dynamic way of preserving and revitalizing traditional spiritual practices.

It is important to note that not all Yoruba practitioners participate in these syncretic religions. Many Yoruba people in Nigeria and other parts of West Africa continue to practice traditional Yoruba religion without any influence from Christianity or Islam. Nonetheless, the emergence of these syncretic religions is a testament to the resilience and adaptability of the Yoruba religion in the face of cultural and historical challenges.

Santeria

Santeria is a syncretic religion that developed in Cuba among Afro-Cuban communities in the 19th century. Santeria combines elements of the Yoruba religion with Catholicism, reflecting the historical context in which it emerged. Santeria is sometimes referred to as "the way of the saints" because of its focus on the veneration of saints, which are often associated with Orishas in Santeria.

Like the Yoruba religion, Santeria places a strong emphasis on divination. Santeria practitioners use a variety of divination tools, including cowrie shells, cards, and coconut shells, to communicate with the Orishas and seek guidance. Santeria also incorporates a wide variety of rituals and ceremonies, including initiation ceremonies, drumming and dance ceremonies, and offerings to the Orishas.

The practice of Santeria involves the creation of altars or shrines dedicated to the Orishas, often containing various offerings such as candles, flowers, and fruits. These offerings are intended to honor and appease the Orishas, and are believed to be essential for maintaining a harmonious relationship with them. Santeria rituals often involve music, dance, and the use of sacred objects such as drums and rattles.

Santeria has also evolved and adapted over time, particularly as it spread from Cuba to other parts of the world. In the United States, for example, Santeria has become more closely associated with the practice of hoodoo, a form of African American folk magic that combines elements of African religions, European folk magic, and Christianity. This has resulted in the emergence of a distinct form of Santeria that incorporates a variety of new practices and beliefs.

Despite its syncretic nature, Santeria has faced significant challenges and persecution over the years. In Cuba, for example, Santeria was suppressed by the government for many years, and practitioners were often subject to harassment and discrimination. In the United States, Santeria has faced legal challenges related to animal sacrifice, which is a common ritual practice in the religion. Some practitioners have argued that these challenges represent a violation of their religious freedom.

Overall, Santeria remains a vibrant and important religious tradition, with millions of followers around the world. Its syncretic nature and rich history reflect the ways in which African religions have evolved and adapted over time, while also highlighting the ongoing challenges and obstacles faced by practitioners.

Vodun

Vodun, also known as Voodoo, is a religion that developed in West Africa and was brought to the Americas through the transatlantic slave trade. Vodun is practiced primarily in Haiti, where it has had a profound influence on Haitian culture and society. Vodun incorporates elements of the Yoruba religion as well as other African spiritual traditions.

One of the key features of Vodun is the belief in spirits, known as lwa, which are similar to the Orishas in the Yoruba religion. Vodun practitioners believe that the lwa can possess individuals during ceremonies and provide guidance and healing. Vodun also places a strong emphasis on ancestor veneration and the use of herbal medicine.

Another important aspect of Vodun is the use of magical charms and amulets, known as gris-gris, which are believed to offer protection and enhance one's luck and fortune. Gris-gris can be made from a variety of materials, such as herbs, animal parts, and crystals, and are often personalized to the individual's specific needs and desires.

Vodun ceremonies and rituals often involve drumming, singing, and dancing, which are believed to facilitate communication with the lwa and create a trance-like state in which possession can occur. These ceremonies can vary in size and complexity, ranging from small, private gatherings to large, public celebrations.

Despite its rich history and cultural significance, Vodun has often been misunderstood and stigmatized by outsiders, particularly through the lens of Hollywood movies and popular culture. This has led to the perpetuation of harmful stereotypes and the demonization of Vodun practitioners.

However, Vodun continues to be an important and vibrant religion in Haiti and other parts of the world. It has been adapted and syncretized with other religions and cultural traditions, such as Catholicism and Hoodoo, to form unique and dynamic spiritual practices.

Exploring Origins, Traditions, and Contemporary Relevance

Exercise:

What are some similarities and differences between Vodun and other African diaspora religions, such as Santeria and Candomble?

How has Vodun been adapted and syncretized with other religions and cultural traditions?

Discuss the challenges and opportunities facing Vodun practitioners in the modern world.

Problem:

Research and analyze a case study of how Vodun has been portrayed in popular culture, such as movies or television shows, and discuss the impact of these portrayals on Vodun practitioners and the broader public perception of the religion.

Candomble

Candomble is a religion that developed in Brazil among Afro-Brazilian communities. Candomble combines elements of the Yoruba religion with other African spiritual traditions, as well as Catholicism and indigenous South American religions. Candomble is characterized by its focus on the worship of Orixas, which are similar to the Orishas in the Yoruba religion.

Candomble incorporates a wide variety of rituals and ceremonies, including offerings to the Orixas, drumming and dance ceremonies, and initiation ceremonies. Candomble also places a strong emphasis on the use of herbal medicine and healing practices.

One of the unique features of Candomble is its emphasis on community and social justice. Candomble practitioners believe that everyone has a role to play in society and that it is important to work towards social justice and equality. Candomble ceremonies often include prayers for the wellbeing of the community and the world as a whole.

Initiation is an important aspect of Candomble, as it allows individuals to connect with the Orixas and become part of the Candomble community. Initiation involves a period of preparation and purification, and the individual is guided through the process by a spiritual leader known as a pai or mae de santo. During initiation, the individual is crowned with a beaded headdress and given a special name, symbolizing their connection to the Orixas.

Drumming and dance ceremonies are an integral part of Candomble, as they are believed to be a way of connecting with the Orixas and receiving their blessings. The drumming and dance rhythms are specific to each Orixá, and practitioners believe that each rhythm has its own unique energy and purpose. During these ceremonies, the Orixas are often invoked and offerings are made to them in the form of food, drink, and other items.

Herbal medicine is also an important part of Candomble, as it is believed to have the power to heal both physical and spiritual ailments. Candomble practitioners use a wide variety of herbs and other natural substances in their healing practices, often combining them with prayers and rituals. Candomble also emphasizes the importance of spiritual hygiene, and practitioners may use herbal baths and other cleansing practices to purify themselves and their environment.

Candomble has faced significant challenges over the years, including persecution and marginalization by the Brazilian government and the Catholic Church. However, Candomble has continued to thrive and evolve, and today it is estimated that there are millions of Candomble practitioners around the world. Candomble has also had a significant impact on Brazilian culture and society, influencing art, music, and literature, as well as social and political movements.

In conclusion, Candomble is a rich and complex religion that combines elements of the Yoruba religion with other African spiritual traditions, as well as Catholicism and indigenous South American religions. Candomble places a strong emphasis on the worship of the Orixas, as well as community and social justice. Candomble also incorporates a wide variety of rituals and ceremonies, herbal medicine, and healing practices. Despite facing significant challenges over the years, Candomble has continued to thrive and evolve, and it remains an important part of Brazilian culture and society.

Conclusion

These four examples provide a glimpse into the diversity of African religions and the many ways in which they have evolved and adapted over time. While they may share some common elements, each religion has its own unique beliefs, practices, and cultural influences.

It is important to note that these examples only scratch the surface of the many African religions that exist. There are countless other religions, both ancient and modern, throughout the continent that offer their own insights into the spiritual and cultural heritage of Africa.

Furthermore, the practice of African religions has spread beyond the continent and can now be found in many other parts of the world. For example, Santeria has a significant presence in Cuba and other Latin American countries, while Candomble is practiced in Brazil.

Despite the diversity of African religions, they have often been misunderstood and marginalized by outsiders. This is due in part to the legacy of colonialism, which sought to eradicate or assimilate traditional African religions in favor of Christianity or Islam.

Today, many practitioners of African religions continue to face discrimination and persecution. It is important for those outside of these traditions to approach them with respect and an open mind, recognizing their rich cultural and spiritual significance.

In conclusion, African religions offer a window into the complex and diverse spiritual traditions of the continent. By studying these religions, we can gain a deeper understanding of the cultural heritage of Africa and the ways in which these traditions continue to evolve and adapt in the modern world.

Similarities and differences between African religions and other spiritual paths

African religions, such as Vodun, Candomble, and Yoruba, share many similarities with other spiritual paths found around the world, while also possessing distinct differences that set them apart. In this section, we will explore the similarities and differences between African religions and other spiritual paths, including Witchcraft, Divination, Herbalism, Shamanism, and Ecospirituality.

Similarities

One of the key similarities between African religions and other spiritual paths is the belief in spirits or deities. In Vodun, for example, practitioners believe in lwa, while in Candomble, practitioners worship Orixas. In many Shamanic traditions, spirits are an integral part of the cosmology, and in Witchcraft, there is often a belief in the Goddess and the God. Additionally, in many herbal traditions, plants are believed to have their own spirits, and divination often involves communing with spiritual entities.

Another similarity is the emphasis on ritual and ceremony. African religions, like Candomble, place a strong emphasis on drumming and dance ceremonies as a way to connect with the divine. Similarly, in Witchcraft, ritual and ceremony are used to mark the changing of the seasons and to honor the deities. In Shamanism, ceremonies often involve drumming, chanting, and dancing as a way to enter into an altered state of consciousness and connect with the spirits.

Another similarity is the use of divination. Divination is used in African religions, such as Yoruba, to communicate with the Orishas and receive guidance. Similarly, in Witchcraft, divination is used to gain insight and guidance from the divine. In Shamanism, divination often involves journeying to other realms to receive messages from the spirits.

Differences

One of the key differences between African religions and other spiritual paths is the way in which they view the world and our place in it. In many African religions, the world is seen as interconnected, with humans, animals, plants, and spirits all playing a role in the web of life. This interconnectedness is often expressed through the belief in ancestor veneration and the use of herbal medicine to heal both physical and spiritual ailments. In contrast, in many Western spiritual traditions, the emphasis is often on the individual's journey and personal growth.

Another difference is the role of initiations and community. In African religions, such as Candomble and Vodun, initiations are an important part of the spiritual path, with individuals undergoing a series of rituals and ceremonies to become fully initiated into the community. In Witchcraft, initiation is often a personal journey, with individuals undertaking their own study and practice to become a Witch. Similarly, Shamanic traditions often involve an individual's personal journey, with the guidance of a mentor or teacher, rather than initiation into a larger community.

Another difference is the way in which the divine is viewed. In many African religions, the deities are seen as part of the natural world, with each one having its own specific qualities and energies. In contrast, in many Western spiritual traditions, the divine is often viewed as separate from the natural world, with humans striving to connect with the divine through meditation and other practices.

Finally, there is often a difference in the way in which African religions and other spiritual paths are perceived by mainstream society. African religions, such as Vodun and Candomble, have often been demonized and marginalized by Western culture, while other spiritual paths, such as Witchcraft and Shamanism, have gained more mainstream acceptance.

Exploring Origins, Traditions, and Contemporary Relevance

Exercises:

Compare and contrast the belief in spirits or deities in African religions with other spiritual paths.

Discuss the role of ritual and ceremony in African religions and compare it to its role in other spiritual paths.

Analyze the differences in the use of herbal medicine in African religions compared to other spiritual paths.

Research and compare the belief in spirits or deities in African religions with those in indigenous South American religions.

Analyze the role of ritual and ceremony in African religions and compare it to its role in modern neo-pagan religions.

Compare and contrast the use of herbal medicine in African religions with traditional Chinese medicine.

Similarities and Differences between African Religions and Other Spiritual Paths

African religions are characterized by a strong belief in spirits, deities, and ancestors. These beliefs are also found in other spiritual paths, such as indigenous South American religions, neo-paganism, and traditional Chinese medicine. However, the specifics of these beliefs and their practices vary significantly between different cultures and traditions.

One of the key similarities between African religions and indigenous South American religions is the belief in spirits or deities that can possess individuals and provide guidance and healing. In African religions, these spirits are often known as lwa or orishas, while in South American religions, they may be known as ayahuasca spirits or plant teachers. The belief in ancestral spirits is also common in both African and South American religions.

However, there are also significant differences in the way these beliefs are practiced. For example, in African religions, the emphasis is often on possession by the lwa or orishas during ceremonies, while in South American religions, the emphasis may be on the use of entheogenic plants to facilitate communication with the spirits. Additionally, African religions may incorporate more drumming and dance in their ceremonies, while South American religions may incorporate more chanting and singing.

In modern neo-paganism, the use of ritual and ceremony is also central to the practice. However, the specific rituals and beliefs vary significantly between different neo-pagan traditions. Some neo-pagan traditions may incorporate elements of African religions, such as the belief in deities or the use of herbal medicine, while others may draw from European folklore or mythology.

One of the key differences between African religions and neo-paganism is the emphasis on nature and the environment. African religions often incorporate the natural world into their beliefs and practices, with a focus on the interconnectedness of all things. In contrast, neo-paganism may emphasize the individual's connection to nature and the importance of ecological sustainability.

Herbal medicine is also a common practice in many African religions, where it is used for healing and spiritual purposes. Similarly, traditional Chinese medicine also emphasizes the use of herbs and other natural remedies for healing. However, the specific herbs and remedies used may differ significantly between these two traditions, as well as the way they are prepared and administered.

In conclusion, while there are many similarities between African religions and other spiritual paths, such as the belief in spirits or deities and the use of ritual and ceremony, there are also significant differences in the way these beliefs and practices are expressed. Understanding these similarities and differences can provide insight into the unique contributions and perspectives of different spiritual paths, and encourage a greater appreciation for cultural diversity and spiritual pluralism.

Exercises:

Research and compare the belief in spirits or deities in African religions with those in indigenous South American religions.

Analyze the role of ritual and ceremony in African religions and compare it to its role in modern neo-pagan religions.

Compare and contrast the use of herbal medicine in African religions with traditional Chinese medicine.

CHAPTER 7: THE INFLUENCE OF COLONIALISM AND GLOBALIZATION ON AFRICAN RELIGIONS

African religions have been influenced by external factors, such as colonialism and globalization. The arrival of European colonizers brought with it the imposition of Christianity and Islam, which challenged traditional African religions. In addition, globalization has brought new ideas, beliefs, and practices, which have also impacted African religions. This chapter will explore the impact of colonialism and globalization on African religions, including the spread of Christianity and Islam, the effects of globalization, and the resistance and adaptation of African religions to these external influences.

The Impact of Colonialism on African Religions

The arrival of European colonizers in Africa had a profound impact on traditional African religions. European colonizers viewed African religions as primitive and barbaric, and sought to impose Christianity and Islam on the African population. In some cases, the imposition of Christianity and Islam was violent, with European colonizers destroying shrines and temples, and punishing those who continued to practice traditional African religions. This had the effect of suppressing traditional African religions, and forcing many Africans to convert to Christianity or Islam.

The spread of Christianity and Islam in Africa

Christianity and Islam were introduced to Africa through the arrival of European colonizers. These religions offered an alternative to traditional African religions, and were often associated with education and social advancement. Many Africans converted to Christianity and Islam in order to access education and employment opportunities. In addition, European colonizers used Christianity and Islam as a means of control, as these religions emphasized obedience to authority and the importance of hierarchy.

African Religions

The effects of globalization on African religions

Globalization has had a significant impact on African religions. The spread of technology, media, and communication has brought new ideas, beliefs, and practices to Africa, which have challenged traditional African religions. For example, the rise of social media has enabled people in Africa to access information about different religions and spiritual practices from around the world. This has led to a growing interest in alternative spiritual practices, such as yoga and meditation, which are not traditionally associated with African religions.

In addition, globalization has brought new economic opportunities to Africa, which have also impacted African religions. The growth of international tourism has created a demand for African spiritual tourism, which has led to the commercialization of traditional African religions. This has led to concerns about the exploitation of African religions for commercial gain, and the loss of cultural authenticity.

The resistance and adaptation of African religions to these external influences

Despite the impact of colonialism and globalization on African religions, many traditional African religions have survived and continue to be practiced today. This is due in part to the resistance and adaptation of African religions to these external influences. For example, many African religions have incorporated elements of Christianity and Islam into their practices, while also maintaining their own unique traditions and beliefs.

In addition, there has been a growing movement to reclaim and revive traditional African religions in response to the impact of colonialism and globalization. This has led to a resurgence of interest in traditional African religions, and a growing awareness of the importance of preserving and protecting these religions for future generations.

Exercises:

Discuss the impact of colonialism on traditional African religions, including the role of European colonizers in the suppression of African religions.

Compare and contrast the spread of Christianity and Islam in Africa, including their impact on traditional African religions.

Exploring Origins, Traditions, and Contemporary Relevance

Analyze the effects of globalization on African religions, including the role of technology, media, and communication in shaping African religious beliefs and practices.

Discuss the resistance and adaptation of African religions to external influences, including the incorporation of elements of Christianity and Islam into traditional African religions, and the growing movement to reclaim and revive traditional African religions.

The impact of colonialism on African religions

African religions have a long history of resilience, adaptability, and survival. These religions have been shaped by the various cultural and historical influences that have impacted the continent. One of the most significant impacts on African religions has been colonialism. The arrival of European powers in Africa in the 19th century brought with it a period of rapid change and transformation, which had a profound impact on African religions. In this chapter, we will examine the impact of colonialism on African religions, focusing on the ways in which European powers sought to suppress, control, and transform these religions.

The Impact of Colonialism on African Religions

The colonial period in Africa lasted from the late 19th century until the mid-20th century. During this time, European powers established colonies across the continent, taking control of land, resources, and people. One of the key ways in which colonialism impacted African religions was through the imposition of Christianity and Islam. European missionaries and colonial officials viewed traditional African religions as primitive and backward, and sought to convert Africans to Christianity or Islam. Missionaries believed that they were saving Africans from the darkness of paganism and idolatry, and saw their work as a civilizing mission. As a result, Christianity and Islam became major religions in many parts of Africa.

The imposition of Christianity and Islam had a profound impact on traditional African religions. Many Africans converted to these religions, and as a result, the traditional religions lost many of their followers. The loss of followers had a significant impact on the ability of traditional religions to maintain their practices and beliefs. In addition, Christianity and Islam brought with them new ways of understanding the world, new moral codes, and new practices. These new ways of understanding the world often conflicted with traditional African beliefs, leading to a gradual erosion of traditional practices and beliefs.

African Religions

Another way in which colonialism impacted African religions was through the suppression of traditional religious practices. European colonial powers viewed traditional African religions as a threat to their control over the continent. As a result, they sought to suppress traditional practices and beliefs. In many cases, traditional religious practices were banned, and those who practiced them were punished. This had a significant impact on the ability of traditional religions to maintain their practices and beliefs. Many traditional religious practices went underground, and were only practiced in secret.

The imposition of Christianity and Islam, and the suppression of traditional religious practices, also had a profound impact on the relationship between African religions and the natural environment. Traditional African religions are closely connected to the natural environment, and many of their practices and beliefs are centered on the idea of living in harmony with the natural world. Christianity and Islam, on the other hand, tend to view the natural world as a resource to be exploited. As a result, the imposition of these religions led to a gradual erosion of traditional practices that were centered on the natural world.

Resistance and Adaptation

Despite the many challenges posed by colonialism, African religions have proven to be remarkably resilient. Traditional practices and beliefs have survived, even in the face of concerted efforts to suppress them. In many cases, traditional practices and beliefs have been adapted to new circumstances, and have been fused with elements of Christianity or Islam.

One example of this is the syncretism that has occurred between traditional African religions and Christianity. In many parts of Africa, Christianity has been fused with traditional practices and beliefs, creating a hybrid form of religion. This has allowed traditional practices and beliefs to survive, even in the face of Christian evangelization.

Another example of adaptation can be seen in the way that traditional African religions have been used as a form of resistance against colonialism. Traditional practices and beliefs were often used as a way of asserting African identity in the face of European domination. For example, during the early years of colonialism, many Africans were forcibly converted to Christianity, and traditional practices were banned. However, Africans often continued to practice their traditional religions in secret, using them as a way of resisting the imposition of European culture and religion.

In some cases, traditional African religions were even used as a means of political resistance. For example, during the Mau Mau rebellion in Kenya, traditional religious practices played an important role in mobilizing resistance against British colonial rule. The Mau Mau relied heavily on traditional African beliefs and practices, such as oathing ceremonies, to inspire and unify their followers.

Despite the challenges posed by colonialism, many African religions have continued to evolve and adapt in response to changing circumstances. Today, African religions continue to be an important part of the religious landscape of many African countries, and they continue to exert a powerful influence on the lives of millions of people.

However, it is important to note that the impact of colonialism on African religions has not been entirely negative. In some cases, colonialism has actually helped to spread African religions beyond their traditional borders. For example, the spread of Islam across West Africa was largely facilitated by the activities of Muslim traders and scholars who traveled to the region from the north. Similarly, the spread of Christianity in Africa was often facilitated by European missionaries who established schools, hospitals, and other institutions that provided services to African communities.

In conclusion, the impact of colonialism on African religions has been complex and multifaceted. While colonialism has undoubtedly had a profound and lasting impact on African religions, it is important to recognize that these religions have also been resilient and adaptable. Traditional practices and beliefs have survived and evolved, and in some cases, have even been used as a means of resistance against colonialism. Today, African religions continue to be an important part of the religious landscape of many African countries, and they continue to play an important role in the lives of millions of people.

The spread of Christianity and Islam in Africa

The spread of Christianity and Islam in Africa has had a profound impact on African religions. The introduction of these two religions was a major turning point in African history and has had far-reaching consequences for the continent and its people.

The Spread of Christianity in Africa

Christianity was first introduced to Africa in the first century AD, when Ethiopian eunuch was converted by Philip the Evangelist (Acts 8:26-40). However, it was not until the 19th century that Christianity began to spread in Africa in a significant way. This was largely due to the efforts of European missionaries who saw Africa as a fertile ground for evangelization.

The spread of Christianity in Africa was facilitated by the colonial powers who used religion as a tool of colonization. European colonizers saw Christianity as a way of civilizing the "uncivilized" Africans and saw themselves as bringing enlightenment to the "dark continent". They also used religion as a means of dividing and conquering the Africans, pitting Christianized Africans against their non-Christianized counterparts.

Christianity spread rapidly in Africa in the late 19th and early 20th centuries, with many Africans converting to the new religion. This was partly due to the fact that Christianity promised to provide relief from the hardships of colonialism, and partly due to the fact that Christianity was associated with modernity and progress.

The Spread of Islam in Africa

Islam was introduced to Africa in the 7th century AD, during the lifetime of the Prophet Muhammad. However, it was not until the 8th century that Islam began to spread in Africa in a significant way. This was largely due to the efforts of Arab traders and missionaries who saw Africa as a potential market for their goods and religion.

Islam spread rapidly in North Africa and the Sahel region in the 8th and 9th centuries, with many African rulers converting to the new religion. This was partly due to the fact that Islam promised to provide protection and support to rulers who converted to the religion, and partly due to the fact that Islam was associated with trade and commerce.

Islam continued to spread in Africa in the 10th and 11th centuries, with the establishment of the Almoravid and Almohad dynasties in North Africa. These dynasties expanded the reach of Islam to the southern parts of the continent, including West Africa and the East African coast.

Impact of Christianity and Islam on African Religions

The spread of Christianity and Islam in Africa had a profound impact on African religions. Traditional African religions were gradually marginalized as Christianity and Islam gained ground. Many Africans converted to these new religions and abandoned their traditional practices and beliefs.

Exploring Origins, Traditions, and Contemporary Relevance

The impact of Christianity and Islam on African religions was not uniform. In some parts of Africa, the new religions were accepted and assimilated into the existing religious practices and beliefs. In other parts, the new religions were rejected and resisted, leading to conflicts and tensions between the new and traditional religions.

In many cases, traditional African religions were adapted and transformed in response to the new religions. Elements of Christianity and Islam were incorporated into traditional practices and beliefs, creating a syncretic form of religion that reflected both the old and the new.

Christianity and Islam also had an impact on the political and social structures of African societies. In many cases, the new religions were used to legitimize and reinforce colonial rule, leading to the suppression of African cultures and traditions. However, in other cases, the new religions were used as a form of resistance against colonialism, leading to the emergence of new forms of African nationalism and identity.

The spread of Christianity and Islam in Africa has had a profound impact on African religions. Traditional practices and beliefs have been marginalized, adapted, and transformed in response to the new religions. However, African religions have proven to be remarkably resilient, and have managed to survive in the face of significant challenges.

It is important to note that the impact of Christianity and Islam on African religions is not a one-way street. African religions have also influenced Christianity and Islam in Africa, leading to the development of unique forms of Christianity and Islam that incorporate African practices and beliefs.

Furthermore, it is essential to recognize that the history of Christianity and Islam in Africa is not entirely negative. These religions have brought significant social, economic, and political changes to Africa, and have played an important role in the continent's history. They have also provided a framework for resistance against colonialism and have been used as a means of promoting social and political change.

However, it is also important to acknowledge the negative impact that these religions have had on African religions. The forced conversion of Africans to Christianity and Islam, the destruction of traditional religious practices, and the imposition of Western values and beliefs have all had a profound impact on African societies.

African Religions

In conclusion, the spread of Christianity and Islam in Africa has had a complex and multifaceted impact on African religions. While traditional practices and beliefs have been marginalized and transformed, African religions have proven to be remarkably resilient, and have adapted to new circumstances. The history of Christianity and Islam in Africa is not entirely negative, and these religions have played an important role in the continent's history. However, it is important to acknowledge the negative impact that they have had on African religions and to work towards a greater understanding and appreciation of the diversity and complexity of African spiritual practices and beliefs.

The effects of globalization on African religions

Globalization refers to the interconnectedness and interdependence of nations, cultures, and economies across the world. The increasing globalization of the world has had a significant impact on African religions. As African societies become more connected to the global community, they are exposed to new ideas, beliefs, and practices that challenge traditional African religions. This section will explore the effects of globalization on African religions, including the rise of new religious movements, the impact of the internet and social media, and the challenges faced by traditional healers and spiritual leaders.

The rise of new religious movements

Globalization has led to the spread of new religious movements across Africa. These movements, often originating in the West, offer a new perspective on spirituality and religion. Some of these movements have been successful in attracting followers in Africa, particularly among the younger generation. One example of this is the rise of Pentecostalism in Africa. Pentecostalism emphasizes personal experiences of the Holy Spirit and emphasizes the importance of charismatic leadership. This movement has grown rapidly in Africa, particularly in urban areas.

Another example of a new religious movement that has gained popularity in Africa is Rastafarianism. This movement originated in Jamaica and emphasizes the importance of African identity and the use of cannabis as a sacrament. Rastafarianism has spread to many African countries, particularly in the Caribbean and West Africa, and has had a significant impact on local culture and spirituality.

The impact of the internet and social media

The rise of the internet and social media has had a significant impact on African religions. These technologies have made it easier for people to access information about different religions and spiritual practices. They have also made it easier for people to connect with others who share their beliefs and practices, regardless of geographic location.

One example of the impact of the internet on African religions is the growth of online spiritual communities. These communities allow people to connect with others who share their beliefs and practices, even if they are not able to meet in person. They also allow people to access information about different spiritual practices and traditions from around the world.

The internet has also had an impact on traditional African religions. It has made it easier for traditional healers and spiritual leaders to connect with each other and share information. However, it has also led to concerns about the commercialization of traditional African religions. Some traditional healers and spiritual leaders have expressed concern that the internet has made it easier for outsiders to exploit their practices for profit.

Challenges faced by traditional healers and spiritual leaders

Globalization has presented a number of challenges for traditional healers and spiritual leaders in Africa. These challenges include the marginalization of traditional practices, the loss of traditional knowledge, and the erosion of traditional values and beliefs.

One of the main challenges faced by traditional healers and spiritual leaders is the marginalization of traditional practices. As Western medicine becomes more widely available in Africa, traditional healers are often viewed as less important. This has led to a decline in the number of people who practice traditional healing and a loss of traditional knowledge.

Another challenge faced by traditional healers and spiritual leaders is the loss of traditional knowledge. As younger generations become more connected to the global community, they are often less interested in traditional practices and beliefs. This has led to a decline in the transmission of traditional knowledge from one generation to the next.

Finally, globalization has led to the erosion of traditional values and beliefs. As African societies become more connected to the global community, they are exposed to new ideas and beliefs that challenge traditional African values and beliefs. This has led to a decline in the importance of traditional values and beliefs, and has made it more difficult for traditional healers and spiritual leaders to maintain their practices.

African Religions

Conclusion

Globalization has had a significant impact on African religions. The rise of new technologies, the spread of global capitalism, and the increased interconnectedness of the world have all contributed to the changing landscape of African religious practices and beliefs. While globalization has brought about many positive changes, such as increased access to education and healthcare, it has also had many negative effects on traditional African religions.

One of the most significant effects of globalization on African religions has been the homogenization of religious practices and beliefs. As Western cultural values and religious beliefs become more widespread, traditional African religious practices and beliefs are being replaced by Westernized versions of Christianity and Islam. This has led to a decline in the diversity of African religions and the loss of many unique and valuable cultural practices.

Another effect of globalization on African religions has been the erosion of traditional values and beliefs. As African societies become more connected to the global community, they are exposed to new ideas and beliefs that challenge traditional African values and beliefs. This has led to a decline in the importance of traditional values and beliefs, and has made it more difficult for traditional healers and spiritual leaders to maintain their practices.

Globalization has also had an impact on the practice of traditional African religions by changing the way that people interact with their religious beliefs. As people become more connected to the global community, they are increasingly turning to the internet and social media as sources of information and guidance. This has led to the rise of online communities dedicated to African religions, and has allowed people to connect with like-minded individuals from all over the world. However, it has also led to a decline in face-to-face interactions between spiritual leaders and their followers, and has made it more difficult for traditional healers to pass on their knowledge and skills to the next generation.

Despite these challenges, African religions have proven to be remarkably resilient. Traditional practices and beliefs have survived, even in the face of concerted efforts to suppress them. In many cases, traditional practices and beliefs have been adapted to new circumstances, and have been fused with elements of Christianity or Islam. The future of African religions remains uncertain, but one thing is clear: these religions will continue to evolve and adapt in response to the changing needs of their followers and the wider world.

Exploring Origins, Traditions, and Contemporary Relevance

The resistance and adaptation of African religions to these external influences

The resistance and adaptation of African religions to external influences is a complex and ongoing process that has been shaped by a range of historical, social, political, and economic factors. Throughout the centuries, African religions have faced many challenges, including colonialism, slavery, and globalization, which have threatened their survival and continuity. Yet, despite these challenges, African religions have demonstrated remarkable resilience, resistance, and adaptation to these external influences.

Resistance

One of the key ways in which African religions have resisted external influences is through the preservation of their core beliefs and practices. African religions are founded on a deep sense of ancestral connection and respect for the natural world, and these values have remained central to their beliefs and practices despite the pressures of colonization, slavery, and globalization. By maintaining these core beliefs and practices, African religions have been able to resist the imposition of foreign values and beliefs that would undermine their identity and integrity.

Another way in which African religions have resisted external influences is through the use of secrecy and hidden knowledge. Many African religions have developed complex systems of initiation, ritual, and symbolism that are only accessible to members of the community who have undergone rigorous training and testing. This secrecy has allowed African religions to maintain their identity and integrity in the face of external pressures, and has also enabled them to preserve their knowledge and traditions over long periods of time.

Adaptation

While African religions have demonstrated a remarkable ability to resist external influences, they have also shown a willingness to adapt and incorporate new ideas and practices into their belief systems. This adaptability has been driven by a range of factors, including the need to survive in changing social, political, and economic environments, and the desire to connect with other cultures and communities.

One example of adaptation can be seen in the way that African religions have incorporated elements of Christianity and Islam into their belief systems. As we saw in the previous chapter, many African religions have developed hybrid forms of religion that blend traditional beliefs and practices with Christian or Islamic elements. This has allowed African religions to maintain their identity and integrity while also connecting with other cultures and communities.

Another example of adaptation can be seen in the way that African religions have responded to the challenges of globalization. As African societies become more connected to the global community, African religions have had to adapt to new forms of communication, transportation, and media. This has led to the emergence of new forms of African religions that incorporate elements of modern technology and popular culture, such as hip-hop, social media, and fashion. By adapting to these new forms of expression, African religions have been able to remain relevant and engaging for younger generations.

Conclusion

The resistance and adaptation of African religions to external influences is an ongoing process that reflects the dynamic and complex nature of African cultures and societies. While African religions have faced many challenges over the centuries, they have demonstrated a remarkable ability to resist, adapt, and transform in response to these challenges. By preserving their core beliefs and practices while also incorporating new ideas and practices, African religions have been able to maintain their identity and integrity while also connecting with other cultures and communities. This dynamic and adaptable nature of African religions is a testament to the resilience, creativity, and diversity of African cultures and societies.

CHAPTER 8: AFRICAN TRADITIONAL RELIGIONS AND THEIR ROLE IN SOCIETY

African traditional religions have played a significant role in the spiritual and cultural lives of African societies for centuries. These religions are diverse and complex, encompassing a variety of beliefs, practices, and customs. Despite the influence of colonialism and the spread of Christianity and Islam, traditional African religions have persisted and continue to be an important part of African society.

In this chapter, we will explore the definition and characteristics of African traditional religions, the role of ancestors and spirits, the significance of rituals and ceremonies, and the relationship between African traditional religions and African society.

Definition and Characteristics of African Traditional Religions

African traditional religions are a diverse set of beliefs and practices that have developed over thousands of years across the African continent. They are characterized by their emphasis on the spiritual and mystical aspects of life and their close relationship with nature. Unlike many Western religions, African traditional religions do not have a central holy book or religious figure, but instead rely on oral traditions passed down through generations.

One of the defining characteristics of African traditional religions is their focus on the relationship between humans and the natural world. Many African religions hold that all living beings, including plants and animals, have a spiritual essence or soul. This belief is reflected in the rituals and ceremonies associated with African traditional religions, which often involve offerings and sacrifices to appease spirits or ancestors.

The Role of Ancestors and Spirits in African Traditional Religions

Ancestors and spirits play a significant role in African traditional religions. In many African societies, ancestors are believed to have the power to influence the lives of their descendants, and are often venerated through rituals and offerings. Ancestors are also believed to have the ability to communicate with the living, and are often consulted for guidance or protection.

Spirits are also an important part of African traditional religions. They are believed to inhabit the natural world, and can be found in trees, rocks, and other natural features. Many African societies believe in the existence of both benevolent and malevolent spirits, and engage in rituals and offerings to appease or ward off these spirits.

The Significance of Rituals and Ceremonies in African Traditional Religions

Rituals and ceremonies are an integral part of African traditional religions. They serve to connect the living with the spiritual realm, and are often used to mark important life events, such as birth, initiation, marriage, and death. Many African societies believe that certain rituals and ceremonies have the power to heal, protect, or bring good fortune.

The specific rituals and ceremonies associated with African traditional religions vary widely depending on the region and culture. However, many African religions share certain common elements, such as the use of music, dance, and drumming to invoke spirits or ancestors.

The Relationship Between African Traditional Religions and African Society

African traditional religions have played a central role in African society for centuries. They have served as a source of spiritual guidance, moral values, and social cohesion. In many African societies, traditional religious practices are intertwined with daily life, and are reflected in art, music, and literature.

Despite the influence of Christianity and Islam, traditional African religions continue to be an important part of African society. In some cases, African traditional religions have adapted and incorporated elements of Christianity or Islam, while in other cases they have resisted external influences.

Conclusion

African traditional religions are a diverse and complex set of beliefs and practices that have evolved over thousands of years across the African continent. They are characterized by their emphasis on the spiritual and mystical aspects of life, their close relationship with nature, and their reliance on oral traditions.

Ancestors and spirits play a central role in African traditional religions, and are often venerated through rituals and offerings. Rituals and ceremonies are also an integral part of African traditional religions, and serve to reinforce the connection between the spiritual and physical worlds. These rituals can include offerings to ancestors, sacrifices of animals or crops, and dancing and music.

African traditional religions have played a significant role in shaping African society. They have provided a sense of community and identity, and have helped to maintain social order by providing a framework for moral and ethical behavior. They have also served as a means of coping with adversity and loss, and have provided individuals with a sense of purpose and meaning in life.

Despite the influence of external forces such as colonization and globalization, African traditional religions continue to play an important role in the lives of many Africans. They have proven to be resilient and adaptable, and have been able to integrate elements of other religions and belief systems into their own practices.

In recent years, there has been a growing interest in African traditional religions among scholars and practitioners alike. This interest has led to a greater understanding and appreciation of these religions, and has helped to promote their preservation and continuation for future generations.

As African society continues to evolve, it is likely that African traditional religions will continue to adapt and change in response to new challenges and opportunities. However, their importance in shaping African culture and identity will remain a significant and enduring legacy for generations to come.

Definition and characteristics of African traditional religions

African traditional religions are a diverse and complex set of beliefs and practices that have evolved over thousands of years across the African continent. They are often characterized by their emphasis on the spiritual and mystical aspects of life, their close relationship with nature, and their reliance on oral traditions. Despite their diversity, African traditional religions share several common features that set them apart from other religious traditions. In this chapter, we will explore the definition and characteristics of African traditional religions.

Definition of African Traditional Religions

Defining African traditional religions is a complex task, as these religions are not centralized or organized in the same way as many Western religious traditions. In general, African traditional religions are defined as the indigenous religious beliefs and practices of African people before the arrival of Christianity and Islam. These beliefs and practices are often characterized by a strong connection to the natural world, a focus on ancestral spirits and other supernatural beings, and a reliance on oral tradition rather than written texts.

Characteristics of African Traditional Religions

African traditional religions share several characteristics that set them apart from other religious traditions. These characteristics include:

Connection to Nature: African traditional religions emphasize the interconnectedness of all living things and the importance of maintaining a harmonious relationship with the natural world. This connection to nature is reflected in many aspects of African traditional religions, from the veneration of natural landmarks such as mountains and rivers to the use of natural materials in religious ceremonies.

Ancestral veneration: Ancestors and ancestral spirits play a central role in many African traditional religions. Ancestors are often seen as intermediaries between the living and the divine, and are venerated through offerings and rituals.

Oral Tradition: African traditional religions are often passed down through oral tradition rather than written texts. This means that the history, beliefs, and practices of these religions are preserved and transmitted through stories, songs, and other forms of oral communication.

Rituals and Ceremonies: African traditional religions place a strong emphasis on rituals and ceremonies as a way of connecting with the divine and maintaining balance in the natural world. These rituals may involve offerings of food or other gifts, dance, music, and other forms of artistic expression.

Syncretism: African traditional religions are often characterized by a high degree of syncretism, or the blending of different religious traditions. This syncretism reflects the complex history of Africa, which has been shaped by centuries of cultural exchange and migration.

Conclusion

African traditional religions are a diverse and complex set of beliefs and practices that have evolved over thousands of years across the African continent. They are often characterized by their emphasis on the spiritual and mystical aspects of life, their close relationship with nature, and their reliance on oral traditions. Despite their diversity, African traditional religions share several common features, including a connection to nature, a focus on ancestral veneration, a reliance on oral tradition, an emphasis on rituals and ceremonies, and a high degree of syncretism.

The role of ancestors and spirits in African traditional religions

The role of ancestors and spirits is a central aspect of African traditional religions. In many African cultures, ancestors and spirits are believed to have the power to influence the lives of the living. This belief is based on the idea that death is not the end of life, but rather a transition to another state of existence. Ancestors and spirits are believed to be able to communicate with the living through dreams, visions, and divination. They are also believed to have the ability to intervene in the affairs of the living, both positively and negatively.

Ancestors are considered to be the first line of defense against evil and malevolent spirits. They are believed to have a protective role over their living descendants, and are often venerated through offerings and rituals. In many African cultures, ancestors are believed to be able to intercede on behalf of the living, and to have the power to bring good fortune or to ward off misfortune.

The veneration of ancestors is an important aspect of African traditional religions. Ancestors are often believed to be the source of wisdom, guidance, and protection for their living descendants. They are also believed to be able to influence the natural world, and are often venerated through offerings and rituals. Ancestor veneration is often accompanied by the belief in a shared identity between the living and the dead, and the idea that the dead continue to play a role in the lives of the living.

In addition to ancestors, spirits are also an important aspect of African traditional religions. Spirits are believed to be supernatural entities that inhabit the natural world. They are often associated with specific places, such as trees, rivers, and mountains. Spirits are believed to have the power to influence the natural world, and are often venerated through offerings and rituals.

In many African cultures, spirits are believed to have a particular interest in human affairs. They are often associated with specific aspects of life, such as fertility, health, and prosperity. Spirits are believed to have the power to intervene in these aspects of life, both positively and negatively. They are often venerated through offerings and rituals, which are designed to appease them and to ensure their favor.

The relationship between ancestors and spirits is complex and multifaceted. In some African cultures, ancestors are believed to become spirits after death, and to continue to play a role in the lives of the living. In other cultures, ancestors and spirits are seen as separate entities, with different roles and functions. However, in all cases, the veneration of ancestors and spirits is a fundamental aspect of African traditional religions.

One example of the role of ancestors and spirits in African traditional religions is the practice of divination. Divination is the practice of seeking guidance or insight from the supernatural realm. It is often used to address specific problems or issues, such as illness, infertility, or financial difficulties. Divination is often performed by a diviner, who is believed to have the ability to communicate with the supernatural realm.

In many African cultures, divination is performed through the use of divinatory tools, such as bones, shells, or cards. These tools are believed to be able to communicate with the supernatural realm, and to provide insight into the problems or issues that are being addressed. Divination is often accompanied by the veneration of ancestors and spirits, who are believed to be able to provide guidance and insight through the divinatory process.

Another example of the role of ancestors and spirits in African traditional religions is the practice of ancestor veneration. Ancestor veneration is the practice of honoring and venerating the ancestors, and is often accompanied by offerings and rituals. Ancestors are believed to have the power to influence the lives of the living, and to provide guidance and protection. Ancestor veneration is often accompanied by the belief in a shared identity between the living and the dead, and the belief that ancestors continue to play a role in the lives of their descendants.

In some African traditional religions, ancestors are believed to be able to intervene in the affairs of the living, and to provide blessings or punishments as needed. Ancestors are often seen as intermediaries between the living and the supernatural realm, and are believed to be able to communicate with spirits and deities on behalf of the living.

Ancestor veneration is often accompanied by the creation of ancestor altars or shrines, which are typically located in the homes of individuals or in communal spaces. These altars are often adorned with offerings such as food, drink, and other objects, and are used as a focal point for ancestor veneration and communication.

The role of ancestors and spirits in African traditional religions is closely tied to the concept of communal identity and responsibility. In many African cultures, the well-being of the community is believed to be dependent on the ancestral and spiritual realm. As a result, ancestors and spirits are often seen as guardians and protectors of the community, and their veneration is seen as a way to maintain the harmony and balance of the community.

Overall, the role of ancestors and spirits in African traditional religions is multifaceted and complex, and varies across different cultures and regions. However, a common thread throughout these religions is the belief in the power and influence of the supernatural realm on the lives of the living, and the importance of maintaining a connection with this realm through rituals, offerings, and veneration.

The significance of rituals and ceremonies in African traditional religions

The significance of rituals and ceremonies in African traditional religions cannot be overstated. Rituals and ceremonies are an integral part of the religious practices of African traditional religions, and serve as a means of establishing and maintaining a connection between the physical world and the spiritual world.

Rituals and ceremonies are performed for a variety of reasons in African traditional religions, such as to honor the ancestors, to mark important life events, to seek guidance and protection from the spirits, and to celebrate the changing of the seasons. These rituals and ceremonies are often accompanied by music, dance, and other forms of artistic expression.

One of the most important rituals in African traditional religions is the initiation ceremony. Initiation ceremonies are rites of passage that mark the transition from one stage of life to another, such as from childhood to adulthood. These ceremonies are often accompanied by teachings about the spiritual and cultural values of the community, and serve as a means of transmitting these values from one generation to the next.

In some African traditional religions, such as the Yoruba religion of Nigeria, initiation ceremonies are performed to initiate individuals into specific religious traditions or priesthoods. These ceremonies are often accompanied by the performance of specific rituals, such as the pouring of libations or the sacrifice of animals, and the wearing of specific clothing or jewelry.

Another important type of ritual in African traditional religions is the healing ritual. Healing rituals are performed to heal individuals who are suffering from physical or spiritual ailments, and are often accompanied by the use of herbal medicines, divination, and other forms of spiritual and physical healing.

In some African traditional religions, such as the San religion of southern Africa, the healing ritual is performed through the use of trance dancing. Trance dancing is a form of ecstatic dance in which individuals enter into a trance state and communicate with the spirits through their movements and gestures.

The role of music and dance in African traditional religions cannot be overstated. Music and dance are used to establish a connection between the physical world and the spiritual world, and to create a sense of community and shared experience. In some African traditional religions, such as the Bantu religion of southern Africa, music and dance are used to invoke the spirits and to communicate with the ancestors.

In the Bantu religion, for example, the dance known as the ngoma is performed to honor the ancestors and to seek their guidance and protection. The ngoma is a form of group dancing that is accompanied by the singing of traditional songs and the playing of traditional instruments, such as drums and rattles.

The use of sacred spaces and objects is another important aspect of the rituals and ceremonies of African traditional religions. Sacred spaces, such as groves of trees or specific locations in nature, are believed to be places where the physical world and the spiritual world intersect. Sacred objects, such as masks or statues, are believed to be imbued with the power of the spirits or the ancestors, and are used in ritual contexts to establish a connection between the physical and spiritual worlds.

In the Yoruba religion, for example, sacred objects known as orishas are used in ritual contexts to honor specific deities or spirits. These orishas are often depicted as statues or masks, and are believed to be able to communicate with the spirits and the ancestors.

In conclusion, the significance of rituals and ceremonies in African traditional religions cannot be overstated. These rituals and ceremonies serve as a means of establishing and maintaining a connection between the physical world and the spiritual world, and are used to honor the ancestors, seek guidance and protection from the spirits, mark important life events, and celebrate the changing of the seasons. The use of music, dance, sacred spaces, and sacred objects are all important aspects of these rituals and ceremonies, and serve to create a sense of community and shared experience among those who participate in them.

The relationship between African traditional religions and African society

The relationship between African traditional religions and African society is complex and multifaceted. African traditional religions have had a profound impact on the social, cultural, and political structures of African societies, and have been both shaped by and shaped these structures in turn.

One of the most notable aspects of the relationship between African traditional religions and African society is the extent to which they are intertwined. African traditional religions are deeply embedded in African society, and are intimately connected with the social and cultural practices of the communities in which they are practiced. For many African societies, traditional religious beliefs and practices are an integral part of daily life, and are woven into the fabric of social and cultural life.

African traditional religions also play an important role in shaping the political structures of African societies. In many African societies, traditional religious leaders hold positions of power and authority, and are often closely connected to political leaders. Traditional religious beliefs and practices are also frequently invoked in political discourse, and are used to legitimize political authority and establish political legitimacy.

Despite their deep connections to African society, African traditional religions have also faced challenges and obstacles in the face of modernization and globalization. The spread of Christianity and Islam throughout Africa has led to the marginalization and even persecution of traditional religious beliefs and practices in some areas. Additionally, the rise of secularism and the influence of Western cultural values have also challenged the place of traditional religions in African society.

Despite these challenges, African traditional religions continue to play an important role in shaping the social, cultural, and political landscape of Africa. In recent years, there has been a resurgence of interest in traditional religious beliefs and practices among African youth, as well as a growing recognition of the importance of these beliefs and practices in the preservation of African cultural heritage.

One of the key ways in which African traditional religions have influenced African society is through their emphasis on communalism and social cohesion. African traditional religions place a strong emphasis on community and the collective, and view individuals as part of a larger social unit. This emphasis on communalism has helped to shape the social structures of many African societies, and has contributed to the development of a strong sense of social cohesion and solidarity.

Another way in which African traditional religions have influenced African society is through their emphasis on the environment and the natural world. African traditional religions place a strong emphasis on the relationship between humans and the natural world, and view the natural world as sacred and imbued with spiritual power. This emphasis on the environment has contributed to the development of a strong tradition of environmental stewardship in many African societies, and has helped to shape attitudes towards environmental conservation and sustainability.

African traditional religions have also played an important role in shaping African art, music, and literature. Many traditional religious beliefs and practices are expressed through artistic and literary forms, and have contributed to the development of a rich and vibrant artistic tradition in Africa. African traditional religions have also influenced African music, with many traditional religious practices incorporating music and dance into their rituals and ceremonies.

Despite their importance in shaping African society, African traditional religions have also faced challenges and criticism. Some have argued that traditional religious beliefs and practices are incompatible with modern values and ideals, and that they are a hindrance to social and cultural progress. Others have argued that traditional religions are inherently oppressive and patriarchal, and that they perpetuate inequality and social injustice.

In conclusion, the relationship between African traditional religions and African society is complex and multifaceted. African traditional religions have had a profound impact on the social, cultural, and political structures of African societies, and have been both shaped by and shaped these structures in turn. Despite the challenges they have faced, African traditional religions continue to play an important role in shaping the social, cultural, and political landscape of Africa, and are an important part of the continent's rich and diverse cultural heritage.

CHAPTER 9: THE RELATIONSHIP BETWEEN AFRICAN RELIGIONS AND OTHER RELIGIONS

Religion has always been a complex and multifaceted phenomenon. Throughout history, different religions have coexisted, often shaping each other through interaction and cross-pollination of ideas and practices. Africa is no exception, and its religious landscape is marked by a rich diversity of traditions, beliefs, and practices. However, as the continent has undergone various social, political, and economic changes, so too have its religions.

One of the key features of African religions is their interaction with other religions, particularly the Abrahamic religions of Christianity and Islam. This chapter will explore the relationship between African religions and other religions, examining the ways in which African religions have interacted with and been influenced by other spiritual paths, the challenges and benefits of interfaith dialogue between African religions and other religions, and the syncretism of African religions and other spiritual paths.

The interaction between African religions and Abrahamic religions:

Christianity and Islam were introduced to Africa during the colonial period, and they have since become major religions on the continent. African traditional religions have interacted with these two religions in various ways, sometimes leading to conflicts and sometimes resulting in syncretism.

One of the key points of conflict between African traditional religions and Christianity and Islam is the issue of religious exclusivity. Christianity and Islam are both monotheistic religions that claim to have the only true path to salvation, which often creates tension with African traditional religions that do not necessarily view the world in such black-and-white terms.

The syncretism of African religions and other spiritual paths:

Syncretism is the process by which different religious traditions blend together to create new hybrid religions. In Africa, syncretism has been a common phenomenon, particularly between African traditional religions and Christianity and Islam.

African Religions

One example of syncretism in African religions is the creation of the "Virgin Mary" figure in some African traditional religions. In many African cultures, there were preexisting female deities who were associated with fertility and motherhood. When Christianity arrived in Africa, the figure of the Virgin Mary was introduced, and some African traditional religions adopted her as a form of their existing mother goddess. This resulted in the creation of a new religious figure that was a blend of Christian and African traditional beliefs.

The challenges and benefits of interfaith dialogue between African religions and other religions:

Interfaith dialogue is the process of communication and exchange between people of different religious traditions. In the context of African religions, interfaith dialogue can be challenging, given the diversity of religious beliefs and practices on the continent. However, there are also many potential benefits to interfaith dialogue, including increased understanding, tolerance, and mutual respect.

One of the key challenges of interfaith dialogue between African religions and other religions is the issue of power dynamics. Many African traditional religions have been marginalized and oppressed by colonialism and other forms of imperialism, which can create a power imbalance in interfaith dialogue with more dominant religions like Christianity and Islam. Additionally, some religious traditions may view interfaith dialogue as a threat to their own beliefs and practices.

Despite these challenges, interfaith dialogue between African religions and other religions has the potential to be a fruitful and enriching process. By engaging in respectful and open-minded dialogue, people of different religious traditions can learn from each other and gain a deeper understanding of the similarities and differences between their beliefs and practices. Interfaith dialogue can also help to promote peace and reconciliation in areas where religious conflict has been a problem.

Conclusion:

The relationship between African religions and other religions is complex and multifaceted, marked by interaction, conflict, and syncretism. The arrival of Christianity and Islam in Africa has had a significant impact on African traditional religions, leading to both tension and hybridization. Additionally, interfaith dialogue between African religions and other religions has presented both challenges and opportunities for mutual understanding and cooperation.

As the world becomes increasingly globalized, the need for interfaith dialogue and understanding has become more pressing. In the case of African religions, the importance of interfaith dialogue lies not only in building bridges between different faiths, but also in preserving and promoting the diversity of African spiritual traditions. This requires a recognition of the value and validity of African religions, and a willingness to engage in dialogue and cooperation with practitioners of these traditions.

One of the main challenges of interfaith dialogue between African religions and other religions is the issue of power dynamics. As a result of centuries of colonialism and the imposition of Western values and religious beliefs, African religions have often been marginalized and viewed as inferior. This has led to a lack of recognition and respect for these traditions, and a tendency to view them as primitive or backward.

In order to overcome these power dynamics and promote genuine dialogue, it is essential to approach interfaith dialogue from a place of mutual respect and equality. This requires a willingness to listen to and learn from practitioners of African religions, and a recognition of the unique value and contribution of these traditions to the global spiritual landscape.

At the same time, interfaith dialogue can also present challenges in terms of preserving the integrity and authenticity of African religions. As African religions interact with other spiritual paths, there is a risk of syncretism and dilution of these traditions. In order to prevent this, it is important for practitioners of African religions to be knowledgeable about the core tenets and practices of their traditions, and to be able to articulate these clearly in dialogue with practitioners of other religions.

In conclusion, the relationship between African religions and other religions is complex and multifaceted, marked by both tension and opportunity. Interfaith dialogue presents both challenges and benefits, and requires a willingness to engage in mutual respect and equality. By promoting dialogue and understanding between African religions and other religions, we can not only build bridges between different faiths, but also preserve and promote the diversity of African spiritual traditions for generations to come.

The interaction between African religions and Abrahamic religions

The interaction between African religions and Abrahamic religions, namely Christianity and Islam, has been a topic of ongoing discussion and debate among scholars and practitioners of religion. The arrival of these religions in Africa has had a significant impact on African traditional religions, leading to both tension and hybridization.

Christianity arrived in Africa in the first century, brought by missionaries who sought to spread the gospel and convert Africans to Christianity. The spread of Christianity was aided by the influence of European colonial powers who saw the religion as a tool for cultural assimilation and control. The introduction of Christianity had a profound impact on African traditional religions, leading to the suppression and demonization of traditional beliefs and practices. Many traditional practices, such as ancestor worship and divination, were considered demonic and sinful by Christian missionaries and were actively discouraged or even outlawed.

Despite this suppression, African traditional religions have continued to exist and even thrive alongside Christianity, often adopting Christian practices and beliefs in a process of syncretism. The blending of traditional African beliefs and Christian teachings has resulted in the emergence of new religious movements, such as African Initiated Churches, that incorporate elements of both traditions.

Islam, on the other hand, arrived in Africa in the seventh century through Arab traders and later through the spread of Islamic empires. Like Christianity, Islam had a significant impact on African traditional religions, leading to the suppression of traditional practices and beliefs. However, Islam also introduced new ideas and practices that were incorporated into African traditional religions, such as the use of Arabic script and the adoption of Islamic dietary restrictions.

One of the most significant areas of interaction between African religions and Abrahamic religions is the concept of monotheism. Both Christianity and Islam are monotheistic religions that believe in the existence of one God. This belief is in contrast to many African traditional religions, which often incorporate the worship of multiple gods and spirits. The idea of monotheism has influenced the development of African religions, leading to the emergence of new monotheistic movements, such as the Bahá'í Faith and Rastafarianism.

The interaction between African religions and Abrahamic religions has also led to conflict and tension, particularly in areas where traditional beliefs and practices are seen as incompatible with Christian or Islamic teachings. This tension has been exacerbated by the influence of political and economic factors, such as the competition for resources and power between religious groups.

Despite these challenges, there have been efforts to promote interfaith dialogue and cooperation between African religions and Abrahamic religions. This dialogue has focused on finding common ground between different religious traditions and addressing issues of mutual concern, such as poverty and social inequality.

One of the key challenges in promoting interfaith dialogue is the recognition of the diversity within each religious tradition. African traditional religions, Christianity, and Islam are not monolithic entities, but rather encompass a range of beliefs, practices, and interpretations. Interfaith dialogue requires an understanding of this diversity and a willingness to engage with different perspectives and experiences.

In conclusion, the interaction between African religions and Abrahamic religions has been marked by both conflict and cooperation. The arrival of Christianity and Islam in Africa has had a significant impact on African traditional religions, leading to the suppression of traditional practices and beliefs, as well as the emergence of new religious movements. The promotion of interfaith dialogue and cooperation requires an understanding of the diversity within each religious tradition and a willingness to engage with different perspectives and experiences.

The syncretism of African religions and other spiritual paths

The syncretism of African religions and other spiritual paths is a complex phenomenon that has been ongoing for centuries. Syncretism can be defined as the blending or fusion of different beliefs, practices, and traditions, resulting in the creation of a new religious or spiritual path. In the context of African religions, syncretism has taken place through the interaction between traditional African religions and various other religious and spiritual paths, including Christianity, Islam, Hinduism, Buddhism, and New Age spirituality.

The process of syncretism can be traced back to the early days of European colonialism in Africa, when Christian missionaries sought to convert the indigenous populations to Christianity. In order to achieve this goal, the missionaries often incorporated elements of African traditional religion into their teachings, creating a form of Christianity that was adapted to the African context. This led to the emergence of various syncretic Christian movements in Africa, such as the Ethiopian Orthodox Church and the Kimbanguist Church.

Similarly, Islam also underwent a process of syncretism in Africa. Islam arrived in Africa in the 7th century with Arab traders, and over time it became fused with various elements of African traditional religion. This led to the emergence of new Islamic traditions in Africa, such as the Sufi brotherhoods, which combine Islamic teachings with local beliefs and practices.

African Religions

In addition to Christianity and Islam, African traditional religions have also interacted with other spiritual paths, such as Hinduism and Buddhism. In the 19th century, Hinduism was introduced to Africa by Indian indentured laborers, and it became fused with African traditional religions in places like South Africa and Mauritius. Similarly, Buddhism has been introduced to Africa in recent decades, and it has begun to influence the development of new syncretic spiritual paths, such as Engaged Buddhism.

The New Age movement, which emerged in the West in the 1960s and 1970s, has also had an impact on the syncretic spirituality of Africa. The New Age movement emphasizes the unity of all religions and spiritual paths, and it has inspired the development of new syncretic spiritual paths in Africa that blend elements of African traditional religions with New Age teachings and practices.

One of the most well-known examples of syncretism in African religions is the practice of Vodou in Haiti, which combines elements of African traditional religions with Catholicism. Vodou originated in West Africa and was brought to Haiti by enslaved Africans in the 18th century. In order to escape persecution by the Catholic Church, Vodou practitioners began to incorporate Catholic saints and symbols into their rituals, creating a form of syncretic spirituality that is still practiced in Haiti today.

While syncretism can be seen as a positive development that allows for the creation of new and dynamic spiritual paths, it is also a controversial phenomenon that has been criticized by some for diluting the authenticity of traditional African religions. Some argue that syncretism has led to the loss of traditional African spiritual practices and beliefs, and that it has contributed to the erosion of African cultural identity.

In conclusion, the syncretism of African religions and other spiritual paths is a complex and ongoing process that has been shaped by the interaction between different cultures and traditions. While it has led to the emergence of new and dynamic spiritual paths, it has also been a source of tension and controversy. The study of syncretism in African religions can provide insights into the ways in which cultural and religious traditions are transformed and adapted over time.

The challenges and benefits of interfaith dialogue between African religions and other religions

The interaction between African religions and other spiritual paths, including Abrahamic religions, has not always been harmonious. There have been conflicts, misunderstandings, and even violence between different religious groups, and this has often been the result of a lack of understanding and communication. However, there have also been positive examples of interfaith dialogue and cooperation, which have led to greater understanding, mutual respect, and even syncretism.

Interfaith dialogue can be defined as a conversation or discussion between people of different religious traditions, with the aim of learning from each other and promoting understanding and cooperation. The benefits of interfaith dialogue are numerous and far-reaching, and they apply to all religions, including African religions. Interfaith dialogue can help to promote peace, social cohesion, and respect for diversity. It can also help to challenge stereotypes, promote tolerance, and foster empathy.

One of the challenges of interfaith dialogue is the difficulty of finding common ground between different religious traditions. Religious beliefs and practices can be deeply ingrained and rooted in cultural and historical contexts, and it can be challenging to find shared values and principles that can form the basis of a productive dialogue. Moreover, some religious traditions may be more open to dialogue than others, and some may view dialogue as a threat to their own beliefs and practices.

Another challenge of interfaith dialogue is the issue of power dynamics. In many cases, there is a power imbalance between different religious groups, with one group being more dominant or influential than the other. This can create an uneven playing field and make it difficult for a genuine dialogue to take place. Moreover, some groups may be more marginalized or discriminated against than others, which can further complicate the dialogue.

Despite these challenges, there have been numerous examples of successful interfaith dialogue between African religions and other religions. One example is the Syncretic Movement in Haiti, which emerged as a result of the interaction between African religions and Catholicism. The Syncretic Movement, also known as Vodou, is a blend of African traditional religions and Catholicism, and it has become an important part of Haitian culture and identity.

Another example is the work of the Interfaith Center of New York, which has been promoting interfaith dialogue and cooperation since 1997. The Center has organized numerous events and programs that bring together people of different religious traditions, including African religions. These programs aim to promote understanding, respect, and cooperation between different religious communities, and they have been highly successful in fostering positive relationships between different religious groups.

In conclusion, interfaith dialogue between African religions and other religions can be challenging but also highly beneficial. It can help to promote peace, social cohesion, and respect for diversity, and it can challenge stereotypes, promote tolerance, and foster empathy. However, it also requires a deep commitment to understanding and communication, as well as a willingness to challenge one's own assumptions and biases. Through interfaith dialogue, African religions can play a vital role in promoting a more peaceful and inclusive world.

Exercise:

Reflect on your own experience of interfaith dialogue. Have you ever engaged in interfaith dialogue? If so, what were some of the benefits and challenges of this dialogue? If not, what do you think are some of the benefits and challenges of interfaith dialogue?

Choose a religious tradition that is different from your own and research its beliefs and practices. What are some of the similarities and differences between this tradition and your own? How might you find common ground between these two traditions and engage in a productive dialogue?

Imagine that you are organizing an interfaith dialogue event in your community. What are some of the steps you would take to ensure that the dialogue is productive and respectful? How would you address the challenges of power dynamics and cultural differences?

CHAPTER 10: THE ROLE OF AFRICAN RELIGIONS IN AFRICAN SOCIETIES

African religions have played a significant role in shaping the cultural, political, and economic landscape of African societies. For centuries, African religions have been an integral part of the daily lives of millions of people on the continent. In this chapter, we will explore the ways in which African religions have impacted African societies, focusing on their role in shaping culture, art, and music, influencing politics and economics, promoting social justice and environmental conservation, and inspiring religious movements.

The Impact of African Religions on African Culture, Art, and Music:

African religions have had a profound impact on African culture, art, and music. They have been a source of inspiration for artists and musicians across the continent, influencing the creation of diverse art forms, including sculpture, painting, dance, and music. African religions are characterized by a rich symbolism, which has been reflected in the visual arts. For example, the Yoruba people of Nigeria are known for their intricate woodcarvings and beadwork, which are infused with religious symbolism. Similarly, the Akan people of Ghana have a rich tradition of weaving, which incorporates religious symbolism and mythology.

Music is another area where African religions have had a significant impact. Music has always been an important part of African religious practice, with many religions using music as a means of communicating with the divine. In West Africa, for example, the griots (professional musicians) have played an important role in preserving the religious traditions of their communities. The griots have passed down songs and stories from generation to generation, ensuring that the religious traditions are kept alive.

The Influence of African Religions on African Politics and Economics:

African religions have also had a significant impact on African politics and economics. They have played a role in shaping the political and economic systems of many African societies, influencing everything from leadership structures to trade practices. For example, in many African societies, religious leaders have played a prominent role in political decision-making, serving as advisors to rulers and helping to mediate disputes between communities.

In addition, African religions have played a role in shaping economic practices. For example, many African societies have traditional beliefs about the relationship between humans and the natural environment. These beliefs often involve a deep respect for nature and the need to live in harmony with the environment. This has led to the development of sustainable agricultural practices and a focus on community-based economic systems.

The Role of African Religions in Promoting Social Justice and Environmental Conservation:

African religions have also played a role in promoting social justice and environmental conservation. Many African religions emphasize the importance of community, equality, and social justice. For example, the Ubuntu philosophy, which is found in many African religions, emphasizes the interconnectedness of all things and the need to treat others with respect and dignity.

African religions also emphasize the importance of environmental conservation. Many religions have traditional beliefs about the relationship between humans and the natural environment, emphasizing the need to live in harmony with nature. This has led to the development of sustainable agricultural practices and a focus on community-based economic systems.

Case Studies of African Religious Movements and Their Impact on African Societies:

Throughout history, African religious movements have emerged in response to social, political, and economic challenges. These movements have played a significant role in shaping African societies, challenging traditional power structures and promoting social justice. For example, the Rastafarian movement, which emerged in Jamaica in the 1930s, has its roots in African religious beliefs and practices. The movement has had a significant impact on Jamaican society, promoting social justice and influencing music and art.

Similarly, the Ethiopian Orthodox Church has played a significant role in shaping Ethiopian society. The church, which dates back to the 4th century, is one of the oldest Christian churches in the world and has been a major influence on Ethiopian culture and politics. It has played a pivotal role in the country's resistance against colonialism and foreign occupation. During the Italian occupation of Ethiopia in the 1930s and 1940s, the Ethiopian Orthodox Church became a symbol of resistance and national identity. The church also played a key role in the country's transition to a republic in the 1970s.

Exploring Origins, Traditions, and Contemporary Relevance

In South Africa, the Shembe Church, also known as the Nazareth Baptist Church, has been a significant force for social change. Founded in the early 1900s, the church blended elements of Christianity and Zulu culture, promoting social justice and advocating for the rights of African people in a highly segregated society. The church has played a key role in promoting the empowerment of women and advocating for the rights of marginalized groups in South Africa.

Another notable African religious movement is the Aladura movement, which originated in Nigeria in the early 20th century. The movement emphasized healing and spiritual practices, and promoted the importance of individual spiritual experiences. The Aladura movement played a significant role in shaping Nigerian culture and society, with many members contributing to the country's political and economic development.

In addition to these movements, many African religious practices and beliefs have also influenced popular culture in Africa and around the world. For example, the use of drumming and dance in African religious ceremonies has influenced music and dance genres such as jazz, blues, and hip hop. African traditional religions have also influenced contemporary art, with many artists drawing on African symbolism and spiritual practices in their work.

Overall, African religions have played a significant role in shaping African societies, influencing culture, politics, and economics. The impact of African religious movements and beliefs is far-reaching and continues to influence contemporary society in Africa and beyond.

The impact of African religions on African culture, art, and music

The impact of African religions on African culture, art, and music has been significant and enduring. African religions are deeply ingrained in the cultural and artistic practices of many African societies. From music and dance to visual arts and literature, African religions have influenced and inspired generations of African artists and cultural producers.

One of the most striking examples of the influence of African religions on African culture is the vibrant and diverse music scene that has emerged in many parts of the continent. African music is characterized by its rich rhythms, intricate melodies, and expressive vocals, all of which draw on a range of cultural and religious traditions. From the traditional music of West Africa to the Afrobeat and highlife music of Nigeria and Ghana, African music has a distinctive sound that reflects the complex history and diverse cultures of the continent.

African Religions

One of the most influential African religions on African music is the Yoruba religion, which originated in what is now Nigeria and Benin. The Yoruba religion is characterized by its elaborate pantheon of deities, or orishas, who are believed to control various aspects of the natural world. Yoruba music, which is often used in religious rituals and ceremonies, is characterized by its use of complex rhythms and call-and-response vocals. Many contemporary African musicians, including Fela Kuti and King Sunny Ade, have drawn on the Yoruba tradition to create their own distinctive sound.

Another important influence on African music is the Akan religion, which is practiced in Ghana and Ivory Coast. The Akan religion is characterized by its emphasis on ancestor worship and the use of drumming and dance in religious ceremonies. Akan music is known for its energetic rhythms and intricate polyrhythms, which have been incorporated into many genres of African music, including highlife and hiplife.

In addition to music, African religions have also had a significant impact on the visual arts of the continent. Many African artists, both traditional and contemporary, have drawn on religious themes and imagery in their work. For example, the masks and sculptures of the Dogon people of Mali are heavily influenced by their religious beliefs and practices, which emphasize the importance of ancestors and spirits.

Similarly, the art of the Yoruba people is characterized by its intricate and highly symbolic imagery, which is often used in religious rituals and ceremonies. Many contemporary African artists, such as El Anatsui and Yinka Shonibare, have drawn on the Yoruba tradition to create their own distinctive styles.

African religions have also had a significant impact on literature and storytelling in Africa. Many African stories and legends are based on religious themes and motifs, such as the trickster figure of Anansi in West African folklore. African writers, such as Chinua Achebe and Ngũgĩ wa Thiong'o, have drawn on these traditions to create powerful works of literature that explore the complexities of African culture and identity.

Overall, the impact of African religions on African culture, art, and music is profound and multifaceted. These religions have influenced and inspired generations of African artists, musicians, and cultural producers, and continue to play an important role in shaping the cultural landscape of the continent.

Exploring Origins, Traditions, and Contemporary Relevance

The influence of African religions on African politics and economics

The influence of African religions on politics and economics is complex and multifaceted. African religions have played a significant role in shaping African societies, providing a framework for understanding the world, and promoting social justice. They have also been used to legitimize political power and economic systems, and as a tool for resistance and liberation.

In many African societies, religion and politics are closely intertwined. Religious leaders have played important roles in political processes, serving as advisors to rulers and playing key roles in conflict resolution. In some cases, religious leaders have even become political leaders, using their religious authority to gain popular support.

African religions have also played a role in shaping economic systems. Many traditional African religions have a strong focus on communal values, emphasizing the importance of sharing and cooperation. These values have been reflected in many traditional African economic systems, which prioritize collective ownership and management of resources.

However, with the rise of colonialism and globalization, many traditional African economic systems have been replaced by capitalist economic systems, which prioritize individualism and competition. This has resulted in economic inequality and environmental degradation in many African countries.

In response to these challenges, many African religious movements have emerged that promote economic justice and sustainability. For example, the Green Belt Movement in Kenya, founded by the late Wangari Maathai, is rooted in traditional Kikuyu spiritual beliefs and practices. The movement focuses on reforestation, sustainable agriculture, and women's empowerment, and has had a significant impact on Kenya's environment and economy.

Similarly, the Jubilee South movement, which originated in South Africa in the 1990s, draws on Christian and African religious traditions to promote economic justice and debt relief for developing countries. The movement has been instrumental in advocating for debt cancellation and fair trade policies at the international level.

Despite the positive impact of African religions on politics and economics, they have also been used to legitimize authoritarian regimes and reinforce social inequalities. For example, in some African countries, religious leaders have been co-opted by political leaders to promote their agendas and suppress dissent.

In addition, some traditional African religions have been criticized for promoting practices that are harmful to women and other marginalized groups. For example, in some societies, traditional beliefs about witchcraft have been used to justify violence against women accused of witchcraft.

To address these challenges, there is a need for dialogue and engagement between African religions and other religious and secular movements. This dialogue should aim to promote a more nuanced understanding of the role of religion in politics and economics, and to identify strategies for promoting social justice and sustainability.

Overall, the influence of African religions on politics and economics is complex and multifaceted. African religions have played an important role in shaping African societies, providing a framework for understanding the world, and promoting social justice. However, they have also been used to legitimize authoritarian regimes and reinforce social inequalities. To address these challenges, there is a need for dialogue and engagement between African religions and other religious and secular movements, to promote a more nuanced understanding of the role of religion in politics and economics, and to identify strategies for promoting social justice and sustainability.

The role of African religions in promoting social justice and environmental conservation

The role of African religions in promoting social justice and environmental conservation is a complex and multifaceted topic. African religions have a long history of promoting social justice and environmental conservation, rooted in their beliefs and practices. This section will explore the ways in which African religions have influenced social justice and environmental conservation in African societies, and the challenges that they face in doing so.

Social Justice

African religions have played a significant role in promoting social justice in African societies. From the early days of African civilizations, religion has been a cornerstone of social order and governance. African religions often emphasize the importance of community and social responsibility, and many religious practices are designed to promote social cohesion and well-being. This has helped to promote social justice by fostering a sense of collective responsibility for the well-being of all members of society.

One of the most notable examples of African religions promoting social justice is the role of religious leaders in the anti-colonial and anti-apartheid movements in

Africa. Many African religious leaders were active participants in these movements, and their teachings and practices often provided a moral foundation for resistance. For example, the South African Anglican bishop Desmond Tutu was a key figure in the anti-apartheid movement, and his religious teachings emphasized the importance of nonviolence, reconciliation, and social justice.

Another example of African religions promoting social justice is the role of religious institutions in providing social services in African communities. In many African societies, religious institutions are among the most trusted and respected institutions, and they often provide a wide range of social services, including education, health care, and humanitarian aid. These services are often provided to the most vulnerable members of society, such as the poor, the sick, and the marginalized.

Despite the positive role that African religions have played in promoting social justice, they also face many challenges. One of the biggest challenges is the tension between traditional religious beliefs and modern values. As African societies have become more modern and urbanized, traditional religious beliefs have often come into conflict with modern values such as individualism, secularism, and human rights. This has created tension between traditional religious leaders and modern political leaders, and has sometimes led to conflict and violence.

Another challenge is the tension between religious pluralism and social cohesion. As African societies have become more diverse and pluralistic, religious diversity has become a more prominent feature of African societies. This has led to tension between different religious groups, and has sometimes led to conflict and violence. In order to promote social justice, African religious leaders must find ways to promote religious pluralism while also fostering social cohesion and unity.

Environmental Conservation

African religions have also played a significant role in promoting environmental conservation in African societies. Many African religions emphasize the importance of the natural world, and many religious practices are designed to promote environmental conservation and sustainability. For example, many African religions have traditional beliefs and practices related to the protection of sacred groves, forests, and other natural habitats.

One of the most notable examples of African religions promoting environmental conservation is the role of traditional African religions in the conservation of wildlife. Many traditional African religions have beliefs and practices related to the protection of wildlife, and many African communities have developed systems of traditional conservation that are designed to protect wildlife and their habitats. For example, in many African communities, certain animals are considered sacred, and hunting or killing these animals is forbidden.

Another example of African religions promoting environmental conservation is the role of religious leaders in promoting sustainable development. Many African religious leaders have recognized the importance of sustainable development for the well-being of African societies, and have advocated for policies and practices that promote sustainable development. For example, some African religious leaders have called for the development of renewable energy sources, such as solar and wind power, as a way to reduce dependence on fossil fuels and promote environmental sustainability.

Despite the positive role that African religions have played in promoting environmental conservation, there are also challenges and limitations that need to be addressed. One of the main challenges is the clash between traditional beliefs and practices and modern development. As African societies become more modernized and urbanized, traditional beliefs and practices related to environmental conservation may be lost or weakened. This can lead to a loss of biodiversity and environmental degradation.

Additionally, some traditional African religious practices, such as hunting and fishing, may have negative impacts on the environment if they are not carried out sustainably. For example, overfishing and unsustainable hunting practices can lead to the depletion of fish and wildlife populations, which can have negative impacts on both the environment and the livelihoods of local communities.

Furthermore, some African religions have been criticized for promoting beliefs and practices that are harmful to the environment, such as the use of endangered plant and animal species in traditional medicine. While it is important to respect and preserve traditional African beliefs and practices, it is also important to ensure that they are sustainable and do not harm the environment.

To address these challenges and promote environmental conservation, it is important to find ways to integrate traditional African beliefs and practices with modern development. This can involve developing policies and practices that support sustainable development, promoting education and awareness about environmental conservation, and encouraging the active involvement of local communities and religious leaders in environmental conservation efforts.

In conclusion, African religions have played a significant role in promoting social justice and environmental conservation in African societies. Through their beliefs and practices, African religions have promoted a deep respect for the natural world and the importance of sustainable development. While there are challenges and limitations to the role of African religions in environmental conservation, there are also opportunities to find innovative solutions and promote a more sustainable future for Africa and the world.

Case studies of African religious movements and their impact on African societies

African religious movements have played a significant role in shaping African societies and culture throughout history. These movements have been shaped by various factors, including political, social, economic, and cultural influences. This section will provide case studies of several African religious movements and their impact on African societies.

✦   Rastafarianism

Rastafarianism is a religious movement that originated in Jamaica in the 1930s and is based on the teachings of Marcus Garvey, a Jamaican activist and Pan-Africanist. The movement is characterized by its emphasis on African liberation, social justice, and the use of marijuana as a sacrament. The movement has since spread throughout the African diaspora, including in Africa itself.

In Africa, Rastafarianism has had a significant impact on culture and music. The movement has been influential in the development of reggae music, which has become popular throughout Africa. The lyrics of reggae songs often deal with themes of social justice and African liberation, reflecting the values of the Rastafarian movement.

Rastafarianism has also been influential in promoting African culture and identity. The movement emphasizes the importance of African culture and heritage, and its followers often adopt African names and wear African clothing as a way of expressing their cultural identity. Rastafarians have been involved in various social and political movements throughout Africa, advocating for social justice and the rights of African people.

✦   Candomblé

Candomblé is a syncretic religion that originated in Brazil and is based on African religious practices brought to Brazil during the transatlantic slave trade. The religion blends African religious traditions with Catholicism and indigenous beliefs. Candomblé has since spread throughout the African diaspora, including in Africa itself.

In Africa, Candomblé has had a significant impact on culture and religion. The religion has been influential in promoting African culture and identity, and its followers often adopt African names and wear African clothing as a way of expressing their cultural identity. Candomblé has also been influential in the development of Afro-Brazilian music and dance, which have become popular throughout Africa.

Candomblé has also played a significant role in promoting social justice and the rights of marginalized communities. The religion emphasizes the importance of community and solidarity, and its followers often organize social and political movements to promote social justice and the rights of marginalized communities.

✧ Vodou

Vodou is a syncretic religion that originated in Haiti and is based on African religious practices brought to Haiti during the transatlantic slave trade. The religion blends African religious traditions with Catholicism and indigenous beliefs. Vodou has since spread throughout the African diaspora, including in Africa itself.

In Africa, Vodou has had a significant impact on culture and religion. The religion has been influential in promoting African culture and identity, and its followers often adopt African names and wear African clothing as a way of expressing their cultural identity. Vodou has also been influential in the development of Haitian music and dance, which have become popular throughout Africa.

Vodou has also played a significant role in promoting social justice and the rights of marginalized communities. The religion emphasizes the importance of community and solidarity, and its followers often organize social and political movements to promote social justice and the rights of marginalized communities.

✧ The Aladura Movement

The Aladura Movement is a Christian religious movement that originated in Nigeria in the early 20th century. The movement emphasizes the importance of faith healing and the power of prayer in promoting physical and spiritual healing. The movement has since spread throughout Africa, and its followers often incorporate African religious traditions and practices into their worship.

In Africa, the Aladura Movement has had a significant impact on the practice of Christianity, particularly in Nigeria where it originated. The movement has been successful in spreading its message and attracting a large following, with estimates suggesting that there are over 10 million Aladura members in Nigeria alone.

The Aladura Movement has also had a significant impact on healthcare in Africa. The movement's emphasis on faith healing and prayer has led many of its followers to reject Western medicine in favor of traditional healing methods. This has led to concerns about the safety and efficacy of these methods, particularly in cases where serious medical conditions require prompt and effective treatment.

Another example of an African religious movement is the Rastafarian Movement. The Rastafarian Movement originated in Jamaica in the 1930s, and is based on the belief that the former Ethiopian emperor Haile Selassie is the messiah. The movement emphasizes the importance of African identity and the rejection of colonialism and white supremacy.

The Rastafarian Movement has had a significant impact on music, art, and culture in Africa and throughout the world. The movement's influence can be seen in the music of Bob Marley, who was a prominent Rastafarian, as well as in the reggae and dancehall music scenes in Jamaica and other parts of the world.

The Rastafarian Movement has also had a significant impact on politics and social justice. The movement has been involved in campaigns for reparations for slavery and other forms of colonial exploitation, as well as in campaigns for environmental conservation and sustainable development.

One final example of an African religious movement is the Unity Church of Christ in Zimbabwe. The Unity Church of Christ was founded in Zimbabwe in the 1950s, and emphasizes the importance of African cultural traditions and practices in the practice of Christianity. The movement has been successful in attracting a large following, and has been involved in campaigns for social justice and human rights in Zimbabwe and throughout Africa.

In conclusion, African religious movements have had a significant impact on African societies, both in terms of religious practice and culture, as well as in terms of social and political activism. These movements have incorporated a wide range of religious and cultural traditions, and have helped to shape the identity and worldview of African societies. Despite criticisms and concerns about some of the practices and beliefs associated with these movements, they continue to play an important role in African society and culture.

PART 3: AFRICAN TRADITIONAL RELIGIONS

African traditional religions are a diverse set of religious practices and beliefs that have been passed down through generations in many different African societies. These religions vary widely in their beliefs, practices, and rituals, but they share a common emphasis on the importance of spirituality and the interconnectedness of all living beings.

African traditional religions have played a significant role in shaping African cultures and societies, and have influenced the development of many African religious movements and practices. They have also been a source of inspiration and empowerment for many African people, particularly during times of social and political upheaval.

In this section, we will explore the history and beliefs of some of the most prominent African traditional religions, including Yoruba religion, Santeria, Vodou, and Candomble. We will examine their beliefs and practices related to divination, herbalism, shamanism, and ancestor worship, and their influence on African spirituality and culture. We will also consider the challenges that African traditional religions have faced, including colonialism and religious persecution, and the ways in which they continue to evolve and adapt in the modern world.

CHAPTER 11: THE CONCEPT OF AFRICAN TRADITIONAL RELIGIONS (ATRS)

African Traditional Religions (ATRs) refer to a diverse set of religious beliefs and practices that have developed over thousands of years in Africa. These religions have been shaped by a variety of factors, including geography, culture, and history, and they continue to play an important role in the lives of many Africans today. In this chapter, we will explore the concept of ATRs, their history, and the challenges of studying them in a modern context.

One of the defining features of ATRs is their emphasis on oral tradition. Unlike many Western religions, ATRs do not have a single text or doctrine that serves as the basis of their beliefs. Instead, their teachings and practices are passed down through oral tradition, from one generation to the next. This has made it challenging for scholars to study and understand ATRs, as there is often limited written documentation of their beliefs and practices.

Despite these challenges, there is much to be learned from the study of ATRs. These religions have played a significant role in the history and culture of Africa, and they continue to influence the beliefs and practices of many Africans today. By exploring the concept of ATRs, their history, and the challenges of studying them, we can gain a deeper understanding of the diversity and complexity of religious traditions around the world.

Defining African Traditional Religions and their history

African Traditional Religions (ATRs) are a diverse set of religious practices and beliefs that have been practiced across Africa for thousands of years. ATRs are characterized by a shared belief in a supreme being or creator, ancestral spirits, and a reverence for the natural world. Despite their widespread presence and importance in African societies, ATRs are often overlooked or misunderstood in Western scholarship and popular culture.

Defining African Traditional Religions

The term "African Traditional Religions" is a Western construct that attempts to group together a wide range of religious practices and beliefs found across the African continent. It is important to note that ATRs are not a monolithic or homogeneous set of beliefs and practices, but rather a diverse and complex collection of religious traditions that vary widely from region to region and even from community to community. In some cases, different religious traditions may coexist and even syncretize, incorporating elements from each other.

One of the challenges in defining ATRs is the lack of a single, authoritative text or scripture that outlines their beliefs and practices. Instead, ATRs rely on oral traditions, passed down from generation to generation through stories, myths, and songs. This emphasis on oral tradition means that ATRs are highly decentralized, with beliefs and practices varying widely depending on the specific community and cultural context.

Despite this diversity, there are some common threads that run through many ATRs. One of the defining features of ATRs is a belief in a supreme being or creator, often referred to as "God" or "the creator." This belief is often accompanied by a belief in ancestral spirits or other supernatural beings, such as nature spirits or animal spirits. Ancestor veneration is a key aspect of many ATRs, with ancestors seen as powerful spiritual entities who can intercede on behalf of the living.

Another defining feature of many ATRs is a strong connection to the natural world. ATRs often emphasize the importance of living in harmony with nature and respecting the natural environment. This is reflected in many ATRs' use of natural materials in religious practices, such as the use of leaves, flowers, and herbs in rituals and ceremonies.

The History of African Traditional Religions

The origins of ATRs can be traced back to pre-colonial Africa, where they played a central role in the social, cultural, and spiritual life of many African societies. ATRs were intimately tied to everyday life, with religious practices and beliefs informing everything from marriage and birth to death and burial.

The spread of Islam and Christianity across Africa during the colonial period had a significant impact on ATRs. Many African societies were forced to convert to Islam or Christianity, often through violent means. This led to the suppression and marginalization of ATRs, with many practitioners forced to go underground or practice their beliefs in secret.

In recent decades, there has been a renewed interest in ATRs, both within Africa and around the world. Many African countries have recognized ATRs as legitimate religious practices and have worked to protect and promote them. At the same time, there has been growing interest among scholars and practitioners in the West in learning more about ATRs and their role in African societies.

Conclusion

African Traditional Religions are a diverse and complex set of religious practices and beliefs that have played a central role in African societies for thousands of years. Despite their importance, ATRs have often been overlooked or misunderstood in Western scholarship and popular culture. Defining ATRs is challenging, given their decentralized and diverse nature, but they are characterized by a shared belief in a supreme being or creator, ancestral spirits, and a reverence for the natural world. The history of ATRs is rich and varied, spanning millennia and influenced by countless factors such as migration, colonization, and globalization.

Throughout Africa's history, traditional religions have played a crucial role in shaping the continent's social, cultural, and political landscape. They have provided a foundation for ethical and moral values, guided social norms and practices, and offered comfort and support in times of hardship. Despite the impact of colonialism and the spread of Christianity and Islam, ATRs remain an integral part of many African communities today.

One of the defining characteristics of ATRs is their emphasis on oral tradition. Stories, myths, and rituals are passed down through generations through storytelling, music, dance, and other forms of performance. This has contributed to the resilience and longevity of ATRs, as they are able to adapt to changing social and political conditions while still maintaining their core beliefs and practices.

However, defining ATRs can also be problematic due to the vast cultural and linguistic diversity across the African continent. ATRs are not monolithic and vary widely from region to region and even within specific communities. Additionally, the term "traditional" can be misleading as it suggests that these religions are static and unchanging, when in fact they have evolved and adapted over time.

In conclusion, African Traditional Religions are a rich and multifaceted set of religious practices and beliefs that have shaped African societies for thousands of years. While defining ATRs can be challenging given their diverse and decentralized nature, they are characterized by a shared belief in a supreme being, ancestral spirits, and a reverence for the natural world. The history of ATRs is complex and influenced by countless factors, and they continue to play an important role in many African communities today.

African Religions

The importance of oral tradition in preserving ATRs

The transmission of knowledge, beliefs, and values from generation to generation is essential in preserving cultures and traditions. In Africa, oral tradition has been the primary means of preserving African Traditional Religions (ATRs). This section will explore the significance of oral tradition in the preservation of ATRs and how it has contributed to their longevity and resilience. It will also examine the challenges that come with relying solely on oral tradition for the preservation of ATRs.

The Role of Oral Tradition in ATRs

ATRs are diverse and decentralized, and the practices and beliefs associated with them vary from region to region. A common feature of ATRs is their reliance on oral tradition as a means of preserving knowledge, history, and culture. Oral tradition in ATRs encompasses various forms of communication, including storytelling, songs, proverbs, and rituals. These forms of communication are used to pass on knowledge from one generation to the next, to reinforce cultural values, and to preserve history.

The Importance of Storytelling in ATRs

Storytelling is an essential aspect of oral tradition in ATRs. Stories are used to explain the origins of the world, the creation of humanity, and the relationship between humans, spirits, and the natural world. These stories also serve to pass on moral and ethical values, to educate people about their history and culture, and to create a sense of community and belonging. In some ATRs, storytelling is also used to teach practical skills, such as farming techniques or medicine.

The Role of Songs and Proverbs in ATRs

Songs and proverbs are also essential aspects of oral tradition in ATRs. Songs are used to express emotions, to praise deities and spirits, and to commemorate important events. Proverbs, on the other hand, are used to convey wisdom, to teach ethical values, and to provide guidance on how to navigate life's challenges. Both songs and proverbs are memorable and easy to pass on, making them effective tools for preserving knowledge and culture.

The Importance of Rituals in ATRs

Rituals are another essential aspect of oral tradition in ATRs. They are used to connect humans with spirits, to seek their guidance and protection, and to mark significant life events. These rituals are often accompanied by music, dance, and other forms of expression, making them memorable and easy to pass on. Rituals play an important role in preserving ATRs because they provide a tangible link to the past, reinforcing cultural values and beliefs.

Challenges of Preserving ATRs Through Oral Tradition

While oral tradition has played a vital role in preserving ATRs, it also comes with challenges. The primary challenge is the risk of losing knowledge and culture due to the death of elders and the decline of traditional practices. As younger generations become more exposed to Western culture and education, they may become less interested in preserving their traditional beliefs and practices, leading to the loss of cultural heritage. Another challenge is the risk of misinterpretation and distortion of cultural practices due to the lack of written records. Oral tradition relies on memory, and over time, details may become distorted or lost, leading to misinterpretation of cultural practices and beliefs.

In conclusion, oral tradition plays a significant role in the preservation of African Traditional Religions. Storytelling, songs, proverbs, and rituals are essential tools used to pass on knowledge, culture, and values from one generation to the next. However, the reliance on oral tradition also comes with challenges, such as the risk of losing knowledge due to the decline of traditional practices and the risk of misinterpretation and distortion of cultural practices. It is, therefore, essential to find ways of complementing oral tradition with written records and other forms of documentation to ensure that ATRs continue to thrive and evolve with changing times while preserving their authenticity and cultural heritage.

One way to complement oral tradition is through academic research, which can help to document and analyze ATRs while providing a more accurate and nuanced understanding of these religious practices. Additionally, collaborations between traditional practitioners and academics can lead to a better understanding of ATRs while ensuring that the cultural sensitivity and integrity of these practices are respected.

Another way to complement oral tradition is through the use of technology. Digital tools such as videos, podcasts, and social media platforms can help to preserve and disseminate ATRs to a broader audience. For example, the African Storybook Project is an online platform that features stories written in African languages and aims to promote literacy and preserve African cultural heritage. Similarly, the African Digital Heritage Project is an initiative that aims to preserve and promote African cultural heritage through the use of digital technologies.

It is crucial to acknowledge that the preservation of ATRs is not only important for cultural reasons but also for ecological and environmental reasons. ATRs have a close relationship with nature, and their religious practices reflect a deep reverence and respect for the environment. As such, the preservation of ATRs can contribute to efforts to protect the environment and promote sustainable development.

In conclusion, oral tradition is an essential aspect of African Traditional Religions, and it plays a crucial role in preserving these religious practices. While the reliance on oral tradition comes with challenges, there are ways to complement it, such as through academic research and the use of digital technologies. The preservation of ATRs is not only important for cultural reasons but also for ecological and environmental reasons, and efforts should be made to ensure that these religious practices continue to thrive and evolve while preserving their authenticity and cultural heritage.

The challenges of studying ATRs in a modern context

Studying African Traditional Religions (ATRs) in a modern context comes with a set of challenges that require careful consideration. ATRs are often misunderstood, misrepresented, and marginalized in Western scholarship and popular culture. Furthermore, ATRs have faced significant challenges due to colonialism, modernization, globalization, and religious conversion. These challenges have had a profound impact on the practice and study of ATRs in contemporary times.

One of the significant challenges of studying ATRs in a modern context is the lack of written sources. ATRs rely heavily on oral tradition, which means that knowledge is often passed down through generations orally. This poses a challenge for scholars who are trying to understand and study ATRs since there is limited written documentation of their practices and beliefs. As a result, scholars must rely on interviews with practitioners, observation of rituals, and other methods of ethnographic research to gather information about ATRs. This reliance on oral tradition can also lead to the misinterpretation and distortion of cultural practices, as misunderstandings can easily arise.

Another challenge of studying ATRs in a modern context is the decline of traditional practices. Modernization and globalization have led to the erosion of traditional practices and beliefs in many African societies. This decline has been particularly pronounced in urban areas, where people are exposed to Western values and beliefs. The decline of traditional practices has made it more challenging to study ATRs since many of the practices and beliefs associated with them are no longer in use.

Exploring Origins, Traditions, and Contemporary Relevance

Furthermore, the spread of Christianity and Islam in Africa has also posed a significant challenge to the study of ATRs. Missionaries, colonizers, and other outside groups have historically viewed ATRs as primitive and backward, which has led to their marginalization and erasure. As a result, many African people have converted to Christianity or Islam, which has led to the decline of ATRs. This decline has made it more challenging to study ATRs since there are fewer practitioners and fewer opportunities to observe their practices.

Another challenge of studying ATRs in a modern context is the issue of authenticity. ATRs are not static; they evolve and adapt to changing circumstances. However, this evolution can make it challenging to determine what is authentic and what is not. Furthermore, some practitioners may modify their practices to make them more appealing to outsiders, which can lead to misrepresentations of ATRs. Scholars must, therefore, be careful not to impose their own preconceptions onto ATRs and to respect the diversity and complexity of these religious traditions.

In addition, there is the challenge of reconciling ATRs with modern scientific knowledge. Many ATRs involve practices that are not easily explained by modern scientific knowledge, such as the use of herbal remedies and divination. This can lead to a tension between ATRs and modern scientific knowledge. However, it is essential to understand that ATRs are not necessarily in opposition to modern scientific knowledge, but rather offer a different way of understanding the world. As such, scholars must approach ATRs with an open mind and respect for their unique perspectives.

Finally, there is the challenge of addressing the biases and power imbalances that exist in the study of ATRs. Many scholars who study ATRs come from Western backgrounds and may have biases and assumptions about these religions. Furthermore, there is a power imbalance between Western scholars and African practitioners, as Western scholars have traditionally held more power and authority in the field of academia. It is, therefore, essential for scholars to be aware of their biases and to work towards building collaborative and respectful relationships with African practitioners.

In conclusion, studying ATRs in a modern context poses a set of challenges that require careful consideration. The reliance on oral tradition, the decline of traditional practices, the spread of Christianity and Islam, and the biases and power imbalances in academia are all obstacles that must be addressed in order to better understand and appreciate ATRs. However, despite these challenges, there are also opportunities for growth and collaboration in the field of ATR studies.

African Religions

One approach to addressing these challenges is through collaboration and partnership with African practitioners. Western scholars can work with African practitioners to gain a deeper understanding of ATRs and to ensure that their work is respectful and accurate. Additionally, scholars can engage in efforts to support the preservation of traditional practices and knowledge, such as through funding or advocacy.

Another approach is through education and outreach. By increasing awareness and understanding of ATRs among the general public, scholars and practitioners can work to counter stereotypes and biases. This can be accomplished through academic courses, public lectures, and community events.

Finally, it is important for scholars to engage in ongoing self-reflection and critical examination of their own biases and assumptions. This can be accomplished through attending workshops and conferences, participating in discussions with practitioners, and reading works by scholars from diverse backgrounds.

Overall, studying ATRs in a modern context requires a nuanced and thoughtful approach. By acknowledging and addressing the challenges that exist, scholars can work towards a deeper understanding and appreciation of these important religious traditions.

CHAPTER 12: CHARACTERISTICS OF ATRS AND THEIR PRACTICES

African Traditional Religions (ATRs) are a diverse set of religious practices that are indigenous to Africa. While there is no single definition of ATRs, they share some common characteristics such as a strong connection to ancestors and spiritual entities, the use of rituals and ceremonies, and the presence of traditional healers who use natural remedies and techniques. This chapter will explore some of the key characteristics of ATRs and their practices.

The Role of Ancestors and Spiritual Entities in ATRs

Ancestors play a vital role in ATRs. They are believed to be powerful spiritual entities who can intercede on behalf of the living. Ancestors are believed to be able to influence the lives of their descendants in positive or negative ways, depending on the actions of the living. Therefore, it is essential to maintain a good relationship with one's ancestors through offerings and other rituals.

In addition to ancestors, ATRs also recognize other spiritual entities such as gods and goddesses, nature spirits, and deities associated with particular geographic locations or ethnic groups. These spiritual entities are believed to have their own personalities, powers, and responsibilities, and are often associated with natural elements such as water, earth, and air.

Rituals and Ceremonies in ATRs

Rituals and ceremonies are an essential part of ATRs. They are used to connect with spiritual entities, to honor ancestors, and to mark important life events such as births, weddings, and deaths. Rituals and ceremonies are often performed by trained specialists, such as priests or priestesses, who have knowledge of the appropriate procedures and offerings.

One common ATR ritual is divination, which is the process of seeking knowledge or guidance from spiritual entities. Divination can take many forms, such as the use of a divination board or the interpretation of dreams. Another common ritual is the sacrifice of animals, which is seen as a way to honor ancestors or appease spiritual entities.

African Religions

Traditional Healers and their Practices

Traditional healers are an important part of ATRs. They are believed to have the ability to diagnose and treat illnesses using natural remedies and techniques. Traditional healers often have specialized knowledge of plants and their medicinal properties, as well as knowledge of the spiritual causes of illness.

Traditional healers are typically trained through apprenticeships, and their practices vary widely depending on the region and ethnic group. Some traditional healers use techniques such as massage or acupuncture, while others use herbal remedies or spiritual practices such as chanting or prayer.

Sacred Spaces and Symbols in ATRs

ATRs often have sacred spaces and symbols that are used in rituals and ceremonies. These spaces and symbols are believed to have spiritual significance and to be infused with the power of the ancestors and other spiritual entities.

One common sacred space in ATRs is the ancestral shrine, which is a designated area where offerings and prayers are made to ancestors. Another common sacred space is the forest or other natural areas, which are believed to be inhabited by nature spirits.

Symbols are also an essential part of ATRs. For example, the Adinkra symbols of West Africa are a set of visual symbols that represent concepts such as wisdom, bravery, and unity. These symbols are often used in textiles and other artwork, as well as in rituals and ceremonies.

Conclusion

The characteristics of ATRs and their practices are varied and complex. They reflect the diversity of African cultures and the unique ways in which they have developed over time. An understanding of the role of ancestors and spiritual entities, the use of rituals and ceremonies, the practices of traditional healers, and the importance of sacred spaces and symbols is essential for gaining a deeper understanding of ATRs.

The role of ancestors and spiritual entities in ATRs

The role of ancestors and spiritual entities is fundamental in African Traditional Religions (ATRs). Ancestors are considered to be the foundation of the community and are believed to have the power to influence the lives of their descendants. The relationship between the living and the dead is reciprocal, and ancestors are believed to provide guidance and support to their living descendants. Spiritual entities, on the other hand, are non-human beings that have supernatural powers and are believed to be present in the world around us. In this chapter, we will explore the role of ancestors and spiritual entities in ATRs, examining their significance, practices and beliefs, and how they are perceived in different cultural contexts.

The Significance of Ancestors in ATRs

In ATRs, ancestors are considered to be powerful spiritual entities who are present in the lives of their descendants. Ancestors are believed to be the link between the living and the spiritual world, and they are often revered as deities. Ancestors are believed to have the power to influence the lives of their descendants and to provide guidance and protection. They are also believed to have the ability to intercede on behalf of their descendants with the gods and other spiritual entities.

In many ATRs, ancestors are seen as the foundation of the community. They are the source of wisdom and knowledge, and they are believed to have the power to preserve and transmit cultural values and traditions. Ancestors are also considered to be the guardians of the land and the environment, and they are believed to be responsible for the well-being of the community.

Practices and Beliefs Regarding Ancestors in ATRs

Ancestors are venerated in various ways in ATRs, depending on the specific cultural context. In some cultures, ancestors are honored through elaborate rituals and ceremonies that involve offerings of food, drink, and other gifts. Ancestral altars are set up in homes and other sacred spaces, and offerings are made to them on a regular basis. In some cultures, ancestors are believed to be present in the natural world, and they are honored through the protection and preservation of natural resources.

Ancestors are also believed to have the power to communicate with their living descendants. In many ATRs, mediums and other spiritual practitioners are able to communicate with the ancestors through divination and other methods. The messages and guidance received from the ancestors are highly valued and are believed to be essential for the well-being of the community.

In some ATRs, ancestors are believed to have the power to punish those who do not follow the cultural norms and values. This belief serves as a way of maintaining social order and promoting community harmony. In other ATRs, ancestors are believed to have the power to bring blessings and prosperity to those who honor them and follow the cultural norms and values.

Perceptions of Ancestors in Different Cultural Contexts

The significance of ancestors in ATRs varies from culture to culture. In some cultures, ancestors are seen as benevolent and protective beings who provide guidance and support to their living descendants. In other cultures, ancestors are viewed as malevolent and dangerous beings who must be appeased through offerings and rituals.

For example, in some West African cultures, ancestors are believed to be the source of sickness and misfortune, and they must be appeased through offerings and sacrifices. In other cultures, ancestors are seen as benevolent beings who provide guidance and support to their living descendants.

In many ATRs, the relationship between the living and the dead is seen as a reciprocal one, with both parties benefiting from the relationship. The living are believed to have the responsibility to honor and respect their ancestors, while the ancestors are believed to have the responsibility to provide guidance and protection to their descendants.

In conclusion, the role of ancestors and spiritual entities in ATRs is complex and multifaceted. These entities play a central role in ATRs, serving as intermediaries between humans and the divine. They are revered and honored through various rituals, offerings, and prayers. Through these practices, ATR practitioners establish and maintain a connection with the spiritual realm and the ancestors, who are considered to be a source of guidance, protection, and wisdom.

The importance of ancestors in ATRs goes beyond the individual level, as ancestors are also seen as a source of community identity and cultural continuity. The ancestors are believed to be the guardians of cultural knowledge, and their guidance is sought in matters of governance, social organization, and ethical conduct. Ancestral practices, such as ancestor veneration, serve to reinforce the importance of community and collective memory in ATRs.

It is important to note that the role of ancestors and spiritual entities in ATRs is not static and unchanging. As ATRs have spread and evolved over time, their practices and beliefs have also undergone transformation. For example, some ATRs have incorporated elements of Christianity or Islam, leading to the emergence of syncretic religions. Similarly, the impact of colonialism and globalization has also affected the way in which ATRs are practiced and perceived.

As ATRs continue to face challenges in the modern world, the role of ancestors and spiritual entities remains a vital aspect of these religions. Understanding and respecting these practices is crucial for building meaningful and respectful relationships between ATR practitioners and those outside of these traditions. By recognizing the importance of the ancestors and the spiritual realm in ATRs, we can gain a deeper appreciation for the diversity and richness of these religions.

Rituals and ceremonies in ATRs

Rituals and ceremonies are a central component of African Traditional Religions (ATRs) and serve as a means of establishing and maintaining a connection with the spiritual realm. These rituals and ceremonies are often deeply ingrained in the cultural and religious practices of the people who practice ATRs, and they vary widely in form and function depending on the specific religion and region. In this section, we will explore the diverse range of rituals and ceremonies found in ATRs, examining their purpose, symbolism, and significance within the context of these traditions.

The Importance of Rituals and Ceremonies in ATRs

Rituals and ceremonies in ATRs serve multiple purposes, including connecting individuals to the spiritual realm, promoting social cohesion, and providing a means for individuals to express their devotion and gratitude to the spirits and ancestors. They are often performed in honor of specific deities or spirits, as well as ancestors who are believed to have the ability to intercede on behalf of the living.

Rituals and ceremonies also serve as a means of passing down cultural and religious traditions from one generation to the next. They are an essential component of the social fabric of many African societies, and they provide a sense of continuity and connection to the past. For many practitioners of ATRs, rituals and ceremonies are not simply a means of communicating with the spiritual realm but also a way of connecting with their cultural heritage and identity.

Types of Rituals and Ceremonies in ATRs

The specific rituals and ceremonies practiced in ATRs vary widely depending on the specific religion and region. However, some common types of rituals and ceremonies include:

African Religions

Ancestor veneration: Ancestor veneration is a central component of many ATRs, and many rituals and ceremonies are performed to honor and communicate with the spirits of deceased family members. Ancestral altars are often established in homes or public spaces, and offerings of food, drink, and other items are made to the ancestors to seek their guidance and protection.

Spirit possession: In some ATRs, spirits are believed to possess the bodies of individuals during ritual ceremonies. This is often accompanied by dancing, drumming, and other forms of music, and the person possessed is believed to communicate with the spiritual realm through the possessed body.

Initiation ceremonies: Initiation ceremonies are often used to mark important life transitions, such as entering adulthood or becoming a priest or priestess. These ceremonies are often highly symbolic and involve a series of rituals and tests designed to prepare the individual for their new role in the community.

Harvest ceremonies: Harvest ceremonies are a common feature of many ATRs, and they are often used to give thanks for a successful harvest and to ask for blessings for future crops. These ceremonies often involve offerings of food and drink, as well as dances and other forms of celebration.

Divination ceremonies: Divination ceremonies are used to seek guidance from the spirits or ancestors. These ceremonies often involve the use of tools such as divination rods, cowrie shells, or bones, and the practitioner will interpret the results to provide guidance and insight to the individual seeking answers.

Symbolism and Significance in Rituals and Ceremonies

Rituals and ceremonies in ATRs are often highly symbolic and are designed to communicate specific messages or ideas to the participants. These symbols and metaphors are often deeply ingrained in the culture and religion of the people who practice ATRs, and they serve to reinforce the values and beliefs of the community.

For example, the use of certain colors, such as white, red, and black, may be highly symbolic in ATRs, representing purity, vitality, and death, respectively. Similarly, the use of certain animals, such as snakes or birds , may have deep symbolic significance, representing various traits and characteristics that are valued or feared within the community. These symbols and metaphors are often communicated through ritual and ceremony, where they are imbued with spiritual power and meaning.

Exploring Origins, Traditions, and Contemporary Relevance

One example of a highly symbolic ritual in ATRs is the act of divination. Divination is a practice that involves seeking guidance or insight from spiritual entities or ancestors through the use of various tools, such as bones, shells, or cards. The practice of divination is often highly ritualized, with specific steps and procedures that must be followed in order to communicate with the spiritual world effectively.

In some ATRs, divination is used to help individuals make important decisions, such as choosing a spouse or making a career choice. In other cases, it is used to diagnose and treat illnesses, or to identify the root causes of social or political problems. Whatever its purpose, the practice of divination is deeply rooted in the cultural and spiritual traditions of many African societies, and it is a powerful tool for communicating with the spiritual world.

Another example of a highly symbolic ritual in ATRs is the initiation ceremony. Initiation ceremonies are often highly elaborate and involve a series of rites and rituals that mark the transition of an individual from one social or spiritual status to another. These ceremonies often involve a period of seclusion, fasting, or other forms of deprivation, as well as the performance of specific rituals that are designed to imbue the initiate with spiritual power and knowledge.

The initiation ceremony is an important rite of passage in many ATRs, as it marks the transition from childhood to adulthood, or from outsider to member of the community. The symbolism and significance of the initiation ceremony vary widely depending on the specific ATR and the culture in which it is practiced, but in all cases, it is a powerful and transformative experience that is designed to connect the initiate with the spiritual world and the community.

In conclusion, rituals and ceremonies play a crucial role in the practice of ATRs, serving as powerful tools for communicating with the spiritual world and reinforcing the values and beliefs of the community. These rituals are often highly symbolic and imbued with deep meaning and significance, and they are designed to help individuals navigate the challenges of life and connect with the spiritual forces that guide their journey. Whether it is through the practice of divination, initiation ceremonies, or other forms of ritual and ceremony, ATRs offer a rich and vibrant tradition of spiritual practice that continues to inspire and transform people all over the world.

Traditional healers and their practices

Traditional healers, also known as medicine men and women, are an essential part of many African Traditional Religions (ATRs). These individuals are often respected members of their communities and are seen as healers, spiritual advisors, and guides.

The role of traditional healers in ATRs is multifaceted. They are responsible for treating physical ailments and illnesses, as well as spiritual and emotional ones. They are also tasked with maintaining the balance between the living and the dead, and between the physical and spiritual realms.

Types of Traditional Healers

There are several different types of traditional healers in ATRs, each with their own unique set of skills and abilities. These include:

✧ Herbalists: Herbalists use plants and natural remedies to treat illnesses and ailments.

✧ Diviners: Diviners use a variety of techniques, including throwing bones or shells, reading tea leaves, or interpreting dreams to gain insight into the spiritual and emotional needs of their clients.

✧ Mediums: Mediums communicate with spirits and ancestors to gain guidance and insight into the lives of their clients.

✧ Spiritual healers: Spiritual healers use prayer, chanting, and other spiritual practices to promote healing and balance.

✧ Sangomas: Sangomas are traditional healers found in southern Africa, particularly in South Africa, Lesotho, and Swaziland. They are trained in a specific set of practices and often specialize in certain areas of healing.

Training and Initiation

Traditional healers are not simply born into their roles. Instead, they must undergo a rigorous training and initiation process that can last for several years. This process typically involves being apprenticed to a more experienced healer and learning the traditions, practices, and beliefs of the community.

In many cases, the training process also includes undergoing a spiritual initiation, which can involve a period of isolation, fasting, and other rituals. This initiation is meant to prepare the individual for their role as a healer and to give them a deeper understanding of the spiritual and cultural traditions of their community.

Exploring Origins, Traditions, and Contemporary Relevance

Healing Practices

Traditional healers use a variety of techniques and practices to promote healing and balance in their clients. These include:

✧ Herbal remedies: Many traditional healers rely on plants and natural remedies to treat a variety of illnesses and ailments. They may use a combination of plants to create a specific remedy, or they may use a single plant that has been found to be particularly effective.

✧ Divination: Divination techniques are often used to gain insight into the spiritual and emotional needs of the client. This information can then be used to develop a treatment plan.

✧ Prayer and chanting: Spiritual healing often involves the use of prayer, chanting, and other spiritual practices to promote healing and balance.

✧ Cleansing and purification: Many traditional healers believe that illness and imbalance can be caused by negative energy or spirits. Cleansing and purification techniques, such as smudging or bathing in herbal waters, can be used to remove this negative energy and promote healing.

Rituals and ceremonies: Traditional healers may also use rituals and ceremonies to promote healing and balance. These ceremonies may involve the use of specific symbols, colors, and other elements that are believed to have a particular spiritual significance.

Challenges and Controversies

Traditional healing practices have been the subject of controversy and criticism, particularly in Western countries where they are often viewed as unscientific and ineffective. Some critics have also raised concerns about the safety of certain traditional healing practices, particularly those that involve the use of herbal remedies.

However, many proponents of traditional healing argue that these practices are an important part of the cultural heritage and identity of many communities. They also point out that traditional healing practices have been used successfully for centuries to treat a wide range of physical, emotional, and spiritual ailments.

Conclusion

Traditional healing practices are a vital part of the cultural heritage and identity of many communities around the world. These practices have been developed and refined over centuries and have proven effective in treating a wide range of physical, emotional, and spiritual ailments. Traditional healers play a crucial role in providing healthcare to communities that may not have access to Western medical services.

Despite their effectiveness and cultural significance, traditional healing practices have faced challenges and controversies, particularly in Western countries where they are often viewed as unscientific and ineffective. However, it is important to recognize and respect the diverse range of healing practices that exist in the world, and to acknowledge that different approaches to healthcare may be appropriate for different individuals and communities.

It is also important to ensure that traditional healing practices are safe and accessible to all who seek them, and to support efforts to preserve and promote traditional healing practices as an important aspect of cultural heritage. By doing so, we can help to ensure that these valuable practices continue to benefit individuals and communities for generations to come.

Sacred spaces and symbols in ATRs

In many African Traditional Religions (ATRs), the concept of sacred space is of great significance. These spaces are seen as portals between the spiritual and physical worlds and are used for various purposes, such as worship, ritual, and divination. Sacred spaces can take many forms, from natural locations such as rivers and mountains, to man-made structures such as temples and shrines.

Symbols also play a crucial role in ATRs, as they are used to convey spiritual and cultural values and to facilitate communication with the spirit world. In this section, we will explore the importance of sacred spaces and symbols in ATRs, and how they are used in various contexts.

Sacred Spaces in ATRs

The concept of sacred space is central to ATRs, and it is often expressed through the use of various natural and man-made features. Some of the most common sacred spaces in ATRs include:

✧ Rivers and Waterways: In many African cultures, water is seen as a powerful force of nature that can connect the physical and spiritual worlds. Rivers and waterways are often considered sacred spaces and are used for purification, healing, and divination.

✧ Mountains: Mountains are also considered sacred in many African cultures, and they are often seen as places of spiritual power and connection to the divine. They are used for meditation, prayer, and divination.

✧ Trees: Trees are seen as symbols of life and fertility in many African cultures, and they are often used as sacred spaces for worship and ritual. Certain trees, such as the baobab and the sacred fig, are especially revered and are believed to possess spiritual powers.

✧ Temples and Shrines: Temples and shrines are man-made structures that are used for worship and ritual. They are often dedicated to specific deities or ancestors and are believed to be sacred spaces where communication with the spirit world can take place.

✧ Homes and Ancestral Altars: In ATRs, the home is often considered a sacred space, particularly when it is used as a site for ancestral worship. Ancestral altars are commonly found in homes and are used to honor ancestors and communicate with the spirit world.

The use of sacred spaces in ATRs is not limited to physical locations, as certain objects and artifacts can also be considered sacred. These objects can include religious texts, ritual tools, and even certain types of food and drink.

Symbols in ATRs

Symbols play a significant role in ATRs, as they are used to convey spiritual and cultural values and to facilitate communication with the spirit world. Some of the most common symbols in ATRs include:

Ancestors: Ancestors play a central role in many ATRs, and they are often represented by specific symbols. For example, in Yoruba culture, the ancestor Ogun is often represented by the iron machete, while the ancestor Oya is associated with the wind and storms.

✧ Elements of Nature: Elements of nature, such as the sun, moon, and stars, are also important symbols in ATRs. These symbols are often used to represent the power and influence of the divine in the natural world.

African Religions

- ✧ Animals: Animals are frequently used as symbols in ATRs, with each animal having its own unique meaning and significance. For example, in some African cultures, the lion is associated with strength and courage, while the tortoise is seen as a symbol of wisdom and longevity.

- ✧ Colors: Colors are also significant symbols in ATRs, with each color having its own unique meaning and significance. For example, in Yoruba culture, white is associated with purity and spiritual energy, while black is associated with death and the spirit world.

- ✧ Ritual Tools: Ritual tools , such as the divination board or the sacrificial knife, are also important symbols in ATRs. These tools are used to connect with the spirit world and to perform various rituals and ceremonies.

Sacred Spaces in ATRs

Sacred spaces play a crucial role in ATRs, as they are believed to be the physical locations where the divine and human worlds intersect. These spaces can include natural features, such as mountains, rivers, and forests, as well as man-made structures, such as temples and shrines.

In some ATRs, sacred spaces are believed to be inhabited by spirits or deities, who are considered to be the guardians and protectors of the space. These spirits are often appeased through offerings and rituals performed at the sacred site.

In Yoruba culture, for example, Osun-Osogbo Grove is a sacred forest located in Osun State, Nigeria. The grove is considered to be the abode of the goddess Osun, and it is revered as a place of spiritual power and healing. Each year, a festival is held in honor of Osun, during which offerings are made and rituals are performed in the grove.

Symbols and Sacred Spaces in ATRs

The use of symbols in ATRs is closely intertwined with the concept of sacred spaces. Symbols are often used to identify and mark sacred sites, and they are believed to facilitate communication between the human and spiritual realms.

For example, in Santeria, a syncretic religion that combines elements of African, Indigenous, and Catholic traditions, altars are commonly used to connect with the spirits. These altars are often decorated with symbolic objects, such as candles, beads, and statues, that represent specific spirits or deities.

Exploring Origins, Traditions, and Contemporary Relevance

Similarly, in Vodou, a religion that originated in Haiti, each lwa, or spirit, is associated with specific symbols and colors. These symbols are used in rituals and ceremonies to identify and communicate with the lwa, and they are often displayed on altars or other sacred spaces.

Examples

- ✧ **Santeria:**
  - Orishas: Each Orisha is associated with specific colors, animals, and symbols. For example, Elegua is associated with the color red, the number three, and the symbol of the crossroads.
  - Elekes: Beaded necklaces that correspond to specific Orishas and colors.
  - Potiche: A clay pot used to represent the Orisha Oshun.

- ✧ Vodou:
  - Loas: Each Loa is associated with specific colors, animals, and symbols. For example, Papa Legba is associated with the color red, the dog, and the symbol of the crossroads.
  - Veves: Intricate symbols drawn on the ground or on paper to represent the Loas.
  - Bocor: A type of Vodou priest who uses symbols and magic to heal and harm.

- ✧ **Candomble:**
  - Orixas: Each Orixas is associated with specific colors, animals, and symbols. For example, Oxossi is associated with the color green, the bow and arrow, and the symbol of the forest.
  - Axé: The life force or energy that flows through all living things.
  - Ile Axe: The physical and spiritual home of a Candomble community.

- ✧ Ifa:
  - Orishas: Each Orisha is associated with specific colors, animals, and symbols. For example, Ogun is associated with the color red, the iron machete, and the symbol of the warrior.
  - Odu: A divination system that uses 16 principal signs or symbols.

- Ile Ife: The spiritual and cultural center of the Yoruba people in Nigeria.

✧ **Hoodoo:**
- Saints: Hoodoo practitioners often use Catholic saints as symbols for different purposes. For example, St. Michael is associated with protection and defense, while St. Expedite is associated with quick results and financial gain.
- Mojo Bags: Small bags filled with herbs, stones, and other items used to carry a specific intention or symbol.
- Conjure Hands: Similar to mojo bags, but larger and often used for more complex rituals.
- Please note that these are just a few examples of the many symbols used in each ATR, and that the meanings and associations of these symbols can vary depending on the specific tradition and practitioner.

Conclusion

In conclusion, symbols and sacred spaces play a significant role in ATRs, serving as a means of communication with the divine and a way of reinforcing cultural and spiritual values. By understanding the meanings and significance of these symbols and spaces, practitioners of ATRs are able to deepen their spiritual connection and further their understanding of their religious traditions.

CHAPTER 13: THE DIVERSITY OF ATRS ACROSS DIFFERENT AFRICAN SOCIETIES

African Traditional Religions (ATRs) are a diverse collection of spiritual practices that have been practiced on the African continent for thousands of years. ATRs are not monolithic, but rather represent a complex web of beliefs, practices, and traditions that are unique to each culture and region. As such, it is impossible to speak of ATRs as a single entity; rather, we must consider the diversity of ATRs across different African societies.

Regional and Cultural Variations in ATRs

One of the defining features of ATRs is their diversity across different African societies. Each culture and region has its own unique beliefs, practices, and traditions that are shaped by factors such as geography, history, and social structure. For example, the Akan people of Ghana have a complex system of beliefs and practices centered around ancestor veneration, while the Yoruba people of Nigeria are known for their complex pantheon of deities and their use of divination and herbal medicine.

Despite this diversity, there are also many similarities between different ATRs. Many ATRs share a belief in a supreme being or creator, as well as a belief in the existence of ancestral spirits and other supernatural entities. They also share a strong connection to the natural world and a belief in the interdependence of all living things.

The Impact of Colonialism and Globalization on ATRs

The history of colonialism and globalization has had a profound impact on ATRs. The arrival of Europeans on the African continent brought with it new religions and worldviews that challenged the traditional beliefs and practices of African societies. Many African peoples were forced to convert to Christianity or Islam, and traditional religious practices were often suppressed or banned.

Despite this, ATRs have persisted and even thrived in many parts of Africa. In some cases, they have been adapted and syncretized with other religious traditions, resulting in the emergence of new forms of spirituality. For example, in the Caribbean,

ATRs have been influenced by Christianity and have given rise to syncretic religions such as Vodou and Santeria.

Contemporary Adaptations and Innovations in ATRs

Today, ATRs continue to evolve and adapt to changing social and cultural contexts. In some cases, this has led to new forms of spirituality that blend traditional practices with modern innovations. For example, some ATR practitioners use social media to connect with others and share information about their practices, while others use modern technologies such as smartphones and GPS to navigate sacred spaces and locate sources of spiritual power.

At the same time, there are also concerns about the commercialization and commodification of ATRs. Some practitioners have expressed concern that traditional practices are being exploited for profit, and that the spiritual integrity of these practices is being eroded as a result.

Conclusion

The diversity of ATRs across different African societies is a testament to the richness and complexity of African spirituality. Despite the challenges posed by colonialism and globalization, ATRs have persisted and even thrived, adapting and evolving to meet the needs of contemporary practitioners. As we continue to study and learn about ATRs, it is important to respect the diversity of these traditions and to approach them with a spirit of humility and openness.

Regional and cultural variations in ATRs

African Traditional Religions (ATRs) are a diverse and complex set of spiritual practices that vary widely across different regions and cultures of Africa. The continent of Africa is home to over 1,000 different ethnic groups, each with their own unique cultural traditions, including spiritual and religious beliefs. ATRs are deeply rooted in the cultural heritage of these diverse groups, and as such, they are often shaped by regional and cultural influences.

In this chapter, we will explore the regional and cultural variations in ATRs, examining how different practices and beliefs have emerged in response to the diverse cultural and environmental contexts of different African societies. We will also examine how these variations have been impacted by colonialism and globalization, and how contemporary adaptations and innovations continue to shape the landscape of ATRs today.

Exploring Origins, Traditions, and Contemporary Relevance

✧ Regional Variations in ATRs

The diversity of ATRs across different regions of Africa is vast and reflects the unique cultural and environmental contexts of each region. Here are a few examples of some of the regional variations in ATRs:

✧ West Africa:

West Africa is home to a number of ATRs, including Ifa, Vodou, and Santeria. Ifa is a Yoruba religion that is widely practiced in Nigeria, Benin, and Togo. It is centered around the worship of Orishas, or deities, who are associated with different aspects of nature, such as the ocean, the forest, and the sky. Vodou, which originated in Haiti but has roots in West African religions, is centered around the worship of spirits, or lwa, who are associated with different aspects of life, such as love, fertility, and death. Santeria, which is practiced in Cuba, is also based on Yoruba religion and centers around the worship of Orishas.

✧ Central Africa:

Central Africa is home to a number of ATRs, including Bwiti, which is practiced in Gabon and Cameroon. Bwiti is centered around the use of a hallucinogenic plant called iboga, which is believed to facilitate communication with the spirit world. The religion also incorporates elements of Christianity and indigenous African beliefs.

✧ Southern Africa:

Southern Africa is home to a number of ATRs, including the Zulu religion, which is practiced in South Africa. The Zulu religion centers around the worship of ancestors and includes a number of rituals and ceremonies designed to honor and communicate with them. The religion also incorporates elements of Christianity and traditional African beliefs.

✧ East Africa:

East Africa is home to a number of ATRs, including the Maasai religion, which is practiced in Kenya and Tanzania. The Maasai religion centers around the worship of a god named Enkai and includes a number of rituals and ceremonies designed to honor him. The religion also incorporates elements of traditional African beliefs.

These are just a few examples of the diverse range of ATRs that exist across Africa. Each of these religions has its own unique set of beliefs, practices, and cultural traditions that reflect the unique history, environment, and social context of the people who practice them.

✧   Cultural Variations in ATRs

In addition to regional variations, there are also cultural variations in ATRs that reflect the unique cultural traditions of different ethnic groups within Africa. Here are a few examples of some of the cultural variations in ATRs:

✧   Yoruba:

The Yoruba people are an ethnic group that is primarily located in Nigeria, Benin, and Togo. The Yoruba religion, which is centered around the worship of Orishas, has had a significant influence on many other ATRs, such as Santeria and Candomble. In Yoruba religion, each Orisha has its own unique set of rituals, symbols, and practices. For example, Ogun, the Orisha of iron, is associated with warfare, hunting, and metalworking. His followers may engage in rituals involving the forging of iron tools or weapons. On the other hand, Oshun, the Orisha of love, fertility, and beauty, is associated with fresh water, particularly rivers. Her followers may leave offerings of honey, flowers, or other gifts by a river as a way of honoring her.

✧   Hausa:

The Hausa people are an ethnic group that is primarily located in Nigeria, Niger, and Ghana. Their traditional religion is centered around the worship of spirits known as Bori. Bori worship involves the use of trance states and possession by the spirits, which are believed to have the power to heal illnesses and provide guidance. Bori worship also involves the use of music and dance, with drumming and other instruments playing a central role in the rituals.

✧   Zulu:

The Zulu people are an ethnic group that is primarily located in South Africa. Their traditional religion is centered around the worship of ancestral spirits, who are believed to be able to communicate with the living through dreams and visions. Zulu religious practices involve the use of divination, herbalism, and ritual sacrifice. Divination is often done using bones or other objects, with the diviner interpreting the patterns and symbols that emerge. Herbalism involves the use of plants and other natural substances for medicinal and spiritual purposes, while ritual sacrifice is used to appease the ancestors and gain their favor.

Exploring Origins, Traditions, and Contemporary Relevance

✦ Asante:

The Asante people are an ethnic group that is primarily located in Ghana. Their traditional religion is centered around the worship of a pantheon of gods and goddesses known as Abosom. Each Abosom has its own unique characteristics and associated symbols, and each is believed to have the power to influence human affairs. Asante religious practices involve the use of divination, sacrifice, and ancestor veneration. Divination is often done using palm nuts or other objects, with the diviner interpreting the patterns and shapes that they form. Sacrifice is used to appease the Abosom and gain their favor, while ancestor veneration is used to honor and communicate with the spirits of the deceased.

These are just a few examples of the many cultural variations that exist within ATRs. Each ethnic group within Africa has its own unique cultural traditions, which are reflected in their religious practices. Understanding these cultural variations is essential for gaining a deeper appreciation of the diversity and richness of ATRs.

The impact of colonialism and globalization on ATRs

The arrival of European colonizers in Africa had a profound impact on the continent's religious landscape, including ATRs. Colonizers often viewed ATRs as primitive and pagan, and they sought to replace traditional religions with Christianity and Islam. This led to the forced conversion of many Africans to these new religions and the suppression of ATRs.

In addition to forced conversion, colonizers also sought to eradicate traditional African practices, including those associated with ATRs. For example, in some areas, colonizers banned drumming and other forms of music, which are essential components of many ATRs. They also destroyed shrines and other sacred sites, which resulted in the loss of important cultural and religious artifacts.

The impact of colonialism on ATRs varied depending on the specific region and colonial power involved. For example, the British colonial authorities in Nigeria were more tolerant of ATRs than their French counterparts in neighboring countries. However, even in Nigeria, traditional religious practices were still suppressed and stigmatized.

Globalization has also had a significant impact on ATRs. With the increasing interconnectedness of the world, traditional cultural practices and religions are often seen as outdated and less relevant. This has led to a decline in the number of people practicing ATRs, as many individuals seek to assimilate into mainstream cultures.

African Religions

In addition to the impact of globalization on ATRs, there has also been an appropriation of African spiritual practices by non-Africans. This can be seen in the popularity of practices such as Hoodoo and Voodoo, which are based on ATRs but have been adapted to suit the needs and beliefs of non-African practitioners.

The commercialization of ATRs has also had a significant impact. With the growth of the global market for spiritual products and services, there has been a rise in the commercialization of traditional African religious practices. This has led to the commodification of ATRs and the exploitation of traditional African spiritual beliefs for profit.

Despite the challenges faced by ATRs due to colonialism and globalization, there has been a resurgence of interest in traditional African religions in recent years. This can be seen in the growth of new religious movements such as Ifa and Orisa worship, as well as the increased interest in traditional African spiritual practices among African diaspora communities.

Examples and Exercises:

✧   Research the impact of colonialism on ATRs in a specific African country, such as Nigeria or Ghana. Write a report on your findings, including the specific ways in which colonialism impacted ATRs in that country.

✧   Compare and contrast the impact of colonization and globalization on ATRs. How are the two processes similar, and how are they different? Provide specific examples to support your argument.

✧   Discuss the ethical implications of the commercialization of ATRs. Should traditional African religious practices be commodified and sold for profit? Why or why not?

✧   In what ways have African diaspora communities adapted and reinterpreted ATRs outside of Africa? Provide specific examples to illustrate your point.

Example 1: Research the impact of colonialism on ATRs in a specific African country, such as Nigeria or Ghana. Write a report on your findings, including the specific ways in which colonialism impacted ATRs in that country.

The impact of colonialism on ATRs in Africa cannot be overstated. The arrival of European powers in the 15th century marked the beginning of centuries of exploitation, violence, and cultural destruction. Colonial powers viewed African traditional religions as primitive, savage, and inferior to Christianity and Islam, which they saw as more civilized and advanced. Consequently, they actively suppressed ATRs and promoted the spread of Christianity and Islam.

One country that experienced the devastating effects of colonialism on ATRs is Nigeria. Prior to the arrival of the British, Nigeria was home to numerous ATRs, including the Yoruba, Igbo, and Hausa-Fulani religions. The British colonial government saw these religions as backward and uncivilized, and they actively sought to eradicate them. They used various tactics to achieve this, including the promotion of Christianity and Islam, the destruction of shrines and sacred places, and the suppression of traditional festivals and rituals.

As a result of these actions, many Nigerians converted to Christianity or Islam, abandoning their traditional religions. In some cases, they did so willingly, but in others, they were forced to convert. This led to the loss of cultural heritage and the erasure of centuries of religious and spiritual practices.

However, despite the efforts of colonial powers to suppress ATRs, these religions persisted and adapted to the changing times. Today, many Nigerians still practice ATRs alongside Christianity and Islam. They have found ways to blend their traditional beliefs with modern practices, creating a unique and vibrant religious landscape.

Example 2: Compare and contrast the impact of colonization and globalization on ATRs. How are the two processes similar, and how are they different? Provide specific examples to support your argument.

Colonization and globalization are two processes that have had a significant impact on ATRs in Africa. While they are distinct phenomena, they share some similarities and differences in their impact on ATRs.

One similarity between the two is that they have both contributed to the erosion of traditional African cultures, including ATRs. Colonial powers sought to suppress and eradicate ATRs, while globalization has led to the spread of Western culture and values, which can be at odds with traditional African values and practices.

However, there are also differences between the two processes. Colonization was a violent and oppressive system that sought to dominate and control African societies, while globalization is a more subtle and gradual process that seeks to integrate different cultures and societies.

One specific example of the impact of colonization on ATRs is the imposition of Christianity and Islam on African societies. This led to the suppression and eradication of traditional religions, as well as the loss of cultural heritage and identity. In contrast, globalization has led to the spread of Western culture and values, which can have a homogenizing effect on African societies.

Example 3: Discuss the ethical implications of the commercialization of ATRs. Should traditional African religious practices be commodified and sold for profit? Why or why not?

The commercialization of ATRs has become an increasingly controversial issue in recent years. Some argue that it is a necessary step towards preserving and promoting traditional African religions, while others see it as a form of exploitation and cultural appropriation.

One ethical concern is whether traditional African religious practices should be commodified and sold for profit. Many argue that this is a violation of the sacredness of these practices, as well as a form of exploitation of African cultures. Others argue that it is a way to promote and preserve traditional practices, as well as provide economic opportunities for African communities

Contemporary adaptations and innovations in ATRs

Contemporary adaptations and innovations in African Traditional Religions (ATRs) reflect the dynamic nature of these belief systems and their continued relevance in modern times. As with all religions, ATRs have evolved over time to reflect the changing needs and circumstances of their followers. In this section, we will explore some of the ways in which ATRs have adapted to contemporary realities.

Christianization of ATRs

One of the most significant adaptations of ATRs has been their incorporation into Christianity. This process, known as syncretism, involves the blending of different religious beliefs and practices. Christianity has had a significant impact on ATRs, especially in West Africa, where many people practice a blend of Christianity and traditional African religions.

For example, in Nigeria, many followers of ATRs have incorporated Christian beliefs and practices into their traditional religious practices. This has resulted in the creation of new forms of religious expression, such as Aladura and Celestial churches. These churches incorporate elements of traditional African religions, such as the belief in ancestor spirits and the use of divination, alongside Christian beliefs and practices.

Similarly, in Brazil, the practice of Candomble emerged from the blending of West African religions, including ATRs, with Catholicism. Candomble practitioners believe in a pantheon of deities known as orixas, which are believed to be spiritual forces that govern different aspects of life. Many of these orixas were syncretized with Catholic saints, such as Saint Barbara and Saint Anthony.

New Forms of Spiritual Practice

Another way in which ATRs have adapted to contemporary realities is through the creation of new forms of spiritual practice. As people's lives and circumstances change, new forms of spiritual practice emerge to meet their needs. For example, in urban areas, where traditional religious practices may be difficult to maintain, new forms of spiritual practice have emerged.

One such form is the practice of Neo-Traditional African Religion (NTR). NTR practitioners seek to connect with their African roots through the use of traditional religious practices, such as ancestor veneration and divination. However, NTR also incorporates contemporary elements, such as the use of social media to connect with other practitioners and the incorporation of new forms of music and dance into religious ceremonies.

Innovation in Ritual Practices

Another way in which ATRs have adapted to contemporary realities is through innovation in ritual practices. Rituals play a central role in ATRs, and their performance is often seen as a way to connect with the spiritual world. However, as people's lives and circumstances change, traditional ritual practices may become difficult to maintain.

One way in which ATRs have adapted to these changes is through the use of technology. For example, in South Africa, Sangomas, or traditional healers, have started using cell phones to communicate with their ancestors. The Sangomas will take a photo of the person they are trying to heal and send it to their ancestors, who will then provide guidance and advice.

Similarly, in Ghana, traditional healers have started using video conferencing technology to perform divination ceremonies. This has allowed them to connect with clients who live in other parts of the country or even in other countries.

Reinterpretation of Traditional Beliefs

Finally, ATRs have adapted to contemporary realities through the reinterpretation of traditional beliefs. As people's worldviews change, their understanding of traditional religious beliefs may also change. This can result in the creation of new interpretations of traditional beliefs or the adoption of new beliefs altogether.

For example, in South Africa, traditional beliefs around gender and sexuality have been reinterpreted to be more inclusive of LGBTQ+ people. Some traditional healers now perform ceremonies to bless same-sex marriages, and some Sangomas have started using their healing powers to help transgender people transition.

Another example of reinterpretation of traditional beliefs can be found in the way ATRs have adapted to modern technology. In many African countries, people have started to incorporate modern technology into their traditional religious practices. For instance, in Nigeria, people use smartphones to access traditional divination practices like Ifa or to connect with traditional healers.

Moreover, many practitioners of ATRs have also started to incorporate elements of other spiritual traditions into their practices. For example, in Brazil, the syncretic religion of Umbanda combines elements of traditional African religions with aspects of Catholicism and Spiritism. Similarly, in Haiti, Vodou has incorporated elements of Christianity, particularly Catholicism, and even Freemasonry.

In some cases, these adaptations have resulted in the creation of entirely new religious traditions that draw on both ATRs and other spiritual practices. For instance, in Cuba, Santeria has merged with the Catholic religion to create a new syncretic tradition known as Regla de Ocha.

These contemporary adaptations and innovations in ATRs have been met with both praise and criticism. On one hand, they allow ATRs to remain relevant and adaptable in the face of changing social and cultural realities. On the other hand, some people view these adaptations as a dilution of traditional beliefs or a form of cultural appropriation.

Examples and Exercises:

Research a contemporary adaptation or innovation in ATRs in a specific African country, such as the incorporation of modern technology or the reinterpretation of traditional beliefs to be more inclusive of marginalized communities. Write a report on your findings, including the ways in which these adaptations have affected the practice of ATRs in that country.

Debate the pros and cons of contemporary adaptations and innovations in ATRs. Take one side of the argument and provide evidence to support your position.

Create a new syncretic tradition that incorporates elements of ATRs and another spiritual practice, such as Christianity or Buddhism. Explain the reasoning behind your choices and describe the beliefs and practices of your new tradition.

Research a contemporary adaptation or innovation in ATRs in a specific African country, such as the incorporation of modern technology or the reinterpretation of traditional beliefs to be more inclusive of marginalized communities. Write a report on your findings, including the ways in which these adaptations have affected the practice of ATRs in that country.

One example of a contemporary adaptation in ATRs is the use of social media to connect practitioners and share knowledge. In Nigeria, a group of Ifa priests has created an online platform called Ifa Connect, which allows practitioners to share information and connect with each other. The platform also features live streams of Ifa ceremonies, allowing practitioners who cannot attend in person to still participate.

Another example is the incorporation of modern medical practices into traditional healing. In Zimbabwe, traditional healers known as n'angas have begun working with medical doctors to provide holistic healthcare to patients. This approach recognizes the importance of both traditional and modern medicine and seeks to provide the best possible care for patients.

Debate the pros and cons of contemporary adaptations and innovations in ATRs. Take one side of the argument and provide evidence to support your position.

One argument in favor of contemporary adaptations and innovations in ATRs is that they allow the tradition to adapt to changing circumstances and remain relevant in modern times. For example, the use of social media platforms like Ifa Connect allows practitioners to connect with each other and share knowledge, which can help to preserve and expand the tradition. Similarly, the incorporation of modern medical practices into traditional healing can improve health outcomes for patients and increase the legitimacy of traditional healing practices.

On the other hand, some argue that contemporary adaptations and innovations can dilute the authenticity of ATRs and strip them of their cultural significance. For example, the commercialization of traditional practices can reduce them to mere commodities, divorced from their cultural and spiritual contexts. Similarly, the incorporation of outside influences into ATRs can blur the boundaries between different traditions and erode their unique identities.

Create a new syncretic tradition that incorporates elements of ATRs and another spiritual practice, such as Christianity or Buddhism. Explain the reasoning behind your choices and describe the beliefs and practices of your new tradition.

One possible syncretic tradition that incorporates elements of ATRs and Christianity is called "Afro-Christianity". This tradition combines the belief in a single supreme God with the veneration of ancestors and the use of traditional African spiritual practices. The reasoning behind this syncretism is to bridge the gap between Christianity and traditional African beliefs, which are often seen as incompatible. By incorporating elements of ATRs into Christianity, this tradition seeks to create a more inclusive and culturally relevant form of spirituality for people of African descent.

The beliefs and practices of Afro-Christianity include the belief in a single, all-powerful God who created the universe and governs all of creation. This God is worshipped through prayer, meditation, and ritual. In addition, ancestors are venerated as intermediaries between the living and the divine, and traditional African spiritual practices such as divination and herbalism are incorporated into the tradition. The Bible is also seen as a sacred text, but it is interpreted through an African lens that emphasizes the role of community and the interconnectedness of all things.

CHAPTER 14: THE ROLE OF DIVINATION AND SPIRITUAL PRACTICES IN ATRS

Divination, trance, possession, music, and dance are all important spiritual practices within African Traditional Religions (ATRs). These practices allow practitioners to connect with the divine, seek guidance, and express their devotion to their ancestors and other spiritual entities. In this chapter, we will explore the various forms of divination, trance, possession, music, and dance used in ATRs, as well as their significance and role within the tradition.

The use of divination to connect with spiritual entities:

Divination is a practice used in many ATRs to communicate with the spiritual world. Divination involves seeking guidance and insight from the divine through the interpretation of signs, symbols, and messages. Practitioners of divination are often referred to as diviners or seers, and they may use a variety of tools to aid them in their practice, such as tarot cards, cowrie shells, or divining rods.

In ATRs, divination is often used to communicate with ancestors or other spiritual entities, such as gods or goddesses. Through divination, practitioners seek guidance on important life decisions, such as marriage, childbirth, or business ventures, and they may also seek answers to questions about their health, relationships, or personal growth.

The role of trance and possession in ATRs:

Trance and possession are also important spiritual practices in ATRs. Trance involves entering a state of altered consciousness, often through the use of music, dance, or other sensory stimuli. In this state, practitioners may communicate with spiritual entities or receive messages from the divine. Possession, on the other hand, involves allowing a spiritual entity to enter one's body and speak or act through them.

In many ATRs, trance and possession are used in healing practices, as spiritual entities may offer guidance or healing energy to those in need. Trance and possession may also be used in rituals or ceremonies, such as initiations or funerals, to honor ancestors or other spiritual entities.

African Religions

The importance of music and dance in ATRs:

Music and dance play a vital role in many ATRs. These practices are used to create a sacred space and connect practitioners with the divine. In some ATRs, music and dance are used to induce trance or possession, as practitioners enter a state of heightened awareness and connection with the spiritual world.

Music and dance are also used to honor ancestors and other spiritual entities. In some ATRs, specific dances or songs are associated with particular deities or spirits, and these may be performed as part of a ritual or ceremony. In addition, music and dance may be used to express gratitude or devotion to the divine, or to celebrate important life events such as weddings or births.

Examples and Exercises:

Research the use of divination in a specific African country, such as Nigeria or South Africa. Write a report on your findings, including the specific divination practices used in that country and their significance within the tradition.

Explore the role of trance and possession in ATRs. Choose a specific ATR, such as Vodou or Santeria, and write a paper on how trance and possession are used in that tradition. Provide specific examples of rituals or ceremonies in which trance or possession play a significant role.

Discuss the importance of music and dance in ATRs. Choose a specific ATR, such as Yoruba or Shona, and write a paper on the role of music and dance in that tradition. Provide specific examples of songs or dances that are associated with particular deities or spirits, and explain their significance within the tradition.

The use of divination to connect with spiritual entities

Divination is a practice found in many traditional African religions (ATRs) and involves the use of various tools and techniques to gain insight into the spiritual realm. Divination is used for many purposes, including communicating with ancestors and other spiritual entities, gaining insight into the future, and diagnosing illness.

In many ATRs, the belief is held that the spiritual realm is intricately connected to the physical world, and divination is one way of accessing that realm. The diviner acts as a mediator between the physical and spiritual realms, using their skills and tools to interpret messages from the spirits and ancestors.

Exploring Origins, Traditions, and Contemporary Relevance

There are many forms of divination used in ATRs, including throwing bones, using divination boards, and consulting with divination animals. Each form of divination has its unique techniques, tools, and beliefs. However, the underlying concept of divination is the same: to connect with the spiritual realm and gain insight into the unseen world.

The use of divination is often accompanied by ritual practices, such as the creation of sacred space and the invocation of ancestors and other spiritual entities. Diviners are often trained over many years, learning the techniques and beliefs associated with their chosen form of divination. They are respected members of their communities, acting as spiritual guides and advisors.

One form of divination commonly used in ATRs is bone divination. The diviner casts a set of bones or shells, interpreting the patterns that they form on the ground. Each bone or shell has its meaning, and the patterns they create can be interpreted to reveal messages from the spirits and ancestors. Bone divination is often used for gaining insight into the future, diagnosing illness, and resolving conflicts.

Another form of divination used in ATRs is divination boards. These boards often feature a series of symbols, such as images of animals or abstract patterns. The diviner throws a set of small objects, such as cowrie shells or stones, onto the board, interpreting the patterns they form. Each symbol on the board has its meaning, and the diviner uses their knowledge and intuition to interpret the messages received.

The use of divination is an essential part of many ATRs, providing a way for individuals to connect with the spiritual realm and gain insight into the unseen world. Divination is often used in combination with other spiritual practices, such as offerings and ritual ceremonies, to create a deeper connection with the spirits and ancestors.

However, some people outside of ATRs have criticized divination, calling it superstitious or fraudulent. They argue that there is no scientific evidence to support the validity of divination practices. Nonetheless, divination is still an essential part of many ATRs, and its practitioners believe that it offers a way to connect with the spiritual realm and gain insight into the unseen world.

Examples and Exercises:

Research the use of divination in a specific ATR, such as Yoruba or Vodou. Write a report on your findings, including the techniques and tools used in divination in that tradition and the ways in which divination is integrated into the spiritual practices of that tradition.

Debate the effectiveness of divination as a means of gaining insight into the spiritual realm. Take one side of the argument and provide evidence to support your position.

Create a divination board or set of bones for use in divination. Explain the symbolism and meanings behind each element of your creation and provide instructions on how to use it.

The role of trance and possession in ATRs

The role of trance and possession in African Traditional Religions (ATRs) is central to the spiritual practices and beliefs of many African societies. Trance and possession are altered states of consciousness that allow individuals to connect with spiritual entities, receive guidance and messages, and gain insight into the workings of the universe. In this chapter, we will explore the various forms of trance and possession in ATRs and their significance in the spiritual lives of practitioners.

Trance and Possession in African Traditional Religions

Trance and possession are terms that are often used interchangeably, but they refer to distinct phenomena. Trance is an altered state of consciousness that is induced by various means, such as meditation, drumming, chanting, or dancing. In trance, the individual remains aware of their surroundings but is focused on their internal experience, which can include vivid visions, feelings of ecstasy, and heightened sensitivity to spiritual energies.

Possession, on the other hand, involves the temporary displacement of the individual's consciousness by a spiritual entity. During possession, the individual loses awareness of their surroundings and may exhibit behavior that is characteristic of the possessing entity, such as speaking in a different voice, using unfamiliar gestures, or performing unusual movements.

In ATRs, both trance and possession are used to connect with spiritual entities, receive messages, and gain insight into the workings of the universe. The most common form of possession in ATRs is spirit possession, in which an individual is temporarily possessed by a spirit or ancestor. Spirit possession is often viewed as a positive experience, as it is believed to bring healing, guidance, and blessings to the individual and the community.

Trance and possession are often induced by specific techniques or rituals, such as drumming, dancing, or chanting. These techniques are believed to create a conducive environment for the spiritual entities to manifest themselves and communicate with the individual. For example, in the Yoruba tradition of Ifá, diviners use a divination board called an opon Ifá, along with chanting and drumming, to enter into trance and communicate with the Orishas, the spiritual entities that govern different aspects of life.

The Role of Trance and Possession in ATRs

The role of trance and possession in ATRs is multifaceted, and it varies depending on the specific tradition and the individual's role in the community. Some of the common roles of trance and possession in ATRs are discussed below:

Spiritual Connection and Guidance
Trance and possession are often used to establish a connection with spiritual entities and receive guidance and messages from them. For example, in the Shona tradition of Zimbabwe, spirit possession is believed to bring guidance and healing to the individual and the community. The possessed individual may receive messages from ancestors or spirits that help to resolve conflicts, heal sicknesses, or provide guidance in decision-making.

✧ Healing

Trance and possession are also used for healing purposes in many ATRs. It is believed that the spiritual entities that possess or communicate through the individual have the power to heal physical, emotional, and spiritual ailments. In the Zulu tradition of South Africa, for example, sangomas (traditional healers) use trance and possession to diagnose and treat illnesses. The sangoma may enter into trance and receive messages from ancestral spirits that prescribe specific remedies, such as herbal treatments, animal sacrifices, or spiritual cleansings.

✧ Religious and Cultural Preservation

Trance and possession are also important for preserving the religious and cultural traditions of ATRs. The messages and guidance received during trance and possession are often interpreted in the context of the specific tradition and transmitted to the community through oral tradition, music, and dance. In this way, trance and possession serve as a means of preserving the cultural heritage and spiritual practices of ATRs.

Furthermore, trance and possession can play a role in maintaining the social and political order of the community. In some ATRs, possession may be used to identify and address social issues such as conflicts or injustices within the community. The possessed individual may act as a mediator, bringing attention to the issue and providing guidance for its resolution.

In addition to social and cultural preservation, trance and possession can also serve as a form of resistance to colonialism and oppression. During the era of colonialism and the transatlantic slave trade, ATRs were often suppressed and demonized by colonial powers who sought to impose Christianity and Western values on the colonized populations. Trance and possession were often seen as signs of primitive and savage behavior, and were suppressed by colonial authorities.

However, many ATR practitioners continued to practice their traditions in secret, often incorporating Christian symbols and beliefs into their practices as a form of syncretism. Trance and possession played a crucial role in these practices, allowing practitioners to connect with their ancestors and spiritual entities despite the oppression and suppression of their traditions.

Today, many ATRs have regained recognition and respect as important cultural and spiritual practices, but the legacy of colonialism and oppression still persists in many ways. Trance and possession continue to serve as a means of resistance and cultural preservation in the face of ongoing struggles for autonomy and recognition.

Despite the many positive aspects of trance and possession in ATRs, there are also potential risks and dangers associated with these practices. In some cases, individuals may become possessed by negative or malevolent entities that cause harm or damage. Trance and possession can also be physically and emotionally taxing, and may require extensive training and preparation in order to be performed safely and effectively.

Furthermore, some critics argue that trance and possession can be used as a means of social control, allowing religious and political authorities to manipulate and exploit the community. It is important to approach trance and possession with a critical and discerning eye, recognizing both the potential benefits and risks associated with these practices.

In conclusion, trance and possession play a vital role in ATRs, serving as a means of spiritual connection, healing, cultural preservation, and resistance. These practices offer a powerful way of connecting with spiritual entities and receiving guidance and messages, but also require careful consideration and critical examination in order to ensure their safe and responsible use.

Exploring Origins, Traditions, and Contemporary Relevance

The importance of music and dance in ATRs

The use of music and dance is central to the spiritual practices of many African Traditional Religions (ATRs). Music and dance are seen as powerful tools for invoking and communicating with spiritual entities, creating a sense of community, and reinforcing cultural identity. In this section, we will explore the importance of music and dance in ATRs, the different types of music and dance used, and their significance.

The Importance of Music and Dance in ATRs

Music and dance are integral to the spiritual practices of ATRs. They are used to create a connection with the divine, to facilitate healing and transformation, and to reinforce cultural identity. Music and dance are often performed in groups, creating a sense of community and shared experience.

In ATRs, music and dance are seen as more than mere entertainment. They are a way to communicate with the spiritual world, to invoke spiritual entities, and to enter into a trance state. Music and dance are believed to have the power to transport individuals from the physical world to the spiritual realm. This is why they are often used in ritual and ceremony.

Music and dance are also important for healing and transformation. They are used to help individuals overcome emotional and spiritual blockages and to promote well-being. In many ATRs, music and dance are used to induce trance states, which are believed to facilitate healing and transformation.

In addition to their spiritual significance, music and dance are also important for reinforcing cultural identity. They are often used to celebrate cultural traditions and to transmit cultural knowledge from one generation to the next. In this way, music and dance serve as a means of preserving cultural heritage.

Types of Music and Dance in ATRs

The types of music and dance used in ATRs vary widely depending on the specific tradition and region. However, there are certain types of music and dance that are common across many ATRs.

Drumming is one of the most important forms of music in ATRs. Drums are often used to invoke spiritual entities and to create a sense of community. The rhythms of the drums are believed to have the power to transport individuals into a trance state.

Different types of drums are used depending on the tradition, including the djembe, the dunun, and the talking drum.

Chanting and singing are also important forms of music in ATRs. Chants and songs are often used to invoke spiritual entities and to create a sense of community. They are often performed in call-and-response format, with a lead singer calling out a line and the group responding. The lyrics of the songs often contain messages of spiritual significance.

Dance is another important component of ATRs. Dance is often used to accompany music and to reinforce its spiritual significance. Different types of dance are used depending on the tradition, including circle dances, line dances, and solo dances. Dance movements are often symbolic, representing specific spiritual concepts or entities.

Significance of Music and Dance in ATRs

Music and dance are significant in ATRs for several reasons. First, they are used to communicate with the spiritual world and to invoke spiritual entities. This is particularly important in ATRs, where spiritual entities are seen as integral to daily life.

Second, music and dance are used to create a sense of community. They are often performed in groups, creating a shared experience and sense of belonging. This is particularly important in ATRs, where community is seen as essential to spiritual and social well-being.

Third, music and dance are used for healing and transformation. They are often used to induce trance states, which are believed to facilitate healing and transformation. This is particularly important in ATRs, where physical, emotional, and spiritual well-being are seen as interconnected.

Finally, music and dance are important for preserving cultural identity. They are often used to pass down cultural traditions and stories from one generation to the next. This is particularly important in ATRs, where cultural heritage is seen as essential to spiritual practice and community cohesion.

One example of the importance of music and dance in ATRs can be seen in the Yoruba tradition of Nigeria. In Yoruba culture, music and dance are central to many religious and social events. The Yoruba use drumming, singing, and dancing to communicate with their deities, orishas, and to invoke their presence. Music and dance are also used in initiation ceremonies, where individuals are initiated into specific religious societies or priesthoods. These ceremonies involve complex choreography, music, and costumes, and serve as a means of passing on cultural knowledge and traditions.

Another example can be seen in the Afro-Cuban tradition of Santeria. Santeria is a syncretic religion that emerged in Cuba during the colonial period. It combines elements of Yoruba religion with Catholicism and other African traditions. In Santeria, music and dance are used to communicate with the orishas and to facilitate trance states. The music is played on drums and other percussion instruments, and the dancing is often accompanied by colorful costumes and ritual objects. Santeria music and dance have had a significant influence on popular music in Cuba and beyond, and have helped to preserve and transmit the cultural traditions of the Afro-Cuban community.

Music and dance are also significant in the Vodou tradition of Haiti. Vodou is a syncretic religion that combines elements of West African and Catholic traditions. In Vodou, music and dance are used to communicate with the lwa, or spirits, and to induce trance states. The music is often played on drums and other percussion instruments, and the dancing is accompanied by chanting and singing. Vodou music and dance have had a significant impact on popular music in Haiti and beyond, and have helped to preserve and transmit the cultural traditions of the Haitian community.

In conclusion, music and dance are integral to many ATRs. They are used to communicate with the spiritual world, to create a sense of community, to facilitate healing and transformation, and to preserve cultural identity. By engaging in music and dance, individuals in ATRs are able to connect with their spiritual and cultural heritage, and to pass on that heritage to future generations.

CHAPTER 15: THE IMPACT OF CHRISTIANITY AND ISLAM ON ATRS

Africa is a continent with a rich spiritual and cultural heritage. African Traditional Religions (ATRs) have been practiced for thousands of years and have played an integral role in the lives of African people. However, the arrival of Christianity and Islam in Africa had a significant impact on ATRs, leading to changes in religious practices, beliefs, and cultural traditions.

The history of missionary activity and religious conversion in Africa

The arrival of Christianity and Islam in Africa dates back to the early centuries of the Common Era. The spread of these religions was facilitated by the activities of missionaries and traders who traveled to Africa from Europe and the Middle East. These missionaries often saw ATRs as primitive and pagan and sought to convert Africans to Christianity or Islam.

The process of religious conversion was often accompanied by coercion and force. Missionaries would often use economic incentives, such as access to education and healthcare, to persuade Africans to convert to Christianity or Islam. Some African rulers also converted to Christianity or Islam in order to gain political and economic power.

The impact of missionary activity and religious conversion on ATRs was significant. Many traditional religious practices and beliefs were suppressed or eliminated altogether. Some ATRs were even criminalized, with their practitioners facing persecution and discrimination.

Syncretism and hybridization between ATRs and Christianity/Islam

Despite the efforts of missionaries and colonial authorities to eliminate ATRs, many Africans continued to practice their traditional religions in secret or alongside Christianity or Islam. This led to the emergence of syncretic religions, which combined elements of ATRs with Christianity or Islam.

Exploring Origins, Traditions, and Contemporary Relevance

Syncretism and hybridization allowed Africans to preserve some of their traditional religious practices and beliefs, while also incorporating new elements from Christianity or Islam. For example, in Brazil, the syncretic religion of Candomblé combines elements of Yoruba religion with Catholicism. In Nigeria, the syncretic religion of Ifa combines elements of Yoruba religion with Islam.

The challenges of preserving and revitalizing ATRs in a modern, globalized world

The impact of Christianity and Islam on ATRs has been significant, but it is not the only challenge facing traditional African religions. ATRs are also facing the challenges of modernization and globalization. The spread of Western culture and values, as well as the influence of technology and the internet, has led to the erosion of traditional cultural practices and beliefs.

Furthermore, the younger generation of Africans are often less interested in traditional religions and more attracted to Western-style Christianity or Islam. This has led to a decline in the number of practitioners of ATRs and a weakening of the cultural and spiritual heritage of Africa.

Despite these challenges, there are efforts underway to preserve and revitalize ATRs. Many African scholars and religious leaders are working to document and promote the traditional practices and beliefs of ATRs. They are also working to integrate traditional practices and beliefs into modern contexts, such as healthcare and education.

In conclusion, the impact of Christianity and Islam on ATRs has been significant, but it is not the only challenge facing traditional African religions. The challenges of modernization and globalization are also threatening the cultural and spiritual heritage of Africa. However, efforts are underway to preserve and revitalize ATRs, and it is hoped that the rich spiritual and cultural traditions of Africa will continue to thrive in the modern world.

The history of missionary activity and religious conversion in Africa

The history of Africa is marked by a long and complex process of religious conversion, as various forms of Christianity and Islam spread across the continent. This process began in the early centuries of the Common Era, as the first Christian missionaries arrived on the shores of Africa. Over the centuries, missionaries from Europe and other parts of the world established churches, schools, and hospitals throughout the continent, in an effort to spread their faith and establish a foothold in Africa.

African Religions

The spread of Christianity in Africa was initially slow, as the early missionaries faced significant obstacles and resistance from the local populations. However, over time, Christianity began to gain a foothold in Africa, particularly in regions where the political and economic influence of European colonial powers was strong. In many cases, Christianity was seen as a symbol of modernity and progress, and conversion to the faith was seen as a way of gaining access to European education, healthcare, and other benefits.

Islam, too, began to spread across Africa in the early centuries of the Common Era. The spread of Islam was facilitated by the growth of trade networks that connected Africa with the Middle East and beyond. As Muslim traders and scholars traveled across Africa, they established mosques and schools, and gradually converted local populations to the faith.

The spread of Christianity and Islam across Africa was not a straightforward process, however. In many cases, the early missionaries and converts encountered significant resistance and opposition from traditional African religious practitioners. African Traditional Religions (ATRs) were deeply rooted in local cultures and were seen as integral to the social and spiritual well-being of African communities. As a result, many Africans were reluctant to abandon their traditional beliefs and practices in favor of foreign religions.

Despite these challenges, Christianity and Islam continued to spread across Africa, particularly in regions where European colonial powers were strong. Missionaries established schools and hospitals, and worked to establish a foothold in African societies by providing material and social support to converts. In many cases, the spread of Christianity and Islam was facilitated by colonial policies that favored converts and discriminated against practitioners of traditional African religions.

In the 20th century, as African countries gained independence from colonial powers, the spread of Christianity and Islam began to slow. Many African leaders sought to promote a sense of national and cultural identity, and saw traditional African religions as an important part of this identity. In addition, the rise of African nationalist movements and the growth of pan-Africanism created a renewed interest in traditional African religions and a rejection of foreign religions.

Today, Christianity and Islam remain significant forces in African society, but traditional African religions continue to play an important role as well. Many Africans practice a hybrid form of religion that combines elements of Christianity, Islam, and traditional African religions, reflecting the complex and dynamic nature of religious practice on the continent.

Exploring Origins, Traditions, and Contemporary Relevance

Syncretism and hybridization between ATRs and Christianity/Islam

Syncretism and hybridization between African Traditional Religions (ATRs) and Christianity/Islam have been a significant phenomenon in Africa for centuries. These religious traditions have often interacted and blended with each other, resulting in new forms of religious expression that incorporate elements of both traditions. This process of syncretism has been both creative and contentious, and has shaped the religious landscape of Africa in profound ways.

One of the key factors that contributed to the syncretism between ATRs and Christianity/Islam was the spread of these religions through missionary activity and colonization. Christian missionaries began to arrive in Africa in the early 15th century, with the Portuguese and Spanish leading the way. They sought to convert Africans to Christianity, and they often saw African traditional beliefs and practices as obstacles to this goal. Similarly, Islamic missionaries arrived in Africa in the 7th century and began to spread the religion throughout the continent.

However, rather than completely replacing traditional beliefs and practices, these new religions often blended with and incorporated elements of ATRs. This was partly due to the flexibility of ATRs, which allowed for the incorporation of new beliefs and practices, as well as the persistence of traditional beliefs and practices among Africans despite the influence of Christianity/Islam. For example, in the Yoruba tradition of Nigeria, the Christian Trinity was incorporated into the traditional pantheon of gods and goddesses, resulting in a new syncretic religion called Ifa-Orisha.

The process of syncretism was not always peaceful or voluntary. Some Africans were forced to convert to Christianity or Islam through colonialism and slavery, and their traditional beliefs and practices were suppressed or even criminalized. However, in other cases, the blending of ATRs with Christianity/Islam was a more collaborative process, with traditional leaders and practitioners negotiating with Christian and Islamic leaders to incorporate elements of their traditions into the new religions.

One example of this collaborative process is the syncretic religion of Vodou in Haiti. Vodou incorporates elements of both African Traditional Religion and Catholicism, which was brought to Haiti by French colonizers. The Catholic saints were identified with the traditional spirits of the African pantheon, resulting in a unique religious practice that is a blend of both traditions.

Syncretism between ATRs and Christianity/Islam has also resulted in new forms of music, dance, and ritual. For example, the use of gospel music in Christian churches in Africa has blended with traditional African rhythms and instruments to create a unique style of music. Similarly, the Islamic call to prayer has been accompanied by African drums in some regions, resulting in a blend of Islamic and traditional African musical styles.

The process of syncretism between ATRs and Christianity/Islam has not been without controversy. Some traditionalists have criticized the blending of traditional practices with Christianity/Islam, arguing that it dilutes the integrity of the traditional beliefs and practices. Others have argued that the blending of ATRs with Christianity/Islam is a form of resistance against colonialism and oppression, and a way to maintain traditional beliefs and practices in a changing world.

Regardless of these debates, the blending of ATRs with Christianity/Islam has resulted in a rich and diverse religious landscape in Africa, with a range of syncretic religions that incorporate elements of both traditions. This process has also shaped the cultural identity of African people, as they have negotiated the challenges of colonialism, slavery, and globalization while maintaining their traditional beliefs and practices. The blending of ATRs with Christianity/Islam is an ongoing process, and one that will continue to shape the religious and cultural landscape of Africa in the years to come.

Examples, problems, and exercises:

Research and write a paper on the history of syncretism between ATRs and Christianity/Islam in a specific African country or region, examining the specific ways in which these traditions have blended together and the impact this has had on the religious and cultural landscape.

Discuss the challenges faced by practitioners of ATRs who have adopted elements of Christianity/Islam, including resistance from both traditionalists and practitioners of the adopted religion.

Examine the impact of syncretism on the role of women in ATRs, particularly in societies where Christianity/Islam have historically been patriarchal and male-dominated.

Consider the potential ethical concerns surrounding syncretism, including questions of authenticity and cultural appropriation. Discuss whether it is appropriate for non-African practitioners of Christianity/Islam to incorporate elements of ATRs into their religious practice.

Read and analyze works by scholars and practitioners of syncretic African religions, such as Jacob K. Olupona's "African Traditional Religion and Christianity in

Exploring Origins, Traditions, and Contemporary Relevance

Western Nigeria: A Study in Adaption, Conflict, and Syncretism" or Robert M. Baum's "Shamanic and Christian Cosmologies: A Comparative Analysis of the Symbolism of Healing Power in Vodou and Pentecostalism." Discuss the similarities and differences in their approaches to the study of syncretic religions.

The challenges of preserving and revitalizing ATRs in a modern, globalized world

The challenges of preserving and revitalizing African Traditional Religions (ATRs) in a modern, globalized world are complex and multifaceted. In the face of Westernization, globalization, and the increasing influence of Christianity and Islam, ATRs are at risk of disappearing altogether. However, there are many efforts underway to preserve and revitalize these ancient spiritual practices, and these efforts offer hope for the future of ATRs in Africa.

One of the greatest challenges to preserving and revitalizing ATRs is the lack of understanding and acceptance of these practices by Western societies. ATRs have often been dismissed as "primitive" or "superstitious" by Westerners, and this attitude has contributed to the marginalization and stigmatization of these traditions. This has resulted in the loss of many important cultural artifacts and practices, as well as a lack of support for those who practice ATRs.

Another challenge to preserving and revitalizing ATRs is the influence of Christianity and Islam. While syncretism and hybridization between ATRs and these religions have led to the development of unique and diverse religious practices, they have also resulted in the loss of many traditional ATR practices. This is particularly true in areas where Christianity and Islam have been used as tools of colonization and oppression, as these religions have often been used to suppress and eradicate traditional ATRs.

In addition to external pressures, there are also internal challenges to preserving and revitalizing ATRs. Many young people in Africa are turning away from ATRs in favor of Western religions and practices, viewing ATRs as outdated or irrelevant in the modern world. This is particularly true in urban areas, where young people are often exposed to Western culture and values from an early age.

To address these challenges, there are many efforts underway to preserve and revitalize ATRs. These efforts include the preservation of cultural artifacts and practices, the revitalization of traditional healing practices, and the creation of educational programs to teach young people about ATRs. There are also many organizations working to raise awareness about the importance of ATRs, both within Africa and internationally.

African Religions

One example of an organization working to preserve and revitalize ATRs is the African Cultural Heritage Trust (ACHT), which was founded in 1996 in Kenya. The ACHT works to promote the preservation and revitalization of traditional African culture, including ATRs, through a range of programs and initiatives. These include the restoration of cultural sites and artifacts, the promotion of traditional healing practices, and the creation of educational materials to teach young people about ATRs.

Another example of an organization working to preserve and revitalize ATRs is the African Traditional Religions Forum (ATRF), which was founded in Nigeria in 1989. The ATRF works to promote the study and practice of ATRs, and to foster dialogue and understanding between practitioners of ATRs and other religions. The ATRF also advocates for the protection of ATRs from the influence of Christianity and Islam, and works to address the marginalization and stigmatization of ATR practitioners.

In addition to these organizations, there are also many individuals working to preserve and revitalize ATRs. For example, in South Africa, traditional healers known as sangomas are working to preserve and revitalize traditional healing practices. These healers use a combination of herbs, rituals, and divination to treat a range of illnesses and conditions, and are seen as essential members of their communities.

Examples, problems, and exercises:

Research and write a paper on the impact of globalization on the preservation and revitalization of ATRs.

Globalization, with its attendant cultural, economic, and political changes, has had a profound impact on traditional African religions (ATRs), including the challenges of preserving and revitalizing these practices in a modern, globalized world. One of the primary effects of globalization on ATRs has been the displacement of traditional beliefs and practices by Western religions and secular values. As a result, many ATRs are facing decline and even extinction, as younger generations adopt the values and beliefs of the dominant culture.

Despite these challenges, there are efforts being made to preserve and revitalize ATRs in the face of globalization. One approach is the establishment of cultural and heritage centers, which serve as repositories for traditional knowledge and practices. These centers provide a space for practitioners to gather, share knowledge, and engage in cultural practices. They also offer educational programs and workshops for younger generations, aimed at revitalizing traditional practices and values.

Exploring Origins, Traditions, and Contemporary Relevance

Another approach is the use of technology, such as social media and digital archives, to disseminate information about ATRs to a wider audience. For example, some practitioners have established online forums and blogs to share information and discuss issues related to the preservation and revitalization of their traditions. Similarly, digital archives provide a means of preserving traditional knowledge and practices for future generations, even in the face of physical destruction or displacement.

Additionally, there are efforts being made to incorporate ATRs into mainstream education and policy-making. For example, some African countries have included traditional knowledge and practices in their school curricula, and have established policies that recognize and protect ATRs as part of their cultural heritage. This recognition and protection of ATRs is crucial for their preservation and revitalization, as it acknowledges their cultural significance and provides legal protections against their destruction or exploitation.

Despite these efforts, there are still many challenges facing the preservation and revitalization of ATRs in a modern, globalized world. One major challenge is the lack of resources and funding for cultural and heritage centers, which limits their ability to provide educational programs and outreach to the wider community. Similarly, the use of technology to disseminate information about ATRs is limited by factors such as access to the internet and digital literacy.

Another challenge is the continued influence of Western religions and secular values, which often lead to the marginalization and stigmatization of traditional beliefs and practices. This can make it difficult for practitioners to openly practice their traditions or share their knowledge with others. Additionally, the effects of globalization, such as urbanization and migration, can result in the displacement of traditional communities and the loss of traditional knowledge and practices.

Despite these challenges, the preservation and revitalization of ATRs is crucial for the cultural identity and well-being of African people. It is important for practitioners and supporters of ATRs to continue to work towards their preservation and revitalization, through initiatives such as cultural and heritage centers, the use of technology, and the incorporation of ATRs into mainstream education and policy-making.

Examples, problems, and exercises:

Choose a specific ATR and research the challenges faced by practitioners of that tradition in preserving and revitalizing their practices. Write a report detailing the history and current state of the tradition, the challenges faced by practitioners, and the efforts being made to preserve and revitalize the tradition. In your report, be sure to address the following questions:

What is the history and cultural significance of the chosen ATR?

What challenges are faced by practitioners of this tradition in preserving and revitalizing their practices?

What efforts have been made to preserve and revitalize this tradition?

What is the impact of globalization on the preservation and revitalization of this tradition?

PART 4: THE ROLE OF ANCESTORS IN AFRICAN RELIGIONS

Ancestors play a central role in many African religions, serving as intermediaries between the living and the spirit world. In African traditional religions (ATRs), ancestors are believed to be active participants in the daily lives of their descendants, offering guidance, protection, and blessings. Ancestor veneration is a common practice across many ATRs, and is often accompanied by rituals, sacrifices, and offerings. The belief in ancestors has also been incorporated into syncretic religions that have emerged as a result of the blending of ATRs with Christianity and Islam. In this section, we will explore the multifaceted role of ancestors in African religions, and how they continue to shape the spiritual and cultural practices of African people.

CHAPTER 16: THE CONCEPT OF ANCESTORS IN AFRICAN RELIGIONS

African religions have a rich and complex tradition of ancestor veneration that has played a central role in the religious and cultural practices of many African communities. The concept of ancestors is central to the belief systems of many African religions, which view ancestors as powerful spiritual beings who continue to influence the lives of their descendants.

In African religions, ancestors are often viewed as intermediaries between the living and the divine, able to communicate with and influence the spiritual realm on behalf of their living descendants. Ancestors are often seen as wise and benevolent figures who can offer guidance, protection, and blessings to their living relatives, as well as intercede on their behalf with the divine.

The role of ancestors in African religions is deeply intertwined with the importance of family and community in African societies. In many African cultures, ancestors are seen as members of the extended family, with their influence and support extending beyond individual households to the broader community.

The practice of ancestor veneration is also closely linked to African ideas about the afterlife and the continuation of the soul after death. Many African religions believe that death is not the end of life, but rather a transition to a different realm of existence. In this view, ancestors are seen as continuing to exist in the spiritual realm, able to maintain connections with the living world and influence the lives of their descendants.

However, the concept of ancestors in African religions has not been without controversy. Some critics have viewed ancestor veneration as a form of ancestor worship or idolatry, and have sought to suppress or eliminate these practices in African communities.

Despite these challenges, the practice of ancestor veneration remains a vital and enduring part of many African religions, and continues to play an important role in shaping the spiritual and cultural identities of African communities. This chapter will explore the concept of ancestors in African religions in depth, examining the ways in which ancestor veneration has evolved over time and the challenges and controversies that have surrounded this practice.

Introduction to the concept of ancestors in African religions

The concept of ancestors is a fundamental and pervasive aspect of African religions, with its roots stretching back to the earliest days of human history. In African traditional religions (ATRs), ancestors are believed to be powerful spiritual entities who can influence the lives of their living descendants, providing guidance, protection, and blessings, or conversely, causing misfortune and illness if not properly honored and appeased. Ancestors are revered as guardians and mediators between the living and the divine, occupying a special place in the spiritual hierarchy of African religions.

The role of ancestors in African religions has been shaped by centuries of cultural, social, and religious practices, as well as by historical events such as the transatlantic slave trade and colonization. The preservation and transmission of ancestral knowledge, rituals, and beliefs have been challenging due to factors such as urbanization, globalization, and the erosion of traditional values and practices. Nevertheless, the importance of the ancestor cult remains a defining feature of ATRs and continues to influence the religious and cultural identity of African communities.

This chapter will explore the concept of ancestors in African religions, examining its historical, cultural, and spiritual dimensions. The chapter will begin by providing an overview of the diverse range of ancestral practices and beliefs found in ATRs, highlighting their similarities and differences across different African cultures. It will then discuss the role of ancestors in ATRs, exploring their functions as protectors, mediators, and sources of wisdom and power. The chapter will also examine the challenges faced by contemporary practitioners of ATRs in preserving and revitalizing ancestral practices, as well as the ways in which new forms of religious expression are emerging in response to these challenges.

The concept of ancestors in African religions reflects a complex and dynamic interplay between the spiritual, cultural, and social dimensions of African life. As we have seen, ancestral practices and beliefs vary widely across different African cultures, reflecting the unique histories, geographies, and social structures of each region. Nevertheless, the role of ancestors in ATRs is a testament to the enduring

Ancestors hold a special place in many African cultures. They are believed to be the link between the living and the divine, and are often seen as mediators between the two realms. Ancestors are also believed to have a direct impact on the daily lives of their living descendants, and are revered as sources of guidance, protection, and blessings.

Despite the commonality of ancestor veneration across Africa, the practices and beliefs surrounding ancestors vary greatly across different regions and cultures. In this section, we will explore the diversity of ancestral practices in African cultures, the role of ancestors in different regions of Africa, and the similarities and differences in ancestral practices across different African cultures.

The Diversity of Ancestral Practices in African Cultures:

Ancestor veneration is a common feature of many African cultures, but the practices and beliefs surrounding ancestors vary greatly from one culture to another. For example, in West Africa, ancestral worship is often closely tied to the practice of divination, in which the ancestors are consulted for guidance and advice. In Central Africa, ancestor veneration is often associated with initiation rites and other forms of ritualized behavior.

In some African cultures, ancestors are believed to have the power to influence the natural world, and are therefore honored through offerings and sacrifices. For example, in many cultures, ancestral spirits are believed to inhabit trees, rocks, and other natural objects, and offerings are made to these objects as a way of honoring and appeasing the ancestors.

In other cultures, ancestors are believed to have the power to influence the lives of their living descendants, and are therefore honored through the performance of various rituals and ceremonies. These rituals may include the pouring of libations, the burning of incense, or the offering of food and drink.

The Role of Ancestors in Different Regions of Africa:

The role of ancestors in different regions of Africa can vary greatly. In some cultures, ancestors are seen as the primary source of spiritual power, and are therefore honored above all other deities. In other cultures, ancestors are seen as more minor deities, and are honored alongside other gods and spirits.

In many African cultures, ancestors are believed to have the power to influence the lives of their living descendants. They are seen as sources of guidance, protection, and blessings, and are often called upon in times of need. Ancestors may be asked to intercede on behalf of their living descendants, and may be called upon to provide guidance in matters such as marriage, childbirth, and other important life events.

Exploring Origins, Traditions, and Contemporary Relevance

In some African cultures, ancestors are also believed to have the power to bring misfortune upon their living descendants. They may be seen as the cause of illness, infertility, or other problems, and may be appeased through offerings and sacrifices.

Similarities and Differences in Ancestral Practices Across Different African Cultures:

While ancestor veneration is a common feature of many African cultures, the practices and beliefs surrounding ancestors can vary greatly from one culture to another. However, there are also many similarities in the ways that ancestors are honored and revered across different African cultures.

For example, many African cultures believe that ancestors have the power to influence the lives of their living descendants, and are therefore honored through offerings, sacrifices, and other forms of worship. Ancestors are often seen as sources of guidance, protection, and blessings, and are revered as powerful spiritual beings.

However, there are also significant differences in the ways that ancestors are honored and revered across different African cultures. For example, some cultures believe that ancestors should be honored through offerings of food and drink, while others believe that ancestors should be honored through the pouring of libations or the burning of incense.

Ancestor veneration is a common feature of many African cultures, but the practices and beliefs surrounding ancestors can vary greatly from one culture to another. The diversity of ancestral practices in Africa is a testament to the richness and complexity of African cultures and traditions. Despite these differences, there are certain commonalities that can be observed across many African cultures. For example, ancestors are often believed to be able to intervene in the lives of the living, either to provide blessings or to inflict punishment. Ancestors may also be called upon for guidance, protection, or assistance in various areas of life, such as health, fertility, and success.

The role of ancestors in different regions of Africa is also worth noting. In West Africa, for example, ancestor veneration is often closely linked with the worship of nature spirits and other deities. Ancestors may be viewed as intermediaries between the living and these other spiritual entities, helping to facilitate communication and the exchange of blessings. In Southern Africa, ancestral worship is often associated with the concept of ubuntu, which emphasizes the interconnectedness of all beings and the importance of community.

African Religions

There are also notable differences in ancestral practices across different African cultures. For example, in some cultures, ancestor veneration is primarily a private, family-oriented affair, while in others it is more of a public or community-based activity. Some cultures may view ancestors as benevolent and helpful spirits, while others may see them as potentially dangerous and in need of appeasement. Additionally, the ways in which ancestors are honored and remembered can vary widely, from elaborate ancestral shrines and offerings to simple acts of remembrance and prayer.

In conclusion, the concept of ancestors plays a significant role in many African religions and cultures. The practices and beliefs surrounding ancestors are diverse and complex, reflecting the varied histories, traditions, and experiences of different African peoples. Despite these differences, ancestor veneration remains an important and meaningful aspect of many African cultures today, providing a connection to the past and a source of guidance and inspiration for the present and future generations. As such, it is an area of study that continues to captivate the interest of scholars, practitioners, and anyone interested in exploring the rich tapestry of African spirituality and culture.

The Role of Ancestors in African Religions

The concept of ancestor veneration is an important aspect of African Traditional Religions (ATRs). Ancestors are believed to have a special relationship with the living and are often seen as protectors, mediators, and sources of wisdom and power. In this section, we will explore the different functions of ancestors in ATRs, focusing on their role as protectors and guardians, mediators between the living and the divine, and sources of wisdom and power.

As Protectors and Guardians

In many African cultures, ancestors are believed to have a protective role, guarding and guiding their descendants from the spiritual realm. Ancestors are often seen as the first line of defense against negative forces such as malevolent spirits, witches, and other supernatural entities. Ancestors are also believed to protect the community as a whole, safeguarding them from harm and misfortune.

One example of ancestor veneration as a protective function can be found in the Yoruba tradition of Nigeria. In this tradition, ancestors are believed to have the power to prevent harm from coming to their descendants. The ancestors are said to watch over their descendants, protecting them from danger, and helping them to overcome adversity.

Similarly, in the Shona tradition of Zimbabwe, ancestors are believed to have the power to intervene on behalf of their descendants in times of trouble. Ancestors are believed to be able to communicate with the living and to provide guidance and assistance when needed.

As Mediators Between the Living and the Divine

Ancestors are also seen as mediators between the living and the divine in many African cultures. Ancestors are believed to have a special relationship with the divine, and to be able to communicate with the gods on behalf of their descendants. Ancestors are seen as a bridge between the living and the divine, helping to facilitate communication and maintain balance between the two realms.

One example of this can be found in the Bantu tradition of Southern Africa. In this tradition, ancestors are believed to be able to communicate with the divine through dreams, visions, and divination. Ancestors are also believed to have the power to intercede on behalf of their descendants, acting as mediators between the living and the divine.

Similarly, in the Akan tradition of Ghana, ancestors are believed to be able to communicate with the gods on behalf of their descendants. Ancestors are seen as intermediaries, able to convey the concerns and needs of the living to the divine, and to bring blessings and guidance back to the living.

As Sources of Wisdom and Power

Ancestors are also seen as sources of wisdom and power in many African cultures. Ancestors are believed to have accumulated knowledge and experience throughout their lives, and to have access to a higher level of consciousness in the afterlife. Ancestors are also believed to have the power to bestow blessings and gifts upon their descendants, including spiritual power and knowledge.

One example of this can be found in the Dagara tradition of Burkina Faso. In this tradition, ancestors are believed to have the power to bestow gifts such as healing, divination, and spiritual power upon their descendants. Ancestors are also seen as sources of wisdom, able to provide guidance and insight into the challenges of life.

Similarly, in the Zulu tradition of South Africa, ancestors are believed to have the power to bestow blessings upon their descendants. Ancestors are seen as sources of spiritual power, able to grant their descendants the strength and courage needed to overcome obstacles and achieve their goals.

In conclusion, ancestors play a significant role in African Traditional Religions, serving as protectors, mediators, and sources of wisdom and power. Ancestor veneration is an important aspect of many African cultures, and the functions of ancestors can vary widely across different regions and traditions.

It is important to note that ancestor veneration in African religions is not the same as ancestor worship in Western cultures. While ancestor worship may involve a form of idolization or deification of ancestors, ancestor veneration in African religions is focused on respecting and honoring ancestors as part of a larger spiritual community that includes the living, the dead, and the divine.

Furthermore, the role of ancestors in African religions is not static, but rather dynamic and evolving. As African cultures continue to adapt to modernity and globalization, the practices and beliefs surrounding ancestors may change or be adapted to fit new social and cultural contexts.

It is also important to acknowledge the diversity of African cultures and the complexities of their religious practices and beliefs. This diversity and complexity should be celebrated and respected, rather than simplified or stereotyped.

In conclusion, the role of ancestors in African religions is multifaceted and nuanced, reflecting the rich cultural heritage of the African continent. Understanding the functions of ancestors in African Traditional Religions is an important step towards appreciating and engaging with the diversity of African cultures and spiritual practices.

The spiritual significance of ancestor veneration in ATRs

The spiritual significance of ancestor veneration in African Traditional Religions (ATRs) is rooted in the belief that the ancestors continue to exist in the afterlife and have the ability to influence the lives of their living descendants. In this section, we will explore the three main aspects of ancestor veneration in ATRs: ancestral cosmologies, ancestral rituals, and ancestral divination.

Ancestral Cosmologies and the Role of Ancestors in the Afterlife
In many ATRs, the belief in the afterlife is central to understanding the role of the ancestors in spiritual life. Ancestral cosmologies describe the journey of the soul after death and the various realms or dimensions of existence that the soul may inhabit. In some ATRs, the soul is believed to pass through multiple levels of existence, each with its own challenges and opportunities for growth and development.

Exploring Origins, Traditions, and Contemporary Relevance

The ancestors are believed to occupy a special place in the afterlife, where they continue to exist and are able to influence the world of the living. They are often depicted as guardians of their descendants, watching over them and guiding them through the challenges of life. In some ATRs, the ancestors are believed to have access to spiritual knowledge and power that can be used to help their living descendants.

The belief in the afterlife and the role of the ancestors in that afterlife is often reflected in the funerary practices of ATRs. Funerals are often elaborate and highly symbolic, reflecting the belief that death is not the end of existence, but rather a transition to a new state of being.

Ancestral Rituals and Their Significance in ATRs

Ancestral rituals are an important aspect of many ATRs, and serve as a means of honoring and communing with the ancestors. These rituals may take many forms, from simple offerings of food and drink to elaborate ceremonies involving dance, music, and trance.

One example of an ancestral ritual is the libation ceremony, which is common in many West African ATRs. In this ceremony, a libation is poured out as an offering to the ancestors, often accompanied by prayers or invocations. The libation may be made with water, alcohol, or other substances, and may be poured onto the ground or onto a special altar or shrine.

Other ancestral rituals may involve offerings of food or other gifts, such as clothing or jewelry. These offerings are often made at specific times of the year, such as during harvest festivals or other seasonal celebrations.

The significance of ancestral rituals lies in their ability to establish a connection between the living and the dead. Through these rituals, the living are able to communicate with their ancestors, seeking their guidance and blessings in various aspects of life.

Ancestral Divination and the Use of Oracles in ATRs

Divination is an important aspect of many ATRs, and is often used to seek guidance from the ancestors. Ancestral divination typically involves the use of oracles or other divinatory tools, such as cowrie shells or tarot cards.

The diviner may enter into a trance state in order to communicate with the ancestors, or may interpret the patterns or symbols revealed by the divinatory tool. The ancestors are believed to speak through the diviner, offering guidance and insight into the challenges of life.

In some ATRs, specific ancestors may be invoked during divination, depending on the nature of the question or problem being addressed. For example, a question about health may be directed to a specific ancestor who is believed to have healing powers.

The use of divination and oracles in ATRs serves as a means of seeking guidance and direction from the ancestors. It is a way of accessing the spiritual knowledge and power that is believed to be available through the ancestors. It is also a way of maintaining a connection with the ancestors, and seeking their continued guidance and blessings.

Ancestral divination can take many forms, depending on the specific ATR and the divinatory tools used. In the Yoruba tradition of Nigeria, for example, the diviner may use a divining chain known as an opele or a divination board known as an Ifa tray. The diviner may also consult the Ifa oracle, a complex system of divination that involves the interpretation of 256 possible combinations of 16 palm nuts or cowrie shells.

In the Dagara tradition of Burkina Faso, divination is often performed using divining rods or the throwing of cowrie shells. The diviner may also enter into a trance state in order to communicate with the ancestors directly.

In the Shona tradition of Zimbabwe, divination is often performed using the mbira, a musical instrument that is believed to facilitate communication with the ancestors. The diviner may play specific songs or rhythms on the mbira, and interpret the patterns of notes and tones to gain insight into the question or problem at hand.

The use of divination and oracles in ATRs is often accompanied by ritual and ceremony. Before performing a divination, the diviner may make offerings to the ancestors, such as food, drink, or other gifts. The diviner may also invoke specific ancestors or spirits, and ask for their guidance and protection.

During the divination itself, the diviner may be accompanied by other members of the community, who may sing, dance, or provide other forms of support. After the divination, the diviner may offer thanks and praise to the ancestors, and may provide advice or guidance to the person seeking divination.

In conclusion, ancestral divination and the use of oracles are important aspects of many ATRs. These practices serve as a means of seeking guidance and direction from the ancestors, and of maintaining a connection with the spiritual world. Divination is often accompanied by ritual and ceremony, and may involve the use of specific divinatory tools and the invocation of specific ancestors or spirits. By seeking the guidance and wisdom of the ancestors through divination, practitioners of ATRs are able to draw upon the spiritual power and knowledge that has been passed down through the generations.

The Challenges of Preserving and Revitalizing Ancestral Practices in a Modern, Globalized World

As the world becomes increasingly interconnected, traditional ancestral practices are facing numerous challenges. The forces of urbanization, globalization, and modernization have led to the erosion of traditional values and the loss of ancestral knowledge. This chapter explores the impact of these forces on ancestral practices and the challenges of preserving and revitalizing them in a modern, globalized world.

The Impact of Urbanization, Globalization, and Modernization on Ancestral Practices

Urbanization, globalization, and modernization have brought about significant changes in the way people live, work, and interact with each other. These forces have led to the fragmentation of communities, the erosion of traditional values, and the loss of ancestral knowledge. As people move away from their ancestral homes to pursue better opportunities in urban centers, they often leave behind their traditional ways of life and the knowledge that has been passed down from generation to generation.

In addition, the spread of globalization and modernization has led to the homogenization of cultures around the world. As Western cultural values and practices are exported to other parts of the world, traditional ancestral practices are often marginalized and viewed as backward or primitive. This has led to a loss of cultural identity and a sense of disconnection from one's ancestral heritage.

The Erosion of Traditional Values and the Transmission of Ancestral Knowledge

The erosion of traditional values and the loss of ancestral knowledge are two of the biggest challenges facing the preservation and revitalization of ancestral practices. Traditional values provide a framework for understanding the world and one's place in it. They provide a sense of identity, belonging, and purpose. Without these values, ancestral practices can lose their meaning and significance.

At the same time, the transmission of ancestral knowledge from one generation to the next is essential for the preservation of ancestral practices. As younger generations become disconnected from their ancestral heritage, the knowledge and wisdom that have been passed down through the ages can be lost. This loss of knowledge can make it difficult to maintain and revitalize ancestral practices.

The Role of Education and Cultural Institutions in Preserving and Revitalizing Ancestral Practices

Education and cultural institutions play a critical role in the preservation and revitalization of ancestral practices. Education can help to promote an understanding of the importance of ancestral practices and the role they play in maintaining cultural identity and heritage. This can be done through the inclusion of ancestral practices in school curriculums, the creation of cultural centers and museums, and the promotion of traditional arts and crafts.

Cultural institutions can also play an important role in preserving and revitalizing ancestral practices. These institutions can provide a space for the transmission of ancestral knowledge and the celebration of ancestral practices. They can also provide support for the revival of traditional practices that have been lost or forgotten.

Examples of successful efforts to preserve and revitalize ancestral practices can be found in many parts of the world. For example, the Maori of New Zealand have successfully revitalized their ancestral practices through the establishment of cultural centers and the promotion of traditional arts and crafts. The Navajo of the United States have also been successful in preserving their ancestral practices through the use of storytelling and the transmission of knowledge from one generation to the next.

The preservation and revitalization of ancestral practices is essential for maintaining cultural identity and heritage. However, this task is becoming increasingly difficult in a modern, globalized world. The erosion of traditional values and the loss of ancestral knowledge are two of the biggest challenges facing the preservation and revitalization of ancestral practices. Education and cultural institutions can play a critical role in addressing these challenges and promoting the preservation and revitalization of ancestral practices.

New Forms of Religious Expression in Response to the Challenges of Preserving and Revitalizing Ancestral Practices

The preservation and revitalization of ancestral practices face numerous challenges in the modern, globalized world. These challenges have led to the emergence of new forms of religious expression that seek to adapt to the changing times while still maintaining a connection to ancestral traditions. In this section, we will explore the emergence of neo-traditional religions, the role of syncretism and hybridity in the evolution of ATRs, and the impact of social and political changes on the practice of ancestral religions.

The Emergence of Neo-Traditional Religions and Their Impact on Ancestral Practices

Neo-traditional religions are religious movements that seek to revive or reconstruct traditional beliefs and practices that have been lost or eroded over time. These movements often emerge in response to the challenges of modernization, globalization, and urbanization. They seek to preserve and revitalize ancestral practices while adapting to the changing times.

One example of a neo-traditional religion is the Orisha movement, which emerged in the United States in the 1950s and 1960s. The Orisha movement is a syncretic religion that combines elements of Yoruba religion, Catholicism, and other spiritual traditions. It seeks to revive the worship of the Orishas, deities from Yoruba religion, who were brought to the Americas by enslaved Africans.

The Orisha movement has had a significant impact on the practice of ancestral religions. It has helped to preserve and revitalize the worship of the Orishas, which had been suppressed or marginalized in many parts of the Americas. It has also inspired the emergence of other neo-traditional religions that seek to revive traditional practices in the face of modernization and globalization.

The Role of Syncretism and Hybridity in the Evolution of ATRs

Syncretism is the blending of different religious traditions or practices. It is a common feature of many ATRs, which often incorporate elements of other spiritual traditions. Syncretism can be seen as a form of cultural adaptation, as practitioners adapt to changing social and historical conditions.

Hybridity is the blending of different cultural traditions or identities. It is also a common feature of ATRs, which often incorporate elements of multiple cultures. Hybridity can be seen as a form of cultural creativity, as practitioners combine different cultural elements to create new forms of expression.

The role of syncretism and hybridity in the evolution of ATRs is complex and multifaceted. On the one hand, syncretism and hybridity can help to preserve and revitalize ancestral practices by adapting to changing conditions. On the other hand, they can also lead to the erosion of traditional practices by diluting or distorting them.

The Impact of Social and Political Changes on the Practice of Ancestral Religions

Social and political changes can have a significant impact on the practice of ancestral religions. For example, the spread of Christianity and Islam has often led to the suppression or marginalization of traditional practices. The process of colonization and the imposition of Western values and institutions has also had a profound impact on ancestral religions.

In response to these changes, many practitioners of ancestral religions have sought to adapt their practices to the changing times. They have created new forms of expression that incorporate elements of the dominant culture or that seek to challenge dominant values and institutions. For example, some practitioners have incorporated environmental activism into their spiritual practice, seeing it as a way to honor the ancestors and to protect the earth.

The challenges of preserving and revitalizing ancestral practices in a modern, globalized world are complex and multifaceted. They require practitioners to adapt to changing social and historical conditions while still maintaining a connection to ancestral traditions. The emergence of neo-traditional religions, the role of syncretism and hybridity, and the impact of social and political changes all play a significant role in shaping the future of ancestral religions.

Despite these challenges, many practitioners of ancestral religions remain committed to preserving and revitalizing their traditions. They recognize the importance of ancestral knowledge and wisdom, and seek to transmit this knowledge to future generations. They also recognize the need to adapt their practices to changing circumstances, and to find new ways to express their spirituality and connect with their ancestors.

Education and cultural institutions can play a critical role in this process. By providing access to information, resources, and training, these institutions can help to preserve and revitalize ancestral practices. They can also serve as a bridge between traditional practitioners and the wider society, helping to promote understanding and respect for ancestral traditions.

Ultimately, the preservation and revitalization of ancestral practices depends on the commitment and dedication of practitioners themselves. It requires a deep connection to the ancestors and a willingness to adapt to changing circumstances, while still maintaining a connection to the past. By working together, practitioners can ensure that ancestral traditions continue to thrive and evolve in the modern world.

The various meanings and interpretations of ancestors in different African cultures

Ancestry is a fundamental aspect of African cultures, and the concept of ancestors is deeply ingrained in the traditions and practices of many African societies. The meaning and interpretation of ancestors vary widely across different African cultures, reflecting the diversity of beliefs and practices within the continent. This section will provide an in-depth analysis of the various meanings and interpretations of ancestors in different African cultures, with a focus on the commonalities and differences between these beliefs and practices.

The Ancestral Realm in African Cosmology

In many African cultures, the ancestral realm is considered to be a parallel universe that exists alongside the physical world. This realm is inhabited by the spirits of ancestors who are believed to have the power to influence the lives of their living descendants. Ancestors are often revered and honored as powerful beings who have the ability to grant blessings, protect their descendants, and punish wrongdoers.

Ancestor Veneration and Ancestor Worship

Ancestor veneration and ancestor worship are common practices in many African cultures. In some cultures, ancestors are venerated as powerful spirits who must be honored and respected through the performance of rituals and offerings. In other cultures, ancestor worship involves the construction of shrines or altars dedicated to the ancestors, where offerings and prayers are made.

Ancestor veneration and worship take different forms across African cultures, reflecting the diverse beliefs and practices of each community. For example, in the Yoruba tradition of Nigeria, ancestors are believed to be intermediaries between the living and the divine. Ancestors are considered to be living beings who have transcended physical death and have become spiritual entities capable of guiding and supporting their descendants. Yoruba people believe that ancestors are able to intervene in the lives of their living relatives, and therefore, they are revered and honored through the performance of ceremonies and offerings.

Similarly, in the Akan culture of Ghana, ancestors are believed to be powerful spiritual beings who are responsible for maintaining the balance between the living and the dead. Ancestors are regarded as sources of wisdom, guidance, and protection, and they are honored through the performance of rituals and offerings. The Akan people believe that their ancestors continue to play an active role in the lives of their descendants and that they have the power to influence their fortunes.

Ancestor veneration and worship are not limited to West African cultures but are also found in other parts of the continent. For example, in the Zulu culture of South Africa, ancestors are believed to have the power to protect their living relatives from harm and to bless them with prosperity and good health. Ancestor veneration in the Zulu culture involves the performance of ceremonies and offerings, such as the slaughtering of an animal or the pouring of beer, to honor and appease the ancestors.

Ancestral Lineage and Identity

In many African cultures, ancestral lineage and identity are essential aspects of one's social and cultural identity. Ancestral lineage refers to one's genealogical heritage and the identification of one's ancestors. It is a way of tracing one's roots and understanding one's place in the larger community. Ancestral identity, on the other hand, is the sense of belonging and connection to one's ancestors and the community of descendants.

Ancestral lineage and identity are often expressed through the performance of rituals and ceremonies that affirm and celebrate one's connection to the ancestors. For example, in the Bamana culture of Mali, the Dama ceremony is a celebration of ancestral lineage and identity. The ceremony involves the construction of a large wooden structure that represents the ancestor's house, which is decorated with symbolic objects and offerings. The ceremony also involves the performance of songs, dances, and other rituals that celebrate the connection between the living and the dead.

Ancestor as Moral Guides

In many African cultures, ancestors are not only revered as powerful spiritual beings but also as moral guides who provide wisdom and guidance to their living descendants. Ancestors are believed to have lived exemplary lives and to have embodied the values and virtues that are considered essential to the community. Therefore, they are often invoked as models of ethical behavior and moral conduct.

For example, in the Igbo culture of Nigeria, ancestors are regarded as moral guides who provide guidance and counsel to their living descendants. Ancestors are believed to have lived virtuous lives and to have embodied the values of the community, such as honesty, integrity, and respect for elders. Therefore, they are revered and honored through the performance of ceremonies and offerings that acknowledge their moral authority.

The concept of ancestors holds significant importance in many African cultures, reflecting the importance of community, lineage, and identity. Ancestors are revered and honored as powerful spiritual beings who have the ability to influence the lives of their living descendants. Ancestor veneration and worship take different forms across African cultures, but they are often expressed through the performance of rituals and offerings that honor and appease the ancestors. Ancestors are also regarded as moral guides who provide wisdom and guidance to their living descendants and serve as models of ethical behavior and moral conduct. The multifaceted meanings and interpretations of ancestors in African cultures can be seen in their diverse religious practices, including divination, healing, and ritual.

Divination

Divination is an essential aspect of many African spiritual traditions, and the practice of divination is often used to communicate with the ancestors. Divination involves the use of various methods, such as throwing bones, reading shells, or interpreting dreams, to gain insight into the spiritual world and to seek guidance from the ancestors. The diviner acts as a mediator between the living and the ancestors, interpreting the messages received from the ancestors and communicating them to the living.

Healing

The ancestors are often seen as healers and protectors who have the power to cure illnesses and ward off evil spirits. Healing rituals and practices that involve the ancestors are common in many African cultures, and they often involve the use of herbs, roots, and other natural remedies. These remedies are believed to have spiritual properties that can heal both physical and spiritual ailments. The ancestors are also seen as protectors who can ward off evil spirits and negative energies, and they are often invoked for protection and to prevent harm.

Rituals

Rituals are an integral part of many African spiritual traditions, and they are often used to honor and appease the ancestors. These rituals can take various forms, such as offerings of food, drink, or other items, and they are performed at specific times and places, such as ancestral shrines or burial sites. The performance of these rituals is believed to strengthen the connection between the living and the ancestors and to ensure the well-being and prosperity of the community.

African Religions

The various meanings and interpretations of ancestors in different African cultures reflect the diversity and richness of African spiritual traditions. Ancestors are revered and honored as powerful spiritual beings who have the ability to influence the lives of their living descendants. Ancestor veneration and worship take different forms across African cultures, but they are often expressed through the performance of rituals and offerings that honor and appease the ancestors. The ancestors are also regarded as moral guides who provide wisdom and guidance to their living descendants and serve as models of ethical behavior and moral conduct. Divination, healing, and ritual are essential aspects of many African spiritual traditions, and they are often used to communicate with the ancestors, seek guidance and protection, and ensure the well-being and prosperity of the community.

The Role of Ancestors in Healing and Divination

In many African cultures, ancestors are believed to have the power to heal and to guide their living descendants. Healing rituals often involve the invocation of ancestral spirits and the use of herbs and other natural remedies. Divination practices also often involve the consultation of ancestors, who are believed to provide guidance and insight into the future.

Ancestors as Mediators and Intercessors

In many African cultures, ancestors are seen as mediators between the living and the divine. They are believed to have the power to communicate with the gods and to intercede on behalf of their living descendants. This role as mediators and intercessors is often reflected in the performance of rituals and offerings, which are made to both the ancestors and the gods.

Ancestral spirits are believed to possess the power to heal and guide their living descendants. Healing rituals often involve the invocation of ancestral spirits and the use of herbs and other natural remedies. The belief in ancestral spirits as healers is often linked to the idea that illness and disease are caused by spiritual imbalances or transgressions, and that the ancestors have the power to restore harmony and balance to the spiritual realm, thereby healing the physical body.

Divination practices also often involve the consultation of ancestors. Ancestors are believed to provide guidance and insight into the future and to help their living descendants navigate life's challenges. Divination practices can take many forms, including the interpretation of dreams, the use of divination tools such as cowrie shells or divining rods, and the consultation of oracles.

Exploring Origins, Traditions, and Contemporary Relevance

Ancestors and Identity

The concept of ancestry is often deeply connected to issues of identity in African cultures. Ancestors are seen as a source of cultural continuity and a link to the past, providing a sense of belonging and identity to their living descendants. Ancestors are also often associated with specific cultural practices and traditions, and their worship and veneration can serve as a means of preserving and transmitting these practices to future generations.

For example, in the Akan culture of Ghana, ancestors are believed to be a source of spiritual and moral guidance, as well as a source of identity and belonging. Ancestors are often associated with specific clans or lineages, and their worship and veneration help to reinforce a sense of belonging and identity within these groups.

Ancestors and Power

In many African cultures, ancestors are associated with power and authority. Ancestors are often revered as powerful beings who have the ability to influence the lives of their living descendants, and their worship and veneration can be seen as a means of tapping into this power. This association with power and authority is also reflected in the role of ancestors as mediators and intercessors, as well as in the performance of rituals and offerings, which are often made to seek the blessings and protection of the ancestors.

The meanings and interpretations of ancestors in different African cultures are diverse and complex, reflecting the rich and varied traditions of the continent. Ancestors are often seen as powerful beings who have the ability to influence the lives of their living descendants, and their worship and veneration are common practices across many African cultures. Ancestors are also deeply connected to issues of identity, power, and cultural continuity, and their role in healing, divination, and mediation reflects their importance in the spiritual and social lives of many African societies.

For example, in the Shona culture of Zimbabwe, ancestors are believed to have the power to bestow blessings and prosperity upon their living descendants. Ancestors are often invoked in rituals and offerings that are made to ensure the success of important endeavors such as marriages, births, and harvests. The belief in the power of ancestors is seen as a means of tapping into a source of strength and authority that transcends the limitations of the individual.

In conclusion, the meanings and interpretations of ancestors in different African cultures are diverse and complex, reflecting the rich and varied traditions of the continent. Ancestors are often seen as powerful beings who have the ability to influence the lives of their living descendants, and their worship and veneration are common practices across many African cultures. Ancestors are also deeply

Ancestors as Mediators and Intercessors

In many African cultures, ancestors are seen as mediators between the living and the divine. They are believed to have the power to communicate with the gods and to intercede on behalf of their living descendants. This role as mediators and intercessors is often reflected in the performance of rituals and offerings, which are made to both the ancestors and the gods.

For example, in the Yoruba religion of West Africa, ancestors are believed to serve as intermediaries between the living and the orishas, powerful deities who govern various aspects of the natural world. The ancestors are believed to have the ability to communicate with the orishas and to intercede on behalf of their living descendants. Offerings are made to both the ancestors and the orishas in order to honor and appease them and to seek their blessings and protection.

Comparison with the Western concept of ancestors

While the concept of ancestors is an important part of many African cultures, it is not as prominent in Western cultures. In Western societies, there is often a focus on individualism, and the role of ancestors in shaping one's identity and cultural heritage is not as central as it is in African cultures. However, there are still some similarities and differences between the way that ancestors are viewed in African cultures and in Western cultures.

One key difference between African and Western concepts of ancestors is the idea of the ancestor as a powerful spiritual being who can influence the lives of their living descendants. While there are some Western spiritual traditions that do acknowledge the existence of ancestors and the possibility of communicating with them, the idea of ancestors as powerful mediators between the living and the divine is not as prevalent in Western cultures as it is in African cultures.

Another difference between African and Western concepts of ancestors is the way that ancestors are honored and venerated. In many African cultures, ancestor veneration involves the construction of shrines or altars dedicated to the ancestors, where offerings and prayers are made. In contrast, Western cultures often do not have such specific practices for honoring ancestors. However, many Western cultures do have traditions of visiting gravesites, leaving flowers or other offerings, and holding memorial services to remember and honor deceased loved ones.

Despite these differences, there are also some similarities between African and Western concepts of ancestors. For example, both African and Western cultures often view ancestors as a source of cultural heritage and a link to the past. In Western cultures, this may be expressed through genealogy and family history research, as well as the passing down of family stories and traditions from generation to generation.

Another similarity is the idea that ancestors can provide guidance and wisdom to their living descendants. In both African and Western cultures, ancestors are often seen as moral guides who can offer insight and advice on how to live a good life. This can be seen in Western traditions such as the use of familial proverbs and sayings, as well as the concept of guardian angels in some religious traditions.

While there are both similarities and differences between African and Western concepts of ancestors, it is important to recognize that these concepts are shaped by different cultural traditions and worldviews. The role of ancestors in African cultures reflects the importance of community, lineage, and identity, while the role of ancestors in Western cultures is often shaped by individualism, personal identity, and cultural heritage.

Exercise: Compare and contrast the concept of ancestors in your own cultural heritage with the concept of ancestors in another culture. How are these concepts similar and different? What can we learn from exploring the different ways that cultures view their ancestors?

The role of ancestors in the cosmology of African religions

The role of ancestors in African religions is an integral part of the cosmology of these belief systems. Ancestors are seen as powerful spiritual beings who have the ability to influence the lives of their living descendants. They are revered and honored in various ways across different African cultures, with their worship and veneration being a central aspect of religious practices.

In many African religions, the universe is seen as a complex network of spiritual forces that are interconnected and interdependent. Ancestors are believed to be part of this network, with their influence and power being felt throughout the spiritual realm. Ancestors are often seen as intermediaries between the living and the divine, with their ability to communicate with the gods and to intercede on behalf of their living descendants.

The role of ancestors in African cosmology can be seen in various religious traditions and practices. For example, in Yoruba religion, ancestors are believed to be part of the "orisha" or deity system, with each ancestor having a specific role and function within the spiritual realm. In the Akan tradition, ancestors are seen as a link between the living and the divine, with their worship and veneration being a means of honoring the spiritual forces that sustain life.

Ancestors are also central to the concept of reincarnation in many African religions. The belief in reincarnation is based on the idea that the spirit of the deceased is reborn in a new body, often within the same family or lineage. Ancestors are therefore seen as continuing to play a role in the lives of their descendants, even after death.

The role of ancestors in African cosmology is also reflected in the performance of rituals and ceremonies. Ancestral worship and veneration often involve the use of offerings, such as food, drink, and other gifts, that are believed to appease the spirits of the ancestors and to ensure their continued blessings and protection. These rituals may also involve the use of music, dance, and other forms of artistic expression, which are seen as a means of connecting with the spiritual realm and honoring the ancestors.

One key aspect of the role of ancestors in African cosmology is their connection to identity and community. Ancestors are often associated with specific cultural practices and traditions, and their worship and veneration can serve as a means of preserving and transmitting these practices to future generations. Ancestors are also seen as a source of cultural continuity and a link to the past, providing a sense of belonging and identity to their living descendants.

In contrast to Western religious traditions, which often emphasize the individual's relationship with the divine, African religions tend to focus on the interconnectedness of all things within the spiritual realm. Ancestors are seen as part of this interconnected network, with their influence and power being felt throughout the spiritual realm. This holistic view of the universe is reflected in the role of ancestors in African cosmology, which emphasizes the importance of community, lineage, and identity.

Despite the importance of ancestors in African cosmology, there are also dissenting opinions and counterarguments. Some scholars have criticized the emphasis on ancestors as limiting and potentially harmful, as it may encourage a narrow focus on the past and a reluctance to embrace new ideas and perspectives.

Others argue that the emphasis on ancestors may promote a sense of fatalism and resignation, as it may suggest that one's destiny is predetermined by the actions of one's ancestors.

In conclusion, the role of ancestors in the cosmology of African religions is a complex and multifaceted concept. Ancestors are seen as powerful spiritual beings who have the ability to influence the lives of their living descendants, and their worship and veneration are central to many African religious practices. The role of ancestors in African cosmology reflects a holistic view of the universe that emphasizes the interconnectedness of all things, and their connection to issues of identity, community, and cultural continuity underscores their importance in African societies.

As we have seen, the role of ancestors in African religions is not limited to the individual or familial level, but extends to the community and even to the broader universe. Ancestors are believed to have a role in the maintenance of the natural world, and their worship and veneration are often closely linked to ecological concerns. In many African cultures, the health and well-being of the natural world are seen as being closely tied to the well-being of the ancestors, and the violation of natural resources and ecosystems is believed to incur the wrath of the ancestors.

Furthermore, the role of ancestors in African cosmology is not static but is dynamic and ever-evolving. As African societies continue to face new challenges and changes, the role of ancestors in these societies is also changing. For example, the impact of colonialism and the spread of Christianity and Islam have had a profound effect on African religious traditions, including the role of ancestors. In some cases, the worship and veneration of ancestors have been suppressed or even prohibited, while in other cases, they have been adapted and incorporated into the practices of these new religions.

Overall, the role of ancestors in the cosmology of African religions is a rich and complex concept that reflects the deep spiritual and cultural traditions of the continent. Ancestors are revered and honored as powerful spiritual beings who have the ability to influence the lives of their living descendants, and their worship and veneration are central to many African religious practices. The role of ancestors in African cosmology reflects a holistic view of the universe that emphasizes the interconnectedness of all things, and their connection to issues of identity, community, and cultural continuity underscores their importance in African societies.

Examples and case studies of ancestor veneration and ancestor worship in African cultures

The veneration and worship of ancestors is an integral part of African religions, and there are numerous examples and case studies of how this practice is carried out in different cultures across the continent. In this section, we will explore some of these examples and case studies to gain a better understanding of the diversity and complexity of ancestor veneration and worship in African cultures.

✧ Yoruba Religion

The Yoruba people of Nigeria, Benin, and Togo are well known for their complex religious system, which includes the worship of numerous deities and the veneration of ancestors. In Yoruba religion, ancestors are believed to be powerful spiritual beings who have the ability to influence the lives of their living descendants. They are seen as mediators between the living and the divine, and their worship is central to many Yoruba religious practices.

One example of ancestor veneration in Yoruba religion is the Egungun festival, which is held annually to honor the ancestors. During this festival, masked dancers (known as Egungun) perform rituals and dances to connect with the spirits of the ancestors. The Egungun are believed to be possessed by the spirits of the ancestors, and their performances are seen as a way to communicate with these spirits and seek their guidance and blessings.

Another example of ancestor worship in Yoruba religion is the practice of offering food and drink to ancestors on special occasions, such as weddings, funerals, and religious festivals. Offerings of food and drink are believed to appease the spirits of the ancestors and ensure their continued protection and guidance.

✧ Akan Religion

The Akan people of Ghana and Ivory Coast are known for their belief in a supreme being called Nyame and a pantheon of lesser deities known as Abosom. Ancestors are also an important part of the Akan religious system, and their worship is seen as a way to maintain a connection with the past and ensure the well-being of the community.

One example of ancestor veneration in Akan religion is the practice of pouring libations to ancestors. Libations are offerings of water, alcohol, or other liquids that are poured on the ground or into a container while prayers and invocations are offered to the ancestors. This practice is seen as a way to honor and connect with the ancestors and seek their guidance and blessings.

Another example of ancestor worship in Akan religion is the annual Odwira festival, which is held to purify the community and strengthen its connection to the ancestors. During this festival, offerings of food and drink are made to the ancestors, and rituals are performed to seek their blessings and protection.

✧ Zulu Religion

The Zulu people of South Africa are known for their rich cultural heritage, which includes a complex religious system that incorporates the veneration of ancestors. In Zulu religion, ancestors are believed to be powerful spiritual beings who have the ability to influence the lives of their living descendants.

One example of ancestor veneration in Zulu religion is the practice of offering sacrifices to the ancestors. Sacrifices may include animals such as goats or cattle, or they may consist of other offerings such as beer or tobacco. These offerings are believed to appease the spirits of the ancestors and ensure their continued protection and guidance.

Another example of ancestor worship in Zulu religion is the annual Umkhosi Wokweshwama festival, which is held to honor the ancestors and ensure their continued protection and blessings. During this festival, young men are circumcised as a rite of passage, and offerings of food and drink are made to the ancestors.

✧ Bantu Religion

The Bantu people of central and southern Africa are known for their rich cultural heritage, which includes a complex religious system that incorporates the veneration of ancestors. In Bantu religion, ancestors play a significant role in the spiritual and social lives of the people. The Bantu believe that their ancestors continue to exist in the spirit world and can influence the affairs of the living.

Ancestor veneration is a central practice in Bantu religion, and various rituals and ceremonies are performed to honor the ancestors. One such ritual is the pouring of libations, which involves pouring a liquid offering, such as water or palm wine, onto the ground or into a special vessel, while reciting prayers and invocations to the ancestors. This practice is believed to help establish a connection between the living and the ancestors, and to seek their guidance and blessings.

African Religions

The Bantu also believe that the ancestors can act as intermediaries between the living and the divine. For instance, in some Bantu cultures, it is believed that the ancestors can communicate with the supreme being or creator, and can intercede on behalf of the living in times of need. As such, ancestor veneration is seen as a way of accessing divine power and seeking protection and guidance.

In addition to libations, other rituals and ceremonies are performed to honor the ancestors, such as ancestor altars or shrines, where offerings of food, drink, and other items are made. The Bantu also observe certain festivals and holidays that are associated with ancestor veneration, such as the annual ancestor remembrance day, where families come together to honor their ancestors and seek their blessings.

The Bantu also believe that ancestors can cause harm if they are not properly venerated, and that they can inflict illnesses, misfortunes, and other problems on their living descendants. As such, ancestor veneration is seen as a way of maintaining the balance and harmony between the living and the spirit world, and of ensuring the well-being of the community.

One example of Bantu ancestor veneration is found in the religion of the Zulu people of South Africa. The Zulu believe that their ancestors have the power to protect them from harm, and that they can provide guidance and blessings to the living. Ancestor veneration is practiced through various rituals and ceremonies, such as the pouring of libations and the creation of ancestor altars. The Zulu also observe a holiday called Umkhosi Wokweshwama, where they offer sacrifices and prayers to the ancestors to seek their blessings for the upcoming year.

Another example of ancestor veneration in Bantu culture is found in the religion of the Yoruba people of Nigeria. In Yoruba religion, ancestor veneration is central to the practice of Ifa divination, a system of divination that involves the casting of cowrie shells and the interpretation of their patterns to gain insight into the future. Ancestors are seen as the guardians and custodians of Ifa knowledge, and their guidance and blessings are sought in the practice of divination.

In conclusion, ancestor veneration and worship are important practices in many African cultures, including the Bantu people of central and southern Africa. The veneration of ancestors reflects a deep respect for the spiritual and cultural heritage of the people, and is seen as a way of maintaining a connection between the living and the spirit world. Various rituals and ceremonies are performed to honor the ancestors, and their guidance and protection are sought in times of need. Examples from the Bantu people, such as the Zulu and the Yoruba, highlight the diversity and richness of ancestor veneration practices in Africa.

CHAPTER 17: THE ROLE OF ANCESTORS IN AFRICAN SOCIETIES AND THEIR PRACTICES

Ancestors play a central role in many African religions and societies. The veneration of ancestors is a widespread practice across the continent, with various cultures incorporating ancestor worship into their spiritual beliefs and practices. Ancestors are seen as powerful spiritual beings who have the ability to influence the lives of their living descendants, and their worship and veneration are central to many African religious practices. This chapter will explore the role of ancestors in African societies and their practices, providing a detailed analysis of their significance and impact.

In this chapter, we will first examine the historical and cultural context of ancestor veneration in Africa, providing a foundation for understanding the various practices and beliefs surrounding ancestor worship. We will explore the diversity of African cultures and their unique approaches to ancestor veneration, highlighting the similarities and differences between them.

We will then examine the role of ancestors in African cosmology, exploring how the veneration of ancestors reflects a holistic view of the universe that emphasizes the interconnectedness of all things. We will also examine the relationship between ancestors and other spiritual beings in African religions, such as deities, spirits, and the natural world.

Next, we will delve into the various practices and rituals associated with ancestor veneration, exploring the different ways in which ancestors are honored and celebrated across the continent. We will examine the significance of ancestor altars, offerings, and other rituals, as well as the importance of communal celebrations and festivals.

Finally, we will explore the significance of ancestor veneration in contemporary African societies, examining how it continues to play a vital role in the lives of many Africans today. We will examine the various challenges and controversies surrounding ancestor worship, such as its perceived conflict with Christianity and Islam, as well as its potential for abuse and exploitation.

Throughout this chapter, we will provide numerous examples, case studies, and exercises to illustrate the significance and complexity of ancestor veneration in

African Religions

African societies. These will include examples from a variety of fields, such as Witchcraft, Divination, Herbalism, Shamanism, and Ecospirituality, providing a broad and multifaceted understanding of the topic.

An overview of the different practices related to ancestors in African societies

Ancestors hold a significant place in African societies, and their practices are diverse and varied. While ancestor veneration is a common thread that runs through many African cultures, the ways in which it is practiced can differ vastly depending on the society, region, and time period. In this section, we will provide an overview of the different practices related to ancestors in African societies, highlighting their commonalities and differences.

Ancestor veneration can take many forms in African societies, and it can be practiced both individually and collectively. In some societies, ancestors are seen as benevolent protectors who are always looking out for their living descendants. In others, ancestors are feared and considered to have the potential to cause harm if they are not propitiated.

One of the most common practices related to ancestors in African societies is the use of ancestral shrines or altars. These shrines are often located in a prominent place within the household or community and are used to honor and appease the spirits of the ancestors. The shrine typically contains objects that are associated with the ancestors, such as photographs, personal items, and ritual objects. Offerings, such as food, drink, and incense, are also left at the shrine as a way of honoring the ancestors and seeking their protection and blessings.

Another common practice related to ancestors in African societies is ancestor worship. In some societies, ancestors are worshipped as gods, and temples or other sacred sites are dedicated to their worship. These sites may be visited by individuals or groups seeking to receive blessings, guidance, or protection from the ancestors. Ancestor worship can also involve the use of music, dance, and other forms of artistic expression as a way of communicating with the ancestors.

Divination is another practice related to ancestors in African societies. Divination is the practice of seeking guidance or knowledge from the spirits through a variety of methods, such as reading patterns in bones, shells, or cards. In many African societies, divination is closely tied to ancestor veneration, with ancestors being seen as a source of guidance and wisdom. Diviners are often consulted by individuals seeking guidance from their ancestors, and divination sessions may involve offerings and prayers to the ancestors.

Exploring Origins, Traditions, and Contemporary Relevance

In some African societies, ancestor veneration is closely tied to agricultural practices. Ancestors are seen as the guardians of the land, and offerings and rituals are performed to ensure a bountiful harvest. These practices may involve the planting of specific crops, such as yams, which are associated with ancestors, or the use of specific tools and implements that are believed to have been used by the ancestors.

Ancestor veneration is also common in African initiation ceremonies. Initiation ceremonies are rites of passage that mark the transition from childhood to adulthood and are often overseen by elder members of the community. Ancestors are seen as important guides and protectors during these ceremonies, and offerings and prayers are made to them to ensure a successful initiation.

Finally, ancestor veneration is often closely tied to the concept of ubuntu in African societies. Ubuntu is the belief in the interconnectedness of all things, and the idea that individuals are defined by their relationships with others. Ancestors are seen as an integral part of this interconnectedness, and their guidance and protection are believed to be essential for the well-being of the community as a whole.

In conclusion, ancestor veneration is a complex and multifaceted practice that holds a significant place in African societies. Ancestors are seen as powerful spiritual beings who have the ability to influence the lives of their living descendants, and their worship and veneration are central to many African religious practices. While the ways in which ancestor veneration is practiced can differ greatly depending on the society, region, and time period, the common thread that runs through all of these practices is the belief in the importance

Analysis of the different forms of ancestor worship, including offerings, libations, and ancestor altars

Ancestor worship takes many forms in African societies, and the specific practices vary depending on the culture and region. However, there are some common practices that are found across many African cultures, including offerings, libations, and ancestor altars.

Offerings are a way of showing respect and gratitude to one's ancestors. These offerings can take many forms, including food, drink, and other items that the ancestors are believed to enjoy. The offerings are often left at the ancestor's grave or at a sacred site associated with the ancestor.

In many African cultures, libations are a key part of ancestor worship. A libation is a ritual pouring of a liquid, usually water or alcohol, as an offering to the ancestors.

African Religions

The liquid is poured onto the ground or into a bowl or other container. The pouring of the liquid is accompanied by prayers or other rituals, which are believed to help connect the living with the spirits of the ancestors.

Ancestor altars are another important aspect of ancestor worship in many African cultures. An ancestor altar is a special space set aside for the veneration of ancestors. The altar may include pictures of the ancestors, candles, incense, and other items that are believed to be pleasing to the ancestors. Offerings are often left at the altar, and prayers and other rituals are performed in front of the altar.

The specific practices associated with ancestor altars vary depending on the culture and region. For example, in some African cultures, the altar is a simple wooden shelf or table, while in others, it may be a more elaborate structure made of stone or other materials.

One example of ancestor altars in African culture is the "minkisi" of the Kongo people in central Africa. Minkisi are sacred objects that are believed to be imbued with the power of the ancestors. They are often carved from wood and decorated with other materials such as shells, feathers, and animal hair. Minkisi are often used in healing rituals and other ceremonies, and are believed to have the power to protect individuals and communities from harm.

Another example of ancestor altars in African culture is the "bocio" of the Fon people in Benin. Bocio are wooden figures that are believed to be inhabited by the spirits of the ancestors. They are often carved with symbols and other images that are associated with the ancestor's power and authority. Bocio are used in various rituals, including those related to healing, protection, and justice.

Overall, offerings, libations, and ancestor altars are all important ways that African cultures show respect and veneration for their ancestors. These practices help to maintain a connection between the living and the dead, and ensure that the wisdom and knowledge of the ancestors are not lost.

The role of ancestors in social organization and community life in African societies

The role of ancestors in social organization and community life in African societies is multifaceted and complex. Ancestors are believed to play an important role in the daily lives of their descendants and are seen as active members of the community who continue to have an impact on the world of the living. In this section, we will explore the various ways in which ancestors are believed to influence social organization and community life in African societies.

Exploring Origins, Traditions, and Contemporary Relevance

Ancestors as Guardians of the Community

In many African societies, ancestors are seen as the guardians of the community, responsible for the well-being of their descendants. They are believed to have a special connection with the land and the spirits that inhabit it, and are thought to be able to intercede on behalf of the living in times of need. For example, if a community is suffering from a drought or a plague, the ancestors may be called upon to intervene and bring about a solution.

In some African societies, the ancestors are believed to be able to communicate directly with the living, either through dreams, visions, or other forms of spiritual contact. In these cases, the ancestors are seen as active participants in the daily lives of their descendants, offering guidance and protection as needed.

Ancestors as Moral Guides

Ancestors are also seen as important moral guides in African societies. They are believed to embody the virtues and values that the community holds dear, and are seen as examples to be followed by their descendants. In this way, the ancestors are thought to play a role in shaping the moral character of the community.

In some African societies, ancestors are also believed to be able to punish those who violate community norms and values. For example, if someone breaks a taboo or commits a crime, they may be visited by the ancestor in a dream or vision, or may suffer from a series of misfortunes that are seen as the result of the ancestor's displeasure.

Ancestors as Mediators

Ancestors are often seen as important mediators between the living and the spirit world. They are believed to be able to negotiate with the spirits and deities that govern the natural world, and may be called upon to intercede on behalf of their descendants in times of need.

In many African societies, offerings and sacrifices are made to the ancestors as a way of honoring their role as mediators. These offerings may take the form of food, drink, or other items that are believed to be pleasing to the ancestor.

African Religions

Ancestors as Keepers of Tradition

Finally, ancestors are often seen as the keepers of tradition in African societies. They are believed to embody the cultural values, beliefs, and practices of their community, and are seen as a link between the past and the present. In this way, the ancestors are thought to play a role in maintaining the cultural identity of the community.

In some African societies, ancestor veneration is seen as an important part of maintaining cultural continuity. For example, in the Yoruba religion of Nigeria, ancestors are believed to play a central role in the worship of the orishas, or deities, who are seen as the embodiment of the natural world. Ancestors are honored with offerings of food and drink, and are believed to play an active role in the lives of their descendants.

Exercises and Discussions:

Research and compare the role of ancestors in two different African societies, highlighting their similarities and differences.

Analyze the role of ancestors in shaping social organization and community life in African societies. What impact do they have on community norms and values?

Compare and contrast the different forms of ancestor worship, including offerings, libations, and ancestor altars, in two different African societies.

How has the role of ancestors changed over time in African societies? What factors have contributed to these changes?

The connection between ancestors and the natural world in African religions

The role of the natural world is central to African religions, including those that involve ancestor worship. In these religions, the natural world is seen as interconnected with the spiritual world, and the ancestors play a key role in maintaining this connection. In this section, we will explore the connection between ancestors and the natural world in African religions, including how the ancestors are believed to be present in the natural world and how this connection is expressed through rituals and beliefs.

Exploring Origins, Traditions, and Contemporary Relevance

The Connection Between Ancestors and the Natural World

In many African religions, the ancestors are believed to be present in the natural world in various ways. For example, they may be believed to inhabit certain natural features, such as rocks, trees, or bodies of water. In some cases, these features may be considered sacred, and offerings and other rituals may be performed at these sites to honor the ancestors and ask for their blessings.

Another way in which ancestors are believed to be present in the natural world is through the use of divination. Divination is a practice in which the diviner, often a priest or priestess, communicates with the spirits and ancestors to gain insight into a particular situation or question. Divination often involves the use of natural objects, such as shells, bones, or stones, which are believed to be imbued with spiritual power and are used to facilitate communication with the spiritual world.

The connection between ancestors and the natural world is also expressed through various rituals and beliefs. For example, many African religions include rituals that involve the use of natural materials, such as herbs, plants, and animal parts. These materials may be used in healing rituals, protective charms, or other forms of magic. In some cases, the use of these materials is believed to be a way of connecting with the ancestors and channeling their power.

Additionally, many African religions include beliefs about the importance of maintaining a harmonious relationship with the natural world. This may involve practices such as conservation, sustainable use of resources, and respect for the spirits that inhabit natural features. In some cases, the ancestors are believed to be the guardians of the natural world, and their blessing is seen as necessary for successful farming, hunting, or other activities that depend on the natural environment.

Rituals and Practices Related to the Natural World

One of the most common ways in which the connection between ancestors and the natural world is expressed in African religions is through the use of rituals and practices related to the natural world. These rituals may include offerings, libations, and other forms of tribute to the ancestors, as well as the use of natural materials in magic and divination.

Offerings are a common practice in many African religions, and they may be made to both living and ancestral spirits. Offerings may include food, drink, tobacco, or other materials that are believed to be pleasing to the spirits. In some cases, offerings may be made at natural features, such as rivers, trees, or rocks, which are believed to be inhabited by spirits or ancestors.

African Religions

Libations are another common practice in African religions, and they may be performed as a way of honoring the ancestors and asking for their blessings. Libations involve the pouring of liquid, such as water, wine, or palm oil, onto the ground or onto a special altar or shrine. The libation may be accompanied by prayers, songs, or other forms of communication with the ancestors.

The use of natural materials in magic and divination is also common in African religions. These materials may include herbs, plants, animal parts, and other natural objects that are believed to have spiritual power. In some cases, these materials may be used to make charms or talismans that are believed to protect the wearer or bring good fortune. In other cases, they may be used in healing rituals or to facilitate communication with the ancestors.

In conclusion, the role of ancestors in African religions is complex and multifaceted. Ancestral veneration is a central part of many African religious traditions and is believed to play a vital role in maintaining the spiritual and social well-being of the community. The ancestors are seen as intermediaries between the living and the divine, and their guidance and blessings are sought through various practices such as offerings, libations, and ancestor altars.

Ancestor altars serve as a physical space where the ancestors can be honored and offerings can be made. These altars are often decorated with symbolic objects and may be located in a prominent place within the home or community. Offerings to the ancestors may include food, drink, and other items that are believed to be pleasing to the spirits.

Libations are another common practice in African religions, and they involve the pouring of liquid as a way of honoring the ancestors and asking for their blessings. Libations are often accompanied by prayers, songs, or other forms of communication with the ancestors.

The connection between ancestors and the natural world is also an important aspect of African religions. Natural features such as rivers, trees, and rocks are believed to be inhabited by spirits or ancestors, and offerings may be made at these sites. The use of natural materials in magic and divination is also common, with herbs, plants, animal parts, and other objects being used for their spiritual power.

Overall, the practices related to ancestor worship in African societies are deeply ingrained in the cultural and spiritual traditions of these communities. Through offerings, libations, and other practices, the ancestors are seen as an integral part of the social organization and community life, providing guidance and blessings to the living and maintaining a connection to the divine.

Exercises and discussions on the ways in which ancestors shape the social and cultural practices of African societies

Exercises:

Write a research paper exploring the ways in which ancestors shape the social and cultural practices of African societies. Use at least three examples from different African cultures to illustrate your points.

Interview someone from an African culture that practices ancestor worship. Ask them about the role of ancestors in their culture and how this influences their daily life.

Imagine you are a member of an African community that practices ancestor worship. Write a journal entry describing how your ancestors have influenced your life and the choices you make.

Research the role of ancestors in African art and create a piece of art that honors your own ancestors.

Discussions:

How do you think the belief in ancestors influences the way African societies view death and the afterlife?

In what ways do you think ancestor worship helps to strengthen community ties in African societies?

How does the practice of ancestor worship in African religions compare to other forms of ancestor worship found in other parts of the world?

What challenges do African communities face in maintaining their cultural practices in a rapidly changing world, and how can these challenges be addressed?

How can non-African individuals respectfully engage with African ancestor worship traditions without appropriating or disrespecting these traditions?

In discussing these questions and engaging in these exercises, students can deepen their understanding of the ways in which ancestor worship shapes the social and cultural practices of African societies. These discussions can also help students explore the complexities of cultural exchange and appropriation, and the importance of respecting and preserving diverse cultural traditions.

CHAPTER 18: THE RELATIONSHIP BETWEEN LIVING INDIVIDUALS AND THEIR ANCESTORS

The relationship between living individuals and their ancestors is a topic of great importance in many African societies. Ancestors are believed to play a vital role in shaping the social and cultural practices of these societies, and their influence can be felt in a variety of ways.

In many African cultures, ancestors are believed to be the link between the living and the divine. They are considered to be powerful spiritual entities that have the ability to influence the lives of their descendants in both positive and negative ways. The relationship between living individuals and their ancestors is therefore a complex and dynamic one, shaped by a variety of cultural, social, and historical factors.

This chapter will explore the ways in which ancestors shape the social and cultural practices of African societies. We will examine the role of ancestors in African religions, as well as their influence on traditional social structures and family relationships. We will also discuss the various ways in which African societies honor and communicate with their ancestors, including through ritual practices, offerings, and divination.

Throughout this chapter, we will emphasize the diversity of African cultures and the many different ways in which the relationship between living individuals and their ancestors is expressed. We will also consider the ways in which this relationship has evolved over time, as African societies have undergone significant social, economic, and political changes.

Finally, we will examine the relevance of the relationship between living individuals and their ancestors in contemporary African societies, and the ways in which this relationship continues to shape the lives of millions of people on the continent today. Through a critical examination of the relationship between living individuals and their ancestors, we hope to provide students with a deeper understanding of the complex cultural and social dynamics that underpin African societies.

African Religions

The nature of the relationship between the living and their ancestors in African religions

In African religions, the ancestors play a central role in the lives of the living. The relationship between the living and their ancestors is complex and multifaceted, shaped by a range of cultural and social practices. Understanding this relationship is essential for understanding the role of the ancestors in African societies and the ways in which they continue to shape the lives of the living.

This chapter will explore the nature of the relationship between the living and their ancestors in African religions. We will examine the various ways in which the ancestors are believed to influence the lives of the living, as well as the practices that are used to maintain and strengthen this relationship. We will also consider the role that ancestors play in shaping the social and cultural practices of African societies, and the ways in which this relationship is expressed through art, music, and other forms of cultural expression.

The Influence of Ancestors on the Lives of the Living

In African religions, ancestors are believed to have a direct influence on the lives of the living. They are seen as intermediaries between the living and the spiritual realm, capable of interceding on behalf of their descendants and influencing the course of their lives. Ancestors are believed to be able to provide guidance, protection, and support to their living descendants, as well as to bring blessings and good fortune.

One of the most important ways in which ancestors are believed to influence the lives of the living is through their ability to communicate with them. It is believed that ancestors are able to communicate with their living descendants through dreams, visions, and other forms of spiritual communication. Through these channels, they may provide guidance, warn of impending danger, or offer comfort and reassurance.

Ancestors are also believed to be able to influence the physical world in various ways. They may protect their descendants from harm, or cause harm to befall their enemies. They may bring good fortune and prosperity, or cause misfortune and hardship. In some cases, they may even be able to intervene in the course of natural events, such as droughts, floods, or other disasters.

Practices for Maintaining and Strengthening the Relationship with Ancestors

Given the important role that ancestors play in African religions, it is essential to maintain and strengthen the relationship between the living and their ancestors.

Exploring Origins, Traditions, and Contemporary Relevance

There are a range of practices that are used to achieve this goal, including offerings, prayers, and other forms of communication with the ancestors.

One of the most common practices for maintaining the relationship with ancestors is the making of offerings. Offerings may be made to both living and ancestral spirits, and may include food, drink, tobacco, or other materials that are believed to be pleasing to the spirits. In some cases, offerings may be made at natural features, such as rivers, trees, or rocks, which are believed to be inhabited by spirits or ancestors.

Prayers and other forms of communication with the ancestors are also important for maintaining and strengthening the relationship between the living and their ancestors. These practices may involve speaking directly to the ancestors, or they may involve more formal rituals or ceremonies. In some cases, these rituals may involve the use of divination, such as the throwing of bones or the reading of patterns in natural materials, in order to communicate with the ancestors.

The Role of Ancestors in Shaping Social and Cultural Practices

In addition to their direct influence on the lives of the living, ancestors also play a significant role in shaping the social and cultural practices of African societies. Ancestors are often seen as the guardians of tradition and culture, and their wisdom and guidance are often invoked in the context of social and cultural practices.

One important example of this is in the context of initiation rites. Initiation rites are common in many African societies, and involve a range of practices designed to mark the transition from childhood to adulthood. These rites may include circumcision, scarification, or other physical markings, as well as education and instruction on social and cultural norms and values. The ancestors are often invoked during these rites, with the belief that their guidance and protection will help the initiates navigate the challenges of adulthood and maintain a connection to their cultural heritage.

Ancestors also play a role in shaping social and political structures in African societies. In some societies, for example, the ancestors are believed to have a direct influence on the selection of leaders and the resolution of disputes. Ancestors may be consulted through divination practices or through the mediation of traditional religious leaders, such as priests or priestesses. The ancestors may also be invoked in the context of community decision-making, with the belief that their wisdom and guidance can help to ensure that decisions are made in the best interests of the community as a whole.

African Religions

The influence of ancestors can also be seen in the arts and literature of African societies. Many traditional African stories and myths feature ancestors as central characters, often demonstrating the importance of respecting tradition and maintaining a connection to the past. Ancestor worship is also frequently depicted in African art, with representations of ancestral spirits often taking the form of masks, sculptures, or other visual art forms.

Overall, the relationship between the living and their ancestors in African religions is complex and multifaceted, with ancestors playing a significant role in shaping the lives and identities of individuals and communities. Through their ongoing presence and influence, ancestors help to maintain cultural traditions, provide guidance and protection, and shape social and political structures in African societies.

The ways in which ancestors communicate with the living, including dreams, visions, and divination

The belief in communication between the living and their ancestors is a central aspect of many African religions. Ancestors are believed to be accessible to the living in a variety of ways, including through dreams, visions, and divination. This section will explore the different ways in which ancestors are believed to communicate with the living in African religions.

Dreams

One of the most common ways in which ancestors are believed to communicate with the living is through dreams. Dreams are considered to be a portal through which the living can receive messages from the ancestors. In many African societies, dreams are seen as a sacred realm, a space where the ancestors can enter and communicate with the living. Dreams are often seen as a way for the ancestors to convey important messages to the living, including warnings, advice, and guidance.

In many African societies, there are specific rituals and practices that are designed to facilitate communication between the living and their ancestors through dreams. These may include fasting, prayer, meditation, or the use of specific herbs or other substances. Dreams are often interpreted by trained diviners or spiritual leaders, who can help to decode the messages contained within them. Dreams are also seen as a way for the ancestors to provide healing to the living, whether through physical or emotional means.

Exploring Origins, Traditions, and Contemporary Relevance

Visions

In addition to dreams, visions are another way in which ancestors are believed to communicate with the living in African religions. Visions are typically more intense and vivid than dreams, and are often seen as a direct communication from the ancestors. Visions may come in a variety of forms, including waking visions, trance states, or other altered states of consciousness.

Visions are often seen as a way for the ancestors to provide specific guidance or advice to the living. For example, a vision may reveal the location of a lost object or provide insight into a particular problem or situation. Visions may also be used to impart knowledge or wisdom to the living, such as in the case of a vision that reveals a new healing remedy or spiritual practice.

Divination

Divination is another important way in which ancestors are believed to communicate with the living in African religions. Divination is a practice that involves seeking guidance or insight from the ancestors through a range of different techniques, including the casting of lots, the use of oracle cards or other divinatory tools, or the interpretation of signs and symbols.

Divination is typically performed by trained spiritual practitioners, who have received extensive training in the art of divination. These practitioners may be known as diviners, seers, or spiritual advisors, and are often highly respected members of their communities. Divination may be used to address a wide range of issues, including matters of health, relationships, finances, and spiritual growth.

In conclusion, the belief in communication between the living and their ancestors is a central aspect of many African religions. Ancestors are believed to communicate with the living in a variety of ways, including through dreams, visions, and divination. These forms of communication are often seen as a way for the ancestors to provide guidance, advice, and healing to the living. Through these forms of communication, the ancestors are able to remain an active and vital part of the lives of the living, shaping their beliefs, practices, and worldviews.

The importance of maintaining a positive relationship with ancestors for spiritual and material wellbeing

In African traditional religions, maintaining a positive relationship with ancestors is considered crucial for both spiritual and material wellbeing. Ancestors are believed to have the power to influence the fortunes of their living descendants, and therefore, honoring and appeasing them is seen as essential for ensuring a harmonious and prosperous life.

Spiritual Wellbeing:

In many African traditional religions, ancestors are seen as the intermediaries between the living and the divine. They are believed to have a direct line of communication with the gods and goddesses, and can therefore intercede on behalf of their living descendants. In this sense, ancestors are seen as spiritual guardians who offer protection, guidance, and blessings to those who honor and respect them.

To maintain a positive relationship with ancestors, African traditional religions often involve rituals and offerings that are designed to appease and honor the ancestors. For example, libations are often poured to the ancestors as a way of offering them gifts and showing respect. Ancestor altars are also common in many African cultures, where offerings such as food, drink, and flowers are placed as a way of honoring and communicating with the ancestors.

In addition to these offerings, maintaining a positive relationship with ancestors also involves living a life that is in accordance with their teachings and values. Ancestors are seen as the keepers of tradition and culture, and therefore, following their guidance and wisdom is seen as a way of maintaining a spiritual connection with them.

Material Wellbeing:

In addition to spiritual wellbeing, maintaining a positive relationship with ancestors is also seen as essential for material wellbeing. Ancestors are believed to have the power to influence the material fortunes of their living descendants, and therefore, appeasing them is seen as a way of ensuring prosperity and abundance.

For example, in many African cultures, ancestors are believed to be able to bring rain and fertility to the land. Therefore, honoring the ancestors through rituals and offerings is seen as a way of ensuring a bountiful harvest and good health for both people and animals.

Similarly, ancestors are also believed to have the power to protect their living descendants from harm and misfortune. By maintaining a positive relationship with them, it is believed that the ancestors will intervene on behalf of their living descendants in times of need, providing them with the protection and guidance they need to overcome adversity.

Exploring Origins, Traditions, and Contemporary Relevance

In conclusion, the importance of maintaining a positive relationship with ancestors in African traditional religions cannot be overstated. Ancestors are seen as spiritual guardians who offer protection, guidance, and blessings to those who honor and respect them, and their influence extends to both spiritual and material wellbeing. Through rituals and offerings, as well as by living a life in accordance with their teachings and values, the living are able to establish and maintain a deep and meaningful connection with their ancestors, ensuring their continued guidance and support in all aspects of life.

Case studies and examples of ancestor communication in African cultures

The ways in which ancestors communicate with the living are diverse and multifaceted, and they vary widely from culture to culture. In this section, we will explore some case studies and examples of ancestor communication in African cultures, highlighting the various ways in which ancestors can be contacted and the significance of these interactions for the living.

Example 1: The Dagara People of Burkina Faso

The Dagara people of Burkina Faso in West Africa have a rich and complex system of ancestor veneration and communication. They believe that the ancestors are always present and available to offer guidance and support to the living. Ancestors are considered to be part of a collective wisdom that spans generations and helps to guide the community in all aspects of life, from agriculture to healing to relationships.

One way in which the Dagara communicate with their ancestors is through divination. The Dagara use a divination system called throwing the bones, which involves casting a set of small objects onto a special mat or cloth. The way in which the objects fall and interact with one another is interpreted by a diviner, who is trained to understand the language of the ancestors. The ancestors are believed to speak through the bones, offering guidance and insight into the questions and concerns of the living.

Another way in which the Dagara communicate with their ancestors is through ritual and ceremony. The Dagara hold regular ceremonies to honor the ancestors and ask for their guidance and support. These ceremonies involve offerings of food and drink, as well as dancing, drumming, and chanting. Through these rituals, the living are able to connect with the ancestors and receive their blessings.

Example 2: The Yoruba People of Nigeria

The Yoruba people of Nigeria have a rich tradition of ancestor veneration and communication. Ancestors are considered to be powerful spiritual beings who can offer guidance, protection, and blessings to the living. The Yoruba believe that ancestors are able to communicate with the living through dreams, visions, and divination.

Dreams are considered to be a particularly important way in which the ancestors communicate with the living. The Yoruba believe that dreams are a portal through which the ancestors can enter the consciousness of the living and offer guidance and advice. Dreams are often interpreted by a diviner, who is trained to understand the symbolic language of the ancestors. The Yoruba also believe that ancestors can visit the living in waking visions, offering guidance and support.

Divination is another important way in which the Yoruba communicate with their ancestors. The Yoruba use a divination system called Ifa, which involves casting a set of palm nuts onto a special tray and interpreting the way in which they fall. Ifa is considered to be a sacred knowledge system that is passed down through generations, and the Yoruba believe that it contains the wisdom of the ancestors. Through Ifa, the living are able to connect with their ancestors and receive their guidance and support.

Example 3: The Akan People of Ghana

The Akan people of Ghana have a rich tradition of ancestor veneration and communication. Ancestors are considered to be powerful spiritual beings who can offer guidance and protection to the living. The Akan believe that ancestors are able to communicate with the living through dreams, visions, and divination.

One way in which the Akan communicate with their ancestors is through libation. Libation involves pouring a liquid offering, such as water, palm wine, or gin, onto the ground as a way of honoring and connecting with the ancestors. The pouring of the libation is accompanied by prayers and invocations, asking for the ancestors' blessings and guidance.

Another way in which the Akan communicate with their ancestors is through divination. The Akan use a form of divination known as Afa or Akan-Kete, which involves the use of palm nuts or seeds. The diviner shakes the palm nuts or seeds, interpreting their patterns and configurations to receive messages from the ancestors. The messages may be related to personal issues, such as health or financial matters, or to broader concerns, such as the well-being of the community.

Exploring Origins, Traditions, and Contemporary Relevance

In addition to libation and divination, the Akan also believe that ancestors can communicate with the living through dreams and visions. Dreams are seen as a powerful means of communication between the living and the spiritual realm, and the Akan believe that dreams can convey important messages from the ancestors. For example, a dream in which an ancestor appears may be interpreted as a message of guidance or warning, and the dreamer may seek the advice of a diviner to help interpret the dream.

The Akan also have a strong tradition of ancestor worship, with each family maintaining a shrine or altar to honor their ancestors. Offerings of food and drink are made to the ancestors, and prayers and songs are offered as a way of maintaining a positive relationship with them. The ancestors are seen as an important source of guidance and protection, and their wisdom and knowledge are valued as a means of navigating the challenges of life.

Overall, the examples of ancestor communication in African cultures highlight the important role that ancestors play in the spiritual and material wellbeing of the living. Through dreams, visions, divination, and other practices, ancestors are able to offer guidance, protection, and blessings to those who seek their assistance. By maintaining a positive relationship with their ancestors, individuals and communities are able to tap into a powerful source of spiritual and cultural wisdom that has been passed down through generations.

Exercises and discussions on the relationship between the living and their ancestors and how to foster positive connections

The relationship between the living and their ancestors is an important aspect of many cultures around the world. Ancestors are often seen as powerful spiritual beings who can offer guidance, protection, and blessings to the living. In this section, we will explore some exercises and discussions on how to foster a positive connection with one's ancestors and build a strong and healthy relationship.

Exercise 1: Ancestor Altar

Creating an ancestor altar is a powerful way to honor and connect with one's ancestors. An ancestor altar is a space where one can place objects, pictures, or other items that represent their ancestors. This altar can be as simple or elaborate as one desires, and can include items such as candles, incense, flowers, crystals, or other sacred objects.

To begin this exercise, find a quiet and sacred space where you can create your ancestor altar. Take some time to reflect on your ancestors and think about what items or objects would represent them. Gather these items and place them on your altar in a way that feels meaningful and respectful. As you create your altar, you can also speak to your ancestors and ask for their guidance, blessings, and protection.

Once your ancestor altar is complete, spend some time each day sitting in front of it and meditating on your ancestors. You can light candles, burn incense, or offer prayers as a way of honoring and connecting with them. Over time, you may find that your connection with your ancestors deepens and becomes more powerful.

Discussion 1: Honoring Ancestors in Different Cultures

In this discussion, we will explore how different cultures honor their ancestors and what practices they use to connect with them. This discussion can be done in a group setting, with each person sharing their own cultural traditions and practices.

To begin the discussion, ask each person to share a practice or tradition from their culture that honors ancestors. This can include things like ancestor altars, ancestor veneration ceremonies, or offerings of food or drink. As each person shares, take note of the similarities and differences between the practices and how they relate to the culture and history of each group.

After everyone has shared, discuss what you learned and what stood out to you about the different practices. Ask questions and encourage everyone to share their thoughts and feelings about the importance of ancestor veneration in their own culture.

Exercise 2: Ancestor Meditation

Meditating on one's ancestors is a powerful way to connect with them and receive guidance and wisdom. In this exercise, we will explore how to do an ancestor meditation.

To begin, find a quiet and peaceful space where you will not be interrupted. Sit in a comfortable position and close your eyes. Take a few deep breaths and allow yourself to relax.

Visualize yourself in a peaceful and serene place, such as a garden or a forest. Imagine that you are surrounded by a loving and supportive energy.

Now, visualize one of your ancestors coming to you. This can be a grandparent, great-grandparent, or other ancestor that you feel connected to. Allow yourself to feel their presence and their love.

Ask your ancestor a question or seek guidance on a particular issue. Listen to their response and allow yourself to receive their wisdom and guidance.

When you are ready, thank your ancestor for their guidance and love. Return to the present moment and take a few deep breaths before opening your eyes.

Discussion 2: Overcoming Ancestral Trauma

In this discussion, we will explore how to overcome ancestral trauma and heal ancestral wounds. Ancestral trauma refers to the pain, suffering, and trauma that has been passed down through generations, often as a result of systemic oppression, violence, or other forms of injustice.

To begin the process of healing ancestral trauma, it is important to acknowledge the trauma that exists within your ancestral lineage. This involves recognizing the ways in which your ancestors may have experienced trauma and how this trauma has been passed down to you. This recognition can be achieved through various means, such as meditation, dreamwork, or working with a therapist or spiritual healer.

Once you have acknowledged the existence of ancestral trauma, the next step is to begin the process of healing. This involves creating a safe space to process and release the trauma, and working on cultivating a positive relationship with your ancestors.

One way to create a safe space for healing ancestral trauma is through ritual or ceremony. This can involve setting up an altar or sacred space dedicated to your ancestors, and performing rituals or ceremonies to honor and connect with them. Lighting candles, burning incense, or offering flowers or other offerings can help create a sacred and respectful environment.

Another way to begin the process of healing ancestral trauma is through creative expression. Writing, painting, dancing, or other forms of artistic expression can help you to connect with and process your emotions and experiences related to ancestral trauma.

It is also important to work on cultivating a positive relationship with your ancestors. This involves recognizing the positive qualities and strengths of your ancestors, and honoring and celebrating their contributions to your life. You can do this by researching your ancestral lineage, learning about your ancestors' culture and traditions, and incorporating these traditions into your own life.

In addition to these practices, it can be helpful to work with a therapist or spiritual healer to process and heal ancestral trauma. A trained professional can help you to identify and work through the emotions and experiences related to ancestral trauma, and provide guidance and support throughout the healing process.

Discussion Questions:

How have you experienced ancestral trauma in your life? What steps have you taken to acknowledge and heal this trauma?

How do you cultivate a positive relationship with your ancestors? What practices or rituals do you engage in to honor and connect with your ancestors?

Have you worked with a therapist or spiritual healer to process and heal ancestral trauma? If so, what was your experience like? If not, what barriers have prevented you from seeking this type of support?

Exercise:

Create a ritual or ceremony to honor and connect with your ancestors. Set up an altar or sacred space dedicated to your ancestors, and perform a ritual or ceremony to honor and connect with them. This can involve lighting candles, burning incense, or offering flowers or other offerings. Write about your experience and reflect on how this practice has helped you to cultivate a positive relationship with your ancestors.

CHAPTER 19: ANCESTRAL VENERATION AND ITS SIGNIFICANCE IN AFRICAN RELIGIONS

Ancestral veneration is a significant aspect of African religions. It is a practice that involves honoring, communicating with, and seeking guidance from one's ancestors. Ancestors are believed to be powerful spiritual beings who have a vested interest in the lives of their descendants. African cultures view ancestors as an important link between the living and the divine. In this chapter, we will explore the significance of ancestral veneration in African religions and how it impacts the daily lives of its practitioners.

Historical Context

Ancestral veneration has been practiced in African cultures for thousands of years. It is deeply rooted in the belief that the ancestors continue to exist in the spiritual realm and that they can influence the lives of their descendants. The practice of ancestral veneration is often linked to traditional African religions, which have been practiced for centuries across the African continent. These religions were typically animistic in nature, meaning that they believed that everything in nature possessed a spiritual essence, including animals, plants, and even rocks.

When colonialism swept across the African continent in the 19th and 20th centuries, traditional African religions were suppressed and, in many cases, outlawed by colonial powers. Christianity and Islam became dominant religions, and many Africans converted to these new faiths. However, the practice of ancestral veneration persisted, and it continues to be an important aspect of African cultures and religions today.

Significance of Ancestral Veneration

Ancestral veneration is significant in African religions for a number of reasons. Firstly, it is a way of honoring and showing respect to one's ancestors. African cultures believe that the ancestors are powerful spiritual beings who have the ability to influence the lives of their descendants. By honoring the ancestors, practitioners hope to gain their favor and blessings.

Secondly, ancestral veneration is a way of connecting with the past. In many African cultures, the ancestors are viewed as a link between the living and their history. They are seen as keepers of tradition, and their wisdom and knowledge are passed down through generations. Through ancestral veneration, practitioners can tap into this wisdom and gain a better understanding of their cultural heritage.

Thirdly, ancestral veneration is a way of seeking guidance and protection. African cultures believe that the ancestors have the ability to communicate with the living and offer guidance and protection. Through rituals and offerings, practitioners can establish a relationship with their ancestors and seek their advice and protection in times of need.

Practices of Ancestral Veneration

The practices of ancestral veneration vary across different African cultures and religions. However, there are some common practices that are shared among many of them. One such practice is the offering of food, drink, and other items to the ancestors. This can be done through rituals such as libation, where a liquid offering is poured onto the ground as a way of connecting with the ancestors. Offerings can also be made at ancestral shrines or gravesites.

Another common practice is divination, which is the use of ritual and other methods to communicate with the ancestors. Divination can take many forms, such as the use of oracle bones, tarot cards, or other divinatory tools. Practitioners may also consult with diviners, who have the ability to communicate with the ancestors and provide guidance to the living.

Ancestral veneration is a significant aspect of African religions. It is a practice that honors the ancestors, connects practitioners with their cultural heritage, and seeks guidance and protection from the spiritual realm. Although the practice of ancestral veneration has faced many challenges throughout history, it continues to be an important aspect of African cultures and religions today. By understanding the significance of ancestral veneration, we can gain a better understanding

The significance of ancestor veneration in African religions

Ancestor veneration is a significant aspect of African religions. It is a practice that involves honoring and communicating with deceased ancestors as spiritual beings who continue to play a role in the lives of the living. Ancestors are believed to possess wisdom, guidance, and protection that can be accessed by their living descendants. In this chapter, we will explore the significance of ancestor veneration in African religions and how it is practiced in different cultures.

Exploring Origins, Traditions, and Contemporary Relevance

Historical Background

Ancestor veneration is an ancient practice that dates back to pre-colonial times in Africa. It was a prominent aspect of traditional African religions and played a crucial role in shaping the social, cultural, and political life of African societies. Ancestors were seen as mediators between the living and the divine, and their spiritual presence was believed to be essential for maintaining harmony and balance in the community. Ancestral worship was also a way of preserving the collective memory and identity of a people and reinforcing their cultural traditions.

With the arrival of colonialism and the spread of Christianity and Islam, the practice of ancestor veneration was suppressed and demonized as pagan and primitive. However, in recent years, there has been a revival of interest in ancestral traditions and a recognition of their value and relevance in contemporary African societies. Ancestor veneration is now practiced alongside other religious traditions and has become an important aspect of cultural heritage and identity.

Concepts and Beliefs

The concept of ancestor veneration is based on the belief in the continuity of life and the interconnectedness of the living and the dead. Ancestors are believed to have transcended the physical world and entered into the spiritual realm, where they continue to exist as powerful beings who can influence the course of events in the world. They are regarded as intermediaries between the living and the divine and are believed to have the ability to communicate with both.

Ancestors are also believed to have specific roles and responsibilities within the community. They are considered to be guardians of family, lineage, and community values and are believed to have the power to bless or curse their descendants depending on their behavior. Ancestors are also believed to have knowledge and wisdom that can be accessed by their descendants and used to solve problems, make decisions, and improve their lives.

Practices and Rituals

The practice of ancestor veneration varies across different African cultures and religions. However, there are some common elements that are found in many traditions. One of the most common practices is the use of altars or shrines to honor the ancestors. These shrines are usually located in the home or a designated sacred space and are adorned with images of the ancestors, offerings, and other sacred objects.

African Religions

Another common practice is the use of libations to communicate with the ancestors. Libations involve pouring a liquid offering, such as water, wine, or milk, onto the ground as a way of honoring and connecting with the ancestors. The pouring of the libation is accompanied by prayers and invocations, asking for the ancestors' blessings and guidance.

Divination is another important practice that is used to communicate with the ancestors. In many African traditions, divination involves the use of objects such as cowrie shells, stones, or bones, which are cast or thrown to reveal messages from the ancestors. Divination is often used to seek guidance on important matters such as health, relationships, and business.

Drumming, dancing, and other forms of music and movement are also commonly used in ancestral rituals. These practices are believed to facilitate communication with the ancestors and to invite their presence into the ceremony. In many African cultures, the ancestors are believed to communicate through music and dance, and these practices are used to invoke their spirits and honor their presence.

Significance and Benefits of Ancestor Veneration

The practice of ancestor veneration is highly valued in African religions and cultures, and for good reason. Ancestor veneration serves many important purposes, both on a personal and societal level.

One of the primary benefits of ancestor veneration is the sense of connection and belonging it provides. By honoring and communicating with our ancestors, we acknowledge and affirm our roots and our place within the larger community. This can be especially important for individuals who have been displaced or disconnected from their ancestral cultures due to colonialism, migration, or other factors.

Ancestor veneration also serves as a means of preserving and transmitting cultural knowledge and traditions. Through the stories, teachings, and experiences of our ancestors, we gain insight into the values and practices that have shaped our communities over time. By passing down these traditions to future generations, we ensure their continuity and relevance.

In addition to fostering a sense of connection and cultural continuity, ancestor veneration also has important spiritual benefits. By honoring and communicating with our ancestors, we tap into a powerful source of wisdom, guidance, and protection. The ancestors are believed to possess knowledge and understanding that transcends our individual lifetimes, and can offer valuable insight and perspective on the challenges and opportunities we face in our lives.

Finally, ancestor veneration serves an important social function in many African cultures. By honoring and caring for the ancestors, we demonstrate our commitment to the well-being of our communities and our interdependence with others. This can help to foster a sense of solidarity and mutual support that is essential for building resilient and thriving communities.

Conclusion

Ancestor veneration is a rich and multifaceted practice that plays a vital role in African religions and cultures. By honoring and communicating with our ancestors, we gain a deeper understanding of ourselves, our communities, and our place within the larger cosmos. Through practices such as shrines, libations, divination, and music and movement, we create a sacred space in which we can connect with the ancestors and receive their guidance and blessings. Ancestor veneration serves as a powerful reminder of our interdependence with others and our responsibility to care for the well-being of our communities and the world around us.

The role of ancestors in spiritual protection and guidance

The belief in ancestral spirits is a common feature of many spiritual traditions around the world, and it is particularly prominent in African religions. Ancestors are often viewed as powerful spiritual beings who can offer protection and guidance to their living descendants. In this section, we will explore the role of ancestors in spiritual protection and guidance in African religions.

Protection from Ancestral Spirits

In many African cultures, it is believed that ancestors can offer protection to their living descendants. Ancestors are believed to have the power to intervene in the lives of their living relatives, and to offer protection from harm and danger. This belief is often expressed through the use of amulets and charms, which are believed to be imbued with the protective power of the ancestors.

Amulets and Charms

Amulets and charms are objects that are believed to have magical powers, and they are often used in African religions as a form of protection. These objects can take many different forms, such as beads, stones, shells, or animal parts, and they are often worn on the body or carried in a bag or pouch.

In some African cultures, amulets and charms are specifically associated with the ancestors. For example, in the Yoruba tradition of Nigeria, it is common to wear beads that are believed to be imbued with the power of one's ancestors. These beads are often worn as a form of protection, and they are believed to connect the wearer with their ancestral spirits.

In other cultures, amulets and charms may be associated with specific spirits or deities. For example, in the Akan tradition of Ghana, it is common to wear amulets that are associated with the abosom, or spirits, who are believed to offer protection and guidance to their worshippers.

Divination and Guidance from Ancestral Spirits

Another important role of ancestors in African religions is to offer guidance and wisdom to their living descendants. Ancestors are believed to have a deep understanding of the human experience, and they are often consulted through divination to offer advice and guidance on important matters.

Divination is a complex system of spiritual communication that is used to seek answers to important questions and to gain insight into the future. Divination is often conducted by a trained practitioner, who may use a variety of tools and methods to communicate with the spirits, including casting cowrie shells, interpreting dreams, or using a divination board.

In many African traditions, the ancestors are believed to be particularly skilled at divination. Ancestors are believed to have a deep understanding of the human condition, and they are often consulted through divination to offer advice and guidance on important matters such as health, relationships, and business.

In some cases, ancestors may also communicate with their living descendants through dreams or visions. It is believed that the ancestors may visit their living relatives in their dreams, offering guidance and wisdom on important matters.

The Importance of Ancestral Connection

The belief in ancestral spirits and the practice of ancestor veneration is deeply rooted in many African cultures. Ancestral connection is viewed as a vital component of spiritual wellbeing, and it is believed that a strong connection with one's ancestors can offer protection, guidance, and blessings.

In many African cultures, it is believed that the ancestors continue to play an active role in the lives of their living descendants, and that they are deeply invested in the wellbeing of their families and communities. Ancestral connection is viewed as a reciprocal relationship, with the living offering offerings and prayers to the ancestors in exchange for their protection and guidance.

Ancestor veneration is a central feature of many African religions, and it plays a significant role in spiritual protection and guidance. Ancestors are viewed as powerful spiritual beings who can offer protection from harm and guidance on important matters. The belief in ancestral protection is deeply ingrained in many African cultures and religions, and it has been passed down through generations as a way of preserving cultural identity and spiritual heritage.

The practices and rituals associated with ancestor veneration are diverse and varied across different African cultures and religions, but they all share a common goal of honoring and connecting with the ancestors. The use of altars or shrines, libations, divination, and music and movement are just a few examples of the many ways in which ancestors are honored and communicated with.

In addition to providing spiritual protection and guidance, ancestor veneration also serves as a way of fostering community and social cohesion. The practice of honoring ancestors is often a collective effort that involves the entire community, and it serves as a way of strengthening social ties and reinforcing shared values and beliefs.

Overall, the practice of ancestor veneration is a powerful and important aspect of many African religions. It provides a way of connecting with the past, honoring one's ancestors, and seeking spiritual guidance and protection. As such, it remains a vital part of African spiritual heritage and cultural identity, and it continues to be practiced and celebrated by many people around the world today.

The connection between ancestor veneration and other spiritual practices, such as divination and healing

The practice of ancestor veneration is often connected to other spiritual practices, such as divination and healing. In many African cultures, the ancestors are believed to be powerful spiritual beings who can offer guidance, protection, and healing to their living descendants. As such, ancestor veneration is often integrated into other spiritual practices as a way of connecting with the ancestors and seeking their guidance and assistance.

Divination is one of the most common spiritual practices that is closely connected to ancestor veneration. Divination involves the use of various methods to communicate with the spiritual realm and seek guidance on important matters such as health, relationships, and business. In many African cultures, divination is believed to be a way of communicating with the ancestors, who are believed to be able to offer guidance and wisdom through the messages revealed during divination. For example, in the Yoruba religion of Nigeria, divination is performed using a system of cowrie shells known as Ifa, and it is believed that the messages revealed during divination are messages from the Orishas, the spiritual beings who represent the ancestors.

Another practice that is closely connected to ancestor veneration is healing. In many African cultures, the ancestors are believed to have the power to heal and protect their descendants from illness and disease. As such, healing practices often involve the invocation of the ancestors and the use of rituals and offerings to honor and connect with them. For example, in the Zulu culture of South Africa, traditional healers known as Sangomas use divination and herbal remedies to diagnose and treat illnesses. The ancestors are believed to guide and assist the Sangomas in their healing work, and offerings are made to them to honor their presence and seek their assistance.

Herbalism is another spiritual practice that is often connected to ancestor veneration. Many traditional African healing practices involve the use of herbal remedies and medicines, which are believed to have been passed down from the ancestors. In many cultures, specific plants and herbs are associated with specific ancestors or spiritual beings, and offerings are made to them as a way of honoring their presence and seeking their assistance. For example, in the Akan culture of Ghana, the Adinkra symbol "Akoko Nan" represents the hen, which is associated with fertility and the ancestors. Offerings of eggs and other foods are made to the ancestors as a way of seeking their assistance with issues related to fertility and reproduction.

Shamanism is also closely connected to ancestor veneration in many African cultures. Shamanism involves the use of altered states of consciousness to communicate with the spiritual realm and seek guidance and healing. In many African cultures, the ancestors are believed to communicate through dreams, visions, and other altered states of consciousness, and shamanic practices are often used to connect with them. For example, in the San culture of southern Africa, traditional healers known as "Sanusi" use trance states and ritual dances to connect with the ancestors and seek their guidance and healing.

In conclusion, ancestor veneration is a central feature of many African religions and is closely connected to other spiritual practices such as divination, healing, herbalism, and shamanism. The ancestors are viewed as powerful spiritual beings who can offer guidance, protection, and healing to their living descendants. By honoring and connecting with the ancestors through these practices, African people are able to maintain a strong spiritual connection with their ancestors and draw upon their wisdom and power in their daily lives.

Exploring Origins, Traditions, and Contemporary Relevance

The significance of ancestor offerings and libations in African religions

Offerings and libations are an integral part of African religions and spiritual practices, especially in the context of ancestor veneration. The act of making offerings and libations is a way of showing respect, gratitude, and honor to the ancestors, and it is believed to facilitate communication with the spiritual realm. In this section, we will explore the significance of ancestor offerings and libations in African religions, including their symbolic meaning, their role in spiritual practice, and their connection to other aspects of African spirituality.

✧ **Symbolic Meaning of Offerings and Libations**

In African religions, offerings and libations are not merely material objects or substances, but they have symbolic meanings and spiritual significance. The act of making offerings is seen as a way of establishing a relationship with the ancestors and showing respect for their power and influence. Offerings can take many forms, such as food, drink, flowers, incense, and other objects that are believed to have spiritual value. These offerings are often placed on an altar or shrine, which is considered a sacred space for the ancestors.

Similarly, libations are not just a physical act of pouring liquid onto the ground, but they are a symbolic gesture of communication with the ancestors. The pouring of the libation is accompanied by prayers, songs, or invocations, which are believed to call upon the ancestors and invite their presence into the ritual. Libations are often poured onto the ground or into a designated receptacle, such as a bowl or cup, which is considered a conduit between the spiritual and physical realms.

✧ **Role of Offerings and Libations in Spiritual Practice**

Offerings and libations play an important role in spiritual practice in African religions, particularly in the context of ancestor veneration. These practices are used to establish a relationship with the ancestors, to seek their guidance and protection, and to express gratitude and honor for their influence. Offerings and libations are often made during important life events, such as births, weddings, and funerals, as well as during seasonal and cultural celebrations.

In some African traditions, offerings and libations are also used as a form of divination, or a way of seeking guidance and insight from the ancestors. For example, the position of spilled liquid or the patterns formed by pouring the libation may be interpreted as a message from the ancestors. Similarly, the appearance of certain objects or signs during an offering ceremony may be seen as an indication of the ancestors' presence and influence.

African Religions

✧ **Connection to Other Aspects of African Spirituality**

Offerings and libations are deeply connected to other aspects of African spirituality, including divination, healing, and shamanism. In many African traditions, offerings and libations are used in conjunction with divination practices, such as casting cowrie shells or throwing bones, to communicate with the ancestors and seek their guidance. Offerings and libations may also be used in healing practices, as a way of invoking the ancestors' healing powers and requesting their intervention.

In shamanic traditions, offerings and libations are seen as a way of establishing a connection between the shaman and the spiritual realm. The shaman may make offerings and pour libations as part of their journeying practices, to seek guidance and communicate with the spirits. Offerings and libations may also be used in trance and possession rituals, as a way of inviting the ancestors or spirits to enter the body of the practitioner.

Offerings and libations are a fundamental aspect of African religions and spiritual practices, particularly in the context of ancestor veneration. These practices are deeply symbolic and are used to establish a relationship with the ancestors, seek their guidance and protection, and express gratitude and honor for their influence. Offerings and libations are also connected to other aspects of African spirituality, such as divination, healing, and shamanism, and they have been adapted and incorporated into various other spiritual and religious practices around the world.

It is important to note that the practice of offering and libation varies across different African cultures and religions. The types of offerings and libations, as well as the methods and occasions on which they are performed, differ widely. However, the underlying belief that the ancestors play an important role in spiritual protection and guidance remains a constant across many traditions.

In addition to their spiritual significance, offerings and libations also have cultural and social significance. These practices help to maintain a connection with ancestors and cultural heritage, and they serve as a way of reinforcing social bonds and community cohesion.

Overall, the practice of offering and libation in African religions is a powerful way of connecting with the ancestors and seeking their guidance and protection. It is a deeply symbolic and meaningful practice that has been passed down through generations and continues to be an integral part of many African cultures and spiritual traditions.

Exploring Origins, Traditions, and Contemporary Relevance

Exercises and discussions on the significance of ancestor veneration in African religions and the ways in which it shapes spiritual practices

The significance of ancestor veneration in African religions is vast and complex. It is intertwined with spiritual practices that involve divination, healing, shamanism, and the use of offerings and libations. It is important for students seeking a bachelor's degree to have a deep understanding of the role of ancestor veneration in African religions and how it shapes spiritual practices. In this section, we will provide exercises and discussions to engage students in critical thinking and discussion on this topic.

Exercise 1: Reflecting on Ancestor Veneration in African Religions
The first exercise involves reflecting on ancestor veneration in African religions. Students should take some time to think about the following questions:

1. What are some common beliefs about ancestors in African religions?

2. How do these beliefs influence spiritual practices in African religions?

3. What are some common rituals and practices associated with ancestor veneration in African religions?

4. How do these rituals and practices contribute to the maintenance of social order in African societies?

5. How might the practice of ancestor veneration be relevant to contemporary spiritual practices outside of African religions?

After reflecting on these questions, students should share their thoughts and engage in a group discussion. This exercise will help students to develop a deeper understanding of the significance of ancestor veneration in African religions.

Exercise 2: Divination and Ancestor Veneration
The second exercise focuses on the connection between divination and ancestor veneration. Students should explore the ways in which divination is used in African religions to communicate with the ancestors and seek their guidance. They should also reflect on the following questions:

1. What are some common divination methods used in African religions?

2. How are these divination methods connected to ancestor veneration?

3.   How does divination serve as a means of communication with the ancestors?

4.   How might divination be used in contemporary spiritual practices outside of African religions?

After exploring these questions, students should engage in a group discussion to share their thoughts and insights.

Exercise 3: Healing and Ancestor Veneration
The third exercise focuses on the connection between healing and ancestor veneration. Students should explore the ways in which healing is connected to ancestor veneration in African religions. They should also reflect on the following questions:

1.   What are some common healing practices associated with ancestor veneration in African religions?

2.   How are these healing practices connected to the ancestors?

3.   How does the belief in ancestral power contribute to the effectiveness of these healing practices?

4.   How might healing practices be integrated into contemporary spiritual practices outside of African religions?

After exploring these questions, students should engage in a group discussion to share their thoughts and insights.

Exercise 4: Offerings and Libations in Ancestor Veneration
The fourth exercise focuses on the significance of offerings and libations in ancestor veneration. Students should explore the ways in which offerings and libations are used in African religions to honor and communicate with the ancestors. They should also reflect on the following questions:

1.   What are some common offerings and libations used in ancestor veneration in African religions?

2.   How are these offerings and libations connected to the ancestors?

3.   How do offerings and libations serve as a means of communication with the ancestors?

Exploring Origins, Traditions, and Contemporary Relevance

4.   How might offerings and libations be used in contemporary spiritual practices outside of African religions?

After exploring these questions, students should engage in a group discussion to share their thoughts and insights.

Discussion: The Role of Ancestor Veneration in Shaping African Religions and Spirituality

The final discussion focuses on the role of ancestor veneration in shaping African religions and spirituality. Students should reflect on the following questions:

1.   How has ancestor veneration influenced African religions and spirituality throughout history?

2.   What are some of the key beliefs and practices associated with ancestor veneration?

3.   How has ancestor veneration been adapted and modified in different African cultures and regions?

4.   What are some of the challenges and controversies associated with ancestor veneration in contemporary African societies?

5.   What are some of the similarities and differences between ancestor veneration in African religions and spirituality and other forms of ancestor worship found in other cultures and religions?

After discussing these questions, students should work in small groups to develop a creative project that explores the role of ancestor veneration in African religions and spirituality. The project could take the form of a research paper, a visual presentation, a short film, a theatrical performance, or a musical composition, among other possibilities.

Each group should choose a particular aspect of ancestor veneration to focus on, such as the symbolism of ancestral altars, the role of divination in ancestor communication, the use of dance and music in ancestor rituals, or the relationship between ancestor veneration and healing practices. The project should incorporate a range of sources and perspectives, including scholarly research, personal experiences and insights, and cultural and artistic representations of ancestor veneration.

African Religions

After completing their projects, each group should present their work to the class and engage in a constructive critique and feedback session. The goal of this exercise is to encourage students to explore the complex and multifaceted nature of ancestor veneration in African religions and spirituality, and to develop a deeper understanding and appreciation of the diverse cultural traditions and practices that shape this important aspect of human spirituality.

CHAPTER 20: ANCESTRAL HEALING AND ITS ROLE IN SPIRITUAL WELLBEING

The concept of ancestral healing is present in many cultures and religions around the world. Ancestors are believed to be powerful spiritual beings who can offer guidance, protection, and healing to their living descendants. Ancestral healing is the process of connecting with and honoring these ancestors in order to address and heal familial and ancestral wounds that may be affecting one's physical, emotional, or spiritual wellbeing.

In African religions and spiritual practices, ancestor veneration is a central aspect of spiritual life. Ancestors are believed to be present and active in the lives of their living descendants, and their guidance and protection are sought after in times of need. Ancestral healing is an important aspect of African spirituality and is often used to address familial and ancestral wounds, generational trauma, and other issues that may be affecting one's spiritual and emotional wellbeing.

In this chapter, we will explore the concept of ancestral healing in African religions and spiritual practices. We will examine the role of ancestors in African spirituality, the importance of ancestral healing, and the different methods and practices that are used to connect with and honor ancestors for healing and guidance.

We will also discuss the ways in which ancestral healing can contribute to overall spiritual wellbeing and the importance of addressing familial and ancestral wounds for personal growth and healing. Throughout the chapter, we will provide examples of ancestral healing practices from various African cultures and traditions, as well as exercises and discussion questions to encourage critical thinking and reflection on the topic.

By the end of this chapter, students will have a deeper understanding of the significance of ancestral healing in African spirituality and the ways in which it can contribute to personal growth, healing, and spiritual wellbeing. They will also be equipped with practical tools and techniques for connecting with and honoring their own ancestors for guidance and healing.

African Religions

An overview of ancestral healing practices in African religions

Ancestral healing is a form of spiritual practice that aims to restore balance and harmony between the living and the ancestors. It is based on the belief that the ancestors are not only present but also actively involved in the lives of their descendants, and that their influence can be positive or negative depending on how they are honored and remembered. In African religions, ancestral healing is an important aspect of spiritual wellbeing, and it involves a variety of practices that are specific to each culture and tradition.

One of the primary goals of ancestral healing is to resolve ancestral trauma, which refers to the unresolved emotional and psychological wounds that have been passed down through the generations. This trauma can manifest as physical and mental illness, addiction, relationship problems, and other forms of dysfunction. Ancestral healing seeks to identify and heal these wounds by working with the ancestors directly.

Ancestral healing practices in African religions vary widely depending on the cultural context and the specific tradition. Some of the most common practices include divination, ritual offerings, prayer, meditation, and ancestor altars. Divination is used to communicate with the ancestors and to seek their guidance and wisdom. Ritual offerings, such as food, drink, and other gifts, are used to honor the ancestors and to establish a relationship with them. Prayer and meditation are used to focus the mind and to connect with the spiritual realm.

Ancestor altars are a central feature of many African religions and are used to honor and remember the ancestors. These altars are typically adorned with offerings such as candles, flowers, and other symbolic objects. They are also used as a focal point for meditation and prayer, and as a place to communicate with the ancestors. Ancestor altars are often passed down through the generations and are a powerful symbol of family and cultural heritage.

In addition to these traditional practices, there are also modern forms of ancestral healing that draw on both ancient wisdom and contemporary psychology. For example, some practitioners use guided visualization, group therapy, and other techniques to help people connect with their ancestors and to heal ancestral trauma.

Ancestral healing is not a one-time event but is an ongoing process that requires dedication and commitment. It involves a deep understanding of the interconnectedness of all things, and a recognition that the past, present, and future are all linked together. By healing the wounds of the past, we can create a brighter future for ourselves, our families, and our communities.

Exploring Origins, Traditions, and Contemporary Relevance

In the following sections, we will explore some of the specific ancestral healing practices in African religions, including divination, ritual offerings, prayer, meditation, and ancestor altars. We will also discuss some of the challenges and controversies surrounding these practices, and the ways in which they are being adapted and transformed in response to changing cultural and social contexts.

The role of ancestral healing in promoting spiritual, physical, and emotional wellbeing

The practice of ancestral healing is deeply rooted in African religions and spiritual practices, and it plays a crucial role in promoting spiritual, physical, and emotional wellbeing. Ancestral healing is the process of connecting with and seeking guidance from one's ancestors in order to heal past wounds, resolve ancestral traumas, and restore balance and harmony to one's life. This practice is based on the belief that one's ancestors are powerful spiritual beings who can provide protection, guidance, and wisdom to their living descendants.

Ancestral healing is an important aspect of African spirituality and is used to address a wide range of issues, including physical and emotional health, relationship problems, financial difficulties, and spiritual blocks. This practice recognizes that individuals are not only shaped by their individual experiences but also by the experiences of their ancestors. Therefore, ancestral healing seeks to address the root causes of an individual's challenges by exploring and healing the ancestral lineage.

The role of ancestral healing in promoting spiritual wellbeing is multifaceted. One aspect of this practice involves reconnecting with one's ancestral heritage and cultural traditions. This can involve learning about the history and traditions of one's ancestors, including their spiritual practices, values, and beliefs. By reconnecting with one's ancestral roots, individuals can develop a deeper sense of identity and purpose, which can promote feelings of belonging and connection.

Ancestral healing also promotes emotional wellbeing by helping individuals to heal from past traumas and wounds. This practice recognizes that unresolved trauma can be passed down through generations, leading to patterns of dysfunction and suffering. Through ancestral healing, individuals can identify and heal these traumas, releasing the negative patterns that have been passed down through the generations.

Furthermore, ancestral healing is also used to promote physical wellbeing by addressing health issues that may be related to ancestral trauma or patterns. For example, some African spiritual traditions believe that illnesses may be caused by ancestral spirits seeking attention or healing. By addressing the underlying spiritual issues, ancestral healing can support physical healing as well.

African Religions

The role of ancestral healing in promoting spiritual, physical, and emotional wellbeing is deeply connected to the African concept of ubuntu, which emphasizes the interconnectedness and interdependence of all living beings. In this worldview, healing is not just an individual process but a collective one that involves the entire community, including the ancestors. By healing one's ancestral lineage, individuals can contribute to the healing of their community and the world at large.

In conclusion, ancestral healing is a vital practice in African religions and spiritual traditions, promoting spiritual, physical, and emotional wellbeing by addressing the root causes of challenges and restoring balance and harmony to individuals and their communities. Through ancestral healing, individuals can reconnect with their cultural heritage, heal from past traumas, and contribute to the healing of their community and the world.

The connection between ancestral healing and other forms of healing in African cultures, such as herbal medicine and divination

The practice of ancestral healing in African cultures is deeply interconnected with other forms of healing, such as herbal medicine and divination. These practices are often used in conjunction with one another to promote spiritual, physical, and emotional wellbeing.

Herbal Medicine

Herbal medicine has been used for thousands of years in African cultures for a variety of health purposes, including the treatment of physical ailments and the promotion of spiritual healing. The use of herbs is often based on a deep understanding of the medicinal properties of different plants, as well as a spiritual connection to the natural world.

In many African cultures, ancestral healing is closely linked to herbal medicine. It is believed that the ancestors possess knowledge of the medicinal properties of different plants and can guide healers in their use. Herbal remedies are often used to treat physical ailments, but they can also be used to promote spiritual healing and connection with the ancestors.

One example of the use of herbal medicine in ancestral healing is the use of mugwort in divination. Mugwort, also known as artemisia, is a powerful herb that is believed to have the ability to open the third eye and promote psychic vision. In many African cultures, mugwort is used in divination practices to help connect with the ancestors and receive guidance.

Exploring Origins, Traditions, and Contemporary Relevance

Divination

Divination is a practice that is used in many African cultures to communicate with the ancestors and receive guidance. Divination practices can take many forms, including the use of tarot cards, astrology, and scrying, but in many African cultures, divination is performed through the use of cowrie shells or other natural objects.

The practice of divination is closely linked to ancestral healing, as it is believed that the ancestors can provide guidance and wisdom through the process of divination. Divination is often used to help individuals connect with their ancestors and receive guidance on issues related to their spiritual, physical, and emotional wellbeing.

One example of the use of divination in ancestral healing is the use of the Ifa divination system in Yoruba culture. The Ifa system uses a complex set of symbols and rituals to communicate with the ancestors and receive guidance on a wide range of issues. The Ifa system is deeply interconnected with other forms of healing in Yoruba culture, including herbal medicine and spiritual healing.

Spiritual Healing

Spiritual healing is another form of healing that is closely linked to ancestral healing in African cultures. Spiritual healing practices can take many forms, including prayer, meditation, and ritual, but in many African cultures, spiritual healing is performed through the use of music, dance, and other forms of expressive arts.

In many African cultures, spiritual healing is believed to be a powerful tool for connecting with the ancestors and promoting spiritual, physical, and emotional wellbeing. Spiritual healers are often highly respected members of their communities and are believed to possess a deep understanding of the spiritual world and its connection to the physical world.

One example of the use of spiritual healing in ancestral healing is the use of music and dance in healing rituals in West African cultures. Music and dance are believed to have the ability to connect individuals with the ancestors and promote healing on a spiritual and emotional level.

Ancestral healing in African cultures is deeply interconnected with other forms of healing, such as herbal medicine, divination, and spiritual healing. These practices are often used in conjunction with one another to promote spiritual, physical, and emotional wellbeing. The connection between these different forms of healing is based on a deep understanding of the interconnectedness of all things and the importance of maintaining a connection with the ancestors and the natural world. By understanding the connection between ancestral healing and other forms of healing in African cultures, individuals can gain a deeper appreciation for the power of these practices to promote holistic healing and wellbeing.

Examples and case studies of ancestral healing practices in African cultures

Ancestral healing is a widespread practice in many African cultures, and it takes many forms. These practices are deeply rooted in the belief that ancestors play a vital role in the lives of the living and that they can offer guidance, protection, and healing. In this section, we will examine some examples and case studies of ancestral healing practices in African cultures.

✧   Ancestral healing in South Africa

In South Africa, ancestral healing is a common practice among the Zulu people. They believe that the ancestors are still present and active in the lives of their descendants, and that they can offer protection, guidance, and blessings. One of the ways that the Zulu people honor their ancestors is through the practice of "ukuphahla," which involves burning traditional herbs and incense to communicate with the ancestors. This practice is often performed during family gatherings or other important events, and it is believed to bring good luck and prosperity.

Another example of ancestral healing in South Africa is the practice of "isigodlo," which involves building a shrine to honor the ancestors. The shrine is usually built in a sacred place, such as a forest or a hilltop, and it is believed to provide a direct link to the ancestors. People come to the shrine to pray, make offerings, and seek guidance from their ancestors.

✧   Ancestral healing in West Africa

In West Africa, ancestral healing is a common practice among many ethnic groups, including the Yoruba people of Nigeria. They believe that the ancestors are still present and active in their daily lives, and that they can provide guidance and blessings. One of the ways that the Yoruba people honor their ancestors is through the practice of "egungun," which involves wearing masks and colorful costumes to honor the ancestors.

Another example of ancestral healing in West Africa is the practice of "ifa," which is a form of divination that involves communicating with the ancestors through a trained priest. The priest uses a system of signs and symbols to interpret the messages from the ancestors, and these messages are believed to provide guidance and insight into the future.

Exploring Origins, Traditions, and Contemporary Relevance

✧   **Ancestral healing in East Africa**

In East Africa, ancestral healing is a common practice among many ethnic groups, including the Maasai people of Kenya. They believe that the ancestors are still present and active in their daily lives, and that they can offer guidance and protection. One of the ways that the Maasai people honor their ancestors is through the practice of "enkaji," which involves building a shelter to honor the ancestors. The shelter is usually built from cow dung and sticks, and it is believed to provide a direct link to the ancestors.

Another example of ancestral healing in East Africa is the practice of "divination," which involves communicating with the ancestors through a trained diviner. The diviner uses a system of signs and symbols to interpret the messages from the ancestors, and these messages are believed to provide guidance and insight into the future.

✧   **Ancestral healing in Central Africa**

In Central Africa, ancestral healing is a common practice among many ethnic groups, including the Bantu people of the Congo. They believe that the ancestors are still present and active in their daily lives, and that they can provide guidance and protection. One of the ways that the Bantu people honor their ancestors is through the practice of "nkisi," which involves creating a powerful object, such as a statue or a charm, to honor the ancestors. The object is believed to contain the power and wisdom of the ancestors, and it is used for protection and healing.

Another example of ancestral healing in Central Africa is the practice of "divination," which involves communicating with the ancestors through a trained diviner. The diviner uses various methods, such as throwing bones or interpreting dreams, to receive messages from the ancestors. These messages may provide guidance on important decisions, reveal the causes of illness or misfortune, or offer advice on how to resolve conflicts.

One particular example of divination in Central Africa is the practice of "ngoma," which is used by the Bantu people of southern Africa. Ngoma involves a group of people coming together in a sacred space to sing, dance, and communicate with the ancestors. The ngoma ceremony is led by a trained healer, or "sangoma," who uses drumming, chanting, and divination to connect with the ancestors and receive guidance and healing for the community.

In West Africa, ancestral healing practices are also prevalent, with many cultures believing in the power of the ancestors to protect and heal their descendants. For example, the Yoruba people of Nigeria and Benin believe in the concept of "orisha," which refers to the various deities and spirits that can provide guidance, protection, and healing. The orisha are believed to be the ancestors of the Yoruba people, and they are honored through offerings, prayers, and rituals.

One of the most well-known ancestral healing practices in West Africa is the Ifa divination system, which is used by the Yoruba people to communicate with the orisha. Ifa involves the use of a divination tray and a set of 16 sacred palm nuts, which are thrown to create a pattern that is interpreted by a trained diviner. The diviner then uses the message received from the orisha to provide guidance and healing to the client.

Another example of ancestral healing in West Africa is the practice of "egungun," which is found among the Yoruba and other cultures in Nigeria and Benin. Egungun involves the use of elaborate costumes and masks to honor the ancestors and communicate with them. The egungun dancers, who are often members of a secret society, perform rituals and dances that are believed to connect them with the spirits of their ancestors.

In Southern Africa, the San people, also known as the Bushmen, have a deep connection to their ancestors and the spiritual world. They believe that the ancestors are present in the natural world, and that they can provide guidance and healing to the living. One of the ways that the San honor their ancestors is through the use of trance dances, which involve singing, dancing, and drumming to enter into a trance state and communicate with the ancestors.

In conclusion, ancestral healing practices are a vital part of many African cultures, providing a way to connect with the wisdom and guidance of the ancestors for spiritual, physical, and emotional healing. From divination and nkisi in Central Africa to orisha and egungun in West Africa, and trance dances in Southern Africa, these practices demonstrate the deep respect and reverence that African cultures have for their ancestors and the spiritual world.

Exercises and discussions on the significance of ancestral healing in African religions and its potential benefits for contemporary spiritual practices

Ancestral healing is a vital component of many African religions and spiritual practices. The importance of ancestors is not limited to the African continent but is also a significant aspect of African diasporic religions. In contemporary times, ancestral healing practices are increasingly being recognized as important tools for spiritual growth, healing, and wellbeing. This section will provide exercises and discussions to engage students in critical thinking and reflection on the significance

Exploring Origins, Traditions, and Contemporary Relevance

of ancestral healing in African religions and its potential benefits for contemporary spiritual practices.

Research and discuss the different ways ancestral practices manifest in different African cultures

Ancestral practices vary greatly across different African cultures, and researching these differences can help us better understand the diversity and richness of African spiritual traditions. Some questions to consider when conducting this research include:

1. What are the different ways that ancestors are venerated in African cultures?

2. What types of rituals or ceremonies are associated with ancestor veneration?

3. Are there any differences in how ancestral practices are carried out based on gender or social status?

4. How do different African cultures understand the relationship between ancestors and the living?

Write a reflection on your personal beliefs about ancestor veneration and its role in spiritual wellbeing

Reflection is an essential tool for exploring our own beliefs and values. In this exercise, students are encouraged to reflect on their personal beliefs about ancestor veneration and its role in spiritual wellbeing. Some questions to consider include:

1. What are your beliefs about the existence of ancestors and their influence on the living?

2. How do you feel about practices such as ancestor veneration or divination?

3. Have you had any personal experiences with ancestral healing or communication?

4. Do you think that ancestor veneration can be helpful in achieving spiritual growth or healing?

African Religions

Analyze the ways in which colonialism and globalization have impacted ancestral practices in African societies

Colonialism and globalization have had a significant impact on African societies, including their spiritual traditions. In this exercise, students are encouraged to analyze the ways in which colonialism and globalization have impacted ancestral practices in African societies. Some questions to consider include:

1.   How have colonialism and globalization affected traditional African spiritual practices, including ancestral healing?

2.   Have certain practices been lost or forgotten due to colonialism and globalization?

3.   Are there any examples of African spiritual practices that have adapted to the changing times?

4.   How do contemporary African diasporic religions, such as Vodou or Candomble, reflect the impact of colonialism and globalization?

Compare and contrast the role of ancestors in African religions with that of other spiritual traditions, such as Hinduism or Taoism

While ancestor veneration is a significant aspect of many African religions, it is also present in other spiritual traditions, such as Hinduism and Taoism. In this exercise, students are encouraged to compare and contrast the role of ancestors in African religions with that of other spiritual traditions. Some questions to consider include:

1.   How is ancestor veneration practiced in Hinduism or Taoism, and what are the similarities and differences with African religions?

2.   What are the common themes or values associated with ancestor veneration across different spiritual traditions?

3.   How does the understanding of the afterlife and reincarnation differ across different spiritual traditions?

4.   What can we learn from comparing the role of ancestors in different spiritual traditions?

Exploring Origins, Traditions, and Contemporary Relevance

5.   Create a presentation on the significance of ancestral practices in contemporary African diasporic religions, such as Vodou or Candomble

Contemporary African diasporic religions, such as Vodou or Candomble, often have a strong emphasis on ancestral practices. In this exercise, students are encouraged to create a presentation on the significance of ancestral practices in contemporary African diasporic religions. Some topics to consider include:

1.   What are the core beliefs and practices of Vodou or Candomble that relate to ancestral practices?

2.   How do these religions view the role of ancestors in spiritual life and practice?

3.   How are ancestors venerated and honored in these religions?

4.   What rituals or ceremonies are conducted to connect with ancestors in Vodou or Candomble?

5.   How have these religions adapted to the new cultural and spiritual contexts of the diaspora, while still maintaining a connection to ancestral practices?

PART 5: AFRICAN DIASPORIC RELIGIONS

Part 5 of this discussion delves into the topic of African diasporic religions, which refer to the various religious traditions that have emerged as a result of the forced migration of Africans to the Americas, the Caribbean, and other parts of the world during the transatlantic slave trade. These religions are characterized by their syncretic nature, blending elements of traditional African religions with Christianity and other spiritual traditions.

African diasporic religions are known for their vibrant and colorful rituals, music, and dance, which are used to connect with the divine and honor the ancestors. They have played a significant role in the cultural and social history of the African diaspora, providing a source of spiritual and cultural identity for people who were forcibly removed from their homeland and faced immense hardship and oppression.

In this section, we will explore the history and beliefs of some of the major African diasporic religions, including Vodou, Santeria, Candomble, and others. We will examine their rituals and practices, and explore the ways in which they have evolved and adapted over time in response to changing social and political contexts. Additionally, we will consider the significance of these religions for contemporary spiritual practices and the ways in which they continue to shape the cultural and spiritual landscape of the African diaspora.

CHAPTER 21: OVERVIEW OF AFRICAN DIASPORIC RELIGIONS, SUCH AS VODOU, SANTERIA, AND CANDOMBLE

African diasporic religions are a diverse set of religious practices that developed among African people in the Americas, Caribbean, and other parts of the world as a result of the transatlantic slave trade. These religions are characterized by their syncretism of African beliefs and practices with Christian and Indigenous religions, as well as their emphasis on ancestor veneration, divination, and healing. Some of the most well-known African diasporic religions include Vodou, Santeria, and Candomble.

This chapter provides an overview of African diasporic religions, focusing on their history, beliefs, practices, and contemporary relevance. It begins by discussing the transatlantic slave trade and its impact on African religions, highlighting the ways in which African religious practices were preserved and adapted in the Americas. The chapter then provides an introduction to key concepts and practices in African diasporic religions, including ancestor veneration, divination, and healing.

Additionally, this chapter explores the diversity of African diasporic religions, emphasizing the unique beliefs and practices of different religions, such as Vodou, Santeria, and Candomble. The chapter also addresses misconceptions and stereotypes surrounding African diasporic religions, such as the association of these religions with evil or demon worship. Finally, this chapter discusses the contemporary relevance of African diasporic religions, highlighting their role in cultural identity and political activism.

Overall, this chapter provides a comprehensive introduction to African diasporic religions, demonstrating the diversity, complexity, and importance of these religions in the Americas and beyond.

Topics Covered:

✦ The transatlantic slave trade and its impact on African religions

✦ Key concepts and practices in African diasporic religions, including ancestor veneration, divination, and healing

✧ Overview of specific African diasporic religions, such as Vodou, Santeria, and Candomble

✧ Addressing misconceptions and stereotypes surrounding African diasporic religions

✧ Contemporary relevance of African diasporic religions, including their role in cultural identity and political activism.

Examples, Problems, and Exercises:

Research and discuss the history and impact of the transatlantic slave trade on African religions and cultures

Compare and contrast the beliefs and practices of African diasporic religions with those of other spiritual traditions, such as Hinduism or Taoism

Analyze the ways in which African diasporic religions have influenced and been influenced by mainstream American culture

Create a presentation on the contemporary relevance of African diasporic religions in terms of social justice and political activism

Write a reflection on your personal experiences with African diasporic religions and their significance in your own spiritual journey.

Define African diasporic religions and provide an overview of their main characteristics

African diasporic religions, such as Vodou, Santeria, and Candomble, are a diverse set of religious traditions that emerged in the Americas as a result of the forced migration of Africans during the transatlantic slave trade. These religions are characterized by their syncretic nature, blending elements of African, European, and indigenous religions. They are also marked by a strong emphasis on ancestor veneration, the use of divination, and the belief in spirit possession.

In this chapter, we will provide an overview of the main characteristics of African diasporic religions. We will examine their historical origins, their religious practices and beliefs, and their cultural significance. We will also explore the ways in which African diasporic religions have been impacted by colonialism, racism, and globalization, and how they have evolved and adapted in response to these challenges.

Exploring Origins, Traditions, and Contemporary Relevance

Defining African Diasporic Religions:

African diasporic religions are a group of religious traditions that emerged in the Americas as a result of the forced migration of Africans during the transatlantic slave trade. These religions are syncretic in nature, meaning that they have blended elements of African, European, and indigenous religions. They are also characterized by a strong emphasis on ancestor veneration, the use of divination, and the belief in spirit possession.

The African diaspora refers to the dispersal of Africans across the world, particularly in the Americas, Europe, and the Caribbean, as a result of the transatlantic slave trade. During this period, millions of Africans were forcibly transported from their homelands to work as slaves in the Americas. As a result of this forced migration, African cultural and religious practices were brought to the New World and began to blend with European and indigenous traditions.

African diasporic religions emerged as a result of this blending process, as enslaved Africans sought to maintain their cultural and religious traditions in the face of oppressive conditions. These religions served as a means of resistance and resilience, allowing enslaved Africans to maintain a sense of identity and community in the face of tremendous adversity.

Main Characteristics of African Diasporic Religions:

African diasporic religions are characterized by their syncretic nature, blending elements of African, European, and indigenous religions. They are also marked by a strong emphasis on ancestor veneration, the use of divination, and the belief in spirit possession.

Ancestor veneration is a central aspect of African diasporic religions. Ancestors are believed to be the living link between the living and the dead, and are revered as sources of wisdom, guidance, and protection. Ancestral veneration is often accompanied by offerings, prayers, and rituals, such as the pouring of libations.

Divination is another important aspect of African diasporic religions. Divination is the practice of seeking knowledge or insight through the interpretation of signs or symbols. It is used to gain insight into personal issues, to determine the causes of illness or misfortune, and to gain guidance on important decisions. There are many forms of divination used in African diasporic religions, including the use of shells, bones, cards, and dreams.

African Religions

Spirit possession is a fundamental aspect of African diasporic religions. It is the belief that spirits can enter the bodies of living humans, allowing them to communicate with the living world. Possession is often accompanied by dancing, drumming, and chanting, and is seen as a means of healing, guidance, and empowerment.

African diasporic religions, such as Vodou, Santeria, and Candomble, are a complex and diverse set of religious traditions that have emerged from the experiences of Africans and their descendants in the diaspora. These religions have roots in West and Central Africa, but have also been influenced by the cultures and religions of the Americas, including Christianity and indigenous religions.

Ancestor veneration, divination, and spirit possession are three key aspects of African diasporic religions. Ancestor veneration is the practice of honoring and seeking guidance from one's ancestors, who are believed to be the living link between the living and the dead. Divination is the practice of seeking knowledge or insight through the interpretation of signs or symbols, and is used to gain guidance on important decisions. Spirit possession is the belief that spirits can enter the bodies of living humans, allowing them to communicate with the living world, and is seen as a means of healing, guidance, and empowerment.

Overall, African diasporic religions offer a unique and rich spiritual tradition that draws from a variety of cultural and religious influences. These religions continue to evolve and adapt to new cultural and social contexts, while also remaining deeply rooted in their ancestral traditions. As such, they provide a powerful source of spiritual connection, guidance, and empowerment for individuals and communities across the African diaspora.

The main differences and similarities between Vodou, Santeria, and Candomble

Vodou, Santeria, and Candomble are all African diasporic religions that have been practiced for centuries in various parts of the Americas. Despite their similarities, these religions also have significant differences in terms of their origins, beliefs, practices, and cultural influences. In this section, we will explore the main differences and similarities between Vodou, Santeria, and Candomble.

Origins and Influences:

Vodou originated in Haiti, which was a French colony in the Caribbean. It emerged as a syncretic religion that blended elements of West and Central African religions, Roman Catholicism, and Indigenous spirituality. Vodou was influenced by the forced migration of African slaves to the Americas, the resistance movements that emerged among slaves, and the political and social upheavals that followed the Haitian Revolution. Vodou practitioners believe in a pantheon of spirits or lwa that can be invoked to assist with various aspects of life.

Santeria, on the other hand, originated in Cuba, which was a Spanish colony in the Caribbean. It is also a syncretic religion that blends elements of West and Central African religions, Roman Catholicism, and Indigenous spirituality. Santeria emerged from the slave trade and the forced migration of African slaves to the Americas. Santeria practitioners believe in a pantheon of orishas or deities that can be invoked to assist with various aspects of life.

Candomble originated in Brazil, which was a Portuguese colony in South America. It also emerged from the slave trade and the forced migration of African slaves to the Americas. Candomble is a syncretic religion that blends elements of West and Central African religions, Indigenous spirituality, and Catholicism. Candomble practitioners believe in a pantheon of orixas or deities that can be invoked to assist with various aspects of life.

Beliefs:

Despite their syncretic origins, Vodou, Santeria, and Candomble have distinct beliefs and practices. In Vodou, practitioners believe in a single Supreme Being called Bondye, who is distant and aloof from human affairs. The lwa, or spirits, are intermediaries between Bondye and human beings. Lwa are believed to be able to possess human bodies and communicate with the living world.

In Santeria, practitioners believe in a Supreme Being called Olodumare, who is similar to the Christian God. Olodumare is distant and aloof from human affairs, and is worshipped through the orishas. The orishas are deities that can be invoked to assist with various aspects of life. Orishas are believed to be able to possess human bodies and communicate with the living world.

In Candomble, practitioners believe in a Supreme Being called Olorun, who is distant and aloof from human affairs. The orixas, or deities, are intermediaries between Olorun and human beings. Orixas are believed to be able to possess human bodies and communicate with the living world.

Practices:

Vodou, Santeria, and Candomble have distinct practices, but they all involve ancestor veneration, divination, and spirit possession. Ancestor veneration involves honoring and communicating with the dead, who are believed to be able to assist the living. Divination involves seeking knowledge or guidance from the spirit world through the interpretation of signs or symbols. Spirit possession involves allowing spirits to enter the body and communicate with the living world.

Vodou is known for its use of vodou dolls, which are used in healing and protection spells. Santeria is known for its use of animal sacrifice, which is believed to please the orishas and ensure their assistance. Candomble is known for its use of dance and music in its rituals, which are seen as a means of connecting with the spirits.

One key difference between the three religions is their pantheon of deities. Vodou has a complex pantheon of spirits known as loa, which are associated with different aspects of life and nature. Santeria has a similar system of orishas, but they are often associated with Catholic saints, and their identities are sometimes obscured for the purposes of secrecy. Candomble has a pantheon of orixas, which are associated with various aspects of nature and society, but also have human-like personalities and stories.

Another difference is the degree to which the religions have been syncretized with other religious traditions. Santeria, for example, has incorporated elements of Catholicism, while Vodou has incorporated elements of Christianity and African traditional religion. Candomble, on the other hand, has remained more distinct from other religious traditions, though it has been influenced by them to some extent.

Despite these differences, all three religions share a common history of oppression and marginalization, and have developed as a means of preserving African cultural traditions in the face of colonialism and slavery. They have also evolved over time as a result of migrations and cultural exchanges, and continue to adapt to new contexts and challenges in the modern world.

In terms of similarities, all three religions emphasize the importance of community and the role of the individual in the larger social and spiritual context. They also place a strong emphasis on ritual, which is seen as a means of connecting with the divine and achieving spiritual transformation. Finally, they all prioritize the value of personal agency and responsibility, and emphasize the need for individuals to actively engage with the spirits and the world around them.

In conclusion, while Vodou, Santeria, and Candomble have distinct practices and traditions, they share many commonalities, including a focus on ancestor veneration, divination, and spirit possession, as well as a common history of marginalization and cultural survival. Understanding the similarities and differences between these religions is key to gaining a deeper appreciation of the diverse religious traditions that make up the African diaspora, and the role they continue to play in shaping the spiritual and cultural landscape of the modern world.

Examples of other African diasporic religions and their unique features

African diasporic religions are not limited to Vodou, Santeria, and Candomble. There are many other religions that have emerged in the African diaspora, each with its own unique features and practices. Here are some examples:

Ifa/Orisa: Ifa/Orisa is a Yoruba-based religion that originated in Nigeria and is practiced throughout West Africa and the African diaspora. It is a monotheistic religion that worships Olodumare, the supreme being, and a pantheon of deities known as orishas. Ifa is known for its use of divination, which involves interpreting patterns made by sixteen palm nuts. The religion also emphasizes the importance of community and ancestor veneration.

Hoodoo: Hoodoo is a spiritual practice that developed in the American South among enslaved Africans and their descendants. It incorporates African spiritual beliefs, Native American herbalism, and European folk magic. Hoodoo practitioners use spells, amulets, and talismans to achieve their goals, and often incorporate Christian elements into their practices. Hoodoo is known for its use of "mojo bags," which contain herbs, stones, and other objects used to attract or repel certain energies.

Rastafarianism: Rastafarianism is a religious and cultural movement that originated in Jamaica in the early 20th century. It is a monotheistic religion that worships Haile Selassie I, the former emperor of Ethiopia, as a messiah. Rastafarians also believe in the importance of African identity, social justice, and the use of marijuana as a sacrament. The religion is known for its distinctive dreadlocks hairstyle and reggae music.

Kumina: Kumina is a religion that developed in Jamaica among the descendants of enslaved Africans from the Congo region. It is known for its drumming and dancing rituals, which are believed to allow communication with the spirits of the dead. Kumina practitioners also believe in the importance of ancestor veneration and healing through herbalism.

Voodoo: Voodoo is a religion that originated in Haiti and is practiced throughout the Caribbean and the African diaspora. It is a syncretic religion that combines African spiritual beliefs with Catholicism. Voodoo practitioners believe in a pantheon of deities known as lwa, and use rituals such as animal sacrifice, drumming, and dancing to communicate with them. The religion is also known for its use of voodoo dolls and the practice of zombification, which involves inducing a trance-like state in someone and then bringing them back to life.

Obeah: Obeah is a spiritual practice that developed in the Caribbean among enslaved Africans and their descendants. It incorporates African spiritual beliefs, European folk magic, and Native American herbalism. Obeah practitioners use spells, amulets, and talismans to achieve their goals, and often incorporate Christian elements into their practices. The practice is often stigmatized and has been outlawed in some Caribbean countries.

Espiritismo: Espiritismo is a spiritualist religion that developed in Cuba and is practiced throughout the Caribbean and the African diaspora. It incorporates elements of Catholicism, African spiritual beliefs, and European spiritualism. Espiritismo practitioners believe in communication with the spirits of the dead, and use mediums to facilitate these communications. The religion is also known for its emphasis on healing through herbalism and spiritual practices.

Each of these religions has its own unique features and practices, but they are all united by their roots in the African diaspora and their emphasis on spirituality and community. By exploring these religions and their traditions, we can gain a deeper understanding of the diversity and richness of African diasporic culture.

The transatlantic slave trade and its impact on African religions

The transatlantic slave trade was a period in history that saw the forced migration of millions of African people to the Americas. The trade began in the 15th century and continued until the 19th century, resulting in the displacement of millions of Africans from their homeland. The impact of the slave trade on African religions was significant, as it resulted in the destruction of traditional practices and the forced assimilation of Africans into Christianity.

The slave trade had a profound effect on African religions. Prior to the arrival of European colonizers, African societies were diverse and complex, with a variety of religious beliefs and practices. Many of these practices were based on animistic beliefs, which held that all living and non-living things possessed a spiritual essence. This worldview was fundamental to many traditional African religions, which placed great importance on the veneration of ancestors and the use of divination to communicate with the spirit world.

However, with the arrival of European colonizers and the introduction of the slave trade, the religious landscape of Africa began to change. European colonizers saw traditional African religions as primitive and inferior to their own Christian beliefs. They viewed the spread of Christianity as a way to "civilize" and "enlighten" Africans, and saw the suppression of traditional practices as a necessary step in this process.

As a result, many African religions were suppressed and replaced with Christianity. Missionaries and colonial administrators actively discouraged the practice of traditional beliefs and rituals, and often used violence and coercion to force Africans to convert to Christianity. In many cases, traditional practices were seen as a threat to colonial rule, and were actively suppressed to maintain control over the local population.

The impact of the slave trade on African religions was also felt in the Americas. Many enslaved Africans were brought to the Americas against their will, and were forced to abandon their traditional beliefs and practices. Enslaved Africans were often converted to Christianity by their slave owners, and were prohibited from practicing their traditional religions. This resulted in the loss of much of the cultural heritage of African peoples in the Americas.

Despite the efforts of European colonizers and slave owners to suppress traditional African religions, these practices have continued to survive and evolve over time. Today, many African religions have been revitalized and are experiencing a resurgence in popularity. In many cases, this resurgence has been fueled by a desire to reclaim cultural heritage that was lost as a result of the slave trade and colonialism.

One example of this resurgence is the revival of African traditional religions in Brazil. Many enslaved Africans were brought to Brazil during the slave trade, and were forced to abandon their traditional beliefs and practices. However, over time, African religious practices have survived and have been integrated into Brazilian culture. Today, many Afro-Brazilian religions, such as Candomble and Umbanda, are thriving and have become an important part of Brazilian cultural identity.

Another example is the revival of African traditional religions in the United States. Many African Americans have sought to reconnect with their cultural heritage by embracing African religions and practices. This has led to the growth of religious movements such as Hoodoo and Vodou, which draw on African religious practices and traditions.

In conclusion, the transatlantic slave trade had a significant impact on African religions, resulting in the suppression of traditional practices and the forced assimilation of Africans into Christianity. However, despite these efforts, many

African Religions

African religions have survived and continue to evolve today. The resurgence of these religions is a testament to the resilience of African culture and the enduring power of traditional beliefs and practices.

Key concepts and practices in African diasporic religions, including ancestor veneration, divination, and healing

The African diaspora refers to the dispersion of people of African descent throughout the world, primarily as a result of the transatlantic slave trade. As Africans were forcibly taken from their homelands and brought to the Americas, their religious practices and beliefs were also transported with them. This led to the development of African diasporic religions, which blended elements of traditional African religions with the influences of the cultures they encountered in the new world. These religions continue to be practiced today, and include traditions such as Vodou, Santeria, Candomble, and Lucumi.

Ancestor Veneration

Ancestor veneration is a key concept in many African diasporic religions. In these traditions, ancestors are believed to have the power to influence the lives of their descendants. They are considered to be intermediaries between the physical world and the spiritual world, and are often invoked for guidance, protection, and blessings. Ancestor veneration involves offerings and prayers to these spirits, as well as the use of ritual objects and symbols.

One example of ancestor veneration in African diasporic religions is found in Vodou, a syncretic religion that developed in Haiti. In Vodou, ancestors are known as "lwa," and are believed to be powerful spirits who can offer protection and guidance to their living descendants. Vodou practitioners often create altars and make offerings to their ancestors, which may include food, drink, and other items that were important to the ancestor in life. Ancestor veneration is also an important part of Santeria, a syncretic religion that developed in Cuba. In Santeria, ancestors are known as "eggun," and are believed to have the power to intercede on behalf of their descendants. Offerings to ancestors in Santeria may include candles, flowers, and other items.

Divination

Divination is another important concept in African diasporic religions. Divination involves the use of various methods to gain insight into the future or to gain guidance from the spirits. These methods may include the use of shells, bones, cards, or other objects, and are often performed by specialized practitioners known as diviners.

One example of divination in African diasporic religions is found in Ifa, a religion practiced by the Yoruba people of Nigeria and in the African diaspora. Ifa involves the use of a divination system known as the "odu," which consists of 16 symbols that are used to interpret the messages of the spirits. Ifa divination is performed by a trained priest known as a babalawo, who uses a divination tray and a set of cowrie shells to communicate with the spirits and receive messages.

Healing

Healing is also an important concept in African diasporic religions. In these traditions, illness is often seen as a result of spiritual imbalance or interference from negative spirits. Healing involves the use of various methods to restore balance and harmony to the individual.

One example of healing in African diasporic religions is found in Candomble, a syncretic religion that developed in Brazil. Candomble involves the use of various herbs and plants for medicinal purposes, as well as the use of drumming and dance for spiritual healing. Practitioners of Candomble often consult with diviners to determine the underlying spiritual cause of illness, and may perform offerings or other rituals to restore balance and harmony.

Problems and Exercises

1. Research and compare the concepts of ancestor veneration in Vodou and Santeria. How are they similar, and how are they different? What are the different types of offerings made to ancestors in these traditions?

2. Choose one method of divination from an African diasporic religion, such as Ifa or the use of cowrie shells in Hoodoo, and research its history, techniques, and symbolism. Write a short essay about the cultural significance of this form of divination and its continued use in contemporary African diasporic religions.

3. Analyze the role of healing in African diasporic religions. What methods are used for physical, spiritual, and emotional healing? How do these methods relate to concepts of energy, balance, and harmony? What are some of the challenges faced by African diasporic communities in accessing healthcare and how have these challenges impacted the practice of traditional healing methods?

4.   Research the concept of the trickster in African diasporic religions, such as Eshu in Yoruba religion or Legba in Vodou. What are the characteristics of the trickster, and how do they relate to broader cultural beliefs about power, deception, and morality? What role does the trickster play in religious rituals and practices, and how has the concept of the trickster been adapted in contemporary African diasporic cultures?

5.   Reflect on your own cultural and religious background, and consider the ways in which ancestor veneration, divination, and healing are present (or absent) in your own traditions. How do these practices relate to broader cultural beliefs about family, community, and the natural world? Write a personal essay exploring these themes and reflecting on your own spiritual journey.

6.   Participate in a divination ritual or healing ceremony in an African diasporic religious tradition. Reflect on your experience and write a journal entry discussing the ways in which the ritual or ceremony impacted you personally. How did it challenge your preconceptions about spirituality and religion, and how did it connect you to broader cultural traditions and practices?

Conclusion:

The African diaspora has produced a rich and diverse array of religious traditions, which reflect the experiences and struggles of enslaved Africans and their descendants across the Americas and beyond. Key concepts and practices in these religions, such as ancestor veneration, divination, and healing, are grounded in deep cultural and spiritual traditions that have been maintained and adapted over centuries. Through the study of these traditions, we gain insights into the complex histories and cultural legacies of the African diaspora, as well as the enduring power of spiritual practices in shaping human experience and identity.

Overview of specific African diasporic religions, such as Vodou, Santeria, and Candomble

African diasporic religions, also known as Afro-Caribbean or Afro-Latin religions, are religious traditions that developed among African slaves and their descendants in the Caribbean, Latin America, and the United States. These religions blend elements of traditional African religions with Christian, Native American, and European influences, creating unique spiritual practices that reflect the history and culture of the African diaspora.

Exploring Origins, Traditions, and Contemporary Relevance

Three of the most well-known African diasporic religions are Vodou, Santeria, and Candomble. Each of these religions has its own distinct practices, beliefs, and deities, but they share common roots in West and Central African religions.

Vodou

Vodou, also spelled Voodoo or Vodun, originated in Haiti and is also practiced in parts of West Africa and the United States. Vodou combines elements of traditional West African religion with Catholicism, reflecting the influence of French colonialism and the forced conversion of slaves to Christianity.

Central to Vodou practice is the belief in a supreme creator god, Bondye, who is distant and inaccessible. Practitioners instead worship a pantheon of spirits, or lwa, who act as intermediaries between humans and the divine. Each lwa has a distinct personality, history, and area of influence, such as love, fertility, or wealth.

In Vodou, ancestor veneration is a crucial practice, with ancestors believed to be able to intercede on behalf of the living. Practitioners make offerings to ancestors and ask for their guidance and protection.

Santeria

Santeria, also known as Regla de Ocha or Lukumi, originated in Cuba and is also practiced in parts of the United States and other countries with large Cuban populations. Santeria developed as a syncretic religion, blending elements of Yoruba religion from Nigeria with Catholicism and indigenous Caribbean beliefs.

Central to Santeria practice is the belief in a supreme creator god, Olodumare, and a pantheon of orishas, or deities, who represent different aspects of the natural world. Each orisha has a distinct personality, history, and area of influence, such as healing, wisdom, or divination.

Santeria practitioners also venerate ancestors and make offerings to them. However, in Santeria, ancestors are seen as part of a larger lineage that includes orishas, with whom practitioners have a more direct relationship.

Candomble

Candomble originated in Brazil and is also practiced in other parts of Latin America. Candomble developed as a syncretic religion, blending elements of Yoruba religion, Catholicism, and indigenous Brazilian beliefs.

African Religions

Central to Candomble practice is the belief in a supreme creator god, Oludumare, and a pantheon of orixas, or deities, who represent different aspects of the natural world. Each orixa has a distinct personality, history, and area of influence, such as fertility, agriculture, or hunting.

In Candomble, ancestor veneration is also a crucial practice. Practitioners make offerings to ancestors and ask for their guidance and protection. However, ancestors are seen as part of a larger lineage that includes orixas and other spirits.

Practices and Rituals

Each of these religions has a complex system of practices and rituals, including music, dance, divination, and healing. These practices are used to communicate with spirits, seek guidance, and bring about positive change in the lives of practitioners.

One common practice in all three religions is animal sacrifice, which is used as a way to honor the spirits and gain their favor. Animal sacrifice is controversial and has been a source of conflict between practitioners and critics.

Another important practice is divination, which is used to gain insight into the past, present, and future. In Vodou, divination is done through the use of a special set of cowrie shells called a "boule," which are thrown and interpreted by a trained diviner known as a "houngan" or "mambo." In Santeria, divination is done through the use of a set of sacred palm nuts called "ikines" or through the use of cowrie shells. In Candomble, divination is done through the use of a special set of cowrie shells or through the use of a divination board known as an "opon ifa."

Dance and music are also an important part of these religions. In Vodou, practitioners often dance to the beat of drums called "tanbou" during religious ceremonies, while in Santeria, practitioners dance to the rhythms of the sacred drums called "bata." In Candomble, practitioners dance to the rhythms of the atabaques and other percussion instruments during religious ceremonies.

Healing is also an important aspect of these religions. In Vodou, healing is done through the use of herbal remedies, spiritual baths, and other forms of traditional medicine. In Santeria, healing is done through the use of herbal remedies, spiritual cleansings, and other forms of traditional medicine. In Candomble, healing is done through the use of herbal remedies and spiritual cleansings, as well as through the use of trance possession by the orishas.

Exploring Origins, Traditions, and Contemporary Relevance

Overall, each of these religions has its own unique practices and rituals that reflect the cultural and spiritual traditions of its practitioners. While there are similarities between these religions, such as the use of animal sacrifice and divination, each religion also has its own distinct practices and beliefs.

Problems and Exercises:

7. Research and compare the role of music and dance in Vodou, Santeria, and Candomble. How are they similar, and how are they different? What are the different types of drums and other percussion instruments used in these religions?

8. Choose one of the three religions discussed in this chapter (Vodou, Santeria, or Candomble) and research its history and development. What are some of the key figures and events in the religion's history?

9. Compare and contrast the use of animal sacrifice in Vodou, Santeria, and Candomble. What are the different types of animals that are sacrificed in each religion? What are the reasons for animal sacrifice, and what are the arguments against it?

10. Choose one of the healing practices discussed in this chapter (herbal remedies, spiritual baths, or trance possession) and research its use in one of the three religions discussed (Vodou, Santeria, or Candomble). How is the practice used, and what are its benefits?

Addressing misconceptions and stereotypes surrounding African diasporic religions

African diasporic religions, such as Vodou, Santeria, and Candomble, have long been misunderstood and stigmatized by mainstream society. These religions have been misrepresented in popular culture and media, leading to stereotypes and misconceptions that are harmful and inaccurate. In this section, we will explore some of the most common misconceptions and stereotypes surrounding African diasporic religions and provide a more accurate understanding of these vibrant and complex traditions.

Misconception 1: African diasporic religions are primitive and savage.

One of the most persistent and damaging misconceptions about African diasporic religions is that they are primitive and savage. This stereotype is rooted in colonialism and racism, which portrayed African cultures as inferior to European cultures. The reality is that African diasporic religions are complex and sophisticated systems of beliefs and practices that have evolved over centuries of interaction with diverse cultures.

African diasporic religions incorporate a wide range of practices, including divination, healing, music, dance, and ancestor veneration. These practices are deeply spiritual and serve as a way to connect with the divine and seek guidance and support. Rather than being primitive or savage, African diasporic religions are rich and nuanced traditions that have been shaped by the experiences and histories of the African diaspora.

Misconception 2: African diasporic religions are associated with black magic and evil.

Another common misconception about African diasporic religions is that they are associated with black magic and evil. This stereotype is perpetuated in popular culture, which often portrays African diasporic religions as dark and dangerous practices that involve sacrificing animals and casting spells.

The reality is that African diasporic religions are not about black magic or evil. Rather, they are about connecting with the divine and seeking guidance and support. Animal sacrifice is a common practice in these religions, but it is not about causing harm or suffering to animals. Rather, it is a way to honor the spirits and seek their favor. Similarly, the use of spells and charms in African diasporic religions is not about causing harm or manipulating others, but rather about manifesting positive change and protection.

Misconception 3: African diasporic religions are primitive forms of Christianity.

Another common misconception about African diasporic religions is that they are primitive forms of Christianity. This stereotype is rooted in the history of colonization and slavery, during which African slaves were forced to convert to Christianity and abandon their traditional religious practices.

The reality is that African diasporic religions are distinct and separate from Christianity. While they may incorporate some elements of Christian symbolism and language, they are not based on Christian doctrine or theology. Rather, they are rooted in African spiritual traditions that predate Christianity and have been adapted and transformed over time through the experiences of the African diaspora.

Exploring Origins, Traditions, and Contemporary Relevance

Misconception 4: African diasporic religions are only practiced by black people.

A final misconception about African diasporic religions is that they are only practiced by black people. This stereotype is rooted in the assumption that African diasporic religions are exclusive to African cultures and communities.

The reality is that African diasporic religions are practiced by people of all races and backgrounds. While they may have originated in African cultures, they have evolved and adapted over time through interaction with diverse communities and cultures. Today, African diasporic religions are practiced by people all over the world, including Latin America, the Caribbean, and the United States.

Addressing these misconceptions and stereotypes is important for promoting a more accurate and respectful understanding of African diasporic religions. By recognizing the complexity and diversity of these traditions, we can move beyond harmful stereotypes and embrace the richness and beauty of these vibrant spiritual practices.

Problems and Exercises:

11.   Research and compare the different ways in which African diasporic religions are practiced in different parts of the world. What similarities and differences do you observe?

12.   Choose one of the common misconceptions about African diasporic religions discussed in this section and write an essay addressing it. Provide examples and evidence to support your argument.

13.   Find examples of African diasporic religious practices in popular media, such as movies, TV shows, or music. How are these practices portrayed? Do they reinforce or challenge stereotypes and misconceptions?

14.   Research the history and cultural context of African diasporic religions. How have they been influenced by colonialism, slavery, and other historical factors? How have they adapted and evolved over time?

15.   Choose one African diasporic religious practice, such as music or divination, and research its cultural significance and meaning. How does this practice relate to other aspects of the religion?

16.   Interview someone who practices an African diasporic religion. What inspired them to embrace this spiritual path? How do they navigate the challenges and misconceptions associated with their beliefs?

Contemporary relevance of African diasporic religions, including their role in cultural identity and political activism.

African diasporic religions have maintained a strong cultural and political presence throughout the world, serving as an important tool for cultural identity and political activism. In this section, we will explore the ways in which these religions continue to play a vital role in shaping contemporary culture and politics.

Cultural Identity

For many practitioners of African diasporic religions, their religious beliefs and practices serve as a means of connecting with their cultural heritage. As we have seen, these religions emerged as a result of the transatlantic slave trade, through which millions of Africans were forcibly removed from their homelands and brought to the Americas and other parts of the world.

Despite the traumatic circumstances of their arrival, enslaved Africans were able to preserve aspects of their cultural traditions through their religious practices. Through syncretism with Christian and indigenous spiritual beliefs, these practices evolved into the diverse and dynamic religions we see today.

For many practitioners, these religions provide a sense of cultural continuity and identity, allowing them to connect with their African roots and maintain a connection to their ancestors. This is particularly important in the context of the ongoing legacies of colonization and racism, which have sought to erase or marginalize African cultures and traditions.

Political Activism

In addition to their cultural significance, African diasporic religions have also played an important role in political activism. Throughout history, practitioners of these religions have used their spiritual beliefs and practices to resist oppression and fight for social justice.

One notable example is the Haitian Revolution, in which enslaved Africans and their descendants rose up against their French colonizers to establish the world's first black-led republic. Vodou played a significant role in this revolution, serving as a source of inspiration and solidarity for the revolutionaries.

Similarly, Santeria and other African diasporic religions have been used as a means of resistance and empowerment in the face of colonialism and oppression. In the United States, for example, the Civil Rights movement of the 1950s and 1960s saw many African Americans turning to their spiritual traditions for strength and inspiration. African diasporic religions such as Hoodoo and Conjure played an important role in this movement, providing practitioners with tools for spiritual resistance and empowerment.

Contemporary Issues

African diasporic religions continue to be relevant to contemporary issues as well. For example, in Brazil, the rise of evangelical Christianity and conservative politics has led to increased persecution of practitioners of Candomble and other African diasporic religions. This has prompted a renewed activism and resistance within these communities, as they fight to preserve their religious traditions and defend their rights.

Similarly, in the United States, African diasporic religions continue to face discrimination and marginalization. Despite legal protections under the First Amendment, practitioners often face discrimination in employment, housing, and other areas of life. This has prompted many practitioners to organize and advocate for their rights, as well as to engage in education and outreach to combat stereotypes and misconceptions about their religions.

Exercises:

17.   What role do African diasporic religions play in shaping cultural identity and preserving cultural heritage?

18.   How have African diasporic religions been used as a tool for political activism and resistance throughout history?

19.   What contemporary issues do practitioners of African diasporic religions face, and how are they addressing these issues through activism and education?

20.   How can non-practitioners of African diasporic religions support these communities and combat stereotypes and discrimination?

CHAPTER 22: THE HISTORY AND DEVELOPMENT OF AFRICAN DIASPORIC RELIGIONS

African diasporic religions are a diverse set of religious traditions that originated in Africa and were brought to the Americas through the slave trade. They are characterized by a complex syncretism of African, European, and indigenous American religious beliefs and practices. This chapter will explore the history and development of African diasporic religions, focusing on the impact of the slave trade and colonization on the formation and evolution of these traditions.

Origins of African diasporic religions

The origins of African diasporic religions can be traced back to the traditional religions of West and Central Africa. These religions were characterized by a belief in a supreme creator god, a pantheon of lesser gods and goddesses, ancestor veneration, divination, and spirit possession. They also featured elaborate rituals and ceremonies that were designed to honor the gods and goddesses and to promote health, prosperity, and fertility.

When Africans were brought to the Americas as slaves, they were forced to abandon their traditional religious beliefs and practices and to adopt the religions of their European and American slave owners. However, many Africans were able to preserve elements of their traditional religions by syncretizing them with the religions of their oppressors. This process of syncretism led to the development of new religious traditions that blended African, European, and indigenous American elements.

The impact of the slave trade on African diasporic religions

The slave trade had a profound impact on the development of African diasporic religions. The experience of slavery was characterized by extreme brutality, exploitation, and dehumanization, and many slaves turned to religion as a means of coping with the trauma of their experience. African diasporic religions provided a sense of community, connection to the divine, and a means of resistance against their oppressors.

Exploring Origins, Traditions, and Contemporary Relevance

The slave trade also led to the formation of new religious traditions as Africans from different regions and ethnic groups were forced to interact with each other. These interactions led to the blending of different African religious traditions, resulting in the formation of new syncretic religions. For example, the religion of Vodou in Haiti is a blend of traditional West African religions, European Catholicism, and indigenous American religions.

The impact of colonization on African diasporic religions

Colonization also had a significant impact on the development of African diasporic religions. European colonizers sought to eradicate traditional African religions and to convert Africans to Christianity. This led to the suppression of African religious practices and the persecution of those who practiced them.

However, despite the efforts of colonizers to suppress African religions, many Africans were able to preserve their religious traditions through syncretism. For example, the religion of Santeria in Cuba is a blend of traditional West African religions and Catholicism. Similarly, the religion of Candomble in Brazil is a blend of traditional West African religions and indigenous American religions.

The development of African diasporic religions in the Americas

African diasporic religions developed differently in different parts of the Americas. In the Caribbean, African religions blended with the religions of indigenous Americans and European colonizers to create new syncretic religions such as Vodou, Santeria, and Candomble.

In North America, African diasporic religions developed in the context of slavery and segregation. African slaves in North America were forbidden from practicing their traditional religions and were forced to adopt the religions of their slave owners. However, despite these restrictions, African slaves were able to preserve elements of their traditional religions through syncretism. For example, the religion of Hoodoo in the southern United States is a blend of traditional West African religions, Protestant Christianity, and Native American spirituality.

In South America, African diasporic religions developed in the context of slavery and colonization. Africans brought to South America were also forced to convert to Christianity, but like in North America, they were able to preserve elements of their traditional religions through syncretism. The most well-known African diasporic religion in South America is Candomblé in Brazil, which developed in the 19th century.

African Religions

Candomblé is a syncretic religion that combines elements of traditional West African religions with Catholicism. The religion is based on the worship of orixás, or deities, who are believed to have the power to influence the natural world. Each orixá has its own characteristics and is associated with different elements of nature, such as water, earth, and air. Candomblé also includes ancestor veneration, divination, and spirit possession.

Another African diasporic religion in South America is Santería, which developed in Cuba. Santería is a syncretic religion that combines elements of traditional Yoruba religion with Catholicism. Like Candomblé, Santería is based on the worship of orishas, who are associated with different aspects of the natural world. Santería also includes divination and spirit possession.

In the Caribbean, African diasporic religions developed in the context of slavery and colonialism. One example of a Caribbean African diasporic religion is Vodou, which developed in Haiti. Vodou is a syncretic religion that combines elements of traditional West African religions with Catholicism. The religion is based on the worship of lwa, or spirits, who are believed to have the power to influence the natural world. Each lwa has its own characteristics and is associated with different aspects of human life, such as love, fertility, and wealth. Vodou also includes ancestor veneration, divination, and spirit possession.

In conclusion, African diasporic religions have a complex and varied history that is deeply intertwined with the history of slavery, colonization, and oppression. Despite these challenges, African slaves and their descendants were able to preserve elements of their traditional religions through syncretism, creating new religions that are unique and powerful. Today, African diasporic religions continue to evolve and thrive, providing spiritual guidance and support to millions of people around the world.

Discuss the historical context and conditions that led to the development of African diasporic religions

The history of African diasporic religions is deeply intertwined with the history of the transatlantic slave trade and the colonization of the Americas. The forced migration of millions of Africans to the New World resulted in the creation of new religions that blended African religious practices with those of the Americas.

The transatlantic slave trade, which began in the 15th century, involved the forcible transportation of millions of Africans to the Americas to work as slaves on plantations and in mines. During the journey, slaves were often separated from their families and subjected to brutal treatment, including beatings, rape, and forced labor. Many slaves died during the voyage, and those who survived often suffered from malnutrition and disease.

Once they arrived in the New World, African slaves were forced to abandon their traditional religions and adopt the religions of their captors. This was especially true in North America, where Christianity was the dominant religion among slave owners. However, despite these restrictions, African slaves were able to preserve elements of their traditional religions through syncretism. This led to the development of new religions that blended African religious practices with those of the Americas.

The conditions in which African slaves lived were often harsh and oppressive. Slaves were considered property and were treated as such. They were forced to work long hours in difficult and often dangerous conditions. Slaves were often separated from their families and communities, which made it difficult to maintain their cultural traditions. In addition, slaves were often subjected to brutal punishment for minor infractions, which created an atmosphere of fear and mistrust.

Despite these challenges, African slaves were able to maintain their cultural traditions in a variety of ways. They created new languages and cultural practices that allowed them to communicate and connect with each other. They also formed mutual aid societies and other organizations that provided support and assistance to members of their communities.

One of the most important ways that African slaves maintained their cultural traditions was through religion. African slaves brought with them a rich and diverse array of religious practices, including animism, ancestor veneration, and divination. These practices were adapted to the new environment and blended with the religious practices of the Americas, resulting in the creation of new religions.

The development of African diasporic religions was also influenced by the political and economic conditions of the time. During the colonial period, European powers established a system of mercantilism that allowed them to extract resources from their colonies and export them back to Europe. This system relied heavily on slave labor, which led to the large-scale importation of Africans to the Americas.

The rise of the abolitionist movement in the 19th century also played a role in the development of African diasporic religions. As slaves became more aware of their rights and began to resist their enslavement, they turned to religion as a source of inspiration and strength. African diasporic religions provided a way for slaves to connect with their ancestors, resist oppression, and assert their dignity and humanity.

African Religions

In conclusion, the historical context and conditions that led to the development of African diasporic religions were complex and multifaceted. The transatlantic slave trade and colonization of the Americas created a new cultural and social environment that forced African slaves to adapt and create new religious practices. Despite the oppressive conditions in which they lived, African slaves were able to maintain their cultural traditions and create new religions that continue to thrive to this day.

Examine the role of slavery and the slave trade in the spread and evolution of these religions

The transatlantic slave trade, which took place from the 16th to the 19th centuries, was a brutal and devastating period in world history. Millions of Africans were forcibly taken from their homes and brought to the Americas, where they were sold into slavery. This violent displacement of people and cultures had a profound impact on the development of African diasporic religions.

The slave trade involved the forced migration of millions of people from diverse ethnic and cultural backgrounds. Among these were people who practiced a wide variety of traditional African religions. The enslaved Africans were stripped of their cultures and their languages, and were forced to adopt the religions and cultural practices of their European slave masters.

One of the key ways that African diasporic religions emerged was through syncretism. Syncretism refers to the blending of different religious traditions to create new, hybrid forms. In the context of the slave trade, syncretism allowed enslaved Africans to preserve elements of their traditional religions while also adopting aspects of the religions of their slave masters.

For example, in the Americas, enslaved Africans were often introduced to Christianity. Many slaves adopted Christianity as their religion, but they also incorporated elements of their traditional African religions into their Christian practice. This syncretism led to the development of new religious practices, such as Santeria, which blends elements of Yoruba religion with Catholicism.

In addition to syncretism, slavery and the slave trade played a key role in the spread and evolution of African diasporic religions. As enslaved Africans were transported across the Atlantic, they brought their religious practices with them. These practices were often adapted to the new contexts in which they found themselves, resulting in the emergence of new religious traditions.

For example, in the United States, enslaved Africans from different regions of Africa were brought together and forced to live and work together. This led to the development of new cultural practices, including new religious traditions. In the southern United States, for example, Hoodoo developed as a blend of African traditional religion, Native American spirituality, and Protestant Christianity.

The brutal conditions of slavery also had a profound impact on the development of African diasporic religions. Enslaved Africans were subjected to violence, exploitation, and oppression. In response, they developed religious practices that provided them with a sense of empowerment, resistance, and resilience.

For example, in Haiti, enslaved Africans developed Vodou as a way to resist the violence and oppression of their slave masters. Vodou provided a way for enslaved Africans to connect with their ancestors and the spirits of the natural world, and to draw upon their power and wisdom to resist their oppressors.

Similarly, in Brazil, enslaved Africans developed Candomble as a way to resist the violence and oppression of slavery. Candomble provided a way for enslaved Africans to connect with their ancestors and the orishas, or deities, of the Yoruba religion. By drawing upon the power and wisdom of these ancestral and divine beings, enslaved Africans were able to resist their oppressors and maintain a sense of identity and community.

Overall, slavery and the slave trade had a profound impact on the development of African diasporic religions. Through syncretism, adaptation, and resistance, enslaved Africans were able to preserve and adapt their traditional religious practices in the face of extreme violence and oppression. The resulting religious traditions are a testament to the resilience and creativity of enslaved Africans in the face of unimaginable adversity.

Analyze the ways in which African diasporic religions have evolved over time and adapted to new contexts

African diasporic religions have undergone significant evolution over time, adapting to new contexts and incorporating new beliefs and practices. These religions have been shaped by a variety of factors, including the experiences of the enslaved Africans who brought them to the Americas, the cultural and spiritual practices of the peoples with whom they interacted in the diaspora, and the social and political conditions of the countries where they developed.

One of the most significant ways that African diasporic religions have evolved is through syncretism, which refers to the blending of two or more cultural or religious traditions to create a new hybrid form. Syncretism has played a crucial role in the development of African diasporic religions, as enslaved Africans were forced to adapt their traditional beliefs and practices to the new contexts in which they found themselves.

In the Americas, African diasporic religions blended with the religious traditions of the Europeans and Native Americans, resulting in new forms of worship that combined elements from all three cultures. For example, in Brazil, the Afro-Brazilian religion of Candomblé developed out of the syncretism of West African religious traditions with Catholicism. Similarly, Santería in Cuba is a blend of West African Yoruba religion with Catholicism and indigenous beliefs.

Another way in which African diasporic religions have evolved is through the process of transformation, which involves the adoption of new beliefs and practices in response to changing circumstances. As African diasporic religions spread throughout the Americas and encountered new cultural and spiritual practices, they incorporated these elements into their own belief systems, adapting to new contexts and evolving over time.

For example, in the United States, Hoodoo developed as a form of African American folk magic that incorporated elements of traditional West African religions, Protestant Christianity, and Native American spirituality. Hoodoo practitioners believed in the power of magical objects such as amulets and talismans, and they used herbs, roots, and other natural substances in their magical practices.

In addition to syncretism and transformation, African diasporic religions have also evolved through the process of differentiation, which involves the creation of new religious traditions that are distinct from their parent religions. This process has occurred as African diasporic religions have spread to new regions and encountered new cultural and spiritual practices, leading to the development of new beliefs and practices.

For example, Vodou in Haiti is distinct from its West African roots, incorporating elements of Catholicism and other traditions that were present in Haiti at the time of its development. Similarly, Umbanda in Brazil is a unique form of African diasporic religion that blends African, indigenous, and European traditions.

Overall, the evolution of African diasporic religions has been shaped by a variety of factors, including the experiences of the enslaved Africans who brought these religions to the Americas, the cultural and spiritual practices of the peoples with whom they interacted in the diaspora, and the social and political conditions of the countries where these religions developed. Through processes of syncretism, transformation, and differentiation, African diasporic religions have adapted to new contexts and evolved over time, creating new and unique forms of worship that continue to thrive today.

CHAPTER 23: THE RELATIONSHIP BETWEEN AFRICAN DIASPORIC RELIGIONS AND AFRICAN RELIGIONS

African diasporic religions are a diverse set of religious practices that originated in Africa and were brought to the Americas through the transatlantic slave trade. They developed in the context of slavery, colonization, and cultural hybridization, and have evolved over time to adapt to new contexts and challenges. Despite the challenges of slavery and colonization, African diasporic religions have persisted and continue to thrive in the modern world.

In this chapter, we will explore the relationship between African diasporic religions and African religions. We will examine the historical context and conditions that led to the development of African diasporic religions, the ways in which these religions have evolved and adapted over time, and the similarities and differences between African diasporic religions and African religions.

First, it is important to understand the historical context and conditions that led to the development of African diasporic religions. The transatlantic slave trade, which lasted from the 16th to the 19th century, involved the forced migration of millions of Africans to the Americas. These Africans were taken from their homes and families and brought to the Americas as slaves. As a result, they were cut off from their traditional religious practices and forced to adopt the religions of their slave owners.

Despite these restrictions, African slaves were able to preserve elements of their traditional religions through syncretism. Syncretism is the blending of different religious traditions to create a new and unique religious practice. African slaves in the Americas were exposed to the religions of their slave owners, which included Christianity and indigenous religions, and they blended these practices with their own traditional African religions to create new religions such as Vodou, Santeria, and Candomble.

In contrast to African diasporic religions, African religions have developed and evolved within the African continent. These religions are diverse and include traditional religions such as Yoruba, Akan, and Dinka, as well as newer religions such as Islam and Christianity, which were introduced to Africa through colonization and trade.

African religions are characterized by a strong connection to the natural world and the spiritual realm. They often involve the veneration of ancestors and the use of divination and other spiritual practices to communicate with the spirit world. African religions are also characterized by a focus on communal values and social harmony.

Despite the differences between African diasporic religions and African religions, there are also many similarities. Both sets of religions emphasize the importance of community and social harmony. Both also involve the use of music, dance, and other forms of expression to communicate with the spiritual world. Additionally, both African diasporic religions and African religions have a strong focus on the natural world and the use of natural remedies and practices in healing.

In conclusion, the relationship between African diasporic religions and African religions is complex and multifaceted. While African diasporic religions developed in the context of slavery and colonization and have evolved to adapt to new contexts, African religions have developed and evolved within the African continent. Despite these differences, both sets of religions share many similarities and emphasize the importance of community, social harmony, and a connection to the spiritual world. Throughout this chapter, we will explore these similarities and differences in greater detail and examine the ways in which African diasporic religions have adapted and evolved over time.

Compare and contrast the beliefs and practices of African diasporic religions and African religions

The relationship between African diasporic religions and African religions is a complex and multifaceted one that has evolved over many centuries. African diasporic religions are those religious traditions that have developed among the descendants of Africans who were brought to the Americas as slaves during the transatlantic slave trade. These religions have been shaped by the experiences of African people who were forcibly removed from their homelands and transported to new and unfamiliar environments. In contrast, African religions are the traditional religions that are practiced by various ethnic groups across the African continent. These religions have developed over thousands of years in diverse environments and have been shaped by a variety of cultural and historical factors.

In this section, we will compare and contrast the beliefs and practices of African diasporic religions and African religions. We will explore the ways in which these two types of religions have influenced each other over time and how they have adapted to new contexts. We will also examine the similarities and differences between these religions, including their beliefs about the divine, their rituals and ceremonies, and their concepts of morality and ethics.

Beliefs About the Divine:

One of the primary ways in which African diasporic religions and African religions differ is in their beliefs about the divine. African diasporic religions are often characterized by a syncretic approach to religion, in which elements of various African and European religious traditions have been blended together to form new religions. For example, the religion of Santeria, which developed in Cuba, combines elements of Yoruba religion with Roman Catholicism. Similarly, Vodou, which developed in Haiti, combines elements of West African religion with Catholicism.

In contrast, African religions tend to be more localized and specific to particular ethnic groups. These religions often have complex cosmologies that describe the relationships between various deities, ancestors, and spirits. Many African religions also have a strong emphasis on ancestor veneration, in which ancestors are believed to play a crucial role in the lives of their descendants. African religions often have complex systems of divination, in which priests or diviners use various methods to communicate with the divine and gain insight into the future.

Beliefs about the divine are fundamental to both African diasporic religions and African religions. African diasporic religions often feature a syncretic approach to religion, which means that they incorporate elements of various religious traditions into their belief systems. In contrast, African religions tend to be more localized and specific to particular ethnic groups.

In African diasporic religions, the divine is often conceptualized as a complex and multifaceted entity. For example, in Santeria, the supreme being is known as Olodumare, who is believed to be the creator of the universe. Olodumare is also associated with other deities, known as Orishas, who represent different aspects of nature and human experience. These Orishas are often associated with Catholic saints, which is a result of the syncretic nature of Santeria.

Similarly, in Vodou, the supreme being is known as Bondye, who is believed to be responsible for creating the world and all living things. Vodou also features a complex pantheon of spirits, known as lwa, who are associated with various aspects of human experience, such as love, fertility, and war. These lwa are believed to be able to interact with humans and can be called upon for help in various situations.

In contrast, African religions often feature a more localized and specific approach to the divine. For example, in the Yoruba religion of Nigeria, there are over 400 different Orishas, each with their own specific characteristics and responsibilities. These Orishas are associated with different natural phenomena, such as rivers, thunder, and wind, and are believed to have the power to influence the lives of humans.

African religions also often have a strong emphasis on ancestor veneration. Ancestors are believed to have a direct connection to the divine and are able to act as intermediaries between the living and the divine. Ancestor veneration is also an important aspect of many African diasporic religions, such as Santeria and Vodou.

Another key difference between African diasporic religions and African religions is the role of divination. Many African religions have complex systems of divination, in which priests or diviners use various methods to communicate with the divine and gain insight into the future. In the Yoruba religion, for example, divination is performed using the Ifa system, which involves casting a chain of eight cowrie shells to determine which Orisha is speaking and what message they have.

In African diasporic religions, divination is also an important practice. For example, in Santeria, divination is often performed using a set of cowrie shells or a deck of cards known as the tarot. Divination is used to gain insight into a wide range of issues, including health, relationships, and financial matters.

Overall, the beliefs about the divine in African diasporic religions and African religions reflect their different histories and cultural contexts. African diasporic religions developed as a result of the forced migration of African peoples to the Americas and the Caribbean, and their syncretic nature reflects the blending of African and European religious traditions. African religions, on the other hand, developed in specific cultural contexts in Africa, and often feature complex cosmologies and systems of ancestor veneration and divination.

Rituals and Ceremonies:

Another way in which African diasporic religions and African religions differ is in their rituals and ceremonies. African diasporic religions often include a wide variety of rituals and ceremonies that are designed to honor the divine, ancestors, and spirits. These rituals and ceremonies may include offerings of food, music and dance, and the use of various spiritual tools such as candles, incense, and statues.

In contrast, African religions often have highly structured and elaborate rituals that are specific to particular ethnic groups. These rituals may include sacrifices of animals, offerings of food and drink, and the use of divination to communicate with the divine. Many African religions also have elaborate initiation ceremonies that mark important life transitions such as puberty, marriage, and death.

Rituals and ceremonies are an integral part of both African diasporic religions and African religions, and they play a significant role in establishing and maintaining a connection with the divine. While there are similarities between the two, there are also significant differences in terms of the types of rituals and ceremonies that are practiced.

African diasporic religions, as previously mentioned, often have a syncretic approach to religion, which means that they incorporate elements of various religious traditions. As a result, there is a wide variety of rituals and ceremonies that are practiced in these religions. For example, in Santeria, one of the most well-known African diasporic religions, ceremonies are often held in honor of the Orishas, or deities, and include offerings of food, dance, and music. In Vodou, ceremonies may include offerings to the lwa, or spirits, as well as rituals for healing, protection, and success.

In addition to these ceremonies, African diasporic religions also often incorporate the use of spiritual tools such as candles, incense, and statues. These tools are believed to help facilitate communication with the divine and to provide protection and guidance to practitioners. For example, in Hoodoo, a practice that developed in the southern United States, practitioners may use candles and oils to attract love, money, or protection.

African religions, on the other hand, tend to have highly structured and specific rituals that are tied to particular ethnic groups. For example, in the Yoruba religion, which is practiced in Nigeria and other parts of West Africa, ceremonies are held in honor of various Orishas and may involve animal sacrifices and offerings of food and drink. These ceremonies are often led by priests or priestesses who have been trained in the religion and who have a deep understanding of the complex cosmology and mythology of the religion.

Initiation ceremonies are also an important part of many African religions. These ceremonies mark important life transitions and may involve rituals such as scarification, circumcision, and the wearing of special clothing or jewelry. Initiation ceremonies may also involve the use of divination to determine the person's destiny and to communicate with the divine.

It is important to note that while African diasporic religions and African religions may have different types of rituals and ceremonies, they both share a common belief in the importance of establishing a connection with the divine.

Exploring Origins, Traditions, and Contemporary Relevance

Whether through offerings of food, dance, or animal sacrifices, these rituals and ceremonies serve to create a sacred space in which practitioners can communicate with the divine and receive guidance and protection.

Examples, Problems, and Exercises:

1.   Research and compare the types of rituals and ceremonies that are practiced in Santeria and Vodou. How are they similar, and how are they different?

2.   What are some of the specific rituals and ceremonies that are practiced in the Yoruba religion? How do these rituals reflect the religion's complex cosmology and mythology?

3.   Imagine that you are a practitioner of Hoodoo. What types of spiritual tools would you use to attract love, money, or protection? Explain why you chose these particular tools.

4.   Initiation ceremonies are an important part of many African religions. Research and describe the initiation ceremony for one African religion of your choice. What are some of the key elements of the ceremony, and what is its significance?

Morality and Ethics:

Finally, African diasporic religions and African religions also differ in their concepts of morality and ethics. African diasporic religions often place a strong emphasis on personal responsibility and the importance of living a moral and ethical life. For example, in the religion of Candomble, which developed in Brazil, adherents are expected to follow a strict code of ethics that includes respect for the divine, respect for elders, and respect for the environment.

Similarly, many African religions also emphasize the importance of living a moral and ethical life. However, these religions often have complex systems of morality that are specific to particular ethnic groups. For example, in the religion of the Yoruba people of Nigeria, there is a complex system of ethics known as Ifa divination, which is used to determine the morality of a particular action or decision. In Ifa divination, a diviner uses cowrie shells or other divinatory tools to communicate with the divine and receive guidance on ethical issues.

Another key aspect of morality and ethics in African religions is the importance of community and social responsibility. Many African religions place a strong emphasis on the interconnectedness of all living beings and the importance of contributing to the well-being of the community as a whole. In many African societies, it is believed that individual success and prosperity are dependent on the well-being of the community. This belief is often reflected in the moral and ethical codes of these religions, which emphasize the importance of sharing resources and helping those in need.

However, it is important to note that not all African religions share the same moral and ethical values. For example, some religions may have more lenient attitudes towards certain behaviors, while others may be more strict. Additionally, there may be variations in ethical codes and practices within the same religion, depending on factors such as geographic location and cultural traditions.

It is also worth noting that African diasporic religions and African religions are not the only spiritual traditions that place a strong emphasis on morality and ethics. Many other spiritual traditions, such as Buddhism and Hinduism, also have complex systems of morality and ethics that are specific to their respective cultural contexts.

In order to better understand and engage with the concepts of morality and ethics in African religions, it is important to consider the diverse cultural contexts in which these religions developed. By examining the specific ethical codes and practices of different African religions and ethnic groups, we can gain a deeper appreciation for the rich and diverse spiritual traditions of the African continent. We can also gain insights into how these traditions continue to shape the moral and ethical values of contemporary African communities around the world.

Examples, problems, and exercises:

5. Research the ethical codes of two different African religions and compare and contrast their similarities and differences.

6. Analyze the role of community and social responsibility in African religions and discuss how this relates to contemporary issues such as climate change and global inequality.

7. Explore the ways in which African diasporic religions have adapted and transformed traditional African ethical codes in response to their cultural and historical contexts.

8. Discuss the potential benefits and drawbacks of using divination as a tool for ethical decision-making, drawing on examples from African religions and other spiritual traditions.

Exploring Origins, Traditions, and Contemporary Relevance

Discuss the ways in which African diasporic religions have incorporated elements from African religions

African diasporic religions, such as Santeria, Vodou, and Candomble, have a complex and fascinating history of incorporating elements from African religions. These religions developed in the Americas, the Caribbean, and South America as a result of the transatlantic slave trade, which brought millions of Africans to these regions as slaves. Despite the efforts of slave owners and colonial authorities to suppress African religions, many aspects of these religions managed to survive and evolve in the diaspora. In this section, we will explore some of the ways in which African diasporic religions have incorporated elements from African religions.

One of the most important ways in which African diasporic religions have incorporated elements from African religions is through the preservation of oral traditions. In many African cultures, knowledge of religious practices and beliefs is transmitted orally from generation to generation. This oral tradition has played a crucial role in preserving the cultural and religious heritage of African societies, and it has also played a key role in the development of African diasporic religions. Through the preservation of oral traditions, African diasporic religions have been able to incorporate elements of African religions into their own practices, even in the absence of written records.

Another important way in which African diasporic religions have incorporated elements from African religions is through syncretism. Syncretism is the process by which two or more distinct cultural or religious traditions merge to form a new hybrid tradition. In the case of African diasporic religions, syncretism has often occurred between African religions and Christianity. During the colonial period, European colonizers and missionaries imposed Christianity on African slaves as a means of suppressing their traditional religious practices. However, many African slaves found ways to incorporate elements of Christianity into their traditional religious practices, creating a hybrid form of religion that allowed them to maintain their cultural identity while appeasing their Christian masters.

One example of this syncretism is the religion of Santeria, which developed in Cuba. Santeria is a fusion of Yoruba religion, which was brought to Cuba by African slaves, and Catholicism, which was imposed on the slaves by their Spanish colonizers. In Santeria, the Yoruba gods, or orishas, are often associated with Catholic saints, and many of the rituals and ceremonies of Santeria involve both Yoruba and Catholic elements. For example, the ritual of the Catholic Mass is often incorporated into Santeria ceremonies, and images of Catholic saints are often used to represent the orishas.

Similarly, in the religion of Vodou, which developed in Haiti, the gods of the Fon and Ewe peoples of West Africa were merged with Catholic saints to create a new pantheon of spirits. This pantheon is known as the lwa, and each lwa is associated with a particular Catholic saint. For example, the lwa Legba is associated with Saint Peter, and the lwa Erzulie Freda is associated with the Virgin Mary.

In addition to syncretism, African diasporic religions have also incorporated elements of African religions through the use of herbal medicine and divination. In many African societies, herbal medicine and divination play a central role in religious practices. Herbal medicine is used to treat illness and maintain physical and spiritual health, while divination is used to communicate with the divine and seek guidance on important matters. In the diaspora, African slaves were often denied access to Western medicine and were forced to rely on traditional herbal remedies to treat illness. As a result, African diasporic religions developed a strong tradition of herbal medicine, which continues to be an important part of these religions today.

Divination is also an important part of African diasporic religions. Many of these religions use divination to communicate with the divine and seek guidance on important matters.

Analyze the impact of African diasporic religions on the preservation and revitalization of African religions

The impact of African diasporic religions on the preservation and revitalization of African religions is a complex and multifaceted topic. African diasporic religions, which include religions such as Vodou, Santeria, and Candomble, have played an important role in preserving and revitalizing traditional African religious practices in the Americas and the Caribbean.

One of the primary ways in which African diasporic religions have impacted the preservation and revitalization of African religions is through the retention of traditional African religious beliefs and practices. These religions often incorporate African deities and spiritual practices, such as ancestor veneration, divination, and spirit possession, that were brought over from Africa during the transatlantic slave trade. These practices have been preserved and passed down through generations within African diasporic religions, contributing to the preservation and continuation of African religious traditions.

Another important aspect of the impact of African diasporic religions on the preservation and revitalization of African religions is the role that they have played in creating spaces for the practice of African religious traditions. Due to the persecution and oppression faced by enslaved Africans and their descendants in the Americas and the Caribbean, the practice of African religious traditions was often driven underground. African diasporic religions have provided a means for the practice of these traditions in a relatively safe and secure manner, allowing for the preservation and continuation of these traditions.

In addition to preserving and revitalizing traditional African religious practices, African diasporic religions have also contributed to the development of new religious practices that incorporate elements of both African and non-African traditions. For example, in the religion of Candomble, which developed in Brazil, African spiritual practices were combined with elements of Catholicism and indigenous Brazilian religious traditions. Similarly, in the religion of Santeria, which developed in Cuba, African spiritual practices were combined with elements of Catholicism and indigenous Cuban religious traditions. These hybrid religious traditions have played an important role in preserving and revitalizing African religious practices by adapting to the cultural and social contexts in which they are practiced.

However, it is important to note that the impact of African diasporic religions on the preservation and revitalization of African religions is not without controversy or criticism. Some critics argue that African diasporic religions have distorted or misrepresented traditional African religious practices, while others argue that they have contributed to the erasure of the specific cultural and historical contexts in which these practices were originally developed. It is also important to note that African diasporic religions have not been universally accepted or embraced within African communities, and there are often debates and tensions surrounding their relationship to traditional African religions.

Despite these debates and tensions, the impact of African diasporic religions on the preservation and revitalization of African religions is undeniable. These religions have played a critical role in preserving and passing down traditional African religious practices, creating spaces for their practice, and adapting these practices to new cultural and social contexts. As African diasporic religions continue to evolve and develop, they will undoubtedly continue to shape the ways in which African religious practices are understood, practiced, and transmitted.

Examples and exercises:

Research and write an essay on the role that African diasporic religions have played in preserving and revitalizing specific African religious traditions, such as Yoruba religion or Akan religion.

African Religions

1. Conduct a comparative analysis of the ways in which different African diasporic religions have incorporated elements of African religious traditions. What similarities and differences do you observe?

2. Consider the critiques and criticisms of African diasporic religions that have been raised by scholars and practitioners of African religions. How might these critiques be addressed or responded to?

3. Engage in a discussion or debate on the role of African diasporic religions in the preservation and revitalization of African religions. What are the benefits and drawbacks of these religions, and how might they impact the broader context of African cultural heritage?

Create a case study on a specific African diasporic religion and its relationship to a specific African religious tradition. Analyze the ways in which the diasporic religion has influenced and impacted the traditional religion, as well as how the traditional religion has influenced the diasporic religion.

Read and analyze primary sources related to the history and development of African diasporic religions, as well as scholarly articles and books on the topic. Write a critical analysis of the ways in which these sources represent the relationship between African diasporic religions and African religions, and consider how these representations may be influenced by cultural biases and assumptions.

Conduct an interview with a practitioner of an African diasporic religion or an African religious tradition. Ask them about their beliefs, practices, and experiences, as well as their perspectives on the relationship between these two types of religion.

Explore the role of African diasporic religions in contemporary African society, including their impact on cultural identity, social structures, and political movements. Consider the ways in which these religions are adapting to modern challenges and opportunities, and how they are contributing to the ongoing evolution of African cultural heritage.

Overall, the study of the relationship between African diasporic religions and African religions is a complex and multifaceted topic that requires careful analysis and consideration of a wide range of factors. By engaging in a variety of examples and exercises, students can develop a deeper understanding of this relationship and its significance for African cultural heritage and spiritual traditions.

CHAPTER 24: KEY PRACTICES AND BELIEFS IN AFRICAN DIASPORIC RELIGIONS

African diasporic religions, also known as African-derived religions, are a diverse set of religious practices that emerged in the Americas as a result of the transatlantic slave trade. These religions are often a blend of African religious traditions and elements of Christianity, Islam, and other religious traditions. They are found in various countries and regions, including the United States, Brazil, Cuba, Haiti, Trinidad and Tobago, Jamaica, and others.

African diasporic religions are known for their vibrant and colorful rituals, music, dance, and art. They have a rich history and culture, and have been instrumental in preserving and transmitting African cultural traditions and values across generations. In this chapter, we will explore some of the key practices and beliefs in African diasporic religions, including their cosmology, rituals, divination practices, and beliefs about the afterlife.

Cosmology:

Cosmology refers to the study of the structure, origin, and evolution of the universe. In African diasporic religions, cosmology plays a central role in understanding the nature of the divine, the universe, and humanity's place within it. The cosmology of African diasporic religions is rich and complex, and it varies among different traditions and regions.

One of the most important concepts in African diasporic cosmology is the idea of a Supreme Being or Creator. This being is often viewed as the originator of all creation and is considered the most powerful force in the universe. In Yoruba religion, for example, the Supreme Being is known as Olodumare, who is believed to have created the universe and all living things. In Akan religion, the Supreme Being is referred to as Nyame, who is associated with the sky and is seen as the source of all life and creation.

Another important aspect of African diasporic cosmology is the belief in a pantheon of deities or spirits. These deities are often associated with various natural phenomena, such as rivers, trees, mountains, and animals, and are believed to have the power to intervene in human affairs. For example, in Haitian Vodou, the deity Ezili

Danto is associated with motherhood, fertility, and protection, while in Santeria, the deity Yemaya is associated with the ocean and is revered as the mother of all life.

The cosmology of African diasporic religions also includes beliefs about the nature of the universe and its relationship to humanity. In many traditions, the universe is viewed as a complex and interconnected system, in which all things are linked and dependent on each other. For example, in Ifa, a Yoruba divination system, the universe is seen as a vast web of relationships between the gods, humans, and nature, in which each element plays a vital role in maintaining the balance and harmony of the universe.

The importance of ancestors is also a crucial aspect of African diasporic cosmology. Ancestors are believed to have a special relationship with the living and are often viewed as mediators between the living and the divine. In many African diasporic religions, ancestors are revered and are believed to have the power to influence the lives of their descendants. In Haitian Vodou, for example, the ancestors are called upon to offer guidance, protection, and blessings, while in Ifa, ancestors are believed to have the power to communicate with the gods and influence the outcomes of divination readings.

The cosmology of African diasporic religions is rich and multifaceted, and it reflects the complex and diverse cultural traditions of Africa and the African diaspora. The belief in a Supreme Being, a pantheon of deities, the interconnectedness of the universe, and the importance of ancestors are all essential components of African diasporic cosmology. By understanding these beliefs, we can gain a deeper appreciation for the spiritual traditions and cultural heritage of African diasporic communities.

Examples and exercises:

1.   Research and write an essay on the role of the Supreme Being in African diasporic religions, and compare and contrast the different names and attributes associated with this deity across various traditions.

2.   Discuss the importance of ancestors in African diasporic cosmology, and analyze the ways in which ancestors are revered and celebrated in different traditions.

3.   Conduct a comparative analysis of the ways in which different African diasporic religions conceive of the relationship between the universe and humanity. What similarities and differences do you observe?

Exploring Origins, Traditions, and Contemporary Relevance

4.   Engage in a group discussion or debate on the importance of pantheons of deities in African diasporic religions. What functions do these deities serve, and how do they differ across various traditions

Rituals:

Rituals are an important aspect of African diasporic religions, and they are often performed in public and private settings. These rituals are often designed to honor the ancestors, deities, and spirits, and to seek their blessings and protection. They may include offerings of food, drink, and other items, as well as the singing of hymns and the playing of musical instruments.

Some of the most well-known rituals in African diasporic religions include:

Drumming and dancing: African diasporic religions are known for their lively and rhythmic drumming and dancing, which is often used to invoke the spirits and to achieve a state of trance or possession.

Animal sacrifice: Animal sacrifice is a common practice in many African diasporic religions, and it is often seen as a way to honor the deities and to seek their favor. The animal is usually consumed as part of a communal meal.

Initiation rites: Initiation rites are an important aspect of many African diasporic religions, and they mark a person's entrance into the religious community. These rites may involve fasting, seclusion, and other forms of purification.

They may also include the receiving of special knowledge or skills from the community's elders or initiators. In some cases, initiates may undergo a period of instruction before being allowed to participate fully in the community's religious practices.

Divination: Divination is a practice that is common to many African diasporic religions, and it is used to seek guidance and advice from the spirits and ancestors. Divination can take many forms, including throwing shells, bones, or cards, interpreting dreams, or observing natural phenomena such as the movements of animals or the patterns of clouds.

Ancestor veneration: Ancestor veneration is a central aspect of many African diasporic religions. Ancestors are believed to be present and active in the lives of their descendants, and they are often honored through offerings of food, drink, and other items. Ancestral altars or shrines are common in African diasporic religions, and they may be adorned with photographs or other images of deceased family members.

African Religions

Healing rituals: Healing rituals are common in many African diasporic religions, and they may involve the use of herbal remedies, massage, or other forms of physical and spiritual healing. Healing rituals may be performed for individuals or for the community as a whole.

Each of these rituals has its own unique meaning and purpose, and they are often accompanied by specific prayers, chants, and other forms of sacred language. In addition to these specific rituals, many African diasporic religions also place a strong emphasis on the importance of everyday practices, such as meditation, prayer, and acts of kindness and service to others.

One of the most important aspects of African diasporic rituals is their communal nature. Rituals are often performed in the context of the community, and they serve to strengthen social bonds, foster a sense of shared identity and purpose, and provide a sense of comfort and support in times of difficulty. By participating in rituals, members of the community affirm their connection to their ancestors, deities, and spirits, and reaffirm their commitment to their religious traditions.

Examples of exercises and discussion questions related to rituals in African diasporic religions:

Research and compare the use of animal sacrifice in different African diasporic religions. What are the similarities and differences in how the practice is carried out, and what does it symbolize in each tradition?

Choose a specific ritual from an African diasporic religion and write a detailed analysis of its meaning and significance. What is the purpose of the ritual, and what are the specific actions and words associated with it?

Explore the use of music and dance in African diasporic religions. How do these practices help to create a sense of community and connection to the spirits and ancestors? What role do they play in achieving a state of trance or possession?

Discuss the importance of initiation rites in African diasporic religions. What do these rites symbolize, and how do they mark a person's entrance into the religious community? How do they reinforce social norms and values within the community?

Research and compare the use of divination in different African diasporic religions. What are the similarities and differences in the methods used, and what do these methods tell us about the relationship between humans and the spirits and ancestors?

Exploring Origins, Traditions, and Contemporary Relevance

Divination practices:

Divination is another important aspect of African diasporic religions, and it is often used to seek guidance and advice from the spirits. There are various forms of divination, including:

Ifa: Ifa is a divination system that originated in Yoruba religion, and it is now practiced in many African diasporic religions. It involves the use of divination trays, palm nuts, and other objects to communicate with the spirits and to receive messages and guidance.

Tarot: Tarot cards are used in some African diasporic religions as a form of divination. The cards are shuffled and drawn to reveal insights and advice from the spirits.

Cowrie shell divination: Cowrie shells are a common tool used in African diasporic religions for divination. The shells are usually cast or thrown onto a mat or other surface, and the pattern they form is interpreted by a diviner to reveal insights and guidance from the spirits.

Diloggun: Diloggun is a divination system that originated in the Santeria religion and is also used in other African diasporic religions. It involves the use of 16 cowrie shells or coconut shells that are thrown onto a mat and interpreted to reveal messages from the spirits.

Numerology: Numerology is a form of divination that is used in many African diasporic religions. It involves the interpretation of numbers and their symbolism to reveal insights and guidance from the spirits.

In addition to these divination practices, African diasporic religions also use other forms of communication with the spirits, such as dream interpretation, meditation, and trance work. These practices are often used in conjunction with divination to gain a deeper understanding of the messages and guidance being received from the spirits.

Divination is often performed by a trained practitioner or diviner who has received extensive training and has a deep understanding of the symbolism and meanings associated with the tools and techniques used in divination. In some cases, divination may also be performed by a group of practitioners or by the entire community.

African Religions

One of the key aspects of divination in African diasporic religions is the belief in the interconnectedness of all things. Divination is seen as a way to tap into this interconnectedness and to receive guidance from the spirits and the universe as a whole. It is also seen as a way to gain a deeper understanding of oneself and one's place in the world.

Some critics of divination argue that it is a form of superstition and lacks scientific validity. However, proponents of divination argue that it is a valuable tool for personal growth and spiritual development, and that it can provide valuable insights and guidance to those who seek it.

To practice divination, one must have a deep respect and understanding of the spirits and the universe, as well as a willingness to engage in introspection and self-reflection. It is also important to approach divination with an open mind and a willingness to accept whatever messages and guidance are received from the spirits.

Exercise:

Choose one of the divination practices mentioned in this section and research its origins, symbolism, and techniques. Write a short report on your findings, including any personal insights or reflections on the practice.

Try a divination practice that you have never used before. Reflect on your experience and write a journal entry about what you learned, what insights you gained, and how you felt during the practice.

Beliefs about the afterlife:

Beliefs about the afterlife vary widely among African diasporic religions, but many of them share the belief in reincarnation or ancestral spirits. Some African diasporic religions believe that the soul is reincarnated into a new body upon death, while others believe that the soul travels to an ancestral realm. The concept of ancestral spirits is central to many African diasporic religions, and ancestors are often regarded as protective and benevolent forces that can offer guidance and wisdom to the living.

In Santeria, for example, the spirits of ancestors are called egguns, and they are believed to live in the world of the dead, which is a parallel world to the world of the living. Practitioners of Santeria believe that it is possible to communicate with egguns and seek their guidance and protection through divination and offerings. Similarly, in Vodou, ancestors are believed to be powerful spirits that can intercede on behalf of the living and offer protection and guidance.

Exploring Origins, Traditions, and Contemporary Relevance

In some African diasporic religions, there is a belief in the existence of a divine creator or a supreme being. In Candomble, for example, the supreme being is called Oludumare, and is believed to be the creator of the universe and all living beings. However, the role of the supreme being in African diasporic religions is often less important than the role of ancestral spirits, who are regarded as more accessible and more relevant to the daily lives of practitioners.

Ancestral spirits are often venerated through offerings and ceremonies, and their presence is felt in many aspects of daily life. For example, in the Yoruba religion, ancestors are believed to play a role in the initiation of new priests and priestesses, and they are also believed to protect families and communities. The veneration of ancestors is also important in the Akan religion, where ancestors are believed to serve as intermediaries between the living and the divine.

In addition to the belief in ancestral spirits, some African diasporic religions also believe in the existence of other supernatural beings, such as deities or saints. In Santeria, for example, the spirits of the orishas are believed to be powerful forces that can influence the lives of practitioners. Each orisha is associated with different aspects of life, such as health, love, and prosperity, and devotees may seek their guidance and protection through offerings and ceremonies.

Similarly, in Vodou, the loa are believed to be powerful spirits that can influence the lives of practitioners. Each loa is associated with different aspects of life, such as fertility, prosperity, and healing, and devotees may seek their assistance through offerings and ceremonies. The loa are often depicted as complex and multifaceted beings, and their stories and characteristics may vary depending on the region and the specific tradition.

Beliefs about the afterlife are also influenced by cultural and historical factors. For example, in the Americas, African diasporic religions often developed in the context of colonialism and slavery, and their beliefs and practices were shaped by the experiences of enslaved Africans and their descendants. In some cases, African diasporic religions blended with other religious traditions, such as Christianity, to form new syncretic practices.

In Brazil, for example, the religion of Candomble developed in the context of slavery and was influenced by both African and Christian traditions. In Candomble, the concept of the afterlife is complex and multifaceted, and it is influenced by both African and Christian beliefs. Candomble practitioners believe in the existence of an ancestral realm called the "land of the ancestors," where the spirits of the dead are believed to reside. However, they also believe in the Christian concept of heaven and hell, and they often incorporate elements of Christian iconography and ritual into their practices.

In conclusion, beliefs about the afterlife in African diasporic religions are diverse and complex, and they reflect the cultural, historical, and spiritual experiences of practitioners. Ancestral spirits are often central to these beliefs, and they are venerated through offerings, ceremonies, and divination. Other supernatural beings, such as deities and saints, may also play a role in the afterlife, and their stories and characteristics may vary depending on the region and the specific tradition.

Examples and exercises:

4.   Research and write an essay on the beliefs about the afterlife in a specific African diasporic religion, such as Santeria or Vodou.

5.   Compare and contrast the beliefs about the afterlife in two different African diasporic religions, such as Candomble and Ifa.

6.   Engage in a discussion or debate on the role of ancestors in African diasporic religions. What functions do ancestors serve, and why are they so important in these religions?

Analyze the role of ritual and symbolism in these religions

African diasporic religions are known for their rich and diverse rituals and symbols. These religions are not just about belief in supernatural beings, but also about the relationships between humans, nature, and the divine. The rituals and symbols used in these religions serve as a means of connecting the physical and spiritual worlds and expressing the cultural heritage of African peoples. In this section, we will analyze the role of ritual and symbolism in African diasporic religions, with a focus on their significance and meanings.

✧   Rituals and Symbolism in African Diasporic Religions

African diasporic religions are characterized by their emphasis on community, ancestor veneration, and the use of ritual and symbolism. These religions are not just about individual beliefs but are also about the collective practices of a community. The rituals and symbols used in African diasporic religions serve to create a sense of identity, solidarity, and belonging among the members of the community. Moreover, these rituals and symbols help to reinforce the connections between the physical and spiritual worlds, making the invisible visible and the intangible tangible.

Exploring Origins, Traditions, and Contemporary Relevance

✧ **Rituals in African Diasporic Religions**

Rituals are an important part of African diasporic religions. They serve as a means of establishing and maintaining relationships with the divine, ancestors, and other spiritual beings. These rituals are often performed in public or communal spaces, such as temples, shrines, or outdoor spaces. Rituals can be simple or complex, depending on the occasion and the purpose. Some common rituals in African diasporic religions include:

Ancestor veneration: African diasporic religions place a great emphasis on ancestor veneration. Ancestors are seen as important spiritual beings who can intercede on behalf of the living. Ancestor veneration rituals involve offerings of food, drink, and other items, as well as prayers and songs.

Initiation: Initiation rituals are an important part of African diasporic religions. These rituals mark a person's entrance into a particular religious community and serve as a rite of passage. Initiation rituals involve various symbolic actions and may last several days.

Healing rituals: Healing rituals are another important aspect of African diasporic religions. These rituals are performed to heal physical, emotional, or spiritual ailments. Healing rituals may involve the use of herbs, water, or other materials, as well as prayers and songs.

Divination: Divination is the practice of seeking guidance or insight from the divine or other spiritual beings. Divination rituals may involve the use of various tools, such as cowrie shells, tarot cards, or pendulums.

✧ **Symbolism in African Diasporic Religions**

Symbols are an important part of African diasporic religions. Symbols serve as a means of communicating complex ideas and concepts in a simple and accessible way. Symbols are used to represent various spiritual beings, as well as important values and beliefs. Some common symbols in African diasporic religions include:

The crossroads: The crossroads is a powerful symbol in African diasporic religions. The crossroads represents a place where different worlds intersect and where one can communicate with the divine or other spiritual beings.

African Religions

The color red: The color red is a symbol of life force, vitality, and power in African diasporic religions. Red is often used in rituals and ceremonies as a symbol of strength and vitality.

The sun: The sun is a powerful symbol of life and vitality in African diasporic religions. The sun is often associated with the divine and is seen as a source of energy and power.

The drum: The drum is an important symbol in African diasporic religions. The drum represents the heartbeat of the community and is used in many rituals and ceremonies.

The snake: The snake is a symbol of wisdom, transformation, and healing in African diasporic religions. The snake sheds its skin and is reborn, which is seen as a powerful metaphor for transformation and renewal.

The cowrie shell: The cowrie shell is a symbol of prosperity and wealth in African diasporic religions. The shell is often used in divination and is believed to have the power to bring wealth and good fortune.

The moon: The moon is a symbol of femininity, intuition, and the subconscious in African diasporic religions. The cycles of the moon are often used in rituals and ceremonies as a way to connect with the divine feminine and access deeper levels of intuition and wisdom.

These symbols are often used in rituals and ceremonies to invoke spiritual beings, connect with the divine, and communicate important values and beliefs. For example, the crossroads may be used as a symbol to communicate with the spirits of the ancestors, while the color red may be used in a ritual to invoke the energy and power of the divine.

In addition to symbols, ritual is another important aspect of African diasporic religions. Rituals are formalized actions that are performed in a specific way and have a specific purpose. Rituals serve as a way to connect with the divine, honor ancestors, and communicate with spiritual beings.

Rituals in African diasporic religions often involve the use of music, dance, and other forms of artistic expression. Music and dance serve as a way to connect with the divine and access deeper levels of consciousness. The use of drums, for example, is often used to create a trance-like state that allows individuals to connect with the spiritual realm.

Exploring Origins, Traditions, and Contemporary Relevance

In addition to music and dance, African diasporic religions also use various forms of divination. Divination is the practice of seeking knowledge of the future or the unknown through supernatural means. Divination practices vary widely among different African diasporic religions, but some common forms of divination include:

Tarot reading: Tarot reading is a form of divination that uses a deck of cards to gain insight into a person's life and future. Tarot reading is often used in African diasporic religions to gain insight into spiritual matters.

Bone casting: Bone casting is a form of divination that involves throwing bones or other objects onto a surface and interpreting their placement. Bone casting is often used in African diasporic religions to gain insight into specific questions or situations.

Oracle reading: Oracle reading is a form of divination that involves asking a question and receiving a response through the use of a divination tool, such as a pendulum or crystal ball. Oracle reading is often used in African diasporic religions to gain insight into spiritual matters or to communicate with spiritual beings.

In addition to divination, healing is another important aspect of African diasporic religions. Healing practices vary widely among different African diasporic religions, but some common forms of healing include:

Herbalism: Herbalism is the use of plants for medicinal purposes. Many African diasporic religions use herbs and other natural remedies for healing purposes.

Energy healing: Energy healing is the practice of using energy to promote healing and balance in the body. Energy healing is often used in African diasporic religions to promote physical, emotional, and spiritual healing.

Faith healing: Faith healing is the practice of using prayer and other forms of spiritual intervention to promote healing. Faith healing is often used in African diasporic religions to promote spiritual healing and to connect with the divine.

In conclusion, symbolism, ritual, divination, and healing are all important aspects of African diasporic religions. Symbols serve as a means of communicating complex ideas and concepts in a simple and accessible way, while rituals serve as a way to connect with the divine and communicate with spiritual beings.

African Religions

Discuss the importance of community and collective identity in African diasporic religions

African diasporic religions are communal in nature and emphasize the importance of collective identity. Community is a fundamental aspect of these religions, and it is through communal practices that individuals find connection to their ancestral roots and establish a sense of belonging. In this section, we will explore the importance of community and collective identity in African diasporic religions, including the role of social structures, rituals, and other forms of group participation.

Social Structures

Social structures play a significant role in the formation and maintenance of community in African diasporic religions. These social structures are often hierarchical and are based on the principle of seniority or experience. Elders are respected members of the community who have accumulated knowledge and experience over time. They are often consulted for guidance and advice and play a critical role in transmitting the traditions of the community to younger generations.

In many African diasporic religions, there are also formal organizations, such as churches or temples, that serve as a focal point for community activities. These organizations may be led by a religious leader, such as a priest or priestess, who is responsible for overseeing the spiritual activities of the community. These leaders may also be responsible for providing guidance on other aspects of life, such as health and well-being.

Rituals

Rituals are an important aspect of community life in African diasporic religions. Rituals are often performed collectively, and they serve as a means of strengthening community bonds and establishing a sense of shared identity. Rituals can take many forms, including drumming, dancing, chanting, and other forms of music.

One common ritual in African diasporic religions is the pouring of libations. Libations are offerings of water or other liquids that are poured on the ground as a way of honoring ancestors and other spiritual beings. This ritual serves as a means of connecting with the spiritual world and recognizing the interdependence of the living and the dead.

Another important ritual in African diasporic religions is divination. Divination is the practice of seeking guidance from the divine through various means, such as casting or reading divination tools like cowrie shells, tarot cards, or throwing the bones. Divination is often done in a communal setting and is seen as a way of seeking guidance and wisdom for the community as a whole.

Group Participation

Participation in group activities is another important aspect of community life in African diasporic religions. Many of these religions place a strong emphasis on group participation in order to create a sense of shared experience and identity. This can take many forms, such as attending religious services, participating in festivals and other cultural events, or working together on community projects.

In some African diasporic religions, such as Santeria or Candomble, there are specific roles or initiations that individuals must go through in order to become full members of the community. These initiations often involve a period of study and preparation, as well as participation in specific rituals or ceremonies.

In some cases, African diasporic religions have also been used as a means of political resistance and community empowerment. For example, during the period of slavery in the United States, African slaves used their religious practices as a means of maintaining their cultural heritage and resisting the oppression of their captors. Today, African diasporic religions continue to serve as a source of strength and empowerment for many people of African descent around the world.

In conclusion, community and collective identity are fundamental aspects of African diasporic religions. Social structures, rituals, and group participation all serve to strengthen community bonds and establish a sense of shared identity. These religions emphasize the importance of connection to one's ancestral roots and the interdependence of the living and the dead. African diasporic religions continue to play an important role in the lives of many people of African descent around the world, providing a source of strength, inspiration, and spiritual guidance.

It is important to recognize that African diasporic religions are not monolithic and vary greatly in their practices and beliefs. There are many different traditions, each with their own unique approach to community and collective identity. Additionally, the experiences of practitioners of African diasporic religions can vary greatly depending on factors such as geography, socioeconomic status, and cultural background.

Despite these differences, however, the emphasis on community and collective identity remains a core feature of African diasporic religions. By fostering a sense of shared heritage and interdependence, these religions provide a powerful source of resilience and empowerment for their practitioners.

As society continues to grapple with issues of race, inequality, and social justice, the lessons of African diasporic religions can provide valuable insights and guidance. These religions offer a model for building strong, resilient communities based on a shared sense of history, culture, and spiritual identity. By emphasizing the importance of interdependence and collective action, African diasporic religions offer a powerful antidote to the individualism and fragmentation that can so often characterize modern life.

As we move forward, it is important to continue to study and learn from African diasporic religions, recognizing their unique contributions to the rich tapestry of human spirituality and culture. By doing so, we can deepen our understanding of ourselves and the world around us, and work towards building a more just and equitable society for all.

CHAPTER 25: THE ROLE OF AFRICAN DIASPORIC RELIGIONS IN CONTEMPORARY SOCIETIES

African diasporic religions have been an integral part of the lives of people of African descent for centuries. These religions have played a significant role in shaping the culture and traditions of communities in Africa and its diaspora. African diasporic religions have undergone many changes throughout history, including the transatlantic slave trade, colonization, and migration. Despite these challenges, these religions have persisted and continue to thrive in contemporary societies.

In this chapter, we will explore the role of African diasporic religions in contemporary societies. We will examine the ways in which these religions have evolved over time and how they continue to shape the lives of their followers. We will also discuss the challenges faced by African diasporic religions in modern times and the ways in which they are adapting to changing social and cultural environments.

The evolution of African diasporic religions:

The evolution of African diasporic religions is a complex and multifaceted process that has been shaped by historical, cultural, and social factors. This section will explore the key stages in the development of these religions, from their origins in Africa to their global spread and adaptation in contemporary societies.

Origins in Africa

African diasporic religions have their roots in the traditional beliefs and practices of the various African cultures that were brought to the Americas during the transatlantic slave trade. These beliefs were diverse and varied, reflecting the different cultural, linguistic, and geographical contexts of the African peoples. However, they shared some common characteristics, such as a belief in a supreme being, a reverence for ancestors and spirits, and a close relationship between the natural and supernatural worlds.

The forced migration of Africans to the Americas disrupted their cultural and religious practices, as they were subjected to a brutal and dehumanizing system of slavery. European slave masters sought to erase the cultural identity of their slaves, including their religious beliefs and practices. As a result, many Africans were forced to convert to Christianity, or to adopt syncretic religions that combined African beliefs with elements of Christianity.

Emergence of New Religions

Despite these efforts, many Africans managed to preserve their traditional beliefs and practices in secret, or through syncretic forms of religion that blended African and Christian elements. Over time, these syncretic religions began to evolve into distinct new religions that were centered around African beliefs and practices, but also incorporated elements of Christianity and other religions.

One of the most well-known of these new religions is Vodou, which originated in Haiti in the late 18th century. Vodou combines elements of traditional African religions with Catholicism, and is characterized by a complex pantheon of spirits, rituals, and ceremonies. Another important African diasporic religion is Santeria, which emerged in Cuba in the 19th century. Santeria blends Yoruba beliefs and practices with Catholicism, and is known for its use of divination, sacrifice, and healing practices.

Candomble is another important African diasporic religion, which originated in Brazil in the 19th century. Candomble is based on the religious beliefs and practices of the Yoruba, Fon, and Bantu peoples of West and Central Africa, and is characterized by a complex system of spirits, rituals, and divination practices.

Spread and Adaptation in Contemporary Societies

In the 20th century, African diasporic religions began to spread beyond their countries of origin, as a result of migration, globalization, and cultural exchange. African American culture played a particularly important role in the spread of these religions, as African American musicians, artists, and writers helped to popularize them in mainstream culture.

One example of this is the influence of African diasporic religions on the development of jazz music. Jazz was invented by African American musicians in New Orleans in the early 20th century, and was deeply influenced by African rhythms, call-and-response patterns, and improvisation. Many jazz musicians, such as John Coltrane and Sun Ra, were also practitioners of African diasporic religions, and incorporated elements of these religions into their music.

In contemporary societies, African diasporic religions continue to evolve and adapt to changing social and cultural environments. Many practitioners have incorporated modern technology, such as social media and online forums, into their practice, in order to connect with other practitioners and share knowledge and resources. Others have begun to incorporate elements of Western spirituality, such as yoga and meditation, into their rituals and ceremonies, in order to create a more holistic and integrated spiritual practice.

Conclusion

The evolution of African diasporic religions is a testament to the resilience and creativity of African peoples in the face of oppression and adversity. Despite centuries of forced assimilation and cultural erasure, these religions have survived and thrived, providing a source of comfort and strength for millions of people around the world.

One of the key factors in the evolution of African diasporic religions has been their ability to adapt and incorporate new elements. As African people were forcibly brought to the Americas, they were exposed to new religions and belief systems, including Christianity and Islam. Many enslaved Africans were forced to convert to Christianity, and their traditional beliefs were often suppressed or demonized by their oppressors.

However, African peoples were able to incorporate elements of Christianity and other religions into their traditional beliefs, creating new syncretic religions that blended African and European traditions. For example, in Cuba, Santeria emerged as a blend of Yoruba religion and Catholicism. Similarly, in Brazil, Candomble developed as a fusion of Yoruba, Bantu, and European traditions.

In the 20th century, the spread of African diasporic religions beyond their countries of origin led to further adaptations and innovations. African diasporic religions began to incorporate elements of other world religions, such as Hinduism and Buddhism, as well as New Age spirituality and Western esotericism.

Today, many practitioners of African diasporic religions continue to innovate and evolve their practices, incorporating new technologies, such as social media and online forums, into their rituals and ceremonies. The diasporic nature of these religions has allowed them to spread across the globe, with practitioners in Africa, the Americas, Europe, and beyond.

However, this evolution has not been without controversy. Some traditionalists argue that the incorporation of non-African elements dilutes the authenticity and cultural heritage of these religions. Others argue that the commercialization of African diasporic religions, particularly in the West, has led to a distortion and exploitation of these traditions for profit.

African Religions

Despite these criticisms, African diasporic religions continue to play an important role in the lives of millions of people around the world. They provide a source of cultural identity, spiritual comfort, and social cohesion for communities of African descent. The evolution of these religions is a testament to the resilience and adaptability of African peoples, and a reminder of the ongoing legacy of the transatlantic slave trade and its impact on the global African diaspora.

The role of African diasporic religions in contemporary societies:

Contemporary societies are diverse and complex, and the role of African diasporic religions varies depending on the specific context. However, there are some common themes that are evident across different communities and regions.

One of the primary roles of African diasporic religions in contemporary societies is to provide a sense of community and belonging. Many practitioners of these religions have been marginalized and discriminated against because of their race, ethnicity, or socio-economic status. African diasporic religions offer a space where people can come together to share their experiences, support one another, and celebrate their cultural heritage.

African diasporic religions also play an important role in preserving and promoting cultural traditions. These religions are often based on oral traditions and have been passed down from generation to generation. Through rituals, ceremonies, and other practices, practitioners of African diasporic religions are able to connect with their ancestral roots and maintain cultural continuity.

Another significant role of African diasporic religions is their influence on popular culture. African diasporic religions have had a profound impact on music, art, literature, and other forms of cultural expression. For example, the blues, jazz, and hip hop music genres all have roots in African American culture and are heavily influenced by African diasporic religions. Similarly, the visual arts and literature have been shaped by the cultural and spiritual practices of these religions.

African diasporic religions have also played a role in the development of new religious movements and spiritual practices. For example, the New Age movement, which emerged in the United States in the 1970s, incorporates elements of African diasporic religions, such as spiritualism and divination. This has led to a fusion of different spiritual practices and traditions, creating a rich and diverse spiritual landscape.

Exploring Origins, Traditions, and Contemporary Relevance

In addition to their cultural and spiritual significance, African diasporic religions have also played a role in social and political movements. For example, in the United States, African American religious leaders played a prominent role in the Civil Rights Movement of the 1950s and 1960s. These leaders, such as Martin Luther King Jr. and Malcolm X, drew on the spiritual and cultural traditions of African diasporic religions to inspire and mobilize their followers.

However, the role of African diasporic religions in contemporary societies is not without controversy. Some people view these religions as primitive or superstitious, and there have been instances of discrimination and persecution against practitioners of these religions. For example, in some countries, such as Nigeria, there have been conflicts between practitioners of different religions, including African diasporic religions. Additionally, some people have criticized these religions for their use of animal sacrifice and other practices that are seen as cruel or inhumane.

In conclusion, the role of African diasporic religions in contemporary societies is multifaceted and complex. These religions provide a sense of community and belonging to their followers, preserve cultural traditions, and have influenced popular culture and the development of new spiritual practices. African diasporic religions have also played a role in social and political movements, but have faced discrimination and controversy. As with any religion or spiritual practice, it is important to approach African diasporic religions with an open mind and a willingness to learn about and respect the beliefs and practices of others.

Challenges faced by African diasporic religions:

Despite the continued importance of African diasporic religions, these religions face many challenges in contemporary societies. One of the biggest challenges is discrimination and prejudice from outside communities. Many people hold negative stereotypes and misconceptions about African diasporic religions, which can lead to discrimination and even violence against practitioners.

Another challenge faced by African diasporic religions is the tension between tradition and modernity. As these religions continue to evolve and adapt to changing social and cultural environments, some practitioners may feel that they are losing touch with their traditional roots. This tension can lead to disagreements within communities and a sense of uncertainty about the future of these religions.

Furthermore, African diasporic religions face challenges in terms of their relationship with mainstream religions and religious institutions. In some cases, African diasporic religions are viewed as inferior or primitive by mainstream religions, which can lead to further discrimination and marginalization. In other cases, African diasporic religions are viewed as a threat to the dominance of mainstream religions, leading to persecution and legal restrictions.

African diasporic religions also face challenges in terms of preservation and transmission of their traditions. Many of these religions have been passed down through oral tradition, and as older generations pass away, there is a risk of losing valuable knowledge and practices. Additionally, younger generations may not be as interested in traditional religions and may be more influenced by Western culture and values.

Another challenge faced by African diasporic religions is the issue of authenticity. With the commercialization and popularization of these religions, there is a risk of cultural appropriation and distortion of their practices and beliefs. Non-African practitioners may appropriate these religions without fully understanding their cultural and historical significance, leading to a dilution and misrepresentation of these traditions.

Finally, African diasporic religions also face challenges in terms of gender and LGBTQ+ inclusion. While these religions have historically been inclusive and accepting of diverse identities, there are still instances of discrimination and exclusion within certain communities. Some practitioners may hold onto patriarchal or heteronormative views that can exclude women and LGBTQ+ individuals from leadership roles or certain rituals and practices.

Overall, the challenges faced by African diasporic religions reflect larger societal issues of discrimination, cultural preservation, and social justice. It is important for practitioners and allies to address these challenges and work towards creating more inclusive and equitable communities.

African diasporic religions have played an important role in shaping the culture and traditions of communities of African descent. These religions have evolved over time, adapting to changing social and cultural environments while maintaining their cultural identity. African diasporic religions continue to provide a sense of connection and community for people of African descent around the world.

In contemporary societies, African diasporic religions have faced many challenges, including prejudice, discrimination, and marginalization. Many people have stereotypical views of African diasporic religions, seeing them as primitive or superstitious. In some cases, African diasporic religions have been suppressed or even outlawed, as was the case during the era of slavery and colonization.

Exploring Origins, Traditions, and Contemporary Relevance

Despite these challenges, African diasporic religions have continued to thrive and evolve. In many countries, African diasporic religions have gained legal recognition and protection as legitimate religions. This recognition has helped to increase awareness and understanding of these religions and has provided opportunities for people of African descent to practice their faith more openly and freely.

African diasporic religions have also played an important role in social and political movements. In the United States, for example, African diasporic religions were an important part of the civil rights movement. Leaders such as Malcolm X and Martin Luther King Jr. drew inspiration from African diasporic religions and incorporated their teachings into their activism.

In contemporary societies, African diasporic religions continue to provide a sense of community and belonging for people of African descent. They offer a space for people to connect with their cultural heritage, to honor their ancestors, and to express their spirituality in a way that resonates with their personal experiences and beliefs.

As society becomes more diverse and multicultural, African diasporic religions will continue to play an important role in shaping the cultural landscape. They offer a unique perspective on spirituality, community, and identity that can enrich our understanding of the world around us. By studying and learning about African diasporic religions, we can gain a greater appreciation for the diversity and complexity of human experience.

Discuss the ways in which African diasporic religions have adapted to contemporary societies

African diasporic religions have a long history of adapting to changing social and cultural environments, while still maintaining their core beliefs and practices. In contemporary societies, these religions have continued to evolve and adapt, finding new ways to connect with their followers and remain relevant in a changing world. In this section, we will explore the various ways in which African diasporic religions have adapted to contemporary societies, including changes in ritual practices, the incorporation of new technologies, and the use of social media to connect with followers.

One way in which African diasporic religions have adapted to contemporary societies is through changes in ritual practices. As these religions have spread throughout the world, they have encountered new environments and cultures, which has led to the development of new rituals and practices. For example, in the United States, practitioners of Santeria have incorporated elements of Catholicism into their practice, such as the use of saints and the celebration of the Christian holy days. Similarly, practitioners of Vodou in Haiti have incorporated elements of Christianity and indigenous African religions into their practice, creating a unique syncretic tradition.

Another way in which African diasporic religions have adapted to contemporary societies is through the incorporation of new technologies. For example, practitioners of Hoodoo in the United States have incorporated the use of smartphones and social media into their practice. They use these technologies to share spells, provide guidance to followers, and connect with other practitioners around the world. In Nigeria, practitioners of Ifa have also begun to use new technologies, such as video conferencing and social media, to connect with followers and perform divination rituals.

In addition to the incorporation of new technologies, African diasporic religions have also adapted to contemporary societies through the use of social media. Many practitioners of African diasporic religions have created online communities through social media platforms such as Facebook and Instagram. These communities provide a space for followers to connect with each other, share knowledge and experiences, and provide support to one another. Social media has also been used by practitioners to educate the public about their religions, dispel myths and misconceptions, and promote greater understanding and acceptance.

Another way in which African diasporic religions have adapted to contemporary societies is through the use of music and dance. Music and dance have always been important components of these religions, and in contemporary societies, they have continued to play an important role. For example, practitioners of Candomble in Brazil incorporate music and dance into their rituals, using them to connect with the spirits and create a sense of community among the participants.

African diasporic religions have also adapted to contemporary societies through their engagement with environmental issues. Many practitioners of these religions view the environment as sacred and believe in the importance of protecting the natural world. They have incorporated environmental activism into their religious practices, using rituals and ceremonies to raise awareness about environmental issues and promote sustainable practices. For example, practitioners of the Yoruba religion in Nigeria have created the Ifa Foundation for Environmental Protection, which works to promote environmental conservation and sustainable development.

Finally, African diasporic religions have adapted to contemporary societies through their engagement with politics and social justice issues. Many practitioners of these religions view social justice as an important part of their religious practice, and have been involved in social and political movements around the world. For example, practitioners of Rastafarianism in Jamaica have been involved in the fight for social and economic equality, while practitioners of Vodou in Haiti have been involved in the struggle for democracy and human rights.

In conclusion, African diasporic religions have adapted to contemporary societies in a variety of ways, including changes in ritual practices, the incorporation of new technologies, and the use of social media to connect with followers. These religions have also engaged with environmental issues, politics, and social justice, demonstrating their continued relevance in a changing world. As these religions continue to evolve and adapt, they will undoubtedly face new challenges and opportunities. It is important for practitioners of these religions to continue to engage in critical reflection and dialogue, both within their communities and with the wider society, in order to navigate these changes and ensure the continued relevance and vitality of these traditions.

One important aspect of the adaptation of African diasporic religions to contemporary societies is the incorporation of new technologies. The use of technology has enabled practitioners to connect with one another across vast distances, and has facilitated the dissemination of knowledge and practices. For example, many practitioners of African diasporic religions have created online communities and social media groups where they can share information, ask questions, and provide support to one another.

Another way in which African diasporic religions have adapted to contemporary societies is through changes in ritual practices. While many of these religions are deeply rooted in tradition, practitioners have found ways to modify rituals in order to make them more relevant to contemporary contexts. For example, some practitioners of Santeria in the United States have modified traditional animal sacrifices in order to comply with animal welfare laws.

Finally, African diasporic religions have adapted to contemporary societies through their engagement with politics and social justice issues. Many practitioners of these religions view social justice as an important part of their religious practice, and have been involved in social and political movements around the world. For example, practitioners of Rastafarianism in Jamaica have been involved in the fight for social and economic equality, while practitioners of Vodou in Haiti have been involved in the struggle for democracy and human rights.

It is worth noting, however, that the adaptation of African diasporic religions to contemporary societies has not been without its challenges. As previously discussed, these religions face discrimination and prejudice from outside communities, and there is often tension between tradition and modernity. In addition, the incorporation of new technologies and changes in ritual practices can sometimes lead to disagreements within communities, and there is a risk that these changes may lead to the dilution or loss of traditional practices.

Overall, the adaptation of African diasporic religions to contemporary societies is a complex and ongoing process. While these religions have faced many challenges, they have also demonstrated remarkable resilience and creativity in the face of adversity. As the world continues to change and evolve, it will be important for practitioners of these religions to continue to engage in critical reflection and dialogue, in order to ensure the continued relevance and vitality of these important traditions.

Analyze the role of African diasporic religions in social and political movements

African diasporic religions have played an important role in social and political movements around the world. From the Civil Rights Movement in the United States to the anti-apartheid struggle in South Africa, practitioners of these religions have been at the forefront of movements for justice and equality. This section will analyze the role of African diasporic religions in social and political movements, with a focus on the ways in which these religions have contributed to the struggle for social justice.

Historical Context

To understand the role of African diasporic religions in social and political movements, it is important to first provide some historical context. African diasporic religions have their roots in the spiritual traditions of West and Central Africa, and were brought to the Americas and other parts of the world through the transatlantic slave trade. Enslaved Africans were forced to abandon their traditional religious practices and adopt the religions of their enslavers, such as Christianity and Islam. However, many enslaved Africans secretly maintained their traditional religious practices, which evolved over time to incorporate elements of Christianity and other religions.

During the period of slavery and colonization, African diasporic religions served as a form of resistance against the oppressive systems of slavery and colonialism. Enslaved Africans used these religions to preserve their cultural heritage, resist cultural assimilation, and create a sense of community and solidarity. African diasporic religions also provided a source of spiritual strength and resilience in the face of hardship and oppression.

As African diasporic religions spread throughout the Americas and other parts of the world, they continued to evolve and adapt to new social and cultural environments. In the 20th century, practitioners of these religions began to play a more active role in social and political movements.

The Civil Rights Movement

One of the most significant social and political movements in which African diasporic religions played a role was the Civil Rights Movement in the United States. During the 1950s and 1960s, African Americans and their allies fought for equal rights and an end to segregation and discrimination. Many of the leaders of the Civil Rights Movement were practitioners of African diasporic religions, including Martin Luther King Jr. and Malcolm X.

King was a Baptist minister, but he was also influenced by the teachings of Mahatma Gandhi and the nonviolent resistance movement in India. King saw his struggle for civil rights as a spiritual and moral struggle, and he believed that the principles of justice and equality were rooted in the teachings of the Bible. King often spoke about the need for a "beloved community" in which all people were treated with dignity and respect.

Malcolm X, on the other hand, was a Muslim who was heavily influenced by the teachings of the Nation of Islam. Malcolm X was a strong advocate for black nationalism and self-determination, and he believed that African Americans needed to take control of their own communities and institutions. Malcolm X also believed that African Americans should be proud of their African heritage and culture, and should reject the cultural assimilation that had been forced upon them by white supremacy.

Other practitioners of African diasporic religions also played important roles in the Civil Rights Movement. For example, Fannie Lou Hamer, a leader in the Mississippi Freedom Democratic Party, was a practitioner of Hoodoo, an African American folk religion that incorporates elements of African spirituality, Christianity, and Native American spirituality. Hamer used her religious beliefs to inspire and motivate others in the struggle for civil rights.

The Anti-Apartheid Struggle in South Africa

Another significant social and political movement in which African diasporic religions played a role was the anti-apartheid struggle in South Africa. Apartheid was a system of racial segregation and discrimination that was implemented by the white minority government in South Africa in 1948. The anti-apartheid struggle was a long and difficult one, spanning several decades, and involved a wide range of social and political actors, including African diasporic religions.

African Religions

Many practitioners of African diasporic religions in South Africa were involved in the struggle against apartheid. They played a crucial role in mobilizing communities and providing spiritual support to activists. For example, the Zion Christian Church, which is one of the largest African-initiated churches in South Africa, was a strong supporter of the anti-apartheid movement. The church provided material and spiritual support to activists, and its members participated in protests and boycotts.

Another example of African diasporic religions' involvement in the anti-apartheid struggle is the role played by traditional healers. Traditional healers, also known as sangomas, are highly respected members of many African communities. They are believed to have the ability to communicate with ancestors and spirits, and to use this knowledge to heal physical, mental, and spiritual illnesses. During the anti-apartheid struggle, many sangomas were involved in providing spiritual support to activists and in mobilizing communities to resist the apartheid government. They also used their knowledge of herbs and traditional medicine to treat activists who were injured or ill.

The anti-apartheid struggle in South Africa also saw the emergence of a new religious movement, known as the Church of the Nazarene. The Church of the Nazarene was founded by Isaiah Shembe in the early 1900s and combines elements of Christianity and traditional African religion. The church played a significant role in the anti-apartheid struggle, with many of its members participating in protests and boycotts. The church's focus on African identity and pride also provided a powerful alternative to the apartheid government's message of white supremacy.

Overall, the role of African diasporic religions in the anti-apartheid struggle in South Africa was significant. Practitioners of these religions played an important role in mobilizing communities, providing spiritual support to activists, and challenging the apartheid government's message of white supremacy.

The Civil Rights Movement in the United States

Another example of the role of African diasporic religions in social and political movements is the Civil Rights Movement in the United States. The Civil Rights Movement was a struggle for racial equality that took place primarily in the 1950s and 1960s. It involved a wide range of social and political actors, including African diasporic religions.

One of the most prominent examples of the role of African diasporic religions in the Civil Rights Movement is the Reverend Dr. Martin Luther King Jr. Dr. King was a Baptist minister who played a central role in the Civil Rights Movement. He was a charismatic leader who inspired millions of people with his message of nonviolent resistance to racial injustice. Dr. King's religious faith was a crucial part of his activism, and he often cited biblical passages and religious themes in his speeches and writings.

Another example of the role of African diasporic religions in the Civil Rights Movement is the Nation of Islam. The Nation of Islam is a religious movement that was founded in the United States in the early 20th century. It combines elements of Islam and traditional African religion, and has a strong focus on black nationalism and self-reliance. The Nation of Islam played a significant role in the Civil Rights Movement, with many of its members participating in protests and advocating for racial equality.

Other African diasporic religions also played a role in the Civil Rights Movement. For example, the Black Church, which is a term used to describe the various African American Protestant denominations, played a significant role in the movement. The Black Church provided a space for African Americans to organize and mobilize, and many prominent Civil Rights leaders were members of Black Churches.

In conclusion, African diasporic religions have played an important role in social and political movements throughout history. From the anti-colonial struggles of the 19th and 20th centuries to the Civil Rights Movement in the United States, these religions have provided a framework for resistance, empowerment, and mobilization.

Through their emphasis on community, ritual, and social justice, African diasporic religions have provided a space for individuals and groups to come together and work towards a common goal. They have offered a sense of identity, purpose, and belonging to those who have been marginalized or oppressed, and have helped to foster a sense of pride and empowerment.

However, it is important to note that not all African diasporic religions have played a positive role in social and political movements. Some have been associated with violence, extremism, and intolerance, and have been criticized for their treatment of women and other marginalized groups.

For example, the controversial practice of female genital mutilation has been associated with some African diasporic religions, and has been the subject of much debate and controversy. Similarly, some practitioners of these religions have been criticized for their treatment of LGBTQ+ individuals, with some advocating for their exclusion or persecution.

Despite these challenges and criticisms, however, African diasporic religions continue to play an important role in contemporary societies. They provide a space for individuals and communities to come together and celebrate their cultural heritage, and offer a framework for social and political action. As such, they represent a vital aspect of the rich and diverse tapestry of religious and spiritual traditions that make up our world today.

Examine the challenges and opportunities facing African diasporic religions in the modern world

African diasporic religions have a long and complex history that spans centuries and continents. From their origins in West Africa to their spread throughout the Americas and beyond, these religions have undergone numerous changes and adaptations over time. In the modern world, African diasporic religions face a number of challenges and opportunities that are shaped by a variety of factors, including globalization, migration, and cultural exchange. This section will examine some of the most important challenges and opportunities facing African diasporic religions in the modern world, and will explore how these religions are adapting to changing circumstances.

Challenges Facing African Diasporic Religions

✦ Stereotyping and Misconceptions

One of the biggest challenges facing African diasporic religions in the modern world is the persistence of stereotypes and misconceptions. Many people still associate these religions with negative stereotypes, such as voodoo dolls, black magic, and animal sacrifices. These stereotypes are not only inaccurate, but they also perpetuate harmful ideas about African cultures and contribute to discrimination and prejudice against practitioners of these religions.

✦ Marginalization and Discrimination

African diasporic religions have often been marginalized and discriminated against throughout history, and this continues to be a major challenge in the modern world. In many places, practitioners of these religions face discrimination in the workplace, in housing, and in other areas of life. This discrimination can take many forms, including verbal harassment, physical violence, and exclusion from mainstream society.

Exploring Origins, Traditions, and Contemporary Relevance

✧ **Globalization and Cultural Appropriation**

Globalization has brought both opportunities and challenges for African diasporic religions. On the one hand, it has allowed for greater communication and exchange between different cultures, which has led to the spread of these religions to new parts of the world. On the other hand, globalization has also led to cultural appropriation, with aspects of African diasporic religions being taken out of context and commodified for profit. This can lead to the distortion and misrepresentation of these religions, and can also undermine their cultural significance and authenticity.

✧ **Political and Legal Restrictions**

In some parts of the world, African diasporic religions face political and legal restrictions that can limit their practice and expression. For example, in some countries, these religions are not recognized as legitimate and are therefore not protected under the law. This can make it difficult for practitioners to practice their religion openly and freely.

Opportunities Facing African Diasporic Religions

✧ **The Growth of Interfaith Dialogue**

One of the most promising opportunities facing African diasporic religions is the growth of interfaith dialogue. In recent years, there has been a growing recognition of the importance of religious diversity and the need for greater understanding and cooperation between different faith traditions. African diasporic religions have an important role to play in this dialogue, as they offer unique perspectives on spirituality, culture, and community that can enrich our understanding of the world around us.

✧ **The Rise of Global Consciousness**

Another opportunity facing African diasporic religions is the rise of global consciousness. As people become more aware of the interconnectedness of the world and the importance of environmental sustainability, there is a growing recognition of the value of indigenous knowledge and traditional practices. African diasporic religions have a long history of connection to the natural world and can offer valuable insights into sustainable living and environmental stewardship.

African Religions

✧   The Empowerment of Marginalized Communities

African diasporic religions have the potential to empower marginalized communities and provide a sense of belonging and identity for those who have been excluded from mainstream society. By providing a space for cultural expression and community building, these religions can help to create a sense of pride and empowerment among their practitioners.

✧   The Growth of African Diasporic Religions in the Diaspora and Africa

Another opportunity facing African diasporic religions is their growing popularity both within the diaspora and in Africa itself. In the diaspora, African diasporic religions have seen a resurgence in recent years, with more and more people seeking to connect with their ancestral roots and reclaim their cultural heritage. In Africa, these religions have been experiencing a similar growth, as many Africans turn to traditional religions as a way to resist the influence of colonialism and embrace their cultural identity.

However, this growth also presents challenges for African diasporic religions. As these religions become more popular, there is a risk of commercialization and commodification. Some practitioners may seek to capitalize on the popularity of these religions, turning them into profitable enterprises and exploiting their followers. Additionally, the growing popularity of these religions may lead to cultural appropriation and the dilution of their traditions as they become more mainstream.

✧   The Challenge of Maintaining Authenticity

African diasporic religions face a challenge in maintaining their authenticity and resisting the pressures of assimilation. As these religions become more mainstream and attract a wider audience, there may be a tendency to dilute their traditions or conform to mainstream norms in order to appeal to a broader audience. This can be a difficult balance to strike, as practitioners seek to maintain the integrity of their traditions while also adapting to changing cultural and social contexts.

✧   The Impact of Globalization

Globalization has had a significant impact on African diasporic religions, both positive and negative. On the one hand, globalization has facilitated the spread of these religions and allowed them to reach new audiences around the world. It has also enabled practitioners to connect with each other and share knowledge and resources across geographic and cultural boundaries.

Exploring Origins, Traditions, and Contemporary Relevance

On the other hand, globalization has also contributed to the erosion of traditional cultures and the homogenization of global cultures. The influence of Western culture and capitalism can be seen in the way African diasporic religions are sometimes commercialized and commodified, and the pressure to conform to Western norms can lead to the loss of cultural diversity and traditional knowledge.

In conclusion, African diasporic religions face both challenges and opportunities in the modern world. While globalization and the rise of global consciousness present new opportunities for these religions, they also face the challenges of commercialization, assimilation, and dilution of their traditions. As practitioners navigate these challenges, it is important to maintain the authenticity and integrity of these religions while also adapting to changing cultural and social contexts.

Examples, problems, and exercises to illustrate topics and engage students in critical thinking and discussion:

Research and discuss the historical roots of a specific African diasporic religion and its contemporary practices

Problem: Based on their research, students will identify and analyze the ways in which Santeria reflects the syncretic nature of African diasporic religions, specifically the blending of Yoruba spirituality with Catholicism. They will consider the implications of this syncretism for the development of the religion and the experiences of its practitioners.

Exercise: Students will create a chart comparing and contrasting Yoruba religion and Santeria in terms of their beliefs, practices, and cultural context. They will then write a reflective essay discussing the similarities and differences between the two religions and their insights into the nature of diasporic religious traditions.

Analyze the role of African diasporic religions in addressing issues of social justice and human rights

Problem: Based on their analysis, students will consider the potential of religious movements for addressing contemporary issues of social justice and human rights, such as the Black Lives Matter movement. They will evaluate the benefits and limitations of using religious frameworks for social and political activism.

Exercise: Students will participate in a debate on the topic of whether African diasporic religions have a significant role to play in contemporary social justice movements. They will prepare arguments for and against this proposition and engage in critical discussion and analysis of the issues involved.

Write a reflection on the impact of African diasporic religions on your personal spiritual beliefs and practices

Problem: Based on their reflections, students will identify the challenges and opportunities involved in engaging with diasporic religious traditions and the role of cultural appropriation in their adoption and practice. They will consider how to navigate these issues in a respectful and ethical manner.

Exercise: Students will engage in a group discussion on the topic of cultural appropriation in diasporic religious traditions. They will examine the different perspectives on this issue and consider strategies for engaging with these traditions in an ethical and respectful manner.

Create a visual representation of the key beliefs and practices of a specific African diasporic religion

Exercise: Students will participate in a group activity in which they create a mock debate on the topic of the role of African diasporic religions in contemporary society. The class will be divided into two groups, with one group arguing for the positive impact of African diasporic religions and the other group arguing against it. Students will be assigned a position and will be required to research and prepare arguments and counterarguments for their side. The debate will be moderated by the instructor, and students will be graded on their preparation, participation, and use of evidence to support their arguments.

Problem: Following the mock debate, students will reflect on their own biases and assumptions about African diasporic religions and the impact these may have on their analysis of the traditions. They will consider how their personal experiences and cultural background may shape their understanding of these religions, and how they can work to overcome these biases in their research and analysis.

Exercise: Students will participate in a guided meditation or visualization exercise that draws on elements of African diasporic religions, such as drumming or chanting. They will reflect on the experience and consider how it has impacted their understanding of these religions and their own spirituality.

PART 6: AFRICAN FEMINIST THEOLOGIES

African feminist theologies emerged in the late 20th century as a response to the patriarchal structures of African societies and the dominance of Western Christianity in Africa. These theologies seek to challenge and subvert patriarchal norms and promote the full participation and empowerment of women in religious and social life. African feminist theologians draw on both African traditional religions and Christianity to develop a unique theological perspective that centers women's experiences and perspectives.

In this section, we will explore the key themes and ideas of African feminist theologies, as well as their historical and cultural context. We will examine the ways in which African feminist theologians have drawn on indigenous African beliefs and practices to challenge patriarchal interpretations of Christianity, and the impact that these theologies have had on African societies and religious communities.

Historical and Cultural Context

In this chapter, we will provide a historical and cultural context for the emergence of African feminist theologies. We will explore the ways in which African societies have been shaped by patriarchy and colonialism, and the impact of these forces on women's lives. We will also examine the history of Christianity in Africa, including the role of colonialism and the ways in which Christianity has been used to reinforce patriarchal norms.

Key topics in this chapter will include:

✧ The impact of colonialism on African societies and the suppression of indigenous knowledge and practices
✧ The role of Christianity in colonialism and the development of African Christian traditions
✧ The history of women's activism in Africa, including the role of women in anti-colonial struggles

✧   The emergence of feminist movements in Africa in the late 20th century and their influence on African feminist theologies

Key Themes and Ideas

In this chapter, we will explore the key themes and ideas of African feminist theologies. We will examine the ways in which these theologies seek to challenge patriarchal interpretations of Christianity and promote women's empowerment and liberation. We will also explore the ways in which African feminist theologians have drawn on indigenous African beliefs and practices to develop a unique theological perspective.

Key topics in this chapter will include:

✧   The centrality of women's experiences and perspectives in African feminist theologies

✧   The use of indigenous African beliefs and practices to challenge patriarchal norms and develop a unique theological perspective

✧   The concept of God/dess in African feminist theologies, including the importance of a gender-neutral or female image of the divine

✧   The role of women in religious leadership and ritual practices

✧   The impact of African feminist theologies on African societies and religious communities

Critiques and Challenges

In this chapter, we will explore some of the critiques and challenges facing African feminist theologies. We will examine the ways in which these theologies have been criticized for being too Western or too secular, and the tensions that exist between African feminist theologies and more traditional interpretations of Christianity.

Key topics in this chapter will include:

✧   The tension between African feminist theologies and traditional interpretations of Christianity

Exploring Origins, Traditions, and Contemporary Relevance

✧   The challenges of integrating feminist perspectives into traditional African societies

✧   The critiques of African feminist theologies as being too Western or too secular

✧   The challenges of building solidarity across different religious and cultural communities

In conclusion, African feminist theologies represent an important and growing movement within African religious and social thought. These theologies seek to challenge and subvert patriarchal norms and promote the full participation and empowerment of women in religious and social life. By drawing on both African traditional religions and Christianity, African feminist theologians have developed a unique theological perspective that centers women's experiences and perspectives.

As we have seen in this section, African feminist theologies have the potential to bring about significant social and religious change in Africa and beyond. However, they also face significant

CHAPTER 26: OVERVIEW OF AFRICAN FEMINIST THEOLOGIES

African feminist theologies emerged in the 1980s and 1990s as a response to the Eurocentric and patriarchal nature of Christian theology in Africa. These theologies challenged the idea that Christianity was a universal and neutral religion that could be practiced without regard to gender, race, or culture. Instead, African feminist theologians argued that Christianity had been used to justify the oppression of women, people of color, and other marginalized groups in Africa and around the world.

African feminist theologies are diverse and multifaceted, reflecting the many cultural and linguistic traditions of the continent. Some African feminist theologians draw on traditional African religions and practices, while others engage with Western feminist theory and Christian theology. Many African feminist theologians are also activists, working to empower women and promote social justice in their communities.

This chapter provides an overview of African feminist theologies, exploring their historical and cultural contexts, key themes and concepts, and their contributions to the larger field of feminist theology. We will examine the ways in which African feminist theologies challenge patriarchal and colonialist assumptions in Christianity, and how they offer a unique perspective on the relationship between religion, culture, and gender in Africa.

Historical and Cultural Contexts

African feminist theologies emerged in the context of a larger movement for social and political liberation in Africa. In the 1960s and 1970s, many African nations gained independence from colonial powers, leading to a renewed interest in African cultures and traditions. At the same time, the women's liberation movement was gaining momentum around the world, challenging patriarchal norms and advocating for women's rights.

In this context, African feminist theologians began to question the ways in which Christianity had been used to justify the subordination of women in Africa. They argued that traditional Christian theology was based on a patriarchal and hierarchical worldview that had been imposed on African societies by colonial powers. This theology had been used to justify the exclusion of women from leadership roles in the church, as well as their subordination in the family and society.

African feminist theologians also drew on traditional African religions and practices to develop a new understanding of Christianity that was more inclusive and empowering for women. They emphasized the importance of community, ritual, and artistic expression in African cultures, and argued that these practices could be integrated into Christian worship to create a more diverse and inclusive religious experience.

Key Themes and Concepts

African feminist theologies are characterized by several key themes and concepts that reflect their commitment to social justice and gender equality. These include:

Intersectionality: African feminist theologians recognize the ways in which gender intersects with other forms of oppression, such as race, class, and sexuality. They argue that a feminist theology must take into account the complex ways in which these different forms of oppression intersect in the lives of women in Africa.

Contextualization: African feminist theologians emphasize the importance of understanding the cultural and historical contexts in which religious practices take place. They argue that Christianity cannot be understood or practiced outside of these contexts, and that a feminist theology must take into account the diversity of cultural and linguistic traditions in Africa.

Liberation: African feminist theologians advocate for the liberation of women from patriarchal norms and structures in both the church and society. They argue that women must be empowered to take on leadership roles in the church and to participate fully in all aspects of religious life.

Community: African feminist theologians emphasize the importance of community and collective action in their work. They argue that social change can only be achieved through collective action and solidarity among women and other marginalized groups.

Contributions to Feminist Theology

African feminist theologies have made significant contributions to feminist theology by challenging the patriarchal nature of traditional Christian theology and offering alternative perspectives on God, the divine, and human existence. These theologies have emphasized the interconnectedness of all life and the importance of community, challenging the individualistic and hierarchical tendencies of Western theology.

One of the key contributions of African feminist theology has been its focus on the experiences and perspectives of women in African societies. This has led to a greater recognition of the diversity of women's experiences and the ways in which gender intersects with other forms of oppression, such as race and class. African feminist theologians have also emphasized the importance of African cultural and religious traditions, reclaiming and celebrating the spiritual practices and beliefs of their ancestors.

Another important contribution of African feminist theology has been its emphasis on the social and political dimensions of theology. African feminist theologians have challenged the notion that theology is purely a theoretical or abstract discipline, arguing that it is intimately connected to the lived experiences of people and the struggles for justice and liberation. They have emphasized the importance of engaging in concrete action to address issues of poverty, violence, and oppression, and have called for the development of theological frameworks that reflect the realities of African societies.

African feminist theology has also made important contributions to the broader field of feminist theology, challenging the Eurocentric and androcentric biases of traditional feminist theology and offering alternative perspectives on the nature of power and oppression. By foregrounding the experiences and perspectives of African women, African feminist theologians have expanded the scope of feminist theology, highlighting the diversity of women's experiences and the need for intersectional analyses of oppression.

Overall, African feminist theology has made significant contributions to feminist theology, offering new perspectives on the divine, the nature of human existence, and the ways in which theology can be engaged with social and political struggles for justice and liberation. In the following chapters, we will explore some of the key themes and debates within African feminist theology, including the relationship between tradition and innovation, the role of religion in African societies, and the challenges of engaging with contemporary social and political issues.

Define African feminist theologies and provide a brief history of its development.

African feminist theologies are a relatively new development in the field of feminist theology, emerging in the late 1980s and early 1990s as a response to the feminist movement in Africa. African feminist theologies have sought to address the intersection of gender and religion within African contexts, taking into account the unique cultural, social, and political factors that shape women's experiences.

Exploring Origins, Traditions, and Contemporary Relevance

African feminist theologies are rooted in the larger tradition of feminist theology, which emerged in the 1960s and 1970s in North America and Europe as a response to the second wave of feminism. Feminist theologians sought to challenge the patriarchal assumptions and structures within traditional religious institutions, and to develop new theologies and practices that centered the experiences and perspectives of women. African feminist theologians drew on these broader feminist theological trends, but also developed their own distinctive approaches to gender and religion within the African context.

One of the key figures in the development of African feminist theology was Mercy Amba Oduyoye, a Ghanaian theologian and founder of the Circle of Concerned African Women Theologians. Oduyoye and other African women theologians argued that traditional African religions and Christianity had often marginalized women's experiences and perspectives, and that feminist theology could offer a way to address this issue.

African feminist theologians have also been influenced by the larger African feminist movement, which emerged in the 1970s and 1980s as a response to colonialism and neo-colonialism in Africa. African feminist theologians have sought to engage with this movement, and to incorporate its insights into their theological work.

African feminist theologies are characterized by a commitment to challenging patriarchal structures and assumptions within religious institutions, and to centering the experiences and perspectives of African women in their theological work. African feminist theologians have developed a wide range of approaches and perspectives on gender and religion, and have drawn on a variety of religious and spiritual traditions, including Christianity, Islam, and traditional African religions.

African feminist theologians have also sought to engage with broader social and political issues, such as poverty, gender-based violence, and environmental degradation. They have emphasized the importance of women's leadership and empowerment, and have sought to develop new models of religious and spiritual practice that are more inclusive and egalitarian.

Overall, African feminist theologies represent an important and growing area of theological inquiry, one that is deeply rooted in African contexts and perspectives, and that offers new and innovative ways of thinking about gender and religion. In the following sections, we will explore some of the key themes and contributions of African feminist theologies in more detail.

The significance of African feminist theologies in the broader context of African religious traditions.

African feminist theologies have emerged as a significant movement in the broader context of African religious traditions. They offer a unique perspective on the intersection of religion, culture, gender, and social justice in Africa. In this section, we will explore the significance of African feminist theologies in the broader context of African religious traditions.

✦   Challenging Patriarchy and Gender Inequality

African feminist theologies have challenged patriarchy and gender inequality in African religious traditions. They have criticized the patriarchal structures and practices that have marginalized women in African societies, including religious institutions. African feminist theologians argue that women's experiences, perspectives, and contributions have been neglected or suppressed in African religious traditions. They seek to reclaim and reconstruct African religious traditions from a feminist perspective that values and promotes gender equality.

For instance, African feminist theologians have critiqued the African traditional religion's male-dominated priesthood and leadership roles. They have challenged the gendered language and symbols used in African religious practices and rituals, which often exclude or diminish women's experiences and perspectives. African feminist theologians also advocate for women's full participation in religious practices, including ordination, leadership roles, and ritual activities.

✦   Reclaiming African Women's Spirituality

African feminist theologies have also sought to reclaim African women's spirituality, which has been marginalized or erased in patriarchal religious traditions. African feminist theologians argue that African women have their own spiritual practices and experiences that have been neglected or suppressed in African religious traditions. They seek to rediscover and promote African women's spirituality from a feminist perspective that values and affirms their experiences and perspectives.

For instance, African feminist theologians have explored the role of African women's spirituality in healing and resilience in the face of social injustices such as colonialism, slavery, and poverty. They have also examined the significance of African women's spirituality in fostering community building and social activism. African feminist theologians have emphasized the need to recognize and respect the diversity of African women's spiritual practices and experiences, which are often shaped by their cultural, social, and historical contexts.

✧ Promoting Social Justice and Human Rights

African feminist theologies have also promoted social justice and human rights in the broader context of African religious traditions. They have critiqued the patriarchal structures and practices that have contributed to social injustices such as gender-based violence, economic exploitation, and political oppression in African societies. African feminist theologians seek to promote social justice and human rights from a feminist perspective that values and promotes the dignity and well-being of all persons, regardless of their gender, ethnicity, or social status.

For instance, African feminist theologians have advocated for the rights of marginalized groups such as women, children, and LGBTQI+ individuals in African societies. They have critiqued the ways in which religious institutions have contributed to the stigmatization and discrimination of these groups. African feminist theologians have also called for the integration of feminist principles and values into African religious traditions, including the promotion of non-violent conflict resolution, respect for diversity, and the pursuit of social justice.

✧ Engaging in Interfaith Dialogue and Collaboration

African feminist theologies have also engaged in interfaith dialogue and collaboration in the broader context of African religious traditions. They seek to promote mutual understanding, respect, and collaboration among different religious traditions in Africa. African feminist theologians recognize that African societies are diverse and pluralistic, with multiple religious traditions coexisting in complex ways. They seek to promote interfaith dialogue and collaboration from a feminist perspective that values and affirms the diversity of religious traditions and perspectives.

For instance, African feminist theologians have engaged in interfaith dialogue with Christian, Muslim, and traditional African religious leaders to explore common ground and areas of difference. They seek to build bridges and promote mutual understanding, respect, and collaboration among different religious traditions. African feminist theologians recognize that religious traditions in Africa have historically been used to justify patriarchal norms and practices that marginalize women and other marginalized groups. Therefore, they seek to promote a more inclusive and equitable understanding of religion that recognizes the dignity and worth of all people.

African feminist theologians have also engaged in interfaith collaboration to address social and environmental issues in Africa. For example, they have collaborated with religious leaders from different traditions to address issues such as poverty, HIV/AIDS, and environmental degradation. They seek to promote a holistic understanding of the interconnectedness of social, economic, and environmental issues, and to work together to address these challenges.

In addition to interfaith dialogue and collaboration, African feminist theologies also recognize the importance of intrafaith dialogue and collaboration. They seek to engage with different theological perspectives within their own religious traditions in order to promote a more inclusive and equitable understanding of their faith.

For example, within Christianity, African feminist theologians have engaged with both conservative and liberal theological perspectives to promote a more inclusive and equitable understanding of Christianity that affirms the dignity and worth of all people. They seek to challenge patriarchal interpretations of scripture and tradition that have been used to justify the marginalization of women and other marginalized groups, and to promote a more just and equitable understanding of Christian theology.

Similarly, within Islam, African feminist theologians have engaged with different theological perspectives to promote a more inclusive and equitable understanding of Islam that affirms the dignity and worth of all people. They seek to challenge patriarchal interpretations of scripture and tradition that have been used to justify the marginalization of women and other marginalized groups, and to promote a more just and equitable understanding of Islamic theology.

Overall, African feminist theologies are committed to promoting interfaith and intrafaith dialogue and collaboration in the broader context of African religious traditions. They seek to promote a more inclusive and equitable understanding of religion that recognizes the dignity and worth of all people, and to work together to address social, economic, and environmental challenges facing Africa.

The intersectionality of gender, race, and class in African feminist theologies.

Intersectionality is a key concept in African feminist theologies. Intersectionality refers to the interconnectedness of different social identities, such as gender, race, class, and sexuality, and how they interact to shape experiences of oppression and privilege. African feminist theologians recognize that African women's experiences of oppression are shaped by multiple and intersecting factors, including their gender, race, class, and other social identities.

One of the main contributions of African feminist theologies has been to highlight the intersectionality of gender, race, and class in African women's experiences of oppression. African feminist theologians have argued that gender cannot be understood in isolation from other social identities and structures of oppression, such as race and class. They have critiqued earlier feminist theologies for ignoring the ways in which African women's experiences of oppression are shaped by multiple and intersecting factors.

African feminist theologians have also critiqued African traditional religious and cultural practices that perpetuate gender, race, and class inequalities. They have argued that many African traditional religious and cultural practices are patriarchal and oppressive to women. They have also highlighted the ways in which race and class intersect with gender to shape African women's experiences of oppression. For example, African women who belong to lower social classes or who belong to marginalized racial or ethnic groups may face additional barriers and challenges in accessing resources and opportunities.

African feminist theologians have also highlighted the importance of intersectionality in addressing the root causes of oppression and working towards social justice. They have argued that social justice movements must recognize the interconnectedness of different forms of oppression and work towards addressing them in an intersectional and holistic manner. This means that movements for gender equality must also address issues of race and class, and vice versa.

In African feminist theologies, intersectionality is not just a theoretical concept but also a practical framework for action. African feminist theologians have worked to develop practical strategies and approaches for addressing the intersectional nature of oppression. For example, they have worked to develop programs and initiatives that address the needs of marginalized groups of women, such as women living in poverty, women with disabilities, and women from minority ethnic or racial groups.

African feminist theologians have also worked to develop intersectional approaches to theology and religious practice. They have sought to develop theologies and religious practices that are inclusive of different social identities and that affirm the dignity and worth of all individuals. They have also worked to develop approaches to spirituality that are grounded in the experiences and perspectives of African women and that challenge patriarchal and oppressive religious practices.

In conclusion, intersectionality is a key concept in African feminist theologies. African feminist theologians recognize that gender cannot be understood in isolation from other social identities and structures of oppression, such as race and class. They have critiqued earlier feminist theologies for ignoring the ways in which African women's experiences of oppression are shaped by multiple and intersecting factors. African feminist theologians have also worked to develop practical strategies and approaches for addressing the intersectional nature of oppression, and to develop intersectional approaches to theology and religious practice.

CHAPTER 27: KEY THEMES IN AFRICAN FEMINIST THEOLOGIES

African feminist theologies have emerged as a significant academic and religious discourse that seeks to engage with the lived experiences of African women, who are often marginalized and oppressed due to their gender, race, and class. African feminist theologies are concerned with the theological, cultural, and political dimensions of African women's experiences, and they seek to develop a feminist theology that is grounded in African cultural and religious traditions.

In this chapter, we will explore the key themes in African feminist theologies, including the intersectionality of gender, race, and class; the role of women in African traditional religions; the role of women in Christianity and Islam in Africa; the use of the Bible and Quran in African feminist theologies; the concept of spirituality and its relationship to African feminist theologies; and the significance of African feminist theologies in the broader context of African religious traditions.

We will begin by discussing the intersectionality of gender, race, and class in African feminist theologies. Intersectionality is a key concept in African feminist theologies, as it acknowledges that women's experiences are shaped not only by their gender, but also by their race, class, sexuality, and other social identities.

Next, we will explore the role of women in African traditional religions. African traditional religions are diverse and varied, and women play different roles in different religious traditions. African feminist theologies seek to challenge patriarchal norms and practices in African traditional religions and to promote the empowerment of women.

We will then turn to the role of women in Christianity and Islam in Africa. Both Christianity and Islam have a significant presence in Africa, and African feminist theologians have engaged with these religions to develop a feminist theology that is relevant to the experiences of African women.

The use of the Bible and Quran in African feminist theologies is another important theme that we will explore in this chapter. African feminist theologians have used these texts to challenge patriarchal interpretations and to develop a feminist theology that affirms the dignity and agency of women.

African Religions

The concept of spirituality and its relationship to African feminist theologies is also a key theme that we will discuss. African feminist theologians view spirituality as an important dimension of women's lives, and they seek to develop a feminist spirituality that is grounded in African cultural and religious traditions.

Finally, we will examine the significance of African feminist theologies in the broader context of African religious traditions. African feminist theologians seek to promote interfaith dialogue and collaboration, to challenge patriarchal norms and practices, and to promote the empowerment of women in African religious traditions.

In this chapter, we will engage with a variety of texts and authors to explore these key themes in African feminist theologies. We will also provide examples, problems, and exercises to illustrate these themes and to engage students in critical thinking and discussion. By the end of this chapter, students will have a deep understanding of the key themes in African feminist theologies and the significance of this discourse in the broader context of African religious traditions.

Introduction: African Feminist Theologies in Context

African feminist theologies are a vibrant and dynamic field of inquiry that seeks to explore the intersections of gender, race, and class in the context of African religious traditions. These theologies emerged in the late 20th century as a response to the marginalization of African women in the broader discourse of African theology and religious studies. African feminist theologians sought to challenge patriarchal interpretations of religious traditions and to develop new modes of theological inquiry that centered the experiences and perspectives of African women.

This chapter will explore the key themes and contributions of African feminist theologies, as well as the challenges and opportunities facing this field of inquiry. Specifically, this chapter will examine the intersectionality of gender, race, and class in African feminist theologies, the contributions of African feminist theologians to feminist theology as a global field, the development of African feminist theologies and their relationship to African religious traditions, the significance of African feminist theologies for women's empowerment and social justice in Africa, the challenges faced by African feminist theologians in their work, the importance of interfaith dialogue and collaboration in African feminist theologies, the diversity of African feminist theologies and the need for intersectional approaches, the role of African feminist theologies in shaping the broader discourse around gender and religion in Africa and beyond, and the potential for African feminist theologies to inform and enrich the practices of witchcraft, divination, herbalism, shamanism, and ecospirituality in Africa and the diaspora.

The Intersectionality of Gender, Race, and Class in African Feminist Theologies

At the heart of African feminist theologies is a commitment to exploring the intersections of gender, race, and class in the context of African religious traditions. African feminist theologians recognize that African societies are diverse and pluralistic, with multiple religious traditions coexisting in complex ways. They seek to promote interfaith dialogue and collaboration from a feminist perspective that values and affirms the diversity of religious traditions and perspectives.

Central to this project is an understanding of the complex ways in which gender, race, and class intersect in the lives of African women. African feminist theologians seek to challenge the patriarchal norms and structures that perpetuate gender inequality, while also recognizing the ways in which gender intersects with other forms of oppression, such as race, class, and colonialism.

African feminist theologians recognize that the experiences of African women are shaped by their social and historical contexts, which include the legacy of colonialism and ongoing neocolonialism. They recognize that African women have often been excluded from formal education and political power, and that their economic opportunities have been limited by patriarchal norms and practices.

By examining the intersections of gender, race, and class, African feminist theologians are able to offer nuanced and context-specific analyses of the experiences of African women. They recognize that African women are not a monolithic group, but rather are shaped by a range of intersecting identities and experiences.

Moreover, African feminist theologians recognize the importance of centering the experiences and perspectives of marginalized women, including LGBTQ+ women, women with disabilities, and women living in poverty. By acknowledging the ways in which different forms of oppression intersect in the lives of these women, African feminist theologians are able to offer a more comprehensive and inclusive vision of feminist theology.

In addition, African feminist theologians recognize the importance of addressing the ways in which gender, race, and class intersect in their own lives and work. They recognize that they are not immune from the influence of patriarchal norms and structures, and seek to promote self-reflection and critical analysis as a means of challenging their own biases and assumptions.

Overall, the intersectionality of gender, race, and class is a central theme in African feminist theologies, shaping the way in which African feminist theologians approach their work and engage with broader discussions around gender, race, and social justice.

The Contributions of African Feminist Theologians to Feminist Theology as a Global Field

African feminist theologians have made significant contributions to feminist theology as a global field. They have challenged dominant Western feminist perspectives that have often overlooked the experiences of women in the Global South. They have also developed new modes of theological inquiry that are rooted in African religious traditions and that center the experiences and perspectives of African women.

One key contribution of African feminist theologians has been their use of the concept of Ubuntu, a traditional African philosophy that emphasizes interconnectedness and community. African feminist theologians have used this concept to challenge individualistic and patriarchal understandings of Christianity and to develop a more communal and egalitarian vision of the church.

Another contribution of African feminist theologians to feminist theology as a global field is their critique of the Eurocentric and androcentric biases of traditional theological discourses. By foregrounding the voices and experiences of African women, African feminist theologians have highlighted the ways in which dominant theological paradigms have marginalized and excluded women's perspectives. They have also challenged the normative assumptions underlying traditional theological discourse, such as the universalization of male experience, the prioritization of rationality over emotion, and the separation of the sacred and the secular.

In addition to their critiques, African feminist theologians have also developed new theological frameworks that emphasize the embodied and experiential dimensions of faith. They have emphasized the importance of lived experience, embodiment, and emotion in shaping religious belief and practice, and have challenged the hierarchical and dualistic nature of traditional theological frameworks.

African feminist theologians have also contributed to the development of intercultural and interfaith dialogue. By engaging with diverse religious traditions and perspectives, African feminist theologians have broadened the scope of feminist theological inquiry and fostered new forms of collaboration and exchange. They have emphasized the importance of mutual respect, empathy, and solidarity in building more inclusive and just communities.

Exploring Origins, Traditions, and Contemporary Relevance

Overall, the contributions of African feminist theologians to feminist theology as a global field have been significant and wide-ranging. They have challenged dominant paradigms, developed new frameworks, and fostered new forms of collaboration and dialogue. Through their work, they have enriched and expanded our understanding of religion, gender, and social justice.

The Development of African Feminist Theologies and Their Relationship to African Religious Traditions

African feminist theologies have developed in the context of African religious traditions, which are diverse and complex. African feminist theologians draw on a range of religious traditions, including Christianity, Islam, and traditional African religions, to develop their theological perspectives.

Central to the development of African feminist theologies is a commitment to engaging with African religious traditions on their own terms, rather than simply importing Western feminist perspectives. African feminist theologians seek to develop new modes of theological inquiry that are grounded in African religious traditions and that center the experiences and perspectives of African women.

African feminist theologies emerged as a response to the marginalization of African women in both African societies and in the broader field of theology. African feminist theologians recognized that African religious traditions had often been used to justify gender-based oppression, and they sought to challenge these patriarchal norms and structures from within their own religious traditions.

One of the central challenges facing African feminist theologians has been how to engage with African religious traditions in ways that are both critical and respectful. African religious traditions are diverse and complex, and they are often deeply intertwined with social and cultural practices. African feminist theologians recognize that African religious traditions have the potential to promote positive social change, but they also recognize that these traditions have been used to justify oppression.

To address these challenges, African feminist theologians have developed new modes of theological inquiry that are grounded in African religious traditions and that center the experiences and perspectives of African women. These modes of inquiry include a focus on women's experiences and perspectives, an emphasis on the intersectionality of gender, race, and class, and a commitment to promoting social justice and women's empowerment.

In addition, African feminist theologians have drawn on a range of religious traditions, including Christianity, Islam, and traditional African religions, to develop their theological perspectives. They have sought to engage with these religious traditions on their own terms, rather than simply importing Western feminist perspectives. This has involved a critical examination of the ways in which these religious traditions have been used to justify gender-based oppression, as well as a recognition of the potential for these traditions to promote positive social change.

Overall, the development of African feminist theologies has been driven by a commitment to engaging with African religious traditions in ways that are both critical and respectful, and that center the experiences and perspectives of African women. By developing new modes of theological inquiry that are grounded in African religious traditions, African feminist theologians have made significant contributions to the broader field of theology, as well as to efforts to promote gender equality and social justice in Africa and beyond.

The Significance of African Feminist Theologies for Women's Empowerment and Social Justice in Africa

African feminist theologies have been instrumental in promoting women's empowerment and social justice in Africa. By centering the experiences and perspectives of African women, African feminist theologians have challenged patriarchal religious and societal norms that have perpetuated gender-based oppression and inequality.

One key contribution of African feminist theologies has been to offer a critical analysis of the ways in which religion has been used to justify and perpetuate gender-based oppression. African feminist theologians have exposed the ways in which patriarchal interpretations of religious texts and traditions have been used to justify gender-based violence, discrimination, and marginalization.

In addition to offering critical analysis, African feminist theologies have also provided frameworks for reimagining and transforming religious and societal norms in ways that promote women's empowerment and social justice. For example, African feminist theologians have drawn on traditional African religious concepts of community and interconnectedness to develop new models of social organization that prioritize collective well-being over individual gain.

African feminist theologies have also been influential in promoting women's leadership and participation in religious communities. By challenging patriarchal interpretations of religious texts and traditions that have excluded women from leadership roles, African feminist theologians have worked to create space for women to take on leadership roles within their religious communities.

Exploring Origins, Traditions, and Contemporary Relevance

Furthermore, African feminist theologies have been instrumental in promoting women's agency and autonomy in decision-making processes related to their bodies, sexuality, and reproductive health. African feminist theologians have challenged religious and societal norms that have limited women's control over their own bodies and have advocated for policies and practices that promote women's reproductive rights and health.

Overall, African feminist theologies have been significant in promoting women's empowerment and social justice in Africa by providing critical analysis, offering new frameworks for social organization, promoting women's leadership and participation in religious communities, and advocating for women's agency and autonomy.

The Challenges Faced by African Feminist Theologians in Their Work

Despite their significant contributions, African feminist theologians face numerous challenges in their work. One of the most significant challenges is opposition from patriarchal religious institutions and societal norms. Many religious institutions in Africa are patriarchal and hierarchical, and they may view the work of African feminist theologians as a threat to their authority and legitimacy.

Moreover, African feminist theologians may face resistance and hostility from broader society, which may view their perspectives as subversive or anti-traditional. African feminist theologians may also face challenges in terms of resources and institutional support, as they may not have access to the same funding or opportunities as their male counterparts.

Another challenge that African feminist theologians face is the lack of recognition and visibility within the broader field of theology. Western feminist theology has historically dominated the field and has often overlooked the experiences and perspectives of women in the Global South, including Africa. This lack of recognition and visibility can make it difficult for African feminist theologians to gain access to resources and platforms to share their work.

Additionally, African feminist theologians may face challenges in balancing their academic work with their commitments to activism and community organizing. Many African feminist theologians are deeply engaged in social justice movements and community-based initiatives, but may face difficulties in finding support and resources for this work.

Finally, African feminist theologians may face challenges in building bridges across different religious traditions and communities. African societies are diverse and pluralistic, with multiple religious traditions coexisting in complex ways. African feminist theologians seek to promote interfaith dialogue and collaboration from a feminist perspective that values and affirms the diversity of religious traditions and perspectives, but this can be a complex and challenging process.

The Importance of Interfaith Dialogue and Collaboration in African Feminist Theologies

Given the diversity of African religious traditions and the complex challenges faced by African feminist theologians, interfaith dialogue and collaboration are critical components of African feminist theologies. Interfaith dialogue and collaboration enable African feminist theologians to engage with diverse religious perspectives and to develop new modes of theological inquiry that are grounded in African religious traditions while also being inclusive and respectful of diverse perspectives.

Moreover, interfaith dialogue and collaboration can help to bridge the gap between African feminist theologians and broader society, by demonstrating the value and relevance of their perspectives for addressing critical social and religious issues in Africa.

The Diversity of African Feminist Theologies and the Need for Intersectional Approaches

African feminist theologies are diverse and multifaceted, reflecting the diverse religious, cultural, and historical contexts in which they have developed. As such, African feminist theologians recognize the importance of intersectionality in their work, as they seek to develop perspectives that are inclusive and responsive to the diverse experiences and perspectives of African women.

Intersectionality involves recognizing and addressing the ways in which different forms of oppression, such as gender, race, class, and sexuality, intersect and shape the experiences of individuals and communities. By adopting an intersectional approach, African feminist theologians can develop more nuanced and complex perspectives that reflect the diverse experiences of African women.

The Role of African Feminist Theologies in Shaping the Broader Discourse around Gender and Religion

African feminist theologies have made significant contributions to the broader discourse around gender and religion, both in Africa and beyond. By exposing the ways in which religious texts and traditions have been used to justify gender-based oppression, African feminist theologians have contributed to broader efforts to promote gender equality and social justice.

Moreover, African feminist theologians have offered new perspectives on religious traditions and practices, demonstrating the potential for these traditions to promote positive social change. By highlighting the ways in which religious and societal norms can be transformed to promote women's empowerment and social justice, African feminist theologians have contributed to broader efforts to reimagine religion as a force for positive social change.

The Potential for African Feminist Theologies to Inform and Enrich the Practices of Witchcraft, Divination, Herbalism, Shamanism, and Ecospirituality in Africa and the Diaspora

In addition to their contributions to feminist theology and religious studies, African feminist theologies have the potential to inform and enrich the practices of witchcraft, divination, herbalism, shamanism, and ecospirituality in Africa and the diaspora.

For example, African feminist theologians have highlighted the role of divination in promoting women's empowerment and social justice. They have argued that divination can serve as a tool for identifying and addressing social issues such as gender-based violence, poverty, and environmental degradation. By emphasizing the role of diviners as agents of social change, African feminist theologians have offered new perspectives on traditional African religious practices.

Similarly, African feminist theologians have explored the potential of herbalism and other traditional healing practices to promote women's health and wellbeing. By highlighting the connections between traditional healing practices and broader efforts to promote women's empowerment and social justice, African feminist theologians have contributed to the development of more holistic approaches to healthcare and wellbeing.

Moreover, African feminist theologians have emphasized the importance of ecological consciousness in African religious traditions. They have argued that traditional African religious practices offer important insights into sustainable and harmonious relationships between humans and the natural world. By emphasizing the importance of ecological consciousness in religious practice, African feminist theologians have contributed to broader efforts to promote environmental sustainability and social justice.

The Need for Continued Engagement with African Feminist Theologies and Their Ongoing Contributions to Feminist Theology and Religious Studies

In conclusion, African feminist theologies have emerged as a dynamic and important field of inquiry within feminist theology and religious studies. African feminist theologians have made significant contributions to our understanding of the intersectionality of gender, race, and class in African religious traditions, as well as to broader efforts to promote women's empowerment and social justice in Africa and beyond.

As the field of African feminist theologies continues to develop, it is important for scholars and practitioners to engage with these perspectives and to recognize their ongoing contributions to feminist theology and religious studies. By centering the experiences and perspectives of African women, African feminist theologians offer new insights into the ways in which religious traditions and practices can be transformed to promote positive social change.

Conclusion: The Ongoing Relevance of African Feminist Theologies.

The contributions of African feminist theologians have been significant and continue to be relevant today. African feminist theologies offer critical perspectives on the intersection of gender, religion, and society in Africa, and provide frameworks for reimagining and transforming religious and societal norms in ways that promote women's empowerment and social justice.

African feminist theologians have challenged dominant Western feminist perspectives that have often overlooked the experiences of women in the Global South. They have developed new modes of theological inquiry that are rooted in African religious traditions and that center the experiences and perspectives of African women. One key contribution of African feminist theologians has been their use of the concept of Ubuntu, a traditional African philosophy that emphasizes interconnectedness and community. African feminist theologians have used this concept to challenge individualistic and patriarchal understandings of Christianity and to develop a more communal and egalitarian vision of the church.

The significance of African feminist theologies for women's empowerment and social justice in Africa cannot be overstated. By centering the experiences and perspectives of African women, African feminist theologians have challenged patriarchal religious and societal norms that have perpetuated gender-based oppression and inequality. African feminist theologians have offered critical analysis of the ways in which religion has been used to justify and perpetuate gender-based oppression, and provided frameworks for reimagining and transforming religious and societal norms in ways that promote women's empowerment and social justice.

Exploring Origins, Traditions, and Contemporary Relevance

However, despite their significant contributions, African feminist theologians face numerous challenges in their work. One of the most significant challenges is opposition from patriarchal religious institutions and societal norms. Many religious institutions in Africa are patriarchal and hierarchical, and they may view the work of African feminist theologians as a threat to their authority and legitimacy. African feminist theologians may also face resistance and hostility from broader society, which may view their perspectives as subversive or anti-traditional. African feminist theologians may also face challenges in terms of resources and institutional support, as they may not have access to the same funding or opportunities as their male counterparts.

To address these challenges, it is essential that African feminist theologians receive more institutional and financial support. This can be done through the creation of academic programs and institutions that prioritize the study and advancement of African feminist theologies, and through the provision of funding and resources to support research, publication, and advocacy efforts. It is also essential that African feminist theologians continue to engage in critical and constructive dialogue with religious institutions and broader society, in order to challenge and transform patriarchal religious and societal norms.

Moreover, African feminist theologies offer important insights and perspectives that can inform and enrich global conversations on gender, religion, and society. African feminist theologians provide critical perspectives on the intersection of gender and religion, and offer frameworks for reimagining and transforming religious and societal norms in ways that promote gender equity and social justice. As such, African feminist theologies are an essential component of global conversations on gender, religion, and society, and their ongoing relevance cannot be overstated.

In conclusion, African feminist theologies have made significant contributions to feminist theology as a global field. They have challenged dominant Western feminist perspectives, developed new modes of theological inquiry, and provided critical perspectives on the intersection of gender, religion, and society. African feminist theologies have also been instrumental in promoting women's empowerment and social justice in Africa, and their ongoing relevance cannot be overstated. It is essential that African feminist theologians receive more institutional and financial support, and that they continue to engage in critical and constructive dialogue with religious institutions and broader society, in order to challenge and transform patriarchal religious and societal norms.

CHAPTER 28: THE INTERSECTION OF GENDER AND RELIGION IN AFRICAN SOCIETIES

Religion and gender are two intersecting and interdependent social constructs that have shaped human societies throughout history. In African societies, religion and gender have played a significant role in shaping social norms, cultural practices, and power dynamics. This chapter explores the intersection of gender and religion in African societies, with a focus on the ways in which religion has been used to justify gender-based oppression and the efforts to challenge and transform these dynamics.

Religion and Gender in African Societies

African societies are characterized by diversity in terms of ethnicity, culture, and religion. Religion in Africa is not a monolithic entity but is rather a complex and diverse set of beliefs and practices that vary across regions and communities. Despite this diversity, there are certain patterns and trends that are observable in the intersection of religion and gender in African societies.

One of the key features of religion in African societies is its patriarchal nature. Many religious traditions in Africa, both indigenous and introduced, are characterized by hierarchical power structures that prioritize men over women. This is reflected in religious texts, which often portray women as subordinate to men and limit their roles and opportunities within religious institutions.

Moreover, religious practices in African societies often reinforce gender-based oppression and discrimination. For example, many traditional African religious practices involve female genital mutilation, which is a harmful and dangerous practice that perpetuates gender-based violence and reinforces patriarchal norms. Similarly, many African religious institutions restrict women's participation in religious activities, such as preaching or leading prayers, on the basis of their gender.

Challenging Patriarchal Religious Norms

Despite the prevalence of patriarchal religious norms in African societies, there have been efforts to challenge and transform these dynamics. African feminist theologians have been at the forefront of these efforts, seeking to develop new modes of theological inquiry that are grounded in African religious traditions and that center the experiences and perspectives of African women.

One of the key contributions of African feminist theologians has been to offer a critical analysis of the ways in which religion has been used to justify and perpetuate gender-based oppression. African feminist theologians have exposed the ways in which patriarchal interpretations of religious texts and traditions have been used to justify gender-based violence, discrimination, and marginalization.

In addition to offering critical analysis, African feminist theologians have also provided frameworks for reimagining and transforming religious and societal norms in ways that promote women's empowerment and social justice. For example, African feminist theologians have drawn on traditional African religious concepts of community and interconnectedness to develop new models of social organization that prioritize collective well-being over individual gain.

The intersection of gender and religion in African societies is a complex and multifaceted issue that requires careful and nuanced analysis. While patriarchal religious norms continue to shape social norms and practices in many African societies, there are also efforts to challenge and transform these dynamics. African feminist theologians have been at the forefront of these efforts, seeking to develop new modes of theological inquiry that center the experiences and perspectives of African women and that promote women's empowerment and social justice. By continuing to engage with these issues, we can work towards a more just and equitable society for all.

Examine the relationship between gender and religion in African societies, including the impact of colonialism and globalization.

The relationship between gender and religion in African societies is complex and multifaceted, shaped by a variety of factors including history, culture, and politics. In this chapter, we will examine the ways in which gender and religion intersect in African societies, exploring how these intersections have been shaped by both colonialism and globalization. We will begin by providing an overview of traditional African religious beliefs and practices, paying particular attention to the roles and status of women in these societies. We will then turn to the impact of colonialism on gender and religion in Africa, examining how European colonial powers sought to impose their own religious beliefs and gender norms on African societies. Finally, we will explore the ways in which globalization has impacted gender and religion in Africa, highlighting both the opportunities and challenges that arise from increased interconnectedness and cultural exchange.

African Religions

Traditional African Religious Beliefs and Practices:

Traditional African religious beliefs and practices are diverse and complex, varying significantly across different regions and cultural groups. However, there are certain commonalities that can be identified across many African societies. One of the most prominent features of traditional African religion is a belief in the interconnectedness of all things, including humans, animals, and the natural world. This belief is often expressed through the veneration of ancestors and the use of ritual practices to maintain a harmonious relationship between humans and the natural world.

In many traditional African societies, gender roles and expectations were highly differentiated. Women were often responsible for domestic labor, including cooking, cleaning, and childcare, while men were more involved in activities such as hunting, farming, and political leadership. However, this division of labor did not necessarily correspond to a hierarchy of value, as both men and women were seen as essential to the functioning of society.

The Impact of Colonialism:

The arrival of European colonial powers in Africa had a profound impact on gender and religion in African societies. European colonial powers sought to impose their own religious beliefs and gender norms on African societies, viewing traditional African religion and gender roles as primitive and inferior.

One of the most significant ways in which colonialism impacted gender and religion in Africa was through the introduction of Christianity. European Christian missionaries sought to convert African peoples to Christianity, viewing traditional African religion as pagan and idolatrous. As a result, many African peoples were forced to abandon their traditional religious beliefs and practices, and adopt Christian beliefs and practices.

This process of Christianization often involved the imposition of European gender norms on African societies. European missionaries viewed African gender roles as backwards and primitive, and sought to promote European gender norms, such as the idea of separate spheres for men and women. This led to the marginalization and subordination of women in many African societies, as European gender norms often privileged men over women.

Exploring Origins, Traditions, and Contemporary Relevance

The Impact of Globalization:

Globalization has had both positive and negative impacts on gender and religion in African societies. On the one hand, increased interconnectedness and cultural exchange has led to the emergence of new religious and cultural movements that challenge traditional gender norms and promote gender equality. For example, the rise of feminist and queer movements in Africa has led to a greater awareness of issues related to gender and sexuality, and has challenged traditional patriarchal religious and cultural beliefs.

On the other hand, globalization has also led to the spread of Western cultural values and beliefs, including Western gender norms. This has led to a homogenization of culture in some parts of Africa, and has undermined the diversity of traditional African religious beliefs and practices. Moreover, globalization has often been associated with economic inequality and political instability, which can have negative impacts on gender equality and the status of women in African societies.

In conclusion, the relationship between gender and religion in African societies is complex and multifaceted, shaped by a variety of factors including history, culture, and politics. Traditional African religious beliefs and practices often involved a deep respect for the interconnectedness of all beings, and many African societies held women in high regard as spiritual leaders and healers. However, the introduction of colonialism and globalization brought with it patriarchal attitudes and practices that have had a lasting impact on gender relations in many African societies.

African feminist theologians have played a vital role in challenging patriarchal religious and societal norms and promoting women's empowerment and social justice. By centering the experiences and perspectives of African women, African feminist theologians have been able to offer critical analyses of the ways in which religion has been used to justify and perpetuate gender-based oppression. They have also provided frameworks for reimagining and transforming religious and societal norms in ways that promote women's empowerment and social justice.

The ongoing relevance of African feminist theologies cannot be overstated. Despite the many challenges faced by African feminist theologians in their work, their contributions have been significant in promoting gender equality and social justice in Africa. Moreover, the insights and frameworks developed by African feminist theologians can be valuable resources for individuals and communities working towards gender equality and social justice around the world.

Moving forward, it is important to continue supporting and amplifying the voices of African feminist theologians and other advocates for gender equality and social justice in Africa. This includes providing resources and institutional support, promoting education and awareness around these issues, and creating spaces for dialogue and collaboration between diverse groups. By working together, we can continue to promote gender equality and social justice in Africa and beyond.

The ways in which African feminist theologies challenge patriarchal structures within African religions.

African feminist theologians have made significant contributions to the study of religion and gender in African societies. They have worked to challenge patriarchal structures within African religions and to promote more inclusive and equitable religious practices. In this section, we will discuss the ways in which African feminist theologies have challenged patriarchal structures within African religions.

One of the primary ways in which African feminist theologians challenge patriarchal structures within African religions is through their critiques of traditional religious practices. Many traditional African religions have patriarchal structures and practices that limit the participation of women and reinforce gender inequalities. African feminist theologians have argued that these practices are not in line with the principles of equality and justice, and they have called for their reform.

For example, African feminist theologians have critiqued the practice of female genital mutilation, which is still practiced in many African communities. They argue that this practice is a form of violence against women that is not supported by any religious text or tradition. African feminist theologians have also critiqued the practice of polygamy, which is still legal and practiced in many African countries. They argue that this practice reinforces gender inequalities and can have negative consequences for women's health, economic security, and social status.

Another way in which African feminist theologians challenge patriarchal structures within African religions is through their efforts to promote women's leadership and participation in religious communities. Many traditional African religions do not allow women to hold leadership positions or to participate fully in religious rituals. African feminist theologians have called for the inclusion of women in leadership positions and for the creation of more inclusive religious practices.

For example, African feminist theologians have worked to promote the ordination of women in Christian churches. They argue that women have the same spiritual gifts and calling as men and should have the same opportunities to serve as religious leaders. African feminist theologians have also called for the inclusion of women in traditional African religious rituals, which are often restricted to men. They argue that women have valuable knowledge and perspectives that should be included in these rituals.

In addition to their critiques of traditional religious practices and their efforts to promote women's leadership and participation in religious communities, African feminist theologians have also worked to develop new theological frameworks that are more inclusive and equitable. They have developed new ways of understanding the relationship between God and humanity that challenge traditional patriarchal assumptions.

For example, African feminist theologians have developed the concept of "Mother God," which emphasizes the maternal aspects of the divine and challenges the patriarchal assumption that God is exclusively male. They argue that a more inclusive and diverse concept of God can help to promote gender equality and social justice. African feminist theologians have also developed the concept of "ubuntu," which emphasizes the interconnectedness and interdependence of all people and promotes a more communal and inclusive approach to religion.

Despite the significant contributions of African feminist theologians, their work is not without challenges. As we discussed earlier, African feminist theologians face opposition from patriarchal religious institutions and societal norms. They may also face challenges in terms of resources and institutional support. However, despite these challenges, African feminist theologians continue to work towards more inclusive and equitable religious practices that promote gender equality and social justice.

In conclusion, African feminist theologians have made important contributions to the study of religion and gender in African societies. Through their critiques of traditional religious practices, their efforts to promote women's leadership and participation in religious communities, and their development of new theological frameworks, they have challenged patriarchal structures within African religions and promoted more inclusive and equitable religious practices. Although their work is not without challenges, African feminist theologians continue to work towards a more just and inclusive future for all.

CHAPTER 29: AFRICAN WOMEN'S SPIRITUAL PRACTICES AND THEIR SIGNIFICANCE

Women have played a critical role in African spirituality, contributing to the development of religious practices and beliefs throughout the continent. However, the contribution of women to African spirituality is often overlooked, undervalued, and sometimes even suppressed, due to the patriarchal nature of many African societies. In recent years, scholars and practitioners of African spirituality have begun to recognize the importance of women's spiritual practices and their significance in shaping African religious traditions.

This chapter explores the spiritual practices of African women, highlighting their contributions to African spirituality, and examining the ways in which their practices challenge patriarchal structures within African religions. We will explore the diversity of spiritual practices among African women, from divination and healing to rituals and ceremonies, and we will examine the ways in which these practices reflect the experiences, values, and beliefs of African women.

The significance of African women's spiritual practices goes beyond the realm of spirituality. These practices are essential to understanding African women's lives, experiences, and struggles, as well as the social, political, and economic challenges they face. Through their spiritual practices, African women assert their agency, resist oppression, and create spaces for healing, empowerment, and social change.

This chapter is divided into three sections. The first section provides an overview of African women's spiritual practices, highlighting their diversity, complexity, and significance. The second section examines the role of African women's spiritual practices in challenging patriarchal structures within African religions. Finally, the third section explores the political, social, and economic implications of African women's spiritual practices.

African Women's Spiritual Practices

African women's spiritual practices are diverse, complex, and rooted in their experiences, histories, and cultures. These practices are shaped by a variety of factors, including geography, ethnicity, and religious traditions. However, despite this diversity, there are common themes and practices that are shared among African women across the continent.

One of the most prominent spiritual practices among African women is divination. Divination is the process of seeking knowledge about the future, the present, or the past through supernatural means. In many African societies, divination is a central part of religious practice and is often performed by women. Women who perform divination are often highly respected and valued members of their communities. They are seen as mediators between the spiritual and physical worlds and are called upon to help people navigate the challenges of life.

Another important spiritual practice among African women is healing. Healing practices among African women are holistic, incorporating physical, emotional, and spiritual dimensions. African women healers use a variety of methods, including herbal medicine, massage, energy work, and prayer, to help people recover from illness, injury, and trauma. Healing practices among African women are often passed down through generations and are deeply connected to cultural traditions and beliefs.

Rituals and ceremonies are also important spiritual practices among African women. These practices are performed for a variety of reasons, including initiation, marriage, childbirth, and death. Rituals and ceremonies are often highly structured and are performed with the participation of the entire community. They are seen as opportunities for spiritual growth, transformation, and communal bonding.

In addition to these practices, African women also engage in prayer, meditation, and other forms of spiritual contemplation. They draw upon a variety of religious traditions, including Christianity, Islam, and traditional African religions, to develop their own unique spiritual practices. These practices reflect the diverse experiences, beliefs, and values of African women and are essential to their spiritual and emotional well-being.

Furthermore, African women's spiritual practices are often linked to broader political and social movements. For example, many African women have used their spiritual practices as a means of resistance against colonialism, racism, and patriarchy. In the face of these oppressive forces, African women have turned to their spiritual practices as a source of empowerment and as a means of building community and solidarity.

One example of this is the use of spiritual practices during anti-colonial and anti-apartheid struggles in Africa. Women played a key role in these struggles and often turned to their spiritual practices as a means of organizing, mobilizing, and sustaining resistance. For example, in South Africa, women in the anti-apartheid movement formed prayer groups and performed ceremonies as a means of expressing their political beliefs and building solidarity.

African women's spiritual practices have also been central to feminist movements on the continent. African feminist theologians have sought to reclaim and reinterpret traditional African religious beliefs and practices from a feminist perspective. They argue that many traditional African religions have been distorted and patriarchalized by colonialism and that there is a need to reclaim and revalue the spiritual practices of African women.

In conclusion, African women's spiritual practices are rich and diverse, reflecting the experiences, histories, and cultures of African women across the continent. These practices are deeply connected to broader political and social movements and have been used as a means of resistance, empowerment, and community-building. By exploring and celebrating African women's spiritual practices, we can gain a greater appreciation for the rich diversity of African cultures and the important role that African women have played and continue to play in shaping them.

Challenging Patriarchal Structures within African Religions

African women's spiritual practices challenge patriarchal structures within African religions in a number of ways. Patriarchal structures within African religions are deeply ingrained and reflect broader patriarchal structures in African societies. They are often based on the assumption that men are superior to women, and that women should be subordinate to men in both public and private spheres. These patriarchal structures can manifest in various ways, such as through exclusion of women from leadership positions, restrictions on women's access to certain religious spaces and rituals, and the subjugation of women's bodies and sexuality.

Despite these challenges, African women have been actively challenging and subverting patriarchal structures within African religions through their spiritual practices. One way in which they do this is by creating alternative spaces for spiritual practice that are centered around women's experiences and perspectives. These spaces often allow for more egalitarian forms of worship and provide a sense of community and empowerment for women who may otherwise feel marginalized within mainstream religious institutions.

In addition to creating alternative spaces, African women's spiritual practices also challenge patriarchal structures through the re-interpretation and re-appropriation of traditional religious beliefs and practices. For example, African women have re-interpreted traditional concepts of motherhood and fertility to challenge patriarchal notions of women as passive and subordinate. They have also reappropriated traditional rituals and symbols to create new forms of spiritual expression that prioritize women's experiences and perspectives.

Furthermore, African women's spiritual practices challenge patriarchal structures by providing a platform for activism and social justice work. Many African women's spiritual practices are grounded in principles of social justice and community building, and women have used these practices to advocate for issues such as women's rights, LGBTQ+ rights, and environmental justice. Through their spiritual practices, African women have been able to mobilize and organize communities around issues that are often neglected or marginalized within mainstream religious institutions.

Overall, African women's spiritual practices are significant because they challenge patriarchal structures within African religions and provide a platform for women's empowerment and activism. By creating alternative spaces, re-interpreting traditional beliefs and practices, and advocating for social justice, African women are contributing to the transformation of African religions and societies more broadly. In the following sections, we will explore some of the specific spiritual practices of African women and their significance in more detail.

Analyze the spiritual practices of African women, including divination, herbalism, and ritual practices.

African women's spiritual practices are diverse and multifaceted, and they reflect the experiences, beliefs, and cultural traditions of women across the continent. In this section, we will analyze some of the most prominent spiritual practices among African women, including divination, herbalism, and ritual practices. We will examine the cultural contexts and beliefs that underpin these practices, as well as their social and political significance.

Divination is one of the most widely practiced spiritual traditions among African women. It is a process of seeking knowledge about the future, the present, or the past through supernatural means. Divination is often performed by women, who are seen as mediators between the spiritual and physical worlds. In many African societies, divination is considered a central part of religious practice, and it is used to help people navigate the challenges of life.

There are many different forms of divination practiced across Africa, including cowrie shell divination, geomancy, and tarot. However, one of the most well-known and widely practiced forms of divination is Ifá, a system of divination that originated in Nigeria and is now practiced throughout West Africa and the diaspora.

African Religions

Ifá divination is based on the principles of a complex system of binary arithmetic known as Odu, which consists of 256 different possible combinations of two binary digits. Each Odu is associated with a set of stories, myths, and proverbs, and each one represents a specific energy or force in the universe. During a divination session, the diviner uses a divination chain or set of divination objects to generate a random sequence of Odus, which is then interpreted to provide guidance and insight to the seeker.

Herbalism is another important spiritual practice among African women. African women have a long history of using medicinal plants to heal a variety of physical and emotional ailments. The use of herbal medicine is deeply connected to cultural traditions and beliefs, and it is often passed down through generations of women healers.

In many African societies, women are the primary caretakers of their families and communities, and they play a central role in the provision of healthcare. Women healers use a variety of methods, including herbal medicine, massage, energy work, and prayer, to help people recover from illness, injury, and trauma. They also provide support and guidance to people who are struggling with emotional and spiritual challenges.

Ritual practices are also an important part of African women's spiritual traditions. Rituals and ceremonies are performed for a variety of reasons, including initiation, marriage, childbirth, and death. These rituals are often highly structured and are performed with the participation of the entire community. They are seen as opportunities for spiritual growth, transformation, and communal bonding.

One of the most well-known examples of ritual practices among African women is the practice of female genital cutting. This practice is deeply controversial and has been the subject of intense debate and activism in recent years. Supporters of female genital cutting argue that it is an important part of cultural tradition and that it is necessary for the social and sexual well-being of women. However, critics argue that it is a harmful and traumatic practice that violates women's human rights and undermines their health and well-being.

In conclusion, African women's spiritual practices are diverse and multifaceted, and they reflect the experiences, beliefs, and cultural traditions of women across the continent. Divination, herbalism, and ritual practices are just a few of the many spiritual traditions that are practiced by African women. These practices are deeply connected to cultural traditions and beliefs, and they play an important role in the spiritual and emotional well-being of African women. However, they are also deeply influenced by social and political factors, and they are often the subject of intense debate and activism. As we continue to study and learn from the spiritual practices of African women, it is important to acknowledge and honor their contributions to the spiritual and cultural heritage of the continent.

One of the key themes that emerges from the study of African women's spiritual practices is the importance of community and interconnectedness. Many of the spiritual practices discussed above are performed in communal settings and involve the participation of the entire community. This reflects the belief that individual well-being is connected to the well-being of the community as a whole. Moreover, these practices serve as a means of strengthening social ties and fostering a sense of belonging and connection.

Another important theme is the centrality of the natural world in African women's spiritual practices. The use of herbalism, for example, reflects a deep reverence for the healing power of the natural world. Moreover, many of the ritual practices discussed above are performed in natural settings, such as forests or rivers, and involve the participation of natural elements, such as plants or animals. This reflects a belief in the interconnectedness of all living things and the spiritual power of the natural world.

It is important to note that African women's spiritual practices are not static, but are constantly evolving and adapting to changing social and political contexts. For example, the introduction of Christianity and Islam to Africa has had a significant impact on traditional African spiritual practices, leading to the development of new syncretic forms of spirituality that blend traditional African beliefs with elements of Christianity or Islam.

Moreover, the rise of feminist and women's rights movements in Africa has led to a re-examination of traditional gender roles within African religious communities and a push for greater inclusion of women in leadership roles and decision-making processes. This has resulted in the emergence of new forms of spiritual practice that challenge patriarchal structures and promote gender equity and social justice.

In conclusion, the study of African women's spiritual practices reveals a rich and complex tapestry of beliefs and practices that are deeply connected to the cultural traditions and experiences of African women. Divination, herbalism, and ritual practices are just a few of the many spiritual traditions that are practiced by African women, and they reflect a deep reverence for community, interconnectedness, and the natural world. As we continue to study and learn from the spiritual practices of African women, it is important to recognize and honor their contributions to the spiritual and cultural heritage of the continent, and to work towards greater inclusion and equity within African religious communities.

The significance of these practices in African feminist theologies and their role in empowering women.

African feminist theologies have emerged in response to the marginalization and subordination of women in African societies. These theologies aim to challenge patriarchal structures and to create spaces for women's empowerment and agency. In this section, we will explore how the spiritual practices of African women, including divination, herbalism, and ritual practices, have played a significant role in the development of African feminist theologies and in empowering women.

One of the ways in which African feminist theologies have been shaped by the spiritual practices of African women is through the use of divination. Divination is often seen as a form of resistance against patriarchy, as it allows women to access knowledge and power that is often denied to them in patriarchal societies. In African feminist theologies, divination is often viewed as a tool for spiritual and political liberation. It is seen as a means of resisting oppression and as a way of reclaiming agency and autonomy.

Another important spiritual practice in African feminist theologies is herbalism. Herbalism is a form of traditional medicine that has been practiced by African women for centuries. In African feminist theologies, herbalism is viewed as a way of healing not only the physical body, but also the spiritual and emotional aspects of a person. It is seen as a form of self-care and self-empowerment, as women are able to take control of their own health and well-being. Additionally, herbalism is often connected to the idea of ecological justice, as it emphasizes the importance of preserving the natural environment and the biodiversity of plant species.

Ritual practices are also significant in African feminist theologies. Rituals and ceremonies are often used to mark important life events, such as birth, marriage, and death. In African feminist theologies, these rituals are seen as a way of affirming the dignity and worth of women. They are viewed as opportunities for women to come together in community and to celebrate their collective strength and resilience. Additionally, rituals are often used to challenge patriarchal norms and to create new ways of understanding and practicing spirituality.

The spiritual practices of African women have played a crucial role in empowering women in African feminist theologies. These practices have been used to challenge patriarchal structures and to create spaces for women's agency and autonomy. Additionally, they have been used to create new ways of understanding spirituality that prioritize the experiences and perspectives of women.

Exploring Origins, Traditions, and Contemporary Relevance

However, it is important to note that the spiritual practices of African women are not without their challenges and limitations. In some cases, these practices have been co-opted by patriarchal structures, and women have been denied access to them. Additionally, there are debates within African feminist theologies about the role of traditional spiritual practices in a modern world. Some argue that these practices are inherently patriarchal and need to be abandoned, while others argue that they can be reinterpreted and transformed in ways that empower women.

To engage with these debates and to deepen our understanding of the role of spiritual practices in African feminist theologies, we can consider the following questions:

How have the spiritual practices of African women been used to challenge patriarchal structures?

In what ways do these practices contribute to the empowerment of women?

How do these practices intersect with other social and political factors, such as colonialism and globalization?

How can these practices be transformed to better serve the needs and aspirations of women in contemporary African societies?

What are the risks and limitations of relying on traditional spiritual practices in the struggle for gender justice and equality?

By engaging with these questions and by critically examining the role of spiritual practices in African feminist theologies, we can gain a deeper appreciation of the diversity and complexity of African women's spiritual lives and the ways in which they intersect with larger social and political struggles for justice and equality.

CHAPTER 30: THE ROLE OF AFRICAN WOMEN IN RELIGIOUS LEADERSHIP

African women have played a vital role in the development and sustenance of various religious traditions on the continent. Despite their important contributions, African women have often been marginalized and excluded from positions of religious leadership due to patriarchal attitudes and practices. This chapter will explore the role of African women in religious leadership, focusing on their historical contributions, contemporary challenges, and emerging opportunities.

Historical Contributions

African women have a long history of serving as religious leaders and spiritual guides. In many traditional African societies, women held positions of authority and respect within religious institutions. For example, in the Yoruba tradition of West Africa, women played important roles as priestesses and diviners. They were responsible for performing rituals and interpreting the will of the gods. In the Akan tradition of Ghana, women served as adehye mogya, or "blood mothers," who oversaw the spiritual health of their communities. They were responsible for maintaining altars, making offerings, and mediating conflicts.

In addition to their roles within specific religious traditions, African women have also played important roles as healers and spiritual advisors. Traditional healers, or herbalists, often included women who were respected for their knowledge of medicinal plants and their ability to communicate with the spirits. Women have also served as mediums, trance dancers, and spirit workers in various African religious traditions.

Furthermore, African women have been instrumental in the spread of new religious movements on the continent. During the colonial era, for example, women played a crucial role in the spread of Christianity, Islam, and other religions. They served as evangelists, teachers, and missionaries, and often played important roles in the establishment of new religious institutions.

In recent years, African women have continued to make significant contributions to religious leadership and spiritual practice. In many cases, they have challenged traditional gender roles and patriarchal power structures within religious institutions, advocating for greater gender equity and inclusivity. They have also worked to develop new forms of spiritual practice that reflect their own experiences and perspectives.

One notable example of this is the rise of African feminist theologies, which seek to articulate a spirituality that is grounded in the experiences and perspectives of African women. These theologies draw on both traditional African spiritual practices and feminist theory to challenge patriarchal power structures and promote greater gender equity and social justice.

African women have also played important roles in the development of ecospirituality, which emphasizes the interconnectedness of all living beings and seeks to promote environmental sustainability and social justice. Through their work as healers, herbalists, and traditional farmers, African women have long recognized the importance of living in harmony with nature. Today, many African women are leading efforts to promote sustainable agriculture, protect natural resources, and combat climate change.

In conclusion, African women have made significant historical contributions to religious leadership and spiritual practice. They have served as priestesses, healers, missionaries, and advocates for social justice. Despite facing significant challenges and obstacles, African women continue to shape the future of religious institutions and communities on the continent, promoting greater gender equity and inclusivity, developing new forms of spiritual practice, and advocating for environmental sustainability and social justice.

Contemporary Challenges

Despite their historical contributions, African women face significant challenges in achieving leadership positions within contemporary religious institutions. Patriarchal attitudes and practices often limit women's access to education, training, and resources needed to become religious leaders. In some cases, women are excluded from leadership positions altogether, while in others, they are relegated to subordinate roles or marginalized within the larger religious community.

One of the most significant challenges facing African women in religious leadership is the persistence of gender-based violence and discrimination. Women who speak out or challenge traditional gender roles and norms may face backlash and violence from their communities and religious institutions. This can include physical violence, sexual harassment, and social ostracism. In addition, women who do manage to achieve leadership positions may face resistance from male colleagues and congregants who are unwilling to accept their authority.

Another challenge facing African women in religious leadership is the intersectionality of discrimination they face. Women who belong to minority ethnic and linguistic groups, women with disabilities, and women who identify as LGBTQ+ may face additional obstacles in their pursuit of religious leadership roles. These women may face multiple forms of discrimination based on their gender, ethnicity, race, sexuality, and ability. This intersectionality of discrimination can create complex challenges that require innovative and intersectional solutions.

Furthermore, globalization and modernization have brought about new challenges to traditional African religions and spiritual practices. The rise of global Christianity and Islam has led to the marginalization of traditional African religions, and the increased influence of Western culture has brought about changes in traditional gender roles and norms. This has resulted in a tension between traditional African religious practices and the expectations of the modern world, which may create challenges for African women seeking leadership positions.

Another challenge that African women face is the lack of institutional support and resources. Religious institutions may not have policies in place to address gender equity and inclusivity or may lack resources to support the training and development of women in leadership positions. This can result in a lack of mentorship, networking opportunities, and funding for research and professional development, which can hinder women's ability to succeed in leadership roles.

Furthermore, African women in religious leadership may face resistance from within their communities, who may not be accustomed to seeing women in positions of authority. This can make it difficult for women to gain the trust and respect of their congregants and to navigate the power dynamics within their communities.

In conclusion, African women in religious leadership face significant challenges that limit their access to leadership positions and opportunities for professional development. These challenges include gender-based violence and discrimination, intersectionality of discrimination, tension between traditional African religious practices and modern expectations, lack of institutional support and resources, and resistance from within their communities. It is important for religious institutions and communities to address these challenges and work towards greater gender equity and inclusivity to build a more just and equitable future for all.

Exploring Origins, Traditions, and Contemporary Relevance

Emerging Opportunities

Despite these challenges, African women are making significant strides in achieving leadership positions within religious institutions. Women's groups and feminist theologians have been instrumental in advocating for greater gender equity and inclusivity within religious institutions. In addition, the growing recognition of women's spiritual gifts and talents has led to the emergence of new religious movements and traditions that prioritize women's leadership.

One example of such a movement is the African Women's Theology Project, which seeks to promote women's leadership and theological scholarship across the continent. The project emphasizes the importance of African women's experiences and perspectives in shaping theological discourse and practice. It also advocates for greater recognition of the spiritual practices and rituals that have been developed and sustained by African women over the centuries.

Another emerging opportunity for African women in religious leadership is the increasing availability of education and training programs. Many universities and religious institutions now offer courses and programs specifically designed to train women for leadership positions within their respective traditions. These programs provide women with the knowledge and skills needed to become effective spiritual leaders, while also helping to challenge and overcome traditional gender barriers.

In addition to formal education and training programs, African women are also leveraging technology to connect with and support one another in their spiritual and leadership journeys. Social media platforms and online forums provide women with opportunities to share their stories and experiences, connect with other women leaders, and build networks of support and advocacy.

Furthermore, the recognition of the critical role that women play in environmental stewardship has led to the emergence of new opportunities for African women to combine their spiritual leadership with environmental activism. Women have long been the primary caretakers of their communities and the natural world, and their traditional knowledge of medicinal plants and other natural resources has been essential to sustainable development. Today, many African women are using their spiritual leadership positions to promote eco-spirituality and advocate for environmental justice.

One example of this is the Green Belt Movement, founded by Kenyan activist and Nobel laureate Wangari Maathai. The movement, which focuses on reforestation and sustainable development, has empowered countless women across Africa to become environmental leaders and advocates.

In conclusion, African women's contributions to religious leadership and spirituality have been significant and varied throughout history, despite facing numerous challenges and obstacles. However, emerging opportunities such as the recognition of women's spiritual gifts and talents, increased access to education and training programs, and the growing importance of environmental stewardship present promising avenues for African women to continue their legacy of spiritual leadership and influence in the years to come.

Conclusion

African women have made significant contributions to religious leadership and spiritual practice throughout history. Despite facing significant challenges and obstacles, they continue to play vital roles in shaping the future of religious institutions and communities on the continent. By advocating for greater gender equity and inclusivity, and by celebrating the unique gifts and talents of women, African religious communities can work to build a more just and equitable future for all.

Furthermore, African women have shown resilience and resourcefulness in navigating patriarchal religious systems and carving out spaces for themselves as leaders, healers, and spiritual authorities. Many have drawn on traditional African spirituality and indigenous knowledge systems to create unique approaches to spiritual practice and leadership that are grounded in local cultures and traditions.

However, despite their contributions and resilience, African women in religious leadership still face significant challenges and barriers. These include gender discrimination, marginalization, and exclusion from decision-making processes. Additionally, the patriarchal structures and values that underpin many religious institutions often limit women's access to leadership positions and opportunities for advancement.

To address these challenges, it is important to recognize and celebrate the diverse experiences and perspectives of African women in religious leadership. This includes acknowledging the contributions of women from different regions, religions, and cultural backgrounds, and recognizing the unique challenges they face.

It is also crucial to work towards greater gender equity and inclusivity in religious institutions. This can include promoting women's leadership and participation in decision-making processes, creating safe spaces for women to share their experiences and concerns, and challenging patriarchal values and norms that perpetuate gender inequality.

Ultimately, by working towards greater gender equity and inclusivity in religious leadership, we can create more diverse, vibrant, and equitable religious communities that reflect the diversity and richness of African spirituality and culture.

Examples, problems, and exercises to illustrate topics and engage in critical thinking and discussion

1.   Research a prominent African woman religious leader and write a report on her life and accomplishments. What challenges did she face in achieving her position? How did she overcome these obstacles? What impact has she had on her community and religious tradition?

2.   Analyze a religious text from an African tradition and identify instances where women's voices and perspectives are present. What insights do these texts offer into women's spiritual experiences and practices? How can this knowledge be used to promote greater gender equity within the tradition?

3.   Attend a religious service led by a woman in an African tradition. What aspects of her leadership style stand out to you? How does she navigate potential resistance or skepticism from male congregants? What impact does her leadership have on the community?

Problems:

1.   Consider the challenges faced by African women seeking leadership positions in religious institutions. What strategies could be used to overcome these challenges? What role can men play in supporting women's leadership?

2.   Research the history of gender relations within a particular African religious tradition. How have women's roles and status evolved over time? What factors have contributed to these changes?

3.   Analyze the impact of colonialism and globalization on African religious traditions. How have these forces influenced attitudes towards gender and leadership? What opportunities and challenges do they present for women seeking leadership roles?

Exercises:

1.   In a group discussion, consider the question of whether women should be allowed to lead religious congregations in African traditions that historically

have been led by men. What are the arguments for and against such a change? What impact might this have on the tradition and its followers?

2.   Create a list of concrete actions that could be taken to promote greater gender equity and inclusivity within African religious institutions. How could these actions be implemented? What challenges might arise in the process?

3.   Write a personal reflection on your own attitudes towards women's leadership in religious contexts. How have your beliefs and values been shaped by your cultural background and experiences? What steps can you take to become a more informed and supportive ally to women seeking leadership roles?

PART 7: CONCLUSION AND FUTURE DIRECTIONS

In this final section, we will summarize the key findings and insights from the previous chapters and offer suggestions for future research directions. Throughout this text, we have explored the complex and multifaceted roles of women in various religious traditions across the globe. We have examined the historical and cultural contexts that have shaped women's experiences in religious contexts and the various challenges they have faced, including discrimination, exclusion, and marginalization.

Despite these challenges, women have played pivotal roles in shaping religious beliefs, practices, and communities, often in the face of significant resistance and opposition. They have challenged traditional gender roles, subverted patriarchal structures, and advocated for greater gender equity and inclusivity within religious institutions.

Looking ahead, there are several areas that warrant further exploration and research. For instance, scholars could investigate the ways in which women's spiritual experiences and practices intersect with environmentalism and eco-spirituality. Additionally, there is a need for more in-depth studies of the experiences of LGBTQIA+ individuals in religious communities, as well as the intersections between race, ethnicity, and religion.

Overall, this text serves as a starting point for further inquiry and reflection on the role of women in religion, highlighting the need for continued efforts towards greater gender equity and inclusivity within religious communities.

CHAPTER 28: KEY INSIGHTS AND TAKEAWAYS

As we come to the end of this book, it is important to reflect on the key insights and takeaways that we have gained from our exploration of spirituality, religion, and the supernatural. This chapter will provide a comprehensive summary of the major themes and ideas discussed throughout the book, highlighting the most important points and insights that we have gained.

At the heart of this book is the idea that spirituality and religion are complex and multifaceted phenomena that can be studied from a variety of perspectives. We have explored a range of different approaches to understanding spirituality, from anthropological and sociological analyses to psychological and neuroscientific investigations. Throughout this journey, we have come to appreciate the diversity and richness of spiritual beliefs and practices around the world, and the many ways in which they shape our individual and collective lives.

One of the central themes of this book has been the tension between traditional and modern forms of spirituality and religion. We have seen how many traditional beliefs and practices are at risk of being lost in the face of modernization and globalization, while at the same time new forms of spirituality are emerging that reflect contemporary social and cultural realities. This tension between tradition and modernity raises important questions about the role of spirituality and religion in contemporary society, and the ways in which we can build a more inclusive and equitable world that respects the diversity of spiritual and religious traditions.

Another important theme that has emerged throughout this book is the relationship between spirituality and social justice. We have seen how many spiritual traditions advocate for social and environmental responsibility, and how they can be powerful tools for promoting social change and addressing systemic inequality. At the same time, we have also explored the ways in which spiritual beliefs and practices can be used to justify or perpetuate social oppression and exclusion. Understanding this complex relationship between spirituality and social justice is essential for developing more ethical and sustainable approaches to spirituality and religion.

Finally, this book has emphasized the importance of critical thinking and reflection in our approach to spirituality and religion. We have seen how many beliefs and practices are deeply ingrained in our social and cultural contexts, and how they can be influenced by a range of psychological and cognitive biases. By critically examining our own beliefs and assumptions, we can develop a more nuanced and informed understanding of spirituality and religion, and be better equipped to engage in constructive dialogue with others who hold different beliefs and perspectives.

In conclusion, this book has been an exploration of the diversity and complexity of spirituality, religion, and the supernatural, and the many ways in which they shape our individual and collective lives. By reflecting on the key insights and takeaways that we have gained throughout this journey, we can deepen our understanding of these important phenomena, and be better equipped to engage with the challenges and opportunities that lie ahead.

CHAPTER 29: FUTURE DIRECTIONS FOR THE STUDY OF AFRICAN RELIGIONS AND THE ORIGINS OF RELIGION

The study of African religions has come a long way since the colonial era, when Western scholars dismissed them as primitive and superstitious. Today, scholars recognize the diversity, complexity, and resilience of African religions and their significant contributions to world religions. However, there is still much to learn about African religions and their origins, as well as the connections and differences between African religions and other religions. This chapter explores some future directions for the study of African religions and the origins of religion.

✧   The Origins of Religion

One of the fundamental questions about religion is its origin. Where did religion come from? What were the earliest forms of religion? What social, cultural, and ecological factors influenced the emergence and evolution of religion? These questions have puzzled scholars and laypeople alike for centuries. There are many theories and hypotheses about the origins of religion, ranging from evolutionary, psychological, sociological, ecological, and cultural perspectives. However, none of these theories can fully explain the complexity and diversity of religion, especially African religions. Therefore, more interdisciplinary and cross-cultural research is needed to shed light on the origins of religion and its global significance.

✧   Comparative Studies of African Religions

Although African religions share some common themes and practices, they are not monolithic or homogenous. African religions are diverse and dynamic, reflecting the cultural and historical contexts of the people who practice them. Therefore, comparative studies of African religions are essential to understanding their similarities and differences, as well as their interactions with other religions. Comparative studies of African religions can also challenge the Eurocentric biases and assumptions that have dominated the study of religion and promote a more inclusive and dialogical approach.

Exploring Origins, Traditions, and Contemporary Relevance

✧   Intersectionality and Social Justice in African Religions

African religions are not just spiritual or religious systems but also cultural, social, and political phenomena. Therefore, they have a significant impact on the lives and identities of the people who practice them, especially women, LGBTQIA+ individuals, and minorities. Intersectionality, a concept that emphasizes the intersection of multiple identities and oppressions, is relevant to the study of African religions and social justice. Scholars of African religions should pay attention to the intersections of gender, sexuality, race, ethnicity, class, and other factors in the analysis of African religions and promote social justice and human rights in their research and advocacy.

✧   Environmentalism and Ecospirituality in African Religions

African religions have a deep connection with nature and the environment, as evidenced by their rituals, myths, and cosmologies. Therefore, they have much to offer to the contemporary debates on environmentalism, sustainability, and ecospirituality. However, the relationship between African religions and the environment is not always harmonious or benign, as environmental degradation and climate change affect the practices and beliefs of African religions. Therefore, scholars of African religions should pay attention to the ecological aspects of African religions and promote ecospirituality and environmental justice in their research and activism.

Conclusion

The study of African religions is a complex and multifaceted field that requires interdisciplinary, comparative, and intersectional approaches. Future research on African religions should focus on the origins of religion, comparative studies of African religions, intersectionality and social justice in African religions, and environmentalism and ecospirituality in African religions. By promoting a more inclusive and dialogical approach to the study of African religions, scholars can contribute to a better understanding of the complexity, diversity, and resilience of African religions and their significance to the global religious landscape.

CHAPTER 30: THE ROLE OF AFRICAN RELIGIONS IN CONTEMPORARY SOCIETY

The role of African religions in contemporary society is a topic that has attracted significant interest and debate among scholars, practitioners, and the general public. African religions, also known as traditional or indigenous religions, are those religious practices that are indigenous to the African continent and have been practiced for centuries. These religions are diverse and vary from one region to another, with each region having its unique beliefs, practices, and traditions. The significance of African religions in contemporary society lies in their ability to provide a sense of identity, community, and spiritual fulfillment to millions of people in Africa and beyond. In this chapter, we will explore the role of African religions in contemporary society, their impact on culture, politics, and social life, as well as their potential for future growth and development.

African Religions and Culture

African religions have played a significant role in shaping the cultural identity of the African continent. These religions are deeply rooted in African culture and have been passed down from generation to generation through oral traditions, myths, and rituals. They provide a framework for understanding the world, the natural environment, and the relationship between humans and the divine. African religions also provide a sense of community and belonging, as they are often practiced within the context of extended family networks and community structures.

One of the most significant contributions of African religions to contemporary society is their role in preserving cultural heritage. In many African societies, traditional religious practices have been under threat from the forces of modernization, globalization, and religious fundamentalism. However, there has been a renewed interest in African religions in recent years, driven by a desire to reconnect with cultural heritage and preserve traditional knowledge and practices. This has led to the establishment of cultural centers, museums, and other initiatives aimed at promoting African culture and preserving its heritage.

African Religions and Politics

African religions have also played a significant role in shaping politics in the African continent. Historically, African religions were often intertwined with political power, as rulers were often seen as being divinely appointed and had a close relationship with the spiritual realm. In many African societies, religious leaders and practitioners have been involved in political activism, advocating for social justice, and challenging oppressive systems of power.

One example of the role of African religions in politics is the anti-colonial struggle in many African countries. During this period, traditional religious practices were often used as a means of resistance against colonial rule. For example, the Mau Mau movement in Kenya was a militant anti-colonial movement that drew inspiration from traditional Kikuyu religion and used traditional rituals and practices as a means of resistance against British colonialism.

In contemporary society, African religions continue to have an impact on politics. In many African countries, traditional religious leaders play a significant role in local governance, conflict resolution, and the promotion of social cohesion. There has also been a growing interest in the role of African religions in promoting sustainable development, with initiatives aimed at promoting environmental conservation and sustainable agriculture.

African Religions and Social Life

African religions have played a significant role in shaping social life in the African continent. These religions provide a framework for understanding social relationships, family structures, and community dynamics. They also provide a sense of identity and belonging, particularly for those who have been marginalized by mainstream society.

One of the most significant contributions of African religions to contemporary society is their role in promoting social justice and human rights. Many African religions have a strong emphasis on social responsibility, community service, and the promotion of the common good. They provide a framework for understanding social inequality and challenging systems of oppression.

African religions have also played a significant role in promoting gender equality and women's rights. In many African societies, traditional religious practices were often used to justify the subordination of women and the denial of their rights. However, many contemporary African religious movements have challenged these patriarchal traditions and advocated for greater gender equality. For example, some African women have become spiritual leaders and have used their positions to advocate for women's rights and social justice.

Furthermore, African religions have played a significant role in promoting environmental conservation and sustainability. Many traditional African religions have a deep respect for the natural world and recognize the interconnectedness of all living things. As such, they often promote sustainable practices that prioritize the protection of the environment.

In contemporary society, African religions continue to play a vital role in providing a sense of community, identity, and belonging for many people. They provide a space for individuals to connect with their cultural heritage, spiritual practices, and social traditions. Furthermore, many African religious practices have been incorporated into mainstream society, influencing art, music, dance, and literature.

However, African religions also face challenges in the modern world. Globalization, urbanization, and the spread of Western values have led to the decline of many traditional religious practices. Furthermore, many African religions have been criticized for promoting superstition, irrationality, and harmful practices such as witchcraft accusations.

To address these challenges, it is essential to promote greater understanding and appreciation of African religions and their contributions to contemporary society. This can be achieved through education, research, and dialogue between practitioners of African religions and those from other faiths. It is also important to address the harmful practices and beliefs that are sometimes associated with African religions, through advocacy and legal action where necessary.

In conclusion, African religions have played a significant role in shaping social life in the African continent and promoting social justice, gender equality, environmental conservation, and sustainability. They continue to provide a sense of community, identity, and belonging for many people and have influenced mainstream society in various ways. However, they also face challenges in the modern world and require greater understanding and appreciation to continue to thrive and contribute to contemporary society.

CHAPTER 31: THE POTENTIAL FOR INTERFAITH DIALOGUE AND COLLABORATION

Interfaith dialogue and collaboration have become increasingly important in contemporary society, particularly as globalization has led to increased cultural and religious diversity. Interfaith dialogue refers to the process of engaging in conversation and exchange of ideas between members of different faiths, while interfaith collaboration refers to the joint efforts of people of different faiths to work together towards a common goal.

African religions have a rich history of interfaith dialogue and collaboration, both within and outside of the continent. Many African religions have incorporated elements of other religions and cultural practices, creating a unique blend of traditions and beliefs. This openness to different perspectives has made African religions particularly well-suited for interfaith dialogue and collaboration.

The potential benefits of interfaith dialogue and collaboration are numerous, including increased understanding and respect between different religious communities, the promotion of peace and social harmony, and the ability to address shared challenges and concerns. However, interfaith dialogue and collaboration can also be challenging, particularly when dealing with deeply held beliefs and values.

In this chapter, we will explore the potential for interfaith dialogue and collaboration in the context of African religions. We will examine the history and current state of interfaith dialogue and collaboration in Africa, as well as the challenges and opportunities that exist for future collaboration. We will also discuss the potential benefits of interfaith dialogue and collaboration, both for individuals and for society as a whole.

History of Interfaith Dialogue and Collaboration in Africa

Interfaith dialogue and collaboration have a long history in Africa, dating back to the pre-colonial era. Many African religions have incorporated elements of other religions, such as Christianity and Islam, into their practices, creating a unique blend of traditions and beliefs. This openness to different perspectives has allowed for greater understanding and respect between different religious communities.

During the colonial period, however, interfaith dialogue and collaboration were often discouraged by European colonizers, who saw African religions as primitive and superstitious. Christian missionaries, in particular, often sought to convert Africans to Christianity and viewed traditional African religions as a barrier to their mission.

Following independence in many African countries, there was a renewed interest in traditional African religions and a push for greater respect and recognition of these religions. This led to increased opportunities for interfaith dialogue and collaboration, both within and outside of Africa.

Today, interfaith dialogue and collaboration continue to play an important role in African society. Many African countries have made efforts to promote interfaith dialogue and collaboration as a means of promoting peace and social harmony. For example, the African Union has established an Interfaith Dialogue Forum to facilitate dialogue and collaboration between different religious communities.

Challenges and Opportunities for Interfaith Dialogue and Collaboration

While there are many potential benefits of interfaith dialogue and collaboration, there are also significant challenges to overcome. One of the biggest challenges is the deeply held beliefs and values that underpin many religious traditions. These beliefs and values can be difficult to reconcile with those of other religions, leading to conflict and tension.

Another challenge is the lack of understanding and knowledge about different religious traditions. Many people may hold stereotypes or misconceptions about other religions, which can make it difficult to engage in meaningful dialogue and collaboration.

Despite these challenges, there are also many opportunities for interfaith dialogue and collaboration. One opportunity is the ability to address shared challenges and concerns. For example, many religious traditions share a concern for social justice and human rights, which can provide a common ground for collaboration.

Another opportunity is the potential for learning and growth. By engaging in dialogue and collaboration with people of different religious traditions, individuals can gain a greater understanding of their own beliefs and values, as well as those of others.

Exploring Origins, Traditions, and Contemporary Relevance

In addition to these efforts, many grassroots organizations and religious leaders are also involved in promoting interfaith dialogue and collaboration. These initiatives often focus on addressing common social and environmental challenges, such as poverty, disease, and climate change, which affect people of all faiths.

One notable example is the work of the Ecumenical Association of Third World Theologians (EATWOT), which was founded in the 1970s and has since become a leading voice in the promotion of interfaith dialogue and collaboration in Africa and other parts of the Global South. EATWOT seeks to promote a deeper understanding of different religions and cultures, and to encourage collaboration among theologians, scholars, and religious leaders from different faiths.

In recent years, there has also been an increasing recognition of the role that traditional African religions can play in promoting interfaith dialogue and collaboration. Many African religions emphasize the importance of community, social justice, and respect for the natural world, values which are shared by many other religions and can provide a basis for collaboration.

Overall, the history of interfaith dialogue and collaboration in Africa is a complex and multifaceted one, shaped by both internal and external factors. However, the ongoing efforts of individuals, organizations, and religious leaders to promote dialogue and collaboration offer hope for a more peaceful and harmonious future for all people, regardless of their religious beliefs.

Benefits of Interfaith Dialogue and Collaboration

There are many potential benefits of interfaith dialogue and collaboration, both for individuals and for society as a whole. One of the most significant benefits is the opportunity for individuals to gain a deeper understanding and appreciation of other religions and cultures. This can lead to increased tolerance, empathy, and respect for diversity, as well as a reduction in prejudice and discrimination.

Interfaith dialogue and collaboration can also promote peacebuilding and conflict resolution. By bringing people of different religions together to discuss shared values and concerns, it is possible to identify areas of common ground and work towards solutions for social, political, and environmental issues. This can help to reduce tensions and promote reconciliation between different groups, particularly in areas where there is a history of conflict or tension.

In addition, interfaith collaboration can provide opportunities for joint action and community service. By working together on social projects or charitable initiatives, individuals and groups from different religious backgrounds can build trust and solidarity, as well as make a positive impact on their communities. This can also help to break down barriers and promote social cohesion.

Another potential benefit of interfaith dialogue and collaboration is the opportunity for religious leaders to address global challenges and promote ethical and sustainable practices. By sharing their perspectives on issues such as climate change, poverty, and human rights, religious leaders can raise awareness and mobilize their followers to take action. This can help to promote social and environmental justice, as well as contribute to the overall wellbeing of society.

Despite these potential benefits, there are also challenges and limitations to interfaith dialogue and collaboration. One challenge is the potential for misunderstandings and miscommunications, particularly when there are language or cultural barriers. It can also be difficult to address deep-seated differences and disagreements on sensitive issues such as theology or morality.

Another challenge is the potential for power imbalances and marginalization of minority groups. In some cases, dominant religious groups may hold more influence or resources, leading to a lack of equal representation and participation in interfaith dialogue and collaboration. It is important to ensure that all voices are heard and that efforts are made to address power imbalances and promote inclusivity.

In conclusion, interfaith dialogue and collaboration have the potential to promote understanding, tolerance, and peace between individuals and communities of different religious backgrounds. By addressing shared values and concerns and working towards joint solutions, it is possible to build trust, solidarity, and social cohesion. However, it is important to be aware of the challenges and limitations of interfaith dialogue and collaboration and to work towards creating a more inclusive and equitable society.

CHAPTER 32: THE IMPORTANCE OF PRESERVING AND PROMOTING AFRICAN RELIGIOUS TRADITIONS

African religious traditions have played a significant role in shaping the cultural and social identity of the African continent. These religious traditions are deeply rooted in the customs, beliefs, and practices of African communities and have been passed down from generation to generation through oral traditions and ritual practices. However, in recent years, African religious traditions have come under threat due to various factors such as globalization, urbanization, and the influence of other religions.

The purpose of this chapter is to explore the importance of preserving and promoting African religious traditions. We will examine the unique features of African religions, their historical and cultural significance, and the challenges they face in contemporary society. Additionally, we will discuss the role of African religious traditions in promoting social cohesion, ecological sustainability, and spiritual well-being.

The Unique Features of African Religions:

African religious traditions are diverse and complex, reflecting the unique cultural and historical experiences of different African communities. However, there are several common features that are shared by many African religions.

One of the defining features of African religions is their emphasis on communal and ancestral connections. In African religions, the individual is seen as part of a larger social and spiritual network that includes ancestors, spirits, and the natural world. These connections are believed to be essential for spiritual well-being and personal growth.

Another key feature of African religions is their use of ritual practices and ceremonies. These rituals are often performed to connect with ancestors, spirits, and deities, and to seek guidance and protection. Examples of African religious rituals include divination, sacrifices, and ancestor veneration.

African religions also place a strong emphasis on the interconnection between humans and the natural world. Many African religions view the natural world as a living, spiritual entity that is intimately connected to human life. This belief has led to a deep respect for the environment and a strong emphasis on ecological sustainability.

Furthermore, African religions often incorporate a holistic approach to healing and well-being. Rather than separating the physical, emotional, and spiritual aspects of an individual, African religions view these aspects as interconnected and interdependent. This has led to the development of a variety of healing practices, such as herbalism, divination, and trance possession, that address the needs of the whole person.

African religions also exhibit a high degree of syncretism, or the blending of different religious traditions. This syncretism is a result of the complex historical and cultural interactions between different African communities, as well as the influence of external religions such as Christianity and Islam. This has resulted in a rich tapestry of religious beliefs and practices that reflect the diversity and complexity of African culture.

Finally, African religions often exhibit a strong sense of resilience and adaptability. Despite the challenges and threats facing African religious traditions, they have managed to survive and adapt to changing circumstances. This resilience is a testament to the enduring cultural and spiritual significance of African religions, and their continued importance for African communities today.

Historical and Cultural Significance:

African religions have a rich historical and cultural significance that spans thousands of years. These religions have been shaped by the complex interactions between different African communities, as well as by external factors such as colonialism and globalization.

One of the most significant contributions of African religions to world culture is their influence on art, music, and literature. African religious practices have inspired a rich tradition of visual and performing arts, including sculpture, dance, and storytelling. These artistic traditions have been instrumental in preserving African cultural identity and promoting intercultural understanding.

African religions have also played a significant role in shaping political and social movements. For example, many African liberation movements were led by religious figures who used religious language and symbols to inspire and mobilize their followers. Additionally, African religious traditions have been instrumental in promoting gender equality, social justice, and human rights.

Exploring Origins, Traditions, and Contemporary Relevance

African religions have also made significant contributions to the field of medicine and healing. Traditional healers, often referred to as medicine men or women, have long been an integral part of African communities. They use a combination of spiritual and herbal remedies to treat a wide range of physical and mental illnesses.

Traditional healing practices are based on the belief that illness is caused by a disruption in the balance between the individual and their environment. Traditional healers work to restore this balance through a variety of techniques, including prayer, divination, and the use of medicinal plants. These healing practices have been passed down through generations and are often closely guarded secrets within families or communities.

In addition to their contributions to the arts, politics, and medicine, African religions have also played an important role in shaping ecological knowledge and practices. Many African religions are grounded in a deep reverence for nature and emphasize the importance of maintaining a harmonious relationship with the natural world. This has led to the development of a rich tradition of ecological knowledge and practices, including sustainable agriculture, hunting, and fishing techniques.

Despite their significant contributions, African religions continue to face challenges and threats to their survival. The erosion of traditional religious practices and beliefs, as well as the influence of other religions and globalization, pose significant challenges. Furthermore, the destruction of the environment and loss of traditional ecological knowledge threaten the survival of many African religious practices and beliefs.

In order to preserve and promote African religious traditions, it is important to recognize their historical and cultural significance, as well as the challenges and threats they face in contemporary society. Efforts to promote intercultural understanding and respect, as well as to protect the environment and preserve traditional knowledge, can help ensure the continued survival and vitality of African religions.

Challenges and Threats:

Despite their historical and cultural significance, African religious traditions face numerous challenges and threats in contemporary society. One of the most significant threats is the influence of globalization and the spread of Western cultural values. Many African communities have been influenced by Western religious and cultural norms, leading to the erosion of traditional religious practices and beliefs.

African Religions

Another challenge facing African religions is the influence of other religions such as Christianity and Islam. While these religions have coexisted with African religions for centuries, their influence has grown significantly in recent years. This has led to conflicts between different religious communities and has threatened the survival of traditional African religious practices.

Finally, many African religious traditions face the threat of environmental degradation and ecological destruction. This is particularly true in rural areas, where traditional agricultural practices are being replaced by industrial farming and mining. This has led to the loss of traditional knowledge and practices related to ecological sustainability and has threatened the survival of many plant and animal species.

The influence of globalization on African religious traditions has been a significant threat to their preservation and promotion. The spread of Western cultural values has led to the erosion of traditional religious practices and beliefs in many African communities. This is especially true for younger generations who are increasingly exposed to Western media and cultural norms. As a result, many African religious practices and beliefs are at risk of disappearing as younger generations are less likely to practice or value them.

Another challenge facing African religions is the influence of other religions such as Christianity and Islam. While these religions have coexisted with African religions for centuries, their influence has grown significantly in recent years. This has led to conflicts between different religious communities and has threatened the survival of traditional African religious practices. For instance, in some African countries, such as Nigeria and Sudan, conflicts have arisen between Christians and Muslims, leading to violence and destruction of cultural heritage sites.

Moreover, the spread of Christianity and Islam has led to the demonization of African religions and the portrayal of traditional religious practices as primitive and superstitious. This has contributed to the stigmatization of African religions and a lack of respect for their cultural significance.

Finally, many African religious traditions face the threat of environmental degradation and ecological destruction. This is particularly true in rural areas, where traditional agricultural practices are being replaced by industrial farming and mining. This has led to the loss of traditional knowledge and practices related to ecological sustainability and has threatened the survival of many plant and animal species. For example, the mining of coltan, a mineral used in the production of electronic devices, has led to the destruction of habitats and the displacement of local communities in the Democratic Republic of Congo.

Exploring Origins, Traditions, and Contemporary Relevance

In light of these challenges and threats, it is essential to recognize the importance of preserving and promoting African religious traditions. This involves educating younger generations about the cultural significance of traditional practices and beliefs and advocating for their inclusion in educational curricula. It also involves raising awareness of the threats facing African religions and advocating for their protection and preservation. Finally, it involves working to promote ecological sustainability and protecting the natural environment, which is essential for the survival of many African religious traditions.

Conclusion:

In conclusion, the preservation and promotion of African religious traditions is of vital importance for the cultural, social, and ecological well-being of the African continent and its people. These traditions provide a rich tapestry of beliefs, practices, and values that are intimately connected to the land, the natural world, and the community.

By preserving and promoting these traditions, we can help to maintain the diversity and richness of African culture and ensure that future generations have access to this valuable heritage. Furthermore, by recognizing the important role that African religions play in promoting social justice, gender equality, and environmental sustainability, we can work towards building a more just and equitable world.

However, the preservation and promotion of African religious traditions must be approached with sensitivity and respect. It is important to recognize the diversity and complexity of these traditions and to avoid essentializing or romanticizing them. It is also important to work collaboratively with African communities and to ensure that their voices and perspectives are valued and heard.

In the following chapters, we will explore different aspects of African religious traditions in more detail, including their historical development, their role in contemporary society, and the challenges they face in the modern world. Through a deeper understanding of these traditions, we can gain a greater appreciation for the rich cultural heritage of the African continent and work towards a more just and sustainable future.

Glossery

A:

Ancestor veneration: Ancestor veneration is a practice found in many cultures, including African diasporic religions, where deceased ancestors are honored and respected. It involves showing reverence, offering prayers, and making offerings to ancestors as a way of maintaining a connection with them and seeking their guidance and protection. Ancestor veneration is based on the belief that ancestors continue to exist in the spiritual realm and can influence the lives of their living descendants.

Animal sacrifice: Animal sacrifice is a ritualistic practice in which an animal, often a specific species or breed, is offered as a sacrifice to a deity or spirit. It is commonly found in various religious traditions, including some African diasporic religions. Animal sacrifice is performed as a means of expressing devotion, seeking blessings or favors, and establishing a reciprocal relationship with the spiritual realm. The sacrificed animal is typically prepared and consumed as part of a communal meal or distributed among participants.

C:

Candomble: Candomble is an African diasporic religion that originated in Brazil, particularly among the Afro-Brazilian communities. It combines elements of various African religious traditions, particularly those from West Africa, with Catholicism. Candomble worships a pantheon of deities known as orixas, who are believed to govern different aspects of nature and human life. Rituals in Candomble involve music, dance, and spirit possession, with the aim of establishing a connection between practitioners and the divine realm. Candomble plays a significant role in Afro-Brazilian cultural and spiritual practices.

Conjure: Conjure, also known as hoodoo, is a system of folk magic and spiritual practices that originated among African Americans in the United States. It blends African, Native American, and European influences and is deeply rooted in African diasporic religions. Conjure involves the use of herbs, roots, candles, and rituals to seek spiritual assistance, protection, and the manifestation of desired outcomes. It encompasses practices such as divination, spellcasting, and the creation of talismans or charms. Conjure has been an important aspect of African American cultural and spiritual traditions.

Cultural identity: Cultural identity refers to a person's sense of belonging and identification with a particular culture or group. It encompasses the shared beliefs, values, customs, traditions, and practices that define a group's way of life. Cultural identity is shaped by various factors, including ethnicity, nationality, language, religion, and heritage. It influences an individual's self-perception, behavior, and social interactions. Cultural identity can provide individuals with a sense of pride, belonging, and community, as well as shape their worldview and understanding of themselves and others. It plays a vital role in shaping personal and collective identities within African diasporic communities and their associated religions and spiritual practices.

D:

Divination: Divination is a practice found in various religious and spiritual traditions that involves seeking insight or knowledge about the future or the unknown. It is a method of gaining guidance, understanding, and answers through supernatural or spiritual means. Divination techniques vary across cultures and religions and can include methods such as tarot card reading, astrology, scrying, pendulum dowsing, and rune casting. Practitioners of divination believe that through these practices, they can tap into higher realms of consciousness, communicate with spirits or deities, and access hidden knowledge.

E:

Ecospirituality: Ecospirituality refers to a spiritual approach that emphasizes the interconnectedness and sacredness of all living beings and the natural world. It recognizes the spiritual dimension of ecological awareness and seeks to foster a deep reverence and respect for the Earth and its ecosystems. Ecospirituality encompasses beliefs, practices, and rituals that promote ecological sustainability, environmental stewardship, and a harmonious relationship with nature. It recognizes the inherent spirituality in the natural world and often integrates environmental activism, sustainable living, and ecological values into religious and spiritual practices.

H:

Healing: Healing refers to the process of restoring physical, emotional, or spiritual well-being and balance. In the context of African diasporic religions and spiritual practices, healing often involves a holistic approach that addresses the interconnectedness of the mind, body, and spirit. It encompasses various methods, including herbal medicine, energy healing, ritual ceremonies, prayer, meditation, and spiritual guidance. Healing practices aim to alleviate physical ailments, emotional distress, and spiritual imbalances by addressing the underlying causes of illness or disharmony. Healing rituals and practices can be performed by practitioners, healers, or religious leaders within the community.

Hoodoo: Hoodoo, also known as conjure or rootwork, is a system of folk magic and spiritual practices that developed among African Americans in the United States. It is characterized by the use of herbs, roots, minerals, candles, and other natural elements to harness spiritual power and manifest desired outcomes. Hoodoo draws from African, Native American, and European folk traditions and incorporates elements of African diasporic religions. It involves spellcasting, divination, herbalism, and the creation of charms or talismans. Hoodoo is deeply rooted in African American cultural and spiritual traditions and often addresses practical needs such as protection, luck, love, and prosperity.

I:

Ifa: Ifa is a system of divination and religious belief that originated among the Yoruba people of Nigeria and has spread to other parts of West Africa and the African diaspora. It is based on the teachings and wisdom of Orunmila, the Yoruba deity of wisdom and divination. Ifa utilizes a complex corpus of oral texts, verses, and symbols called odu, which are consulted by trained priests or priestesses to provide guidance, insight, and solutions to personal and communal issues. Ifa is not only a divination system but also a comprehensive philosophical and ethical framework that guides individual and social behavior, emphasizing the concepts of destiny, personal responsibility, and the interplay between humans and the divine.

M:

Music: Music plays a significant role in African diasporic religions and spiritual practices. It serves as a medium of communication, worship, celebration, and ritual. Music in these contexts often combines traditional African rhythms, melodies, and instruments with elements influenced by the cultures and traditions of the diaspora. It can include drumming, chanting, singing, dance, and the use of various musical instruments such as drums, rattles, bells, and stringed instruments. Music is used to invoke and communicate with spirits, create a sacred atmosphere, induce altered states of consciousness, and facilitate spiritual connection, healing, and transformation.

O:

Orisha: Orisha refers to the deities or divine forces in the Yoruba religion and various African diasporic religions, including Santeria, Candomble, and Vodou. Orishas are considered intermediaries between humans and the supreme deity Olodumare. Each Orisha is associated with specific characteristics, powers, and domains of influence, such as love, fertility, wisdom, healing, and protection. Devotees of African diasporic religions often develop personal relationships with specific Orishas, seeking their guidance, blessings, and assistance through rituals, offerings, prayers, and possession ceremonies. Orishas are represented through symbols, sacred objects, and artistic depictions and play a central role in the religious and spiritual practices of these traditions.

P:

Political activism: Political activism refers to organized efforts and actions undertaken by individuals, groups, or communities to bring about social, political, or cultural change. In the context of African diasporic religions, political activism involves using religious or spiritual beliefs and practices as a foundation for advocating for justice, equality, and the rights of marginalized communities. It can encompass various forms of activism, such as advocating for religious freedom, combating discrimination and stereotypes, addressing social and economic inequalities, promoting environmental sustainability, and engaging in community empowerment and grassroots organizing. Political activism within these religious contexts seeks to challenge oppressive systems, promote social justice, and uplift the voices and rights of marginalized communities.

Practices: Practices refer to the rituals, ceremonies, and activities associated with African diasporic religions. These practices vary depending on the specific tradition, cultural context, and individual preferences. They can include offerings and sacrifices to deities or ancestors, divination, prayer, meditation, chanting, drumming, dance, possession ceremonies, healing rituals, and communal celebrations. Practices often serve multiple purposes, including establishing a connection with the divine, seeking guidance and protection, celebrating important events and milestones, fostering community cohesion, and promoting personal and spiritual growth. Practitioners engage in these practices to deepen their spiritual connection, honor their traditions, and enhance their overall well-being.

R:

Rituals: Rituals are structured and symbolic actions or ceremonies performed within African diasporic religions. These rituals often involve a series of prescribed steps, gestures, prayers, and offerings that are carried out to establish a connection with the divine, invoke spiritual powers, seek guidance, express gratitude, or mark important life events. Rituals serve as a means of communication between the human and spiritual realms, providing a sacred framework for spiritual expression, transformation, and communal bonding. They can range from private, individual rituals to elaborate community ceremonies and may incorporate elements such as chanting, dancing, drumming, purification rituals, and the use of sacred objects and symbols.

S:

Santeria: Santeria, also known as La Regla de Ocha or Lucumi, is an African diasporic religion that developed in Cuba among the descendants of Yoruba slaves. It is a syncretic religion that blends elements of Yoruba spirituality with Catholicism. Santeria centers around the veneration of Orishas, who are seen as intermediaries between humans and the supreme deity. Santeria rituals involve music, dance, offerings, divination, and possession ceremonies. It places emphasis on personal spiritual development, healing, and achieving balance and harmony in life. Santeria has spread to other parts of the Caribbean and the Americas and continues to evolve and adapt in different cultural contexts.

Shamanism: Shamanism refers to a spiritual practice that involves a practitioner, known as a shaman, who acts as an intermediary between the human and spirit worlds. While shamanism is not exclusive to African diasporic religions, it has significant overlaps and influences on various practices within these traditions. Shamans are believed to have the ability to enter altered states of consciousness, communicate with spirits, and facilitate healing, divination, and spiritual guidance. Shamanic practices often involve rituals, drumming, chanting, the use of plant medicines, and journeying into non-ordinary states of consciousness to gain insight, retrieve lost souls, and restore balance and harmony. Shamanism emphasizes a holistic worldview that recognizes the interconnectedness of all living beings and the natural world.

Spirituality: Spirituality refers to an individual's personal quest for meaning, connection, and transcendence, often encompassing beliefs and practices related to the sacred or divine. Within African diasporic religions, spirituality plays a central role as practitioners seek to establish a connection with the divine, deepen their understanding of the spiritual realms, and cultivate a sense of inner peace and harmony. Spirituality encompasses a wide range of experiences and practices, including prayer, meditation, introspection, contemplation, and engaging in rituals and ceremonies. It is a deeply personal and subjective aspect of religious and cultural identity that can shape one's worldview, values, and sense of purpose.

Stereotypes: Stereotypes are simplified and often misleading beliefs or generalizations about a particular group of people or their cultural practices. African diasporic religions have long been subject to stereotypes and misconceptions due to factors such as colonialism, cultural bias, and lack of accurate information. Stereotypes can include assumptions of being primitive, superstitious, or evil, and may overlook the rich history, cultural significance, and spiritual depth of these traditions. Addressing stereotypes requires promoting accurate information, challenging preconceived notions, and fostering respect and understanding for the diversity and complexity of African diasporic religions.

Syncretism: Syncretism refers to the blending or merging of different religious or cultural traditions to create new forms of belief and practice. In the context of African diasporic religions, syncretism is a significant characteristic resulting from the historical encounter between African spiritual beliefs and the dominant religious traditions of the colonizers, such as Christianity and Catholicism. Syncretic religions, such as Santeria and Candomble, have emerged as a result of this blending process.

T:

Traditional religions: Traditional religions refer to the indigenous and pre-colonial belief systems and practices that are deeply rooted in the cultural, spiritual, and social fabric of specific communities or ethnic groups. These religions often emphasize a close connection with nature, the worship of ancestral spirits, and the recognition of sacred forces or deities associated with natural phenomena. Traditional religions are passed down through generations and play a significant role in shaping cultural identity, values, and communal cohesion.

Trans-Atlantic slave trade: The Trans-Atlantic slave trade refers to the forced transportation of millions of African people from their homelands to the Americas and other parts of the world between the 16th and 19th centuries. It was a brutal and inhumane system in which African men, women, and children were captured, enslaved, and transported across the Atlantic Ocean to work on plantations, mines, and other labor-intensive industries. The Trans-Atlantic slave trade had profound and long-lasting effects on the African continent and its diaspora, including the displacement of millions of people, the disruption of African societies, and the intermingling of diverse cultures and traditions.

V:

Vodou: Vodou, also spelled Voodoo or Vodun, is a syncretic religion that originated in Haiti during the period of African enslavement and European colonization. It combines elements of African spirituality, Indigenous Taino beliefs, and Catholicism. Vodou practitioners believe in a supreme creator deity, Bondye, as well as various spirits or loa that can be invoked through rituals, songs, drumming, and dance. Vodou emphasizes ancestor veneration, healing, divination, and the belief in the interconnectedness of the spiritual and physical realms. It has been an integral part of

Haitian culture and identity, serving as a source of resistance, empowerment, and cultural preservation throughout history.

www.ingramcontent.com/pod-product-compliance
Lightning Source LLC
Chambersburg PA
CBHW082139120626
46553CB00010B/2709